Setting Up and Managing Your Own Business

Published by
Kensington West Productions Ltd

Editor
Colin Barrow

Sub Editors
Helen Parker
Nicola Clements
Christine Macgregor

Research
Martin Ellis

Production
Diane Ridley
Mark Scandle

Design
Nick Ridley

Origination by
Pre-Press Ltd, Hong Kong

Printed by
Liang Yu Printing Factory, Hong Kong

KENSINGTON WEST
Productions Ltd

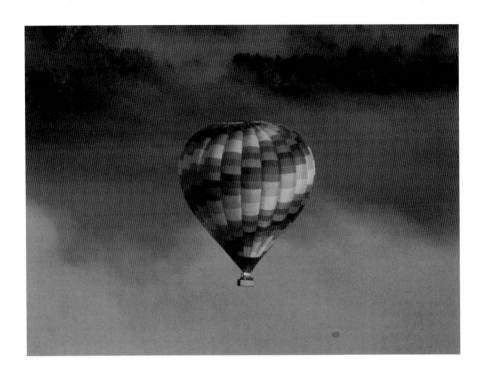

Setting Up
and Managing
Your Own Business

World leaders in PC accounting software

KENSINGTON WEST
Productions Ltd

Acknowledgements

Like many great British inventions and business concepts, the idea for this book was conceived in a pub. However, unlike many public house dreams that flounder amidst the enduring political or sporting debate this idea survived and these pages are the end result. The second edition has come on a lot and I am pleased that we have a strong internet chapter. Naturally, this will need to be updated regularly as the web weaves itself ever more, but it is a great start.

The main thanks for this goes to Sage Group plc. I'm particularly grateful to Paul Stobart, Jo Ray and Dawn Baker for their time and energy. Every article provided has been written without reward by an expert in their field. I have spoken to all the contributors at one time or another and their principal intent was to foster the spirit of small business that is so alive in Britain.

With regard to our leading contributors, well there are many but several of special note should be mentioned. Firstly John Spratt and his team at Shoosmiths - enthusiasm from day one, many phone calls and finally thousands of words from lawyers who really enjoy their business. I would also pay tribute to Business Link. Many small business owners may be wary of government-led business initiatives but believe you me if the representatives of Business Link who contributed to this book are anything to go by, give them a call. Without exception they were receptive, positive and efficient and above all had a sense of humour - and without that it's tough to run a small business! We are also particularly grateful to the Advertising Association, who kindly allowed us to take significant extracts from their booklet "Advertising Means Business," copies of which are available from the Association whose details are listed in chapter 10 along with our other contributors.

To all contributors and to the researchers, editors and designers at Kensington West Productions, I am grateful for a job well done. Finally, thank you for purchasing a copy of this book. We wish you well in your endeavours and dreams in business however they develop.

Julian West

Kensington West Productions Ltd

An introduction from Sage

When we started Sage in 1981 we too were a very small business. We had four employees and 1000 square feet of space in a rented building. In the first few years we spent 40 per cent of our revenue on marketing our products and services to the outside world. We took risks, we were daring, we made good decisions and we also made mistakes. As I write this foreword I can remember vividly the good times and the bad times in those formative years. Today 19 years later, Sage is an international company with 4000 employees, two million customers worldwide and over £300 million turnover. The simple truth is that if we can do it, so can anyone else.

Many books have been written about small businesses but none, in my view, has ever managed to address the real needs of those who actually run a small business.

What we have tried to do in this book is mix management theory with real practical advice. We have tried to make the book easy to read and easy to follow by using examples of good and bad experiences enjoyed or endured by some of our customers. We have also focused on different aspects of managing a small business - how to convince bank managers and venture capitalists to invest, how to manage a company through the good times and the bad times, how to manage people, how to use technology, how to succeed.

Last but not least, we have included a section on how small business can make the most of the opportunities presented by the internet.

You will not find all the answers to every question in the pages of this book, but I do hope you will find a stimulating read full of tips and advice on how to manage your business better.

Good luck!

Graham Wylie

Managing Director, Sage Software Limited.

An introduction from The Association of Chartered Certified Accountants

The Association of Chartered Certified Accountants (ACCA) has 250,000 members and students in 140 countries. Many own, work in or advise small businesses. Support for the small business community is, therefore, central to ACCA's activities. Our small business agenda is the responsibility of ACCA's Small Business Committee, the members of which are drawn from the accountancy profession, small businesses themselves and a range of organisations active in their support.

ACCA recognises that the small business community is complex. Professor Alan Gibb of Durham University Business School has identified seven features common to most small businesses:

- small business is a way of life

- it is about personal risk

- it means managing interdependencies

- know-who and know-how are more important than know-what

- small business means standing alone

- it means the buck really stops with you

- it means learning by doing.

However, there are many different communities and types of small business and a myriad of aspirations for businessmen and women. Too much small business support is oblivious to this complexity and too many packages of help have simply applied big business techniques to small business circumstances.

Business members of ACCA, known as Chartered Certified Accountants, are aware of this complexity, they can offer financial and management advice that will help small firms help themselves, tailoring advice to needs of each individual business. Many Chartered Certified Accountants are now experts in the fields of information technology expertise and raising business finance. Other specialisms range from employment law to human resources issues.

Like Sage, ACCA believes that small business owners know best where they want their business to go. ACCA can provide tools that will help them, but we are realistic enough to know that issues such as cash flow, late payment, regulations, paperwork and a lack of skilled employees are the most significant problems facing most small businesses. We can help resolve these issues, leaving business owners to concentrate on longer-term plans.

Government and the business support community talk incessantly about innovation, entrepreneurship and better management. Many businesses can make practical improvements to their competitiveness and in turn their capacity to add to wealth, employment and growth. However, all of us who seek to advise the small business community do well to remember, and to respect, the aspirations of business people. Running a small business is more than just "business". For many of you reading this book, it is a way of life and no one knows it better.

ACCA is pleased, therefore, to support the second edition of the Sage Guide, which offers excellent practical advice for anyone looking to start up, or to review, his or her business.

David Harvey, Secretary ACCA Small Business Committee

Setting Up
and Managing
Your Own Business

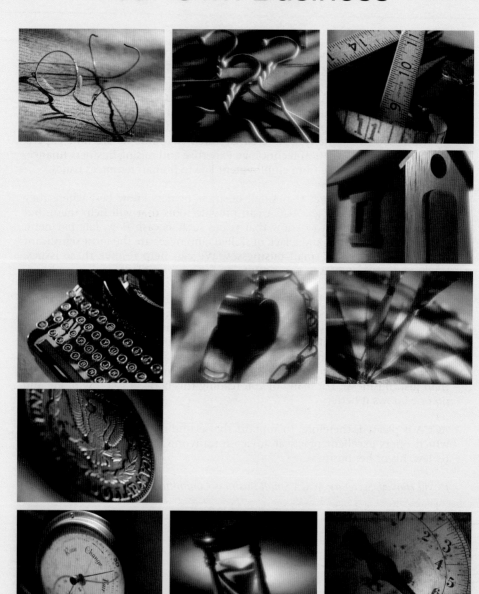

Contents

Chapter 4 Property, People and Practicalities

Chapter 5 Administration, Production and Communication

Chapter 6 Managing Manpower & Money

Chapter 7   The Internet

Chapter 8   Marketing the Business

Chapter 9 International Trade

Chapter 10 Managing Change

Chapter 11 Useful Information

Introduction

Defining a small business can be nearly as difficult as starting one. Size and market share have been tried, as have different definitions for each sector. For example, a manufacturing firm with 200 employees or fewer could be considered small, and a construction company with 26 workers large.

Inevitably the EC has its own definition, the latest version of which emerged in January 1997. To be small you have to employ between 10 and 49 people or turn over more than £5.6 million or have more than £4 million in the balance sheet. Anything smaller is micro and greater is medium.

As most firms in the UK don't publish a balance sheet with this financial muscle, this definition is unhelpful. A more realistic and widely accepted definition of small is any business privately owned. However you describe it, the number of people running their own business is still considerable. In the UK alone the small business population has grown from around two million in 1980 to more than 3.5 million in 1997. Across Europe one worker in eight runs their own business, and in Japan and the USA the figures are higher still. Russia, the former Soviet satellites and even China have all proved fertile ground for the new business starter.

Starting out in business, people rank independence as their primary motivation. Only 14 per cent have money as their foremost reason. By the time they are employing 20 people or more, independence as the primary goal has been supplanted by making money for nearly a third of business owners.

But whatever the motives, launching a small business or expanding an existing one successfully is not a simple task. Good ideas, hard work, enthusiasm, skills and knowledge about your product and how to make it, though essential, are not enough. Evidence for this is the substantial number of business failures and liquidations. By the mid 1990s company failures alone across Europe exceeded 200,000 a year, nearly double the figure for the start of the decade. To be sure, the adverse economic climate was responsible for some of those failures, but even in the relatively buoyant late 1990s over 300,000 businesses of all types die each year in the UK alone.

Most of these failures occur within the first few years. This has made it increasingly clear that small businesses need special help - particularly in their formative period. For example, owners and managers often need help in acquiring business skills in such areas as basic book-keeping and accounting. Most failing businesses simply do not know their financial position. The order book can be full when the cash runs out. Then they need information with which to make realistic assessments of the size and potential of their chosen market. Over-optimism about the size and ease with which a market can be reached is an all too common mistake. This book endeavours to focus on ways to avoid these problems and offers solutions to try to prevent such calamities. It cannot be emphasised enough, however, that good clear planning is essential. You might be the best salesman, or have a great idea, but without an overall plan even you may get into difficulty. Remember in business as in life to really succeed it's as important to work on your weaknesses as well as your strengths.

Owners and managers also need to know what sort of finance is available and how to put themselves in the best possible position to raise it. Surprisingly, there is no shortage of funds. Problems lie, rather, in the business proposition itself, or, more often, in the way in which the proposition is made to the financier. This calls for a business plan - a statement of business purpose - with the consequences spelled out in financial terms. For example, you must describe what you want your business to do, who its customers will be, how much they will spend, who will supply you, how much their supplies will cost. Then you must translate those plans and projections into cash - how much your business will need, how much you already have, how much you expect outsiders to put in. For most people this calls for new knowledge. They have never prepared a business plan before, and they do not know how to start. Naturally, this should not put you off as this book shows there are numerous professionals eager to advise and, in the early stages, particularly if you negotiate well, costs should not be prohibitive. Furthermore, there are numerous bodies such as Business Link who are geared up to assist start ups and expanding businesses. Consider it like this. You have to cross the M1 to pick up £100. You could run randomly across without looking and you'd probably get squished! Alternatively, you could make a plan - I'll go at 5 o'clock in the morning on a mid summer day, look both ways, proceed to the central reservation and use the same process to cross the second carriageway. OK you might get squished but, in business, planning is essential if you want to prosper!

The business plan will also help them to escape the 'graveyard' of small businesses - underestimating the amount of start-up capital they will need. It is difficult, if not impossible, to go back to a bank and ask for another 30 per cent of funding six months after opening the doors and retain any credibility at all. And yet this is what happens. New businesses consistently underestimate how much they will need to finance growth. Most end up struggling where they need not have struggled, or failing where there was no market reason for failure.

Inventors and technologists have special problems of communication and security when they try to translate their ideas into businesses. All too often their inventions have been left for other countries to exploit, or else they feel unhappy about discussing ideas, believing that a patent is their only protection. But more often than not they simply do not know who to talk to, little realising that sophisticated help is often close at hand. Thus a path from the laboratory to the marketplace has to be illuminated so that small firms and inventors can see a clear route. New technologies have to be made available to new businesses. The microcomputer that has revolutionised big business has now begun to knock on the doors of smaller businesses. For this reason these firms have to know how to exploit this technology and so remain competitive - or they may join the ranks of the failures.

This book is aimed at those who either want to start up a business or to review their prospects in the small business world. It brings together, from a wide variety of sources, the essential elements of knowledge that are a prerequisite to understanding the world of small business. This book is not intended to be read at one sitting, or even from beginning to end. Rather you should use it as a guide and mentor when you are reviewing a particular topic. Ultimately, running a business is a tough option but with good planning, despite the statistics, it can be very rewarding.

Colin Barrow

Cranfield

Thoughts, Dreams & Aspirations

Chapter One

THOUGHTS, DREAMS & ASPIRATIONS

To launch a new business successfully calls for a particular type of person. Business founders are frequently seen as people who are always bursting with new ideas, highly enthusiastic and able to talk the hind legs off a donkey. But the more you try to create a picture of the typical small business founder the more elusive they become. For every extrovert, such as Richard Branson, there is a similarly successful entrepreneur who is virtually invisible, such as Barrie Haigh. Barrie founded Innovex which he grew from a modest £8 million annual turnover business in 1990 to one worth £550 million in 1996. He did this whilst giving virtually no interviews to the press and has since all but vanished from view.

Peter Drucker, the great American business guru, summed it up nicely with this definition:

"Some are eccentrics, others painfully correct conformists; some are fat and some are lean; some are worriers, some relaxed; some drink quite heavily, others are total abstainers; some have great charm, some have no more personality than a frozen mackerel."

It seems it is not so much a genetic type that makes for a successful business starter, rather a way of behaving. That behaviour needs to encompass a capacity for hard work and a willingness to accept uncertainty whilst still being prepared to plan.

This chapter gives an insight into how to turn your dreams into a viable business.

In my experience . . .

I would like to pass on a piece of advice that I received a few years ago at a relaxation class. I have found this advice invaluable during the past eighteen months whilst helping my colleagues set up and manage Bishop Financial Management.

"To avoid the stresses of over-commitment, choose between what is achievable and what is a waste of time, then devote your energies only to what you can achieve"

Viki Harwood, Administration Manager, Bishop Financial Management Ltd

Running Your Own Business

So you want to set up and run your own business. Or maybe you are already running your own business and want to make some changes. There are many people who have walked this route, with and without success, so advice is readily available, in fact unavoidable. Let me offer a little more.

To be successful you have to be ambitious, you have to want to achieve, and you have to want to be seen to be successful. You are going to make a poor start if there is no powerful driving force.

However, a desire for success must not be allowed to override common sense. Be flexible and prepared to compromise. A new business needs a plan but more importantly it needs a vision against which everything is set. Flexibility allows you to spot opportunities for achieving the vision in ways which you may not have realised at the outset. Change the plan but maintain the vision.

Be resilient. There will be occasions when you will be set back and things will not turn out as planned. Turn these occasions into opportunities. It is rare to start a new business and not have disappointment as well as success. If you expect some disappointment it is easier to put it behind you quickly and concentrate on the successful aspects. But do learn from the disappointment.

Seek and take advice. There is a network of people whose reputation is enhanced by your success. Let them help you. In particular seek advice on the use of information and communications technology. A special group, known as Technology Means Business Advisors, has been trained to help small businesses use ICT to improve their competitiveness. Seek the support of one before you make any decisions. You will find more about Technology Means Business on the Internet.

Commitment, enthusiasm and good advice, while essential, are not alone sufficient for a successful business start-up. Many of those who are not successful failed to recognise their own lack of business and management skill. Indeed aspiring owner-managers often confuse 'advice' with 'knowhow'.

Starting your own business is similar to climbing mountains. You start with the desire to do it - you want the thrill of the climb and the fulfilment of reaching the top. But being shown the equipment and the best route is not sufficient to start your first ascent. There is a personal development phase. You have identified your first challenge. A good instructor will help you identify your present skill level and the additional skills you require to reach the first peak. With help you can learn to use the right equipment. You need some practice in an exercise environment. Your instructor is in attendance, coaching to ensure that you are well prepared for the real thing. Only when you are ready should you attempt the first climb. With careful preparation it will be successful. Because you had some practice you will be looking for the obvious pitfalls.

When you've completed the first climb, achieved the first challenge, your advisers will tell you what comprises the second challenge. Now is the time to undertake another phase of personal development. Seek the support of your climbing instructor, learn to use new equipment, extend your skills to a level that matches the next challenge. When you feel ready - go for it.

Each new climb will extend your experience, but each should be accompanied by a planned extension of your ability. Your climbing instructor will help you create a personal development plan to ensure that you will always have the skill level to match the severity of the climb and to face new challenges.

This is what it is like when starting your own business. It may be that you already have all the skills you need, in which case you are unlikely to be reading this book. However most people need a range of new skills at each stage. Find out from your advisers what your first challenge will be then seek help to ensure that your skills are matched to the challenge you face. Be selective and develop your skills to match your progress. This way you ensure that you know the challenge of each phase and that you have given yourself the best chance of success. Remember that personal development is not a one-shot process - it is a continuing process of development.

Glyn Macken, Director, The Institute of Management

Planning To Start Your Own Business

Many of us dream of running our own business, eager to enjoy the thrill of working for ourselves and not having to answer to an endless stream of managers. But before starting to run your own business, you must ask yourself some simple, but nonetheless important questions.

One major factor is the number of hours you will need to give to ensure that your business will be a success - the '9 to 5' mentality just doesn't work. Once the working day is over, paperwork, restocking, marketing and the chasing of debt all become part of the routine. Family time, holidays and weekends will be secondary considerations. If the business activity stops and the income dries up, there are very few state benefits to assist the struggling entrepreneur.

During the first few months, the main problem will be building a customer base, funding your initial stock and equipment and managing your cash flow and probably getting paid late on top of all that. Credit facilities are available to new small businesses but bank managers will want to see a cash flow forecast, business plan and probably some sort of security to protect any loans or overdraft facilities they grant. Too many prospective entrepreneurs go into the bank with a great idea, but forget to take along a fully costed, detailed business plan. The bank manager simply isn't interested without one.

A brilliant idea for a business will count for nothing unless it is truly viable and there is a market for it. One thing which tends to get overlooked sometimes is that a great idea may be too specialised - there may be a need for the service, but not enough demand. What a new business needs is a unique selling point to set it apart from its competitors. Finally, small businesses cannot afford big sums on market research, so they have to examine the market as cheaply and thoroughly as possible.

After reading this, you may ask yourself whether it is all worth it. Every year though, thousands believe that it is, and with work and effort, manage to succeed. Each different business will face different, specific problems, but with the right planning your business can be a success!

David Hands, Deputy Head of Press and Parliamentary Affairs, Federation of Small Businesses

THINKING AHEAD

Why be your own boss? The first question you should ask yourself when starting a business is why you want to do it - only then can you ask yourself how.

There may be lots of reasons why you want to do it, but one of them should always be: "I want to make money". At the end of the day that is what every business is about. You must also believe in yourself. You must believe that you will succeed. A brilliant new idea for a product, being the best at what you do, or simply wanting the freedom to be your own boss is not enough unless you are convinced that you will succeed - and succeed financially.

You also need to be sure that it's what you really want to do. Starting a business is a risk. You may have to give up a secure job and borrow money secured on your major assets - usually your family home. It's a brave but potentially rewarding step that you are about to take.

All right, so now you know why you want to do it, the next question is how. Decisions that you take right at the start can make a fundamental difference to the success of your business in the future. Are you going to go it alone, or do you need partners who can bring extra skills and experience that you don't have. You might need a partner today but are you going to want to share the rewards of your hard work in ten years' time? What legal structure is best?

Take the right advice. It may seem expensive to spend money on accountants and lawyers when you're just starting out, but an investment in experienced advisers will reap rewards as your business takes off.

Good advisers will also have contacts that could help you to make sure that you have the appropriate finance in place. Remember that two out of three start-ups will fail in the first three years, and one of the most common reasons is a lack of cash.

When it comes to your business plan you should remember that its main purpose is to convince you of the viability of your venture. It's a realistic working plan, not simply a document to impress the bank manager who will have seen hundreds of plans that attempt to do exactly that. Above all it must be your plan - not your advisers. They are only there to help. You must live, breathe and believe in your plan and be able to justify the figures and underlying assumptions.

In the search for finance you're not limited to borrowing - you can also consider equity investment. But you should remember that while selling 30 per cent of your business for £30,000 may seem like a good deal today, it might not look so good when in five years' time your sleeping partner owns 30 per cent of your £10m business.

You should take care when entering into your first deals with suppliers. It's very easy to get locked into agreements that may solve immediate cash flow problems but can also lock you into long and expensive contracts.

This isn't intended to put off would-be entrepreneurs, rather to serve notice that it's a rocky road ahead but one that can be very rewarding both personally and financially.

Running your own business gives you the freedom to make your own choices and shape your destiny.

Andrew Godfrey, Head of Growth and Development Services, Grant Thornton

STARTING IN BUSINESS

Many businesses start from a glimmer of an idea in an entrepreneur's mind which may develop in many different ways. Generally a business plan is an essential business tool. It is a document that sets out how the business idea will come to fruition and how the business will operate. It helps to focus ideas and push management effort in the right direction and should therefore be produced whether or not you are likely to need additional finance for the business.

The business plan

The business plan is an ongoing document. Its forecasts and assumptions need to be measured against actual costs and sales on a regular basis and updated so that the plan can be used as a yardstick for the ongoing progress of the business.

Preparing a business plan has many important advantages. It means that you have to think carefully about every aspect of the business and explain the reasoning behind the decisions made. Planning ahead in this way helps you to foresee difficulties and make arrangements to deal with any problems well in advance. The business plan itself becomes an operations manual that covers all aspects of the business and which can therefore be used for guidance in day-to-day decision-making. And finally (and the reason many business plans are written) it helps to demonstrate to potential financial backers that you know and understand your business and the market the business operates in.

To be useful in these ways, a business plan should include:

- Introduction
- Management - the people involved and their experience
- Description of the product or service to be supplied
- The market - customers, level of demand, growth potential
- Pricing policies - especially vis-à-vis competitors
- Legal issues - e.g. structure of the business
- Premises and location
- Objectives - short, medium and long term
- Financial information
  - Cash flow forecasts
  - Cash flow assumptions
  - Profit forecasts
  - Break-even point
  - Finance requirements
- Additional information in the form of appendices.

Market Research

Market research forms the bedrock of the business plan. Many businesses are handicapped by a lack of information at the planning stage. To base all strategic decisions or financial forecasts on assumptions rather than on researched fact is a recipe for disaster. It is also essential to recognise that market research is an ongoing activity. Information needs to be gathered regularly and the business plan updated accordingly if the company is to stay ahead of the game.

Do not confuse pure market research with test marketing. Market research involves understanding how your industry works and where your business fits into the marketplace. Test marketing is a process of gauging the likely response of the market to a specific product or service.

The four main areas that require research are:

 Market forces - what governs success in your marketplace

 Customers - demographics of who and where they are

 Competition - who they are, size, market activity, pricing

 Suppliers - size, viability, levels of price competition

The legalities of running the business need to be established before trading starts. Initially it is important to decide on the type of legal structure under which the business will operate (sole trader, partnership, limited company) and to ensure that the way the business is set up ensures that day-to-day operations conform to the relevant aspects of company law.

The main areas to consider are:

- Legal structure
- Business name
- Inland Revenue requirements
- National Insurance requirements
- VAT registration
- Working from home
- Licences required
- Health and Safety regulations
- Fire regulations
- Trading regulations
- Employment requirements and regulations
- Insurances - public liability, employee liability, fire, consequential loss, theft, goods in transit, fidelity, sickness, key person
- Data Protection Act

Why be self-employed?

There may be many reasons for considering self-employment. Most people are attracted by the idea of escaping the daily grind of working for someone else and being in charge of their own destiny. Other reasons frequently given for taking this step are:

- Being able to make your own decisions
- Continuation of the business through the next generation
- Creating employment for the family
- Being able to capitalise on specialist skills
- Earning your own money when you want
- Having flexible working hours for existing or family commitments
- Taking a calculated risk on your own abilities
- Reducing existing stress and worry

- Having satisfaction in your own work and achievements
- Being your own boss
- Working without having to rely on others

All are valid reasons - but some people are more suited to self-employment than others. To assess your own ability for self-employment you need to take a realistic look at your own strengths and weaknesses, the business idea, the existing market and the potential for growth. Businesses fail for a variety of reasons - for example, high costs, low demand, inadequate skills, underpricing. All these areas and more can be addressed by a thoroughly researched and thought through business plan that highlights potential problems and is sufficiently detailed to assist managers in steering the company through them.

Do

Take time to plan

Take professional/expert advice

Research in detail

Consider changing initial plans in response to changing circumstances

Do realistic planning, particularly related to cash flow

Don't

Jump in without thought

Keep all your eggs in one basket - have a range of suppliers/outlets

Don't

Ignore legalities - VAT, Inland Revenue etc

Be afraid to ask for help

Ignore the business plan - it is an ongoing management tool

Graham Bayliss, Business Link, Coventry & Warwickshire

In my experience . . .

With hindsight, my seven rules for starting a new business would be:

- Speak to someone who has run a similar sized company before you go with your idea - many small business owners are likely to help someone they see as being in the same boat
- Cash flow is certainly key for any new business
- Always treat people as you would like to be treated yourself
- If you pay peanuts, you get monkeys
- Information is the key to any business venture - in sales terms this may mean subscribing to the right trade magazines or learning to network properly
- While your business may start off successfully it is always important to think six to twelve months ahead - and beyond if possible
- If you really believe in an idea and have thought it through, then go for it. Before you start up a business many people will be only too keen to tell you all the risks and the down sides - don't dismiss these, but don't let them dampen your enthusiasm

Enthusiasm, fun and belief are my key reasons for having my own business. I believe that the financial upside will happen as a result of this. Yes, you work long hours with your own business but if you enjoy it, why not?

Jamie Cunningham, Professional Sports Partnerships Ltd

COURSES TO CONSIDER

Attending courses can make a real difference to successfully starting your business. Many of those available are run by people who have been through the experience themselves.

Local agencies run workshops where you will find yourself learning alongside people with similar ambitions to your own. The sessions are tailored to benefit individuals who often have limited resources.

Before starting up, you can attend awareness sessions which will point out the ups and downs of running your own business. Courses are also available on sales and marketing, managing money (including how to keep basic books) and preparing a business plan.

Once up and running, you will be able to access a wide range of courses to help make your business grow. Many of these are supported by the government and you will be required only to make a relatively small financial contribution.

You can get advice on :

- Finance
- Marketing
- Exporting
- Strategic business planning
- Time management
- Quality management systems
- Managing people

Information and help is available for employees on training courses, many of which lead to national vocational qualifications (NVQs).

Small businesses are also being encouraged to gain recognition as an Investor in People. This National Standard demonstrates that a company is seeking to achieve the best from its employees by utilising their full potential. Advice can be obtained from local teams of Personal Business Advisers and counsellors. They all have good experience of helping to make businesses grow. Some will provide specialist advice on the area that is of particular interest to you.

Where do I find out about these courses?

The agencies for helping you start and grow your own business are the local Training and Enterprise Council (TEC), Business Link and Enterprise Agency. All of these are listed in the phone book - often at the front with other essential services. These agencies work in partnership with each other, so whoever you call first will put you in touch with exactly the right person to help with your type of business. They will signpost the most appropriate courses and sometimes provide financial support. There is also a wide range of information services which can make a significant difference to the effectiveness of your marketing.

Godfrey Blakeley, TEC National Council

DO YOU WANT TO BE AN ETHICAL BUSINESS?

Over the past twenty years there has been one major business development which has recently gathered even more pace. Increasingly, companies have begun to challenge many of the basic notions of how they should operate, and as a result they have become more open to new ideas about their role in the wider society. As they have tried to develop a socially aware company ethos, so they have prospered.

For some companies this has simply been a recognition that if they treat their staff decently, in return those employees will be more loyal and productive. For others it has been a case of giving a new respect to customers where in the past they may have been taken somewhat for granted.

But the essence of those companies who either are, or are striving to be, ethical businesses is wider and more comprehensive than just these important recognitions. The concept is one which embraces the entire scope of the relationships which the company forms with its work force, with its customers, with its suppliers and with the wider world outside of those 'natural' partners.

As the word ethical implies, an ethical company tries to take the widest view of its responsibilities. It is concerned that it does not contribute to pollution - either on its own doorstep or elsewhere - that it does not benefit from the overuse of scarce natural resources such as fossil fuels and non-replaceable rain forest products, and that it tries to favour socially desirable objectives where all other criteria are equal.

Ethical companies are value driven entities as well as profit making enterprises. They are about long term sustainability as well as shorter term profitability. They foster a greater involvement in the communities they serve, and from which they derive their materials, giving something back as well as taking something away.

Why Bother?

Becoming an ethical company has many advantages:

* You feel more comfortable and confident dealing ethically
* As a marketing and publicity tool - customers like to feel they are involved with honest and caring organisations
* Building client trust leads to repeat business, and enables longer term relationships such as partnering rather than the uncertainty of constant tendering exercises
* As a consistent and fair employer - employees identify more with a company they feel respects them as individuals, and in return they are more loyal, co-operative and productive
* Reduced likelihood of industrial relations and tribunal hassles
* Ability to negotiate lower insurance premiums - less likelihood of professional indemnity claims, pollution clean-up risks etc.
* Changing standards and culture in business allows you to speak to a whole new and growing market in the public, voluntary and not-for-profit sector - as well as traditional ones.

What's Involved, and How Do I Join?

There isn't an Association and it isn't a Club. Anyone can call themselves an ethical business, but unless you really mean it, your customers will pretty soon 'find you out'.

You need to establish clearly what are the company's values and spell them out in plain English for everyone to see - customers, suppliers, work force and partners. As well as the obvious things such as straight and honest dealing, they should address how you deal with the less obvious things like prompt settlement of bills, accidental overcharging or overestimating.

You will need to identify the issues of local sustainability and environmental concern that affect the area of business you are intending to operate within. A car repair business should make appropriate arrangements for the recycling and disposal of oil and scrap metal, as well as taking account of disturbance and disruption to neighbours. A small shop might concentrate on the local provision of goods and the sourcing of products from environmentally friendly organisations.

Drawing up an Ethical Plan (as with your Business Plan), will help you to cover these and such other important points as Quality Assurance, Customer Care, Investing in People, and an Environmental Management Strategy. Similarly, an Ethical Audit (as with your financial audit), will assist you to trace your successes and identify the areas for future attention.

If you embark on this route, you need to be clear that these are not add-ons to your other business aspirations. They must be as central to your core business as the other values you bring.

As a new business you will find that the ethical dimension is rewarding for the range of unexpected opportunities it opens up, as well as the satisfaction you will gain from working in a more rounded environment. Approach it with enthusiasm - but don't let yourself become too 'earnest' or 'worthy'!

Peter Kahn, Director, Ethical Consultancy Services Ltd.

PLANNING YOUR PERSONAL FINANCES

If you are a business owner you probably work very long hours. Probably the last thing that you want to do after a long day is to sit down and sort out your personal financial affairs. But this is the time you should start thinking about yourself and your family.

The danger with being busy is that sometimes we overlook the need for long term planning. But it is important sometimes to reflect on why we are in business, and what we are trying to achieve. Do we want more money, more time, or more fun?

The first step is to bring all your personal financial affairs under control. Decide first on what you want to achieve and ask a few basic questions. What pension arrangements and insurance do you have? Is your borrowing at minimum cost and tax-effective? How are your investments performing? Could your tax situation be improved? Bringing all of these matters together in a comprehensive way should ensure the most effective use of your resources towards achieving your personal goals and aspirations.

The key to personal success is almost certainly the way in which you run the company, how you derive financial benefits from it and ultimately how you sell it. If your pension arrangements are inadequate, then it may be important to find a way in which the company can make the necessary extra profits out of which to pay the pension contributions. The link between yourself and the company is crucial - there is no point in identifying problems alone, we must find solutions to them as well.

How do you plan your income for the coming year? Many business owners decide what they think they can sell; then they look at the level of their existing overheads; and by deducting one from the other, they come up with what is left as their profit share. May I suggest an alternative approach?

I call this upside-down budgeting. Here you put yourself at the front of the queue, not at the back. You first decide what you need as income for the coming year, including any pension contributions that ought to be made. This is the starting point. Then look at your overhead position - what is the expected cost of running the business over the next year? From this you can derive the level of turnover you have to achieve. This is not an optional target - you have to achieve it to meet your income requirement.

This is one example of why planning and being realistic is so important, both in business and in your private life. As an analogy, imagine that you are about to build a new house. You have the land and you have assembled the materials on the site. If you engage a builder, the first thing he will ask for is the plan. It would be laughable to seek to build a house with just materials and land, and no plan. But that is what many of us do, in our businesses and our private lives - assemble the materials and build with no plans at all.

There is an old saying - 'We never plan to fail, we simply fail to plan'. It's sadly true.

David Norton, Norton Partners and the Immediate Past President of the Institute of Financial Planning

PRIVATE PENSION PROVISIONS AND SMALL BUSINESSES

The Main Options

Private Pensions are, in simple terms, a form of investment which enjoy a number of tax privileges, in fact they can be in many instances the most tax efficient retirement savings vehicle available to small business owners and their employees.

The general tax advantages are as follows:-

- Corporation tax relief on employer contributions
- Income tax relief , at the highest rate paid , in employee contributions
- Part of the retirement benefits can be taken as a tax free lump sum
- Lump sums paid on death are normally free of taxes

However, as a result of these tax advantages certain restrictions are placed on private pensions in order to prevent abuse. These are:-

- There are limits that can be contributed, these depend on the type of private pension used
- The benefits can usually only be taken after a certain age, often 50 years old
- A proportion of the benefits must be taken in the form of a pension income, which is subject to tax.
- An employee cannot contribute to an occupational pension and a personal pension at the same time.

Why would a small business consider establishing a pension scheme besides the tax advantages?

- A pre-retirement investment vehicle for some or all employees
- An employee benefit to assist in recruiting and retaining good quality staff
- A useful tax planning tool

Private Pensions can be set up to include all employees or just a few employees, such as the business directors.

There are two main types of pension which have different rules on the level of contributions and the benefits. These are an occupational pensions scheme and a personal pension scheme

Occupational Pension

In general, occupational pension schemes exist to provide employees with retirement benefits.

Occupational pensions must be set up under an irrevocable trust, include a contribution from the company and must be for the benefit of employees. They take one of two main forms.

Money Purchase Scheme: the employer decides how much the company and employee will contribute. The benefits available on retirement depend on the salary at retirement and number of years service as well as the total value of the pension fund.

Final Salary Scheme: the pension scheme guarantees the employee a level of pension benefits on retirement depending on the employee's length of service and level of salary at or near retirement age. The employee pays a percentage of earnings into the scheme and the employer is responsible for meeting the rest of the cost to provide the guaranteed pension benefits.

There are two specific types of money purchase pension schemes which are used by small business directors:

Executive Pension plans or directors pension plans are a form of occupational pension money purchase scheme designed specifically for one or a small number of employees.

They have two closely linked functions, in the first place they are used as a tax planning vehicle turning taxable business profits into tax efficient benefits for the future.

Secondly, they are used to attract and benefit key personnel of the business. Whilst they are subject to the occupational pension tax rules they are more like a personal pension scheme (see below) and are provided by a large number of insurance companies.

A Small Self Administered Scheme (SSAS) is a scheme with fewer than twelve members which has more control over where the contributions and pension fund is invested.

One of the attractions of SSAS for small businesses is the ability to invest in the firm's premises and lend back to the sponsoring company some of the scheme assets. However, this investment flexibility is subject to very strict tax regulations imposed by the Inland revenue on where and how much of the pension scheme funds are used in this way.

Personal Pensions

Personal pensions are an alternative to occupational pension schemes and are individual contracts taken out by an employee with an insurance company.

Personal Pensions are subject to a different tax treatment in which the contributions are limited by a percentage of earnings depending on the age of the individual, subject to an overall maximum level (see table 1 below as the maximum that can be contributed).

The retirement benefits are based on the value of the pension fund at retirement age (any time after 50) and this can all be taken in form of a pension income or up to 25% of the fund can be taken as a tax free lump sum whilst the rest must be a pension income.

Group Personal Pensions provide an alternative for companies to setting up an occupational pension scheme and are currently the preferred choice for many small businesses as they are simpler to operate and not subject to the same administration requirements. Furthermore, an employer can make a group personal pension available to employees but is not obliged to make any contributions.

A personal pension with more investment flexibility is known as a self invested personal pension (SIPP). These allow the pension contribution and fund to invest in a wider range of assets other than just insurance company funds; these include shares and commercial property.

Maximum Contributions to a PPP (1999/2000)

AGE	% of Earnings
35 or less	17.5
36-45	20
46-50	25
51-55	30
56-60	35
61-74	40

By Stephen Ingledew, Head of Corporate Pensions, NPI

The challenge before you start up is to identify your own business strengths and weaknesses. You can top up your skills and learn how to adopt new habits and patterns of behaviour, perhaps by taking a course or by looking carefully at how other successful business people in your field operate. It might pay you to revisit this chapter, certainly before you start up.

In my experience . . .

Some of the best things about running your own business are:

- Taking that order number
- Being paid on time by large organisations
- Making a good profit at the end of the financial year
- Letters of thanks from satisfied customers
- Getting new customers and continually satisfying your existing ones

. . . and some of the worst things:

- The time it takes for capital projects to become real orders and the plethora of in-house organisational politics in other companies that gets in the way
- Always having to stay one step ahead and constantly ask yourself where the new business is coming from
- People who habitually tell lies

Mike Seeley, Hugh Jennings Ltd

In my experience . . .

Always on the lookout for new talent I went to see a young rugby player of whom I had heard great things - Alex King. We met in Bristol where he was a student and the first meeting went very well. We agreed at the time that his best bet was to look at all the options, but I left the meeting confident that Alex would want to sign with us - and he gave the same impression in a subsequent telephone conversation.

Unfortunately I had to go to Portugal on business for a week and in the interim Alex was approached by Peter Powell's organisation. He met Peter and his wife, Anthea Turner, and by the time I returned from Portugal he had signed with Peter Powell's group.

Some may say that I should have acted more quickly and undoubtedly one of the lessons to be taken from this is that one should take nothing for granted. However, I respect Alex for taking the glamour option as opposed to our relatively new company. Yes Anthea's legs are better than mine, but basically Alex went with credibility. Two years on we can compete on an equal footing.

Jamie Cunningham, Professional Sports Partnerships Ltd

The apparent contradiction between the statistics which show manufacturing start-ups rising and the overall contraction of the sector is brought about because the new breed of manufacturer is a high tech, low employment venture. They are more likely to outsource the heavy elements of manufacturing to larger firms. A sort of sub contracting in reverse.

Recent business starters are more likely to be men; however, between a quarter and a third of new businesses are started by women. They are also likely to be older. Ten years ago, two thirds of business starters were under 35. Now it's under a half, although all age groups are well represented. Business starters are now better educated, with only 26% having no qualifications compared with 39 % a decade ago. The self employed who are employing people are likely to be more highly educated still. Over 16% of them have degrees, compared with 11% of those who work alone. However success stories involving entrepreneurs who left school at 16 or less still greatly outnumber those concerning high flying "nerds". The new small business owner works harder than ever. A third work over 57 hours a week, whilst only a fifth of their staff work as long. Interestingly, male business owners with children work longer hours than those without. Female business owners work fewer hours when they have children. Over half of business owners say they have less time for family and friends now than before they started in business. It's hard work running your own business, it can often be worth it . . . but not always!

The Business Structure

Chapter Two

It is pretty frightening to think that many big mistakes are made before the business even gets started. Whilst some founders are debating the colour of the office phone, major decisions on exactly how to trade are going by the board. People find themselves in partnership with the wrong people or even with people they never knew were their partners. They get into 'fifty-fifty' relationships which sound fair but make decision-making all but impossible, just when it is most important for clear and focused leadership.

Too many business starters end up shouldering all the risk personally, when it would make more sense for a company to bear the burden and may be more tax efficient too.

Don't sign anything until you have read this chapter.

YOUR BUSINESS STRUCTURE - THE OPTIONS

The main structures for trading in Great Britain are as a sole trader, a partnership or a limited company. Although commonly regarded as such, a franchise is not a trading structure. The franchisee can adopt any of the three trading formats, but is restricted by the terms of the contract with its franchisor.

Trading as a sole trader

Advantages

This is the simplest business structure. You can trade in your own name, and manage yourself. The minimum administrative requirements apply. If you have no premises or employees and turnover is below the VAT threshold, you need only tell the DSS and the Inland Revenue before you commence trading. The profits from carrying on your trade will be taxed under Schedule D, Case I of the Taxes Act.

Disadvantages

As you trade in your own name, you have unlimited personal liability. This means that you are liable for any debts of the business and your personal assets could be used to pay business debts. Ultimately, your creditors could make you bankrupt.

Other businesses know that sole traders are good for credit only up to the limits of their own wealth. So it may take time to build up good credit terms with your suppliers, and your main source of external funding will be bank overdrafts and perhaps loans from investors.

You may not wish to trade under your own name. Perhaps it is not the most memorable name, or not appropriate for your business image. You can instead trade under a business name. If so, you cannot use certain words and expressions (e.g. 'University', 'Pharmacy') without approval from the DTI and any other relevant bodies. You will also need to display prominently upon all stationery etc., and at places of business to which suppliers or customers have access, your name and an address within Great Britain for service of documents upon you. Companies and partnerships who use business names have similar obligations.

Trading as a partnership

Advantages

A partnership automatically arises where two or more people agree they will share responsibility and decision-making for a business, and do so. There need be no formal written contract. An oral agreement suffices, although the law will imply provisions into the agreement in the absence of express provision. The law also imposes a duty of utmost fairness and good faith in partners' dealings with each other.

Partnerships work well where there is symbiosis - where the skills and contributions of each partner complement each other and where fundamental decisions are reached after full and considered debate. Partnerships are said to have more credibility in the business community than sole traders, probably because professionals, such as accountants and solicitors, have traditionally traded as partners.

Partners are taxed in a similar way to sole traders, upon the taxable profits of the business, divided in accordance with the profit-sharing arrangements of the partnership.

Disadvantages

Some of the largest legal bills arise from partnership disputes, often stemming from personality clashes overriding business sense. Be very wary about with whom you enter partnership, as in general you will be personally liable for business losses of the partnership, even if these were incurred by a partner without actual authority from the other partners. It is always prudent to instruct a solicitor to draw up a partnership deed for you, which will at the least define the commencement date of the partnership, the name of the partnership, who the partners are and the scope of the partnership. It will also modify the terms the law implies in the absence of agreement, regulate dealings between partners and outsiders and set out covenants and profit/loss-sharing ratios for each partner.

The maximum number of partners is 20, with some exceptions such as professional partnerships.

Trading as a company

Advantages

A company is seen as a person in the eyes of the law, and is quite separate from the individuals concerned, even if they are the directors and shareholders of the company. The company can own property, execute contracts, commit crimes, and, crucially, it can owe money. This is the principal advantage of running a limited company - for a hundred years it has been accepted that the liability of shareholders is limited to the amount of capital unpaid on their shares. There are a few instances where Parliament or the courts view it as prudent to 'lift the veil' of incorporation, such as where the directors have been trading fraudulently, but these are few and far between. Generally, if a company goes into liquidation as a result of poor sales or poor management, the shareholders and directors can simply walk away, taking anything that remains of the assets after preferential debtors and creditors have been paid in full.

The corporate form institutionalises the separation of management and ownership because, although the shareholders own the company, it is the directors who run the company on a day-to-day basis. In smaller companies, the directors and shareholders will be one and the same, but as companies grow the amount of issued share capital increases and it becomes increasingly expensive for the directors to amass a significant tranche of the equity of the company. The directors are of course answerable to the shareholders, who can remove any director or the entire board of directors by a simple majority, and on a whim. In larger companies this becomes both difficult, due to the large number of shareholders whose agreement would be required, and expensive, because of the cost of settling any claims of redundancy and/or unfair and/or wrongful dismissal (especially where the directors have 'golden parachutes', i.e. service contracts specifying substantial termination payments).

A limited company is usually regarded as more credible and reliable than a sole trader or partnership, but you should bear in mind that anyone, and in particular any creditor, is free to perform a company search to discover how much (or little) paid-up capital and assets the company has recorded with the Registrar of Companies.

As explained in more detail later in this book, companies enjoy a wide range of opportunities for raising finance. As well as receiving injections of capital in the form of shares and loans, companies can issue 'floating charges' on their changing assets, and successful companies can convert to public limited companies to offer shares to the public, or to 'float' on a stock exchange where the general public can trade those shares.

Forming a company is relatively easy. All it requires is that you send four documents to Companies House in Cardiff together with a cheque for £20.

These are the memorandum (stating the name of the company, the 'objects' for which the company is incorporated, the country of registered office, the names of the founding shareholders etc.), the 'articles' (the rules by which the company is to operate), Form 10 (a standard form containing details of the first directors and secretary of the company etc), and Form 12 (a statutory declaration that all requirements of the Companies Act have been adhered to in the formation). A solicitor will do this for about £300, or you could simply buy an existing 'shelf company' that has not traded and change the name to one of your choice.

Disadvantages

The main difficulty with trading as a company is adhering to the detailed provisions of the Companies Act and case law. To give but a few instances of the administrative difficulties that you will experience, you will be required by statute to maintain a register of shareholders, directors, secretaries, directors' interests in company securities etc., 'mortgages' granted by the company, minutes of board (directors') and general (shareholders') meetings; to maintain accounting records and keep copies of directors' service contracts. All stationery used by the company must bear its name, place of registration, registered number and address and either the names of all the directors or none of them.

Directors of a company are subject to numerous duties to their company, and virtually all company matters will result in legal documentation, a good deal of which you will have to file with Companies House within strict timescales.

Unless you have previous experience of company law and accounting, you will require the advice and assistance of solicitors and accountants in running your company. In the long term this will be expensive, however efficiently you use their services, but is unavoidable if you are to ensure that you do not risk the criminal liability that can arise if you breach company law.

Finally, for directors of many small companies, limited liability can be somewhat illusory. At least in the early years of trading, banks and suppliers will often demand personal guarantees from director-shareholders before advancing cash or supplying goods. If the company fails, the directors' assets are then just as vulnerable as those of the partner or sole trader.

Becoming a franchisee

Any one of the above business structures can be adopted to carry on a franchise business. Franchise agreements are contracts whereby the owners of a business name, trademark or 'unique selling proposition' (the franchisor) grants you, as franchisee, the right to use that device and to 'buy into' that brand.

Advantages

By copying the design of the franchiser's premises, and working to his tried and tested formula, you can gain from the experience and goodwill he has amassed. Additionally, the most successful franchises (e.g. Perfect Pizza, The Body Shop) usually provide training, business guidance and national advertising for the benefit of their franchisees. In return for this, you would typically pay royalties on your sales, and purchase at least part of your stock from the franchisor or associated businesses.

Disadvantages

Although many franchisees have prospered from the dynamism, organisation and marketing of their franchisers, as always take heed of the rule that risk is commensurate with reward. There can be high entry costs for the best known franchises, whilst the growth of franchising has inevitably allowed the existence of poorly organised and structured franchises. As a franchisee, you remain an independent trader, and will be greatly reliant upon your franchisor. Carefully consider the business opportunities involved and take professional advice on the terms of the franchise agreement before you sign.

Scott Halborg and John Spratt, Shoosmiths

In my experience . . .

Like many people I started my business on a shoestring and wanted to save money when I rented offices. The building was old but in a good location and had a bank on the ground floor, which I thought would be an advantage in arranging an overdraft. I met with the bank manager who turned me over to an assistant who assured me there would be no problem.

A few months later, with some business coming in but little cash, I turned to my overdraft for help. The assistant had been transferred and the bank manager said he would never have approved the overdraft. It turned out the building was full of deadbeat businesses and he'd had several bad experiences. I struggled through without the overdraft but it wasn't easy.

- When it comes to banks, a good relationship is better than a good location
- Get all arrangements in writing

Barry Roxburgh, Public Relations Consultant

Your Business Structure
- The Financial Implications

Should your new business be a company or should you set up on your own?

Not all businesses can choose their status freely; for a business that is financed by borrowing, a company is likely to be the only practical option. You should establish whether law, regulation or a franchise agreement requires you to adopt a particular form. If you can choose, the factors to take into account are:

 Are you going into business by yourself (or with your spouse), or are you setting up with one or more partners ?

 How important is it to minimise the administration costs of the business, including taxation ?

 What potential liabilities will the business incur which you cannot insure against at a reasonable cost ?

Partnership

Where more than one person is involved in a business, the relationship between the individuals needs to be agreed in writing, in a partnership or shareholders' agreement. Although both fulfil the same function, their structures differ; generally, a partnership agreement is more flexible.

Minimum content

 Who is to be included and how much their share is, both of capital and profit?

 Decision-making: the authority limit for any one person acting alone and circumstances requiring unanimity?

 What happens if someone wants to leave, or if someone dies?

The first two are not difficult. The value of codifying decision-making is obvious - common sense requires consultation before the firm takes on large liabilities.

Providing for Leavers

However high your hopes when you first start out in business, many partnership arrangements fall apart in less than a year.

Insurance helps protect the business against accidents - keyman insurance for the business and life cover for the family. More commonly disagreement breaks up the partnership. Those continuing want to recover control of the business, continuing shareholders will want to buy back shares; the leaver wants a proper price. Your should specify the procedure and how to value the leaver's share, otherwise resolving the situation will be costly.

Valuing a Leaver's Share

Traditionally, you ask an independent accountant. This is rarely cost-effective. The valuation costs money; worse, it is not definitive. Consequently there is room for argument.

A formula can be agreed - eight times the last audited pretax profits, for example. This approach is simple but difficult to get right. A fast-growing business is undervalued by a formula using historic data unless the multiple is high; a high multiple may overvalue 'hope' or goodwill thus unreasonably profiting the leaver.

Under a third option, one partner offers to buy the others out at a price he specifies. If they do not accept his offer, the continuing partners must buy the leaver out at that price. In theory, such a price should be acceptable to all.

Although possible in unincorporated businesses, these formulae are more common in company-based arrangements. If you expect your partnership may break up because you will want to leave it, then you should probably set up as a company with a shareholders' agreement.

Relative Costs

Although the differential is now smaller, it is still generally more expensive to carry on a small business through a company than as a partnership or trader.

Compliance Costs

All businesses need to keep records of their activities. Various agencies have the right to require businesses to keep records or make periodic returns in a specified form and you will probably need professional help to meet these requirements. These are costs to the business of complying with the law.

Businesses generating turnover of £51,000 or more per year must register for Value Added Tax, record, collect and account for it, usually quarterly. Many businesses with employees are required to deduct income tax under Pay As You Earn from wages and pay it to the Inland Revenue, generally monthly.

There are reliefs from these provisions for smaller businesses, but it is generally irrelevant whether the business is a company or not, though an unincorporated business that has only one member of staff - the proprietor - would escape the PAYE system.

1. The company must make up annual financial statements in the format specified by the Companies Act. These must be audited by a Registered Auditor unless the company's turnover is less than £350,000 (and fixed assets are under £1.4 million or less than 10% of the shareholders request one).

An unincorporated business may make up such financial statements as its owners please providing they satisfy the Inland Revenue (see 3 below).

2. Along with a return detailing the identities of the directors and shareholders, the financial statements need to be filed with the Registrar of Companies each year within specified timescales. Whilst the annual filing fee is modest, late filing generates substantial monetary penalties.

There is no similar requirement for unincorporated businesses, though bankers and any major suppliers will want some financial details.

3. Because it is a separate legal entity, a company must file its own tax return with the Inland Revenue each year with its financial statements.

Sole traders now just complete the business pages in the personal tax return, including simple financial statements. Partnerships complete their own tax return. The Inland Revenue accept financial statements drawn up on recognised accountancy principles consistently applied over time.

Taxation

Companies are liable to corporation tax; individuals pay income tax. Taxable profits are determined similarly for both, but the timing of payment varies. Employees generally pay much more National Insurance than the self-employed who also escape the income tax rules on non-cash benefits in-kind.

Personal circumstances vary so individual calculations are advisable but the following will generally be accurate for 1999/2000:

 If business profits are £54,000 or less, trading through an unincorporated business will be cheaper than doing so through a company - this limit can be doubled to £108,000 if your spouse can work in partnership with you.

 The most important tax advantage of trading through a company is to retain profit to finance future growth under deduction of the (lower) corporation tax rate. If you draw out all the profit for private spending, there is no significant tax advantage to trading through a company at all.

Income tax payable by an individual benefiting from the married person's allowance for 1999/00 on business profits of £54,000 would amount to £14,650. National Insurance Class II and Class IV would also be due giving a total charge of £16,100. This leaves £37,900 to spend or reinvest in the business.

The director of a private company earning similar profits before a salary that keeps him below the 40% top rate of tax has less flexibility. The profits suffer the same total tax but the director has £23,800 to spend and £14,100 to reinvest.

Corporation tax is paid nine months after the company's year end. Employee income tax and National Insurance is paid monthly. The self-employed now pay income tax in two instalments on 31 January during and July following the tax year, with a balancing payment the following January, if necessary.

The change to the current year basis for income tax means that there is now little advantage in a number of common strategies, such as arranging for partners to be employees for the first period of trading. Similarly, all profits are now taxed once only so it is no longer possible to obtain a 22-month deferral between the time the profit is earned and the tax paid on it.

The treatment of non-salary benefits is favourable to the self-employed. The proprietor can generally obtain a tax deduction for the business element of their costs that are only partly business-related, for example using your home as an office and the use of your private car for business.

The director of a private company by contrast will be taxed on 35% of the car's list price each year (reduced by one third for over 2,500 business miles per year and two thirds for over 18,000 business miles). Further, the cost of travel from your home to your office is not a business cost for an employee, even a director.

Respectability

Although it is cheaper for the smaller business to start off unincorporated, many still start up as companies. There is an emotional appeal for some people in being able to describe themselves as having their own company.

The Inland Revenue will now challenge payments to individuals in certain industries - notably building, IT consultancy and the film and music industry. Many employers are cautious over making payments without deducting tax under PAYE and the involvement of a company may help. This is only cosmetic though; at the time of writing, The Inland Revenue are publishing proposed new rules designed to negate the advantages of "personal services companies". The important point is whether you are truly employed or self-employed. Most will accept you as self-employed if the terms of your engagement support you and you provide evidence, such as tax district and reference number, that the Inland Revenue accept your status.

Pension savings

Personal Pension Schemes were created on 1 July 1988. Employees and the self-employed can save a percentage of earned income varying with age (17% for those aged 35 and under, up to 40% for those aged 61 and over), up to a limit of securing maximum pension on a salary of £90,600. These schemes are 'money purchase' schemes - the amount you contribute is controlled, not the benefits drawn.

Alternatively, employees can participate in a company pension scheme. Company schemes have traditionally been 'final salary' schemes, contributions are controlled by restricting the final benefits to two thirds of final salary for each year of service, up to a maximum of 40. Increasingly though, company schemes are becoming 'money purchase' - just the same as personal schemes.

Under each scheme, contributions are tax-deductible but company schemes remain more flexible because they can accept payments at any time before retirement to provide maximum pension. Under a personal scheme, tax relief that is not used within six years is lost. Most people save less towards their pension than their maximum entitlement, particularly when they are younger. Under a company scheme, this can be made good whereas under a personal scheme, it cannot.

Funding and Liabilities

As an unincorporated business, you are liable for the debts you incur without financial limit, while the liability of a shareholder is limited to the paid-up share capital.

The limitation of liability is often seen as a powerful reason for incorporation but is often worth little. Your principal creditors are likely to be the bank, the landlord and one or two important suppliers. It has become standard practice for banks and landlords to seek personal guarantees from the proprietors of smaller private companies and suppliers may do likewise. Personal guarantees, particularly if they are unlimited, expose the owner-manager of the smaller company to the same liability as his self-employed counterpart.

Incorporation does provide protection against unforeseen liabilities - the uninsured disaster, and gives you the ability to create a floating charge over the company's assets, which is now the form of security banks prefer for commercial borrowing.

The Choice

Choosing whether to set up as a company or on your own account is not easy. The costs of trading as a company are high and relatively heavy tax and compliance burdens fall on the smallest companies.

Many businesses start off unincorporated and switch to companies when they have passed through the initial phase. The tax treatment of the transfer to corporate status is beyond this chapter but is a relatively straightforward exercise for which specific tax reliefs are available. There can be a 'catch up' tax charge in the year of change but, with planning, the amount should be considerably less than the savings you will have achieved by trading initially on your own account.

Advantages of a Company

* Limitation of Liability - protection against the unexpected
* Tax efficient reinvestment of profit
* Apparent respectability and status
* Easier to provide for partnership break-up
* Easier to raise bank loans
* May qualify for tax relief on the investment (if less than 30% owned)

Disadvantages of a Company

* Financial data available to the public
* More tax to pay if profits less than £54,000
* Costs of audit, separate tax computation,
* Registrar of Companies' requirements
* No capital gains allowance

Advantages of a Sole Trade or Partnership

* Confidentiality of financial data
* Cheaper tax bill if profits below £54,000
* Lower professional fees
* Initial losses can be relieved against previous year's tax

Disadvantages of a Sole Trade or Partnership

* Unlimited liability
* Partnership break-ups can be acrimonious
* More difficult to secure borrowings

Tony Steinthal

Tony is a partner in Chantrey Vellacott DFK chartered accountants who specialise in the affairs of owner-managed businesses.

Finding a Business - To Start-Up Or Buy?

'To buy or not to buy, that is the question'

Having decided that you want to run your own business, you now have to find a business to run. There are a number of ways that you can bring together the necessary ingredients that make up 'a business'. Generally, they all fall between the two options:

* Set up the business yourself or
* Buy an existing business that has already been set up by somebody else.

There are advantages and disadvantages to both options and these are examined below. In practice, your aspirations, financial resources, and your existing skills will lead you to the most appropriate route.

The start-up - setting up the business yourself

If you wish to develop your own unique ideas for a product or service, then setting up your own business from nothing may be the only option. Many people start businesses because they want to do things 'the right way'. This usually means they want to do things 'their own way'. It is much easier to do things 'your own way' in a new business, rather than in an old business that already has its routines and working practices established.

Often people who start up their own businesses do not have enough money to buy into an existing operation, so the 'Do It Yourself' approach is the only alternative.

Advantages of setting up your own business include:

* You can control the speed at which the business develops. It may be possible to start the business in your spare time. This will allow you to gain more confidence in the future success of your proposed venture before you 'give up the day job'.
* If you have limited money to invest in your new venture, you may not need to spend it all at the start of the project. This means, that if things do start to go wrong, it will be easier to restrict the loss of your own personal financial resources.
* Running a small business requires many different management and administration skills. If your previous experience has been primarily technically related, a start-up situation will allow you to grow your management skills as the business grows.
* Starting a new business is not all about money. Setting up and running a successful business has the potential to give you a feeling of personal achievement which you may have only dreamed of in your past career.

- Your business will take time to grow. It may not be able to support your current personal financial obligations (and those of your dependants) for many months or years. Unless you have another source of income, be prepared for some lean times ahead.
- There is a lot of one-off administration involved in setting up a new business (e.g. becoming registered for VAT and PAYE, printing business stationery, setting up phone and fax lines at your trading premises) in addition to actually trading. These chores can be very time-consuming and frustrating in the short term, and very costly in the long run if you get them wrong. Unfortunately, these tasks are often not easily delegated and can be expensive if you get other people to do them. If you buy a business, these basic administrative tasks should have already been dealt with (but never take this for granted!)
- Statistically, the risk of failure is higher for start-up businesses than for businesses with a trading record of over five years.
- As a result of this, it is generally more difficult to borrow money to fund a start-up' than to borrow to invest in an established profitable business. In fact, the word 'start-up' is enough, on its own, to make some less adventurous bank managers break out into a cold sweat.

Buying a business - hitting the ground running

The main advantage to buying a business is, in theory, that as soon as you have paid your money, you can start making money! This route is particularly well suited to people who have extensive experience of general business management but lack detailed technical or product knowledge.

When you buy an established profitable business, you will not only pay for the basic assets of the business, but also the accumulated time and effort that the previous owners spent growing the business to its present state. This extra asset is called the 'goodwill' of the business. The better the business, the more the 'goodwill' will cost you.

Advantages of buying a business include:

- You will buy some of the experience and expertise you do not have. Nobody can be expected to know how to do everything. It is much easier (and cheaper!) to learn from other people's mistakes that they have made in the past, rather than making all these mistakes again yourself.
- If your new idea needs to be marketed to a specific target customer, buying a business dealing in related goods or services will give you both access to your potential customers and the credibility of a

trading history when you seek to launch your new product.

- Buying an existing business can be a way of gaining access to your chosen market if that market has barriers to entry that would be too difficult or costly for a start-up to overcome.

- When you buy an established business there is always the risk you will buy the existing unsolved problems and mistakes of the person who is selling it.
- Identifying the right potential acquisition and negotiating purchase can take a very long time, especially if you don't succeed at your first attempt.
- The professional fees associated with buying a business can be very significant. Good solicitors and accountants are a necessary evil in this process. They are your safeguard to ensure that you know exactly what you are buying. When purchasing a smaller business, you should expect that the total professional fees associated with the transaction will be a major percentage of the total cost of your investment.

If you want to buy - what can you buy?

If you have decided that you want to buy your way into an existing business, there are a number of ways that this can be achieved. The type of purchase will depend upon whether you are buying the whole business from its existing owners and they will take no further part in its future operation (i.e. a take-over); or, buying a percentage of the business from the existing owners and becoming part of a team to run it with them.

If you want to take over a business, you can buy:

Parts of the business

A business is made up of various assets and liabilities. Some of these will be valuable to you and some may be of no use at all. For example, you may wish to buy the customer list and stocks of an existing business but may not wish to take on the property it trades from or its existing liabilities. Naturally, it will cost you more if you only want to 'cherry pick' the parts of the business that are valuable to you, but this can be a good way of avoiding saddling yourself with problems inherited from the old business.

- This approach is worth pursuing if the current owners need a quick sale
- Make sure you get all you need from the business at the first go, because you may be in a very weak bargaining position if you need to come back for something you missed.

- Make sure you know exactly what assets you're buying and do confirm the exact nature of any obligations you are taking on as part of the deal.

The whole business and nothing but the business

If the business is owned by a company, you can buy all of the business from that company. If the business is a partnership or sole trader, you can buy out the existing owners. This will mean you will get all of the business, both the bad bits and the good bits. If there are some particularly onerous obligations you are taking over from the previous owners, this should be reflected in the price you pay.

Hints and tips

- Make sure you know the reason why the existing owners are selling. If it is because the business is 'sick', are you sure you can cure it?
- Again, make sure you know exactly what you are taking on. Get indemnities from the previous owners to protect against hidden liabilities. You should also check that the previous owners have sufficient assets to cover those indemnities should you need to enforce them.
- Don't pay all the purchase price immediately. Agree to the purchase price being based on continued profitability of the business, part of which will be paid when the future profits are determined.
- Make sure the agreement prohibits the old owners from setting up a new, but identical, business on your doorstep. Agree that they cannot contact old customers.

'I liked the business so much, I bought the company'

If the business you want is owned by a company, you can buy all the shares in that company to acquire the business. This is advantageous if you want to maintain the trading name of the company or do not want to bring the change of ownership to the attention of customers or suppliers.

Hints and tips

- As always, make sure you're buying what you think you are buying. Double check that the company actually owns the assets it uses in its business.
- Large tax liabilities can arise for an owner selling a business. There can be considerable tax advantages to the seller in selling the shares of a company rather than the business contained in that company. Be aware of the seller's tax position because this can be used when negotiating the structure of the deal and the sale price.
- Make sure that the company you are buying is up to date with all its regulatory returns. Just like any individual, a company has to

complete a lot of routine administration to keep its affairs in order. Heavy fines can be levied on the company, regardless of who owns it, if the company's statutory and tax affairs are not up to date.

Buying an interest in an established business

If you want to buy part of a whole business, the form of the interest that you buy will depend upon the corporate structure of the entity that you are buying into.

If you are buying part of a company:

You will buy a percentage of the ordinary share capital. Your relationship with the other shareholders should be set out in a shareholders' agreement or dealt with in the company's Articles of Association.

If you are buying into a partnership:

You will buy an agreed percentage of the partnership, as set out in a revised partnership agreement.

If you are buying a share of the business of a sole trader:

You will enter into partnership with the current owner, having bought an agreed percentage of the business, as set out in the new partnership agreement.

Going into business with other people - the golden rule

When going into business with other people, you should not only consider what you are buying (i.e. the business - as considered above) but also your relationship with your new business partners. The golden rule is:

 Always formalise the relationship with your business partners in a comprehensive and professionally drafted legal agreement.

 Whether it is a shareholders' agreement or partnership agreement, this document should set out what everybody is required to put into the business and what everybody can take out. It should anticipate both the good times (profits) and the bad times (losses). It will also include rules on how important issues are to be dealt with. These will commonly include how important business decisions are to be made and what happens if somebody wishes to sell their interest in the business.

 Do not get drawn into 'gentlemen's agreements' or unwritten undertakings. If your prospective business partners are not willing to sign a properly drafted agreement - don't do the deal.

Other points to consider:

- Be aware of the reputation of your prospective business partners. Ask around and get references if appropriate. Going into business with them means you will take on their reputation by association.
- Be wary of going into business with somebody who has obvious difficulties in their personal life. Sooner or later, these problems are bound to affect their input to the business.

Other ways of buying into a business

Management Buy Outs (MBOs)

This term is applied to the sale of a business to the existing management team. Large companies are continuously reviewing their overall operating strategy. They often seek to dispose of or close down businesses they have acquired in the past that are not sufficiently profitable or that do not fit in with their future plans.

The people in the best position to run these operations are often the people who are running them at the moment, because they have the expert detailed knowledge to do so. When it is known that the business may be sold or shut down, the current management often see this as an opportunity to take over the business. They then form a team to make an offer to the existing owner. Such offers are often viewed favourably because they are strategically more desirable than closing a business down or selling it to a potential competitor.

The major problem for the buy-out team will be to secure enough finance to purchase the business.

Management Buy Ins (MBIs)

This term is applied to the purchase of a stake in a business by an external management team. This opportunity exists where current management are poor or lack expertise and, consequently, the business is underperforming. In this way the business gets the injection of expertise it requires and the new managers share in the future profits they expect to generate.

Both MBIs and MBOs tend to be major transactions backed by external investors and are driven by the skills of the management teams concerned. However, the principles of the 'Buy Out' or 'Buy In' can be applied to many small business situations.

Finding a business to buy

Before you start your search, you will need to have established the characteristics of the business that you are looking for. This will help you to eliminate unsuitable businesses at an early stage. It will also help establish your credibility when you discuss your plans with your advisers or bankers and, at a later stage, with potential sellers. The characteristics of your ideal business will be based upon your future aspirations. However, make sure you are realistic, because this profile must also reflect the money available to pay for the business.

There are two approaches to finding a business to buy:

- Look for a business where the current owners are already offering it for sale
- Look for a business that you want to buy and approach the current owners with a proposal.

Finding out about businesses that are already being offered for sale

Businesses for sale are advertised in regional and national newspapers, trade journals and other related periodicals. Estate agents will often deal with retail businesses. The initial information you receive will be very limited, so it may take you a little time to establish whether the business for sale meets your basic requirements.

The vast majority of businesses for sale are never advertised because a potential purchaser is found through word of mouth or connections in the business community. This means that your best approach will be to talk to the people in your local area, and also your line of business, to find out about potential sales. People to talk to include accountants, solicitors, estate agents and bankers. Try to get involved in the business community that you want to join, so that you get to hear the local business news early.

Receivers and liquidators are regularly instructed to sell businesses, and assets from those businesses, when they have developed serious financial problems. It is worth contacting the local Registered Insolvency Practitioners, who act as receivers and liquidators in your area, to let them know the type of business you are interested in.

Finding and researching target businesses

You will find that identifying a business that you would like to buy or invest in is not as easy as it sounds, especially after you have discarded all those that do not fit your selected characteristics.

The larger accountancy firms offer search services to help identify target businesses and will make initial approaches to the businesses you are interested in. They will charge a finder's fee if a successful purchase is negotiated but, usually, if the potential transaction is big enough, no initial fee will be payable. The advantage in using a professional firm to conduct the initial approach is that it will give the enquiry increased credibility and the owner of the target is less likely to dismiss the approach without consideration.

If you are searching for very small businesses, it will generally be more cost-effective to conduct the target search yourself, but it will still be useful to ask your accountant or solicitor if they will be willing to make the initial approach.

The search and selection procedure can be usefully split into three stages:

Listing initial possibilities

Initial ideas can be gained from numerous sources including trade journals, local directories and the Yellow Pages.

Obtain general information

Once you have prepared a shortlist of possible targets, obtain as much general information as you can about the business without making your intentions known. The best way to do this is to phone or visit the business as a potential customer, so that you can see how they operate. Remember, if it's a small business, you may get straight through to the owner - so be careful what you say, if you want to avoid embarrassment later!

Detailed inquiry

When you have narrowed down your listing to your two or three favourite targets, then spend some time researching each business in detail. For companies, a 'Company Search', which gives you details of the documents lodged with the Registrar of Companies is the place to start. This will give you a copy of the latest set of accounts filed with the Registrar. For sole traders and partnerships you will find it a lot harder to get information, but local papers and trade associations may be a route to more information.

At this stage, it is essential that you find out who actually owns the business, so you can make your initial approach to the right person.

Contacting the owners of a target business

There is no way to guarantee that your approach will not be immediately dismissed without consideration. This is the prerogative of the owners you contact. Remember, your approach will be unsolicited and there is no obligation for them to respond.

The easiest way to make the initial approach is by a short letter introducing yourself and your interest in the business. This can then be followed up by a telephone call. Do make sure that your letter is addressed to the correct person, otherwise, the initial impact of your inquiry will be lost.

The following points are worthy of note:

 Be polite, even if your approach is dismissed out of hand. You never know when you will have to deal with the person or people again.

 'No' means 'No'. Don't be tempted to pester your target, even though you may have put a lot of work into the selection procedure. If you are professional and unambiguous in your approach, the owner may come back to you later if their circumstances change.

 Don't say anything in your initial approach which could bind you in future negotiations.

 If you are fortunate enough to get a positive response, don't rush into the next contact with your target without preparation.

Negotiating a purchase

Whole books are written about this subject, so it is very difficult to do it justice in a few paragraphs. This phase is the most important in the process of buying a business, and the outcome can determine whether your business is a success or failure in the future.

Now is the time to get good professional help. Experience is the key. Very few people have actual practical experience of negotiating the sale or purchase of businesses, so having a 'specialist' on your side at this stage is critical. You wouldn't expect your local doctor to perform major surgery on you, even though he could probably do it; you would expect to be treated by a surgeon. You should apply the same reasoning to your business. If your usual advisers are general practitioners, who don't have relevant experience, ask them to refer you to a specialist for this particular transaction. If you are worried about the level of fees, get a fixed fee quote before you start.

Other key points:

 Like any other major purchase, decide how much you are willing to spend before you start negotiations.

 Always negotiate 'subject to contract'. This means that no negotiations are binding until the final contract is agreed.

 Be prepared to walk away from the deal if it doesn't 'feel' right - first impressions are generally quite accurate.

 Try not to get rushed or bullied into accepting things you are not happy with. Take plenty of time to think things over.

 Remember that it's business - not personal. When people invest a lot of time and effort in a project, they can let their emotions affect their judgment. Try to stay cool and calm - even if the other side don't!

Due diligence

Once both sides are in general agreement over the terms for sale, you should request the opportunity to review the business's affairs, in detail, to check that you are buying what you think you are buying. This checking process is called 'due diligence'.

There will be legal aspects (e.g. confirming ownership of assets in the business and the validity of contracts) and financial aspects (e.g. reviewing asset values and checking for unrecorded liabilities) to the review. These will generally be carried out by your solicitor and accountant. However, if the business you're buying is in an industry that is particularly risky or specialised, it will be worth getting the assistance of an industry expert.

Don't be tempted to do the review by yourself. Accountants and solicitors have checklists and procedures to make sure they cover all the major risk areas, so important issues don't get missed. Taxation related issues also can arise at this stage. These can prove extremely costly in the future if not dealt with correctly in the sale agreement.

Just because your solicitor and accountant are completing the investigation doesn't mean you should stop asking questions. This is your chance to get the answers to all the questions about the operation of the business, before the deal is done.

Finally, if the due diligence work uncovers problems, these must be addressed immediately before the transaction proceeds. In general, there are three possible approaches to resolving this type of issue:

- Adjust the purchase price to take account of the issue that has been identified.
- Obtain a guarantee or indemnity from the seller to protect yourself against any loss arising from the problem. This may include your solicitors holding back purchase monies from the seller until you are happy that the problem identified has been resolved.
- If the problem is fundamental to the operation of the business, abort the transaction.

Start-up or buy - some final thoughts

When I was asked to write this chapter, I was reminded of something my grandma used to say:

'Setting up a new business is like getting married; nobody can guarantee you that your new venture will be a success, but if you work hard at it, you stand as good a chance as anybody'

The comparison may sound a bit glib and simplistic, but please humour me for a moment. It is worth dwelling on this comparison for a minute because it helps to put some important issues in a common context. (Unlike my grandma, I will use bullet points to extend the analogy).

A comparison of starting in business and getting married:

 Both require a positive commitment. Do it or don't do it, but don't be half-hearted.

If you do them well the first time, you may never have to do them again.

They are acknowledged as having the potential to be two of the most stressful things you can do in your life.

Just because a possible business venture or partner initially looks very sexy and exciting doesn't mean they're right for you for the long term.

Both can change your life forever!

Finally, don't automatically believe everything you're told when you're deciding whether to set up in business, especially if you are buying a business. Anecdotal stories about how easy or hard it is to run your own business get passed around, like old wives' tales, with very little truth to them. If you do your own research, take advice from reliable sources and use your common sense, you won't go too far wrong.

Robert Stenhouse, Senior Manager, National Assurance and Advisory, Deloitte & Touche, Chartered Accountants

BUYING INTO AN EXISTING BUSINESS... A SUMMARY

Advantages:

- Existing reputation (good or bad)
- Equipment and employees to operate it
- Regular cash flow
- Established customer and supplier base
- Possibly current financial backers who wish to continue to support the business
- Current employees will also have invaluable experience and technical abilities

Disadvantages:

- Existing problems or liabilities (e.g. poor reputation, debts, litigation, faulty products, poor employee or customer relations)
- Watch out for "skeletons in the cupboard" which have not yet come to light
- Overstaffing or the need to streamline may result in high redundancy payouts and reorganisation costs
- There may be a good reason why the current owners are selling. Beware!

Management Buy Ins (MBIs)

The pros and cons of a management team from outside the business buying into a business are as set out above. In addition to these, often the incoming skills enhance and complement the existing management skills in particular areas. Financial backers will be looking for management skills and comprehensive business plans which will provide the stepping stones to success.

Management Buy Outs (MBOs)

In addition to the advantages set out above, the distinct advantage of the current management team acquiring the business is their knowledge of the business. The hurdle of getting to know how the business operates and establishing a rapport with employees and customers is dispensed with. The only question is whether the management team have sufficient capabilities to replace the seller both in terms of skill and reputation.

Investigation of the business prior to sale

Don't sign until you know what you are buying. The buyers, their solicitors and accountants should endeavour to turn over every leaf to establish what the business does and does not own, what its liabilities (and potential liabilities) are, which will range from financial liabilities to environmental liabilities. This process is of equal importance in an MBO as an MBI as the MBO team may not have been involved in every aspect of the business prior to the sale. Whilst they may wish to speed things on, the buyers should not be rushed.

Peter Seary and Alexandra Martin, Shoosmiths

HOW TO CHOOSE A FRANCHISE

When deciding whether a franchise is right for you, you must, first and foremost, look closely at yourself - at your commitment, your expectations and your qualities. Only then can you make realistic judgments about a franchise that will suit you.

Franchising is no easy option. It requires a lot of hard work, as well as money, over long periods of time and often in unsocial hours. Sometimes you will have to take work home with you, or you may have to take your family to work. Either way the stresses and strains will be as much your family's as your own. The first year will be the hardest, or the first two years, or the first three - it depends as much on you as on the type of franchise.

Your expectations by way of earnings are as important to think about as the amount you will have to invest. If you need £20,000 a year to live on, do not choose a franchise which can only produce £15,000 a year. Although the failure rate in franchising is lower than in most new small businesses (less than

1 in 10) failures are still for the same reason that most new businesses fail - taking too much money out of the business too quickly.

You must take as much responsibility for checking the financial projections as the franchisor. Be sure you know the basis for those projections, and that they apply sensibly to the particular territory you are considering. Be sure you check them against the actual experience of existing franchisees. Do not base your investment on what you hope will happen. Base it on a realistic assessment, a conservative estimate, of what has and could happen. If the difference between profit and loss is only 1 percentage point on the interest rates then you are clearly at risk!

It pays to be realistic about the kinds of business that will suit your own strengths and weaknesses. So take time to find out, preferably from the horse's mouth what franchisees in a particular business really do. Some people go for the first franchise they hear about where the franchisor is willing to take a cheque. Don't. You need time to find out the facts, and to compare the realities of one proposition with the realities of another.

You should be looking for a shortlist of as many as six opportunities, acquiring as much advice as you can get from franchisers, from franchisees, from your bank and from other professional advisers. Organisations such as the British Franchise Association are also there to help. There are also a growing number of books and other publications on franchising.

Looking realistically at your own suitability for any one franchise proposition you will inevitably discover that you cannot offer every bit of knowledge, experience and financial clout that would make you the ideal candidate. Don't worry. If franchising is about anything it is about training people with no experience of printing, for example, to manage a printing business. In any franchise proposition you should see a well organised training programme.

It is often said that franchising is running your own business, but not on your own. You should get lots of support from your franchisor - you are paying for it after all. But you will also have to do many things in the franchiser's way whether you like it or not. After all it is the franchisor who has paid to develop the most successful format for running the business.

In the end it all comes back to realism. Be realistic about what you want out of your own business and what you are prepared to put into it. Then be realistic about how the franchisor can help you and what you need from the franchisor. All BFA members must:

- Be prepared to disclose to you their financial record, the records of their directors, the basis for the financial projections they make on your particular franchise proposition and details of their existing franchisees
- Operate with a franchise agreement which is comprehensive,

protecting your rights as well as theirs
- Have proven that their product or service can be sold profitably in the marketplace
- Have proven that they can deliver the 'knowhow' of their business to a franchisee so that he can be successful in the marketplace

Full members must also have an established track record in franchising that proves that a substantial majority of their franchisees have been successful over an extended period.

If a franchisor is not a member of the BFA, they may still be a good franchisor - but you must then satisfy yourself that they are open, ethical, viable and franchisable and that they have a proven track record. If you take the advice of a franchise consultant on these matters, be careful to ensure that they do not stand to make a commission on your appointment - this is hardly likely to give you the benefit of objective advice. Members of the Franchise Consultants Association never take per capita commissions - so this is often a good place to start.

If all this sounds daunting, it should do. Most franchisees are beguiled by the dreams they see in a crystal ball. Do be persuaded by a balance sheet, by a series of personal recommendations, by accredited expert advisers, by the people who have chosen the same option before you and by the hard-nosed common sense you will need when you are in business.

Simon Wise, British Franchise Association

NOT FOR PROFITS AND THE TRUST ECONOMY

It is increasingly recognised that not all businesses are concerned with maximising personal profit and that an area of activity previously the concern of philanthropic and charitable organisations can legitimately be seen as part of the mainstream economy. For many people, starting their own business is not about making a million, but an opportunity to exercise control over their working environment and to 'make a difference'. As the funding structures of public services have changed, business opportunities can now be found in social and community activities and these often require specific structures and skills - those of the 'social entrepreneur' and 'social business'.

Although these terms may seem contradictory, they are in fact, recognising that for many years individuals and groups have worked in nontraditional businesses to meet social as well as economic objectives. This sector is described variously as the third sector, the independent sector and the social economy. The key features are:

Financially

- Non profit distributing - organisations should aim to make a surplus, but this is not distributed to shareholders, instead it is reinvested in the firm
- Can receive grant funds, social and ethical loan finance at preferential rates
- Is unlikely to have external shareholders

Legally

- Will be formally constituted as a not-for-profit limited company or Industrial and Provident Society, co-operative, community enterprise, development trust
- Will often be accountable to groups such as staff - in a co-op, clients or service users, or the wider community
- Will often trade with public sector organisations such as local councils, health authorities, etc.

Ethically

- Will have social as well as economic objectives, such as accountability to the community, employment creation - often with disadvantaged groups such as the long term unemployed or disabled people
- Will be concerned with long term social, environmental and economic sustainability
- Will aim to offer products or services that meet social needs

Social businesses will often trade in sectors that are characterised by

- Being highly labour intensive - to create and maintain employment
- Being relatively low tech - thus requiring lower capital investment
- Requiring relatively low skills - providing employment in unskilled or semi-skilled occupations
- Examples include: personal care, such as child care or domiciliary care for the elderly; environmental issues, such as recycling, waste handling and habitat management; arts, culture and heritage

What defines these sectors is that the trading relationship is beyond the purely financial and is also one of trust. The purchase of childcare is a hugely emotional transaction and is cast in a different light if the profit motive is not at the root of It. A social childcare business, providing high quality care in a price sensitive market can have a significant business advantage over one that is pricing for profit distribution. As we have witnessed the retraction of public services over the past fifteen years, market opportunities have opened up for social businesses. Public authorities are now operating on the principles of 'best value', recognising that contracts with external agencies must reflect criteria other than the lowest price. Again, the social business is at an advantage. Although we are far from some European models where social firms have preferred status and some tax advantages as a payoff for creating jobs, trends are moving towards businesses that can provide a wide range of social benefits.

Social businesses like any other must identify a market, research the potential, be financially viable, meet legislative requirements and promote themselves effectively.

The relationship with what can still be described as the 'mainstream' business community is an interesting one. An increasing number of businesses are taking into account the social impact of their activities and attempting to contribute to their local community. The effects of this can often be seen as being more well intentioned than strategic and usually as a 'bolt-on' to core business activities. An offer to give old office furniture or computers to a local charity, or a donation to a diabetic support organisation because the managing director's daughter has been diagnosed, are typical examples. Whilst not wishing to suggest that companies should stop making these valuable contributions, I would suggest that a consideration is also given to developing a trading relationship with local social firms. Depending on the availability of local services, these might include contracts to provide recycling, catering, cleaning, product assembly or packaging, with organisations creating employment for long term unemployed people in deprived areas or adults with learning disabilities who have the opportunity to earn a 'real' wage and become involved with aspects of running the business.

These relationships can develop in other ways. Sometimes staff volunteer to get involved with these organisations, resulting in personal and skills development and greater commitment to their own jobs. Companies can also develop a higher profile in their local communities and increase the market for their products.

There is a well-established network of support organisations at local and national levels providing support for social businesses.

ICOM (the Industrial Common Ownership Movement) provides a support service for co-ops, community businesses and other democratically owned structures. It is also the source of information about local Co-op Development Agencies, which offer a wide range of practical support. The Voluntary Service and Rural Community Councils also offer support and many local authorities now employ community economic development officers to promote these kinds of activity.

Sources of finance can include local Single Regeneration Budget (SRB) programmes (check with your Regional Development Agency for information). Social lending organisations include the Charities Aid Foundation, Triodos Bank and local loan funds such as the Aston Reinvestment Trust in Birmingham. The

Development Trusts Association supports asset-based community economic development and has helped establish leading community enterprises such as the Bromley-by-Bow healthy living centre.

This sector is growing and being encouraged to do so by various government initiatives. It is highly innovative and effective and, throughout Europe, is creating an increasing proportion of new employment. It may not be the first approach you think of when planning a new business, but it should not be over-looked or under-valued. Even if your business is a traditional one, you can still trade with, or otherwise provide support to, social firms. And if you want to start one, you're not alone. Many others have tried and tested this approach and will be happy to help you learn from their mistakes (we're like that in the social economy!) Find out what's happening in your area and access the specialist agencies that will provide moral and financial support.

Nicky Stevenson, The Guild

Most people use their own ideas to start up in business and are equally keen to have their name over the door. But then more than half of all new ventures shut down within eighteen months. One of the most successful businesses of all time was founded using someone else's ideas and name. In 1954, Ray Kroc, a Magimixer salesman, became curious as to why a small hamburger stand on the edge of the desert in San Bernardino, California, would need eight multimixers - enough to make more milk-shakes than any other restaurant in America - and decided to fly out and take a look. The restaurant he found, run by the brothers Maurice and Richard McDonald, was only 600 square feet, but the burgers were tasty, the fries crisp, the shakes unusually thick, and it was unquestionably popular with the locals. Kroc at this time was 52 years old, but he saw an opportunity here. He bought into the business and by 1961, when he bought the McDonald brothers out for $2.7 million, there were two hundred McDonalds franchises. Now the company operates in 108 countries, has tens of thousands of outlets and is the biggest real estate business in the world. Not bad for an idea that wasn't even his.

In my experience . . .

I would like to offer the following one sentence top tip:-

'Turnover is vanity, profit is sanity but cash is reality'

This refers of course to the fact that no matter how good or high your turnover and profit is in business, unless you have cash or access to cash to meet your business debts as they fall due, your business is not going to survive very long.

Duncan M. Walker, Premium Accounting & Training Services

In my experience . . .

When we first set up in business, my father, who had worked in insolvency, advised us to start a new company for each new venture so that failure in one area wouldn't pull the whole enterprise down. We followed his advice and the satellites in East Anglia, Bristol and Scotland were set up as separate companies rather than branch offices. This had benefits in many unexpected ways. Not only was the risk spread but the directors of the satellites, feeling free to be innovative in their own companies, came up with a lot of ideas that the sister companies found useful.

When the Bristol managing director suggested we went into manufacture we persuaded him to set up a separate company for this rather than expanding his operations as he had originally planned. The manufacturing company foundered because of technical problems and price competition but the damage was limited to that one company and the other four continued to flourish.

- Don't put all your eggs in one basket - there is some extra administrative work involved in setting up a new company but it is worth it in the long run
- Listen to the Jeremiahs - you need to have confidence and optimism but you also need strategies for damage limitation

John Francis, Leomax Ltd

Planning, Research & Finance

Chapter Three

Who to talk to...

Those would-be entrepreneurs with funds of their own, or worse still, borrowed from innocent friends or relatives, tend to think that the time spent in preparing a business plan could be more usefully (and enjoyably) spent looking for premises, choosing a new car, or buying a computer. In short anything that inhibits them from immediate action is viewed as time-wasting.

In a way, those without money who have to talk to their bank manager or accountant are more fortunate. If they are careful they gain greatly from listening to professionals in the business world, who have seen hundreds, perhaps even thousands of similar ventures start and, all too often, fail.

BUSINESS LINK

Business Link is a network of 81 advice centres with over 180 outlets. It provides affordable advice to all small and medium sized businesses, especially those with the potential to grow.

Each Business Link has two core services, the Information Service and the Advice Service.

Business Information Service

The information service provides a single, local point of access to information on any business query and access to the complete range of business advice delivered by organisations such as local authorities, TECs and Chambers of Commerce or provided by private organisations such as banks, marketing consultants and accountants.

Previously, companies wanting business information or services in their area had to wade through a multiplicity of channels. These sometimes overlapped, were often hard to find and almost always confusing. In the case of export advice, for example, a company would have had to decide whether to approach the local government office, the Chamber of Commerce, the TEC or a private consultancy specialising in the field. Now they can simply contact the local Business Link which will either answer the query itself or bring in the relevant partner organisation, whether public or private sector, or other appropriate outside body.

Business Advice Centre

The second main platform of the Business Link service is the provision of tailored, on-the-spot advice from a range of specialist advisers.

At the heart of the service is the Personal Business Adviser (PBA) who provides independent, affordable and long term help, if necessary over several years. This fills a fundamental gap in the market. Although there is plenty of short term help available for small businesses, most companies need sustained support over a period of time in order to achieve significant change. PBAs will help companies write a business strategy and implement it. In the process, they help overcome many of the classic cultural, organisational and financial barriers to growth. These range from a lack of strategic planning (because management are too busy fire-fighting daily operational pressures) to the need to create a management structure, motivate staff, control cash flow or establish a benchmark against competitors. The PBA can also act as a channel through which other expert resources from the Business Link partnership can be accessed, with the Business Link bringing in the most appropriate partner or other service supplier.

Additionally, Business Links have expert advisers in key areas such as export, finance, innovation and technology, design, marketing and training. These advisers help with all aspects of their speciality and can cover everything from finding innovative sources of finance to new product development.

Cost

Pricing structures vary between Business Links but the fundamental premise is that they should be accessible and affordable, meeting the market need of small and medium sized enterprises unable to afford full market rates. Typically a PBA might undertake an initial business review free of charge and then provide ongoing, subsidised consultancy.

Structure

All 81 Business Links are private sector organisations comprising a number of partners which typically include: TECs, Chambers of Commerce, Local Authorities, Enterprise Agencies, universities, banks and others. Each Business Link's board of directors is drawn from local businesses as well as from its partners. The 81 local partnerships have, between them, a total of around 180 outlets nationally. For businesses wishing to be directed to their nearest Business Link call 0345 567765.

Business Link

WHY TALK TO A BANK MANAGER . . ?
AND WHAT TO ASK

When setting up in business your first thought may be about borrowing. In fact, there is much more to it than that. A bank is one of your suppliers and, as with other suppliers, it makes sense to talk to them about the range of services they can provide. You would not necessarily take the first offer from a supplier and, so, with a bank you should have no hesitation in questioning them, being prepared to negotiate and shop around. After all, you want a good relationship with all your suppliers and the bank is no exception, so it is important to make the right choice at the outset.

What services can a bank offer? What should you ask about? The best starting place is the account you want to open. What will you use it for? If you are opening a shop, you might need a convenient night safe but a small partnership out in the country handling little cash might find a phone or PC based account the most useful.

Think about how you will use the account. List the volume and sort of transactions you expect (cash deposit and withdrawals, cheques paid in and out, credit card payments, electronic payments to suppliers and from customers). That will help the bank manager give you an estimate for the bank charges you will incur.

There are many other services a bank can supply. Here are a few examples:

- Phone/Internet banking - enables you to keep track of your accounts, make payments and access other bank services
- Making and receiving foreign currency payments - vital if you are buying or selling overseas
- Company payment cards - avoids a lot of paperwork if you need to make occasional purchases
- Factoring and invoice discounting - takes the worry out of when you are going to get paid
- Leasing and HP - you may want to buy something or to offer facilities to your customers
- Deposit accounts - make any spare cash work for you.

If you describe your business, the manager will be able to tell you about the full range of services the bank can provide. Don't let him use jargon that you don't understand - ask and he will be happy to explain it further. He will also tell you the cost and may be prepared to negotiate if you are buying a package of services from him.

A major service you may want from your bank is to borrow money. When you talk to a bank manager about borrowing, remember that uppermost in his mind is whether you are going to be able to generate enough money to repay the loan, with interest. The money you are borrowing does not belong to the bank - it belongs to hundreds of thousands of depositors who place it with the bank and who, in turn, want it back with interest.

How would you react if a friend asked for a loan? If you are the sort of person that would give it without any questions, then you are going to find bankers a tough bunch. However, most people would ask the questions a banker will ask you, so you can prepare the sort of information and forecasts that he will want to see. Prepare your case carefully. Someone who thinks things through, considers the risks and allows a margin for error is likely to be a lower risk than someone who can't answer fairly basic questions about their borrowing plans.

Finally, your bank manager can be a valuable source of suggestions and of help about where to get advice. Don't be afraid to ask - if he can't help, he may well know someone who can.

Andy Brenan, Director, British Bankers' Association

WHY TALK TO AN ACCOUNTANT ?

While working 70-90 hours a week setting up your business, you may be tempted to cut corners by cutting out professional accounting advice. True, this might give you a short term saving, but it could prove an expensive mistake later. Depending on the state of the economy, between one third and two thirds of start-ups flounder in their first three years. Invariably poor financial management is a major factor in failure. Many small firms only come across a qualified accountant when he or she is appointed to wind up the business. Chances are that accountant would have been just as well qualified to help turn the business around six months before.

The primary reason for finding an accountant is to draw on his or her experience of hundreds or thousands of start-ups. This may save you days of time or thousands of pounds. While you are on the nursery slopes you will probably hit some problems, but you may well also find some exciting opportunities. It makes sense to have someone to fall back on who knows your business, who can provide you with expertise that you do not have and who has a broader business perspective.

While running your own business you will have a number of obligations to provide financial information to outsiders. This is where an accountant will be able to save you time and money. If you are setting up as a limited company you may need an audit. Subject to your turnover this may no longer be compulsory, but may be required by the bank or an investor. Equally, your accountant will be far better able to keep your tax bill down, with his first-hand knowledge of tax law and the allowances available. Chartered and chartered certified accountants offer expert advice on all general tax matters including the preparation of tax returns, checking assessments and preparing computations for submission to the Inspector of Taxes. They can also advise on matters such as Inheritance Tax, VAT, and Overseas Tax.

Your accountant will also be able to set up record-keeping systems - boring perhaps. But the financial information that you keep in a cash book or on the computer is the core of management information that tells you what is going on and what might be developing. It's one of the few early warning systems that you have - you need to get it right! This includes matters such as stock control (having enough and not too much on the shelves) credit control, being paid on time and, importantly, paying on time to keep your suppliers happy, as well as wages and National Insurance.

Many accountants also have specialist skills that could be useful to your start-up. Some deal with computing and IT. Others are experts in raising investment or government grants.

When you are considering using a new accountant you should take certain basic precautions:

 Check for membership of one of the recognised accounting bodies

 Have a clear idea of what services you require and discuss your needs and likely costs

 Use personal recommendations from business colleagues or Business Link

 If you are not sure, ask for references from the accountant's clients and follow them up

 Make sure that your choice of accountant matches the needs of your business, with experience of your business sector and the right level of service. There is no point in having a one man band if you need a wide range of services. Equally, if your needs are smaller, a large scale practice may be less personal and cost more.

Choosing the right accountant is vital and requires careful consideration. Anyone can set up in practice offering accountancy services to the public. Using a chartered or chartered certified accountant means that you are dealing with someone who has been through a rigorous training and is monitored by a government recognised professional body. Just as important, picking a chartered or chartered certified accountant means that you have a source of redress through the professional body if anything does go wrong.

David Harvey, Secretary Small Business Committee, The Association of Chartered Certified Accountants

WHY USE A SOLICITOR ?

In business, there are countless decisions to be made, whether about the best way forward for the company, or how to deal with an imminent crisis. Success can depend on making the right choice under pressure. As we all well know, effective decision-making is based on having the right information and, where necessary, advice. Professional advisers can bring specialist expertise to a particular situation, enabling the businessman to make the right moves with confidence.

But why go to a solicitor for advice? Isn't a lawyer someone you use to get out of a hole, or when a disagreement is turning into a nasty dispute? After all, if you are looking to establish a successful business, you need constructive advice - not someone to start an argument.

It is probably fair to say that many people see lawyers as the kind of people who will argue about anything. Ask them a simple question and you will be launched into a lengthy discourse on the precise meaning of some obscure term until you no longer remember the nature of your original enquiry.

Most of us will have known lawyers who go at least some way towards living up to this stereotype but, even though the ability to grapple with contentious details is a basic skill for the professional, the job that most lawyers do does not involve being argumentative at every opportunity.

What lawyers really do

A solicitor's work contains a paradox: the time spent arguing is usually aimed at achieving agreement. Be it over a proposed sale, lease or who should take responsibility for the failure of that vital new machinery, the resolution is found by achieving accord. But at the most fundamental level, what a solicitor really does is not to argue with an opponent, but to advise his or her client on a course of action.

Solicitors who are serious about working with businesses do not confine themselves to a knowledge of development in statutes and case law, though this is their stock in trade. Increasingly, solicitors are advisers who understand, and are involved in their client's day-to-day needs and challenges. They advise them not only on the latest transaction or dispute, but on how they can run their business most effectively.

This is, of course, especially true of small businesses, where an experienced adviser can be invaluable during the steep learning curve most entrepreneurs face. For example, inexperienced managers are often concerned exclusively with where the next sale is coming from and how they are going to pay the bills - naturally enough. But this can often lead to them neglecting to protect their ideas - the unique ingredient that lets them compete with, or stay ahead of the competition.

Commercial solicitors can have a much more positive role in advising businesses than many people might believe. They should certainly not be viewed as an 'emergency service'. Businesses who make the best use of a solicitor's services can gain a competitive advantage, as well as having a smoother ride through the inevitable difficulties of running a business.

Prevention is better than cure

The fact is that, in business, you know that one day you will need a lawyer. The complexity of commercial life means that, sooner or later, you will find yourself taking, or defending, legal action. It may be a contract dispute with a customer or supplier, or perhaps the lease on your premises turns out to give you far fewer rights than you hoped. A former employee might claim you fired him without reason. Or the Health and Safety Inspector will call before you get round to fixing some dodgy machinery.

The possibilities are endless, and when things do go wrong, the time and money required to put them right is an enormous drain on your business. However, as the saying goes 'prevention is better than cure' - and many legal problems are, in fact, preventable. By doing things right from the start, you can avoid disputes and cope more easily with catastrophes.

Lawyers For Your Business, the Law Society group which works with owner-managed businesses, stresses that - by taking preventative advice on common legal issues - companies actually save money in the long run, as well as avoiding the stress and disruption litigation can cause.

Using a solicitor to your advantage

In addition to ensuring that contracts are correctly drawn up, leases are free from nasty surprises, and the right health and safety procedures are followed, a solicitor can also advise on choosing the best structure for your company, on protecting your intellectual property, and on how to go about raising money.

It is always best to be well prepared before you go to your solicitor for advice - what is it you need him or her to do? What are the facts of the situation? Many businesses waste time and money with their solicitor simply because they have not thought about the fundamental issues beforehand.

The golden rule is: don't leave it too late. Go to see your solicitor before your problems arise, and find out what he or she can do for you. If they can help you gain an advantage over competitors, or save you money in the long run, a solicitor will be a valuable partner in your business.

Lawyers For Your Business, an initiative run by the Law Society.
For more information contact 0171 405 9075

Five Golden Rules To Make Sure You Receive An Efficient Service From Your Solicitors

Legal advice is a regular and often substantial expense for most businesses and the cost of legal services must be controlled if those services are to be cost-effective. The wind of change that has swept the solicitors' profession in the past decade, in the form of fierce competition amongst firms, has resulted in a cheaper and improved service to clients. Nevertheless, the skills and professionalism of those giving legal advice will always be reflected in their fees, and there are at least five golden rules for ensuring that you receive an efficient service from your solicitors.

Choose the right firm of solicitors

Broadly, there are three types of solicitors' firms:

- The sole practitioner or the small firm, often reliant on legal aid fees, which deals mainly with residential conveyancing, divorce, probate and crime;
- The mid-sized provincial, West End or City firm, with fewer than 30 partners, which deals with a broad mixture of both private client and commercial work, perhaps specialising in several niche areas;
- The major City and regional firms, of which there are probably 20 'key players' dealing almost exclusively in commercial law

For each legal problem select a firm of good repute with specialist knowledge and a proven track record in that field. For example, although you would use a high street practice for residential conveyancing, as a general rule corporate work or substantial pieces of litigation should always be handled by a larger or more specialist firm. The hourly rate of partners in the high street firm may be a fraction of that of the major practice, but it is unlikely that the former could, or would want to devote sufficient resources to the work. Even if it did, much time (and therefore your money) would be wasted 'reinventing the wheel' - for example in researching issues with which the specialist would already be familiar.

Define and cultivate your relationship

Once you have selected some appropriate firm(s), ensure that one of the partners has overall supervision of your legal work. If practical, pass all new instructions to him or her, to avoid duplication of work within the firm, or the more usual problem of conflicting instructions being given to different solicitors in the same firm. Equally, cultivate your relationship with your chosen firm(s). Where relevant, explain the needs and practices of your business and industry, so the lawyers who regularly work for you have a fuller idea of what you require from them. This close working relationship can be a great help to clients. A good solicitor should not only react to problems you ask him or her to solve, but should also be proactive, for example by warning clients of changes in the law that affect them.

Take full advantage of free seminars and other marketing events offered by the larger firms. Where possible, introduce your key solicitors to your key personnel - personal contact can cement excellent solicitor-client relationships.

Talk money at the start

There are few things in life that are non-negotiable, and solicitors' fees are certainly not amongst them. Remember the old adage, "If you don't ask, you don't get", and do not be afraid to enter into full and open discussions about the likely cost of the job at the outset. The best firms no longer have the attitude that clients will simply have to pay what they are billed, but instead recognise that they exist to provide quality service at a reasonable cost. Likewise, if you ever have to instruct counsel (a barrister), ensure that your solicitors negotiate with his or her clerk as to the level of fees, before the barrister is instructed - otherwise the bill may prove an unpleasant shock.

Good firms of solicitors should write to you after you have instructed them, to provide you with cost information or estimates, covering matters such as hourly charging rates, the seniority of lawyer(s) assigned to your file(s), when the work should be completed and billed, and whether a fixed fee is to be charged. If your solicitors do not, write to them to confirm your agreement on costs.

Provide full information and assistance to your solicitor

Firstly, consult in good time. It is a false economy to instruct solicitors only when matters have got out of hand, or you feel that there is no alternative. If lawyers are instructed late, it may be too late to take preventative action, and the lawyers will often have to undertake work as a matter of urgency, which will cost more and involve non-legal work that you could have done if there had been time.

Secondly, keep your solicitors fully informed. Many clients work on the basis that the less information and help they provide to their lawyers, the less time the lawyers will spend and the cheaper they will be. This simply is not true. In fact, the lawyer will either lack the necessary information or assistance to serve you properly, or will be forced to spend additional time obtaining that information from you.

On a similar note, assist your solicitors whenever you can by providing them with documents without them having to ask repeatedly. Wherever possible, do the non-legal work yourself. It is considerably cheaper for you to give substantial amounts of photocopying to your secretary than to pay for a trainee solicitor to do the work.

Closely monitor progress

Discuss the progress of your work at each key stage. Do take the trouble to check that you agree with what your solicitors are doing, to telephone for a general discussion or to warn them that they should brief themselves on a certain problem before a meeting. Here a note of caution must be raised. It is usually best for access to your solicitors to be restricted to key personnel in your business, and for them to be sure what they want before they instruct lawyers. Clients have been known to spend a surprising amount of money paying for solicitors to travel to meetings where their attendance was never required, or instructing solicitors to research irrelevant or trivial points of law or practice. At the end of the day, know what you want from your solicitors, get it (in the context of a good ongoing relationship), and bear in mind that the 'meter is running' until the work is billed.

John Spratt and Scott Halborg, Shoosmiths

Don't be too disheartened if not everyone you talk to is as enthusiastic as you are about your plans. Accountants and lawyers are paid to see that glasses are half empty rather than half full. One highly successful business starter took his proposition to 26 banks before getting backing. He asked everyone why they didn't like his plans and in the process greatly improved them. In hindsight he admitted his initial proposition stood little chance of success.

YOUR BUSINESS PLAN

Nearly two in every three small businesses don't have a business plan - coincidentally the same proportion of businesses that fail within five years of setting up. Or is it such a coincidence? The Oxford dictionary describes a plan as 'a formulated or organised method by which a thing is to be done'. Hardly a revolutionary course of action and one would think a prudent thing for any venture. Only a lunatic would set out to build a house with thirty thousand pounds worth of bricks and a cement mixer. A plan is essential to decide right at the outset how many bricks are needed and of what sort.

Yet still every day a thousand hopeful new business start-ups get under way in the UK, committing their proud proprietors to a whole lot more expense than the average house. And most without a clue as to where they are going.

PREPARING YOUR BUSINESS PLAN

Regular planning is an essential discipline for any business. Just as you wouldn't embark on a journey without having at least some idea of your destination, so you should have a clear vision of where your company is heading.

Frequently business plans are prepared with the primary purpose of raising additional finance, possibly to fund a new development or expansion. However, whilst a plan is likely to be an essential tool in raising additional borrowings, all businesses should plan for the future as a matter of routine.

To understand why there is a need for an organisation to prepare a business plan, it is necessary to first consider the most common reasons for businesses to fail. The office of the Official Receiver lists the following causes for business failures:

- Insufficient turnover
- Poor management and supervision
- Lack of proper accounting
- Competition
- Not enough capital
- Bad debts
- Excessive remuneration to the owners

Without exception these are all matters that could be addressed in advance and the underlying purpose of the business plan is to provide the management with focus and direction. A frequent reason given by those from the ostrich school of management for not preparing a business plan is lack of time. Ironically, it is precisely these people who are most likely to benefit from standing back from the business and preparing a carefully considered plan for the future.

So what is the underlying purpose of the business plan ?

 Providing management with direction. The managers of any business need to have a clear image of how they want the enterprise to progress. This may be tangible, such as increasing turnover by 50 per cent over the next two years, or intangible - for example, being the best known supplier of a particular product in a certain location.

Providing management with focus. Having decided the direction of the business, the next consideration is how you are going to get there. Management focus must be achievable and realistic. Clearly, a bland statement like "My focus is on expanding the company's customer base" is less easy to achieve and monitor than "I will contact five potential new customers each week".

 Determining available and required resources. The resources needed to achieve the business objectives will include funding, staffing, raw materials, accommodation. The planning process will highlight the gap between resources required and those available. The nature of the resource shortage will influence whether a fundamental re-think is required or merely a minor change in the method of achieving the business objectives.

- Obtaining additional resources. Frequently business plans are prepared with the purpose of securing the additional resources required to achieve the business objectives. The most common example is additional bank borrowings but other instances would be government grants, recruiting staff or securing business from a major customer.

- Providing a benchmark against which future performance can be measured. You need to be able to measure the performance of the business both financially and operationally and the progress that is being made to meet your business objectives.

- Identifying parameters within which the business should be operated. Mistakes will be made in any business environment but what is important is to be able to identify the reasons and take corrective action promptly. For example, if the selling price of your products is too low, leading to the business making a loss, it is important that this is identified and corrected before the impact on the business becomes critical. A business plan will provide the parameters for decisions on areas such as pricing, pay rises and the cost of raw materials.

Although a business plan can be used as a marketing document, this is not its primary purpose and indeed it would be inappropriate to circulate the contents of many business plans in their entirety to a wider audience. However, extracts from or an executive summary of a business plan can provide a useful marketing tool and give the management confidence that they know the direction that the business is taking.

The content and structure of your business plan

Turning now to the actual contents and structure of a business plan. First of all there are a number of golden rules.

- Never get someone else to write your business plan for you. The business plan needs to convey enthusiasm and energy which is unlikely to be achieved if the plan is written on your behalf by your accountant or other professional advisers. Take advice on format and contents but write the plan yourself.

- Include a punchy and brief executive summary that puts the business plan into context and explains the key features and conclusions.

- If the plan is to be used for an external purpose (such as raising finance or negotiating terms with suppliers) then make it an attractive and easy to read document. Use tables, graphs and photographs to break up the text.

- Keep the plan brief. As a general rule of thumb a business plan should be no more than 15 pages and if in doubt, err on the side of brevity.

If the business plan is being used to raise funds you must address the concerns the lender will have. It may be obvious, but these will include, "How will I be repaid?", "Will the debt be secured?" and "Will the business generate sufficient cash to service the debt?".

 All detailed financial data including past performance and future projections should be included in appendices, with summaries being provided in the body of the text as relevant.

 To add credibility, always state the source of any statistics provided. Include a contents page with references to section numbers and preferably page numbers.

 If the business plan is to be used for an external purpose, only date it if the date can be changed with relative ease. Even a business plan which is only two months old will be perceived to be tired and out of date by an external reader.

Writing the plan

It's now time to start writing and whilst the business plan must be tailored to meet its underlying objectives it is likely that it will include all or some of the following sections:

Section 1 – Introduction and Executive Summary (2 to 3 pages)

Section 1 should include a brief description of the company, its history and recent business developments, an outline of the senior management and their successes. You should explain the purpose of the business plan and highlight key aspects including business strategy, shareholders' objectives, market opportunities, past and projected financial performance (covering the two most recent years together with the projections for the next three), the requirement for funds or other resources.

Section 2 – The Business (2 to 3 pages)

This section will provide an overview of the business. You should start with a brief description of the history of the company with a focus on recent key developments such as expanding into new markets or gaining additional customers as a result of management actions. You should then give an overview of the products or services provided by the organisation before providing a summarised table of the historical trading results (preferably audited).

Section 3 – The Markets (3 to 4 pages)

In this section you should provide a description of the markets in which the business operates including available data on market size. This will then be followed by an assessment of the opportunities within those markets, details of competitors and, possibly, a SWOT style analysis.

Section 4 – The Business Plan and Strategy (2 to 3 pages)

The business objectives and the detailed steps that will be taken to achieve those objectives will be considered in Section 4. You should also include a timetable and allocate individuals' responsibility for achieving the objectives.

Section 5 – Organisational Structure (1 to 2 pages)

Section 5 will provide an overview of the company's organisational structure in diagrammatic form. This will cover senior personnel and the reporting lines, together with, if applicable, the divisional or group structure. You should also provide brief profiles of the key personnel.

Section 6 – Financial Information (2 to 3 pages)

This final section will give the reader summarised financial information regarding the organisation together with the assumptions adopted in preparing projections. Ordinarily, the financial information should cover the preceding two years and projections for the next three. You should include a profit and loss account for the business, a summarised cash flow statement and a balance sheet. For new businesses a two year cash flow forecast is of prime importance - particularly if you are seeking funds.

Appendices

Any detailed information that is likely to distract the reader if given in the body of the plan should be included as an appendix. Examples will include the detailed financial projections, curricula vitae for the senior management and selected product literature. The financial projections included in the appendix should cover the next three years and be presented on a monthly basis for the first year and quarterly thereafter.

And finally, having prepared your business plan, remember that it is a working document. It will need to be updated and amended on a regular basis to reflect the ever-changing circumstances of the business.

Rhodri Whitlock, Partner, Pannell Kerr Forster

Without a business plan you have no hope of getting financial backing and little chance of success. You do hear of successful people who wing it without a plan. But you also hear of people falling from the 15th floor and living to tell the tale. Not something many people would want to put to the test.

One great and rarely mentioned bonus of writing a business plan is that you will feel more confident in the venture, and that confidence may just rub off on others.

FINANCIAL FORECASTS

Financial and weather forecasts have much in common. For one thing they are frequently both wrong. But most of the time that doesn't matter too much. As far as the weather is concerned, to make a workable plan it's usually enough to know if rain is very likely. In business, peaks and troughs are equally certain, though exactly when is less predictable. Nevertheless a well prepared financial forecast can give you a feeling for those periods when cash may be tight and allow you to plan accordingly. It is certainly worth remembering that profitable businesses can and do fail for lack of cash.

Don't worry too much if, as you read this chapter, you find you don't know all the answers. For example you may not know the monthly rent on premises you haven't even found yet. Make a prudent estimate and put the item down for investigation when you do your market research.

CASH FLOW FORECASTING

What is a cash flow forecast and why is it important?

A cash flow forecast is an estimate of the future movement of cash into and out of the business bank accounts as a result of receipts and payments of money.

It is vital that a business has adequate finance to pay its way. A cash flow forecast will help in determining if and when either further cash will be needed from outside sources or there will be surplus cash to invest. A well prepared cash flow forecast will highlight such situations in advance and hence allow time to put the necessary bank facilities into place and time to plan how best to invest surplus cash.

If a business runs out of cash it will be unable to pay suppliers and staff and as a result will very quickly find it impossible to continue in operation. It is important to realise that sales do not necessarily equal cash.

For example:

XYZ Limited is set up to sell computer hardware from a catalogue.

Customer A orders one computer and therefore XYZ Limited buys one computer for £800 to sell for £1000.

It is probable that XYZ Limited will be required to pay the £800 before receiving the £1000 and will therefore have to fund the purchase until the cash is received from the customer.

When preparing a cash flow forecast it is crucial that all cash inflows and outflows are considered. But even then cash forecasting can still go wrong if:

- Forecasts are incorrect or unrealistic
- No action is taken when problems are highlighted
- The budgeting process is not controlled or monitored
- Unforeseen expenditure arises
- Unexpected delays and time differences occur.

The fortunate ones

Although margins may be small for supermarkets they have a major cash flow advantage over most businesses. Most businesses have to consider how long they can delay paying their suppliers and how quickly they can persuade their customers to pay. Supermarkets, however, are such a powerful purchasing force that they can virtually dictate terms to their smaller suppliers.

In addition, and most importantly, we all pay supermarkets almost immediately. Even if we use a credit card the cash is in their bank in a couple of days.

Therefore supermarkets tend to receive sales proceeds well before they have to pay their suppliers.

How to produce a cash flow forecast

A cash flow forecast is usually prepared on a monthly basis although a weekly basis may well be more appropriate in some cases. The forecast should cover at least the next 12 months. The important point is that it shows a cash balance at the end of each of the periods under consideration, which will highlight any cash shortages. A suggested layout is shown below.

The ABC Co. Limited
Cash flow forecast for the six months to Dec 1999

	July £	Aug £	Sep £	Oct £	Nov £	Dec £
Receipts						
Cash sales						
Cash from debtors						
Payments						
Wages and salaries						
Creditors						
Purchase of fixed assets						
Net cash flow						
Balance brought forward						
Balance carried forward						

Getting it right

To start off you need to build a model using realistic estimates of sales, costs of sales and expenses, and incorporating the timing of receipts and payments. It is best to set up your forecast on a specific software package. The advantage of this is that such packages can be linked directly to your accounting software, ensuring that you have an accurate starting point.

You should also estimate your profit (or loss, where applicable, particularly in the early stages) and gauge the sensitivity of the results to changes in prices, margins, timing of cash flows and market activities so that you can estimate how viable your plans are.

You also would be well advised to remember certain do's and don'ts.

Do

- Research the market thoroughly
- Involve managers from all areas of the business
- Make use of IT and modelling tools, spreadsheets, specific software packages etc
- Use realistic and conservative assumptions
- Flex the forecast for changes in key assumptions, for example price changes
- Link it up with profit and balance sheet forecasts

Don't

- Rush into it
- Forget the possibility of economic changes - inflation, tax, interest rates, VAT and labour supply
- Do it by yourself
- Do it manually
- Overestimate demand or underestimate the cost of labour and supplies
- Ignore the advice of your colleagues and professional advisers

Including all costs

It is important to consider **all** cash inflows and outflows when preparing a cash flow forecast. Often, set-up costs get underestimated and some costs even forgotten.

Always bear in mind such costs as:

Time: Time spent in setting up your business means less time has been spent earning money.

Legal and Professional Fees:	These include company/trade set-up, purchase of licences (for restaurants, betting shops), obtaining professional advice on start up.
Advertising and Marketing:	These costs will have to be incurred to launch the business and its products. Initial costs could be very high.
VAT:	If you are not VAT registered then VAT will have to be paid on most purchases.
	If you are VAT registered the selling price will have to include output VAT and this may affect demand.
	In addition, VAT has important cash implications, since you have to pay any excess of VAT charged over VAT suffered to Customs and Excise every 3 months.
Property Costs:	Include surveyors' costs, lawyers' costs and land registry rates.
Delays:	Delays can cost business a lot of money - e.g. late arrival of plant will result in lost revenue, late moving will result in lost trade and having to pay rent/fixed costs on both premises.
Travel:	Unavoidable travel costs can mount up and are often underestimated in the forecasting process.
Bank interest and charges:	Overdraft interest is usually remembered in a cash flow forecast but bank charges, which can be considerable and are charged by the bank as they arise, are often forgotten.
Increases in raw material prices:	Whilst you can control the selling price of your products, you cannot control raw material prices. Any unforeseen increase in raw material price will affect your cash flow in the same way as it affects your profits.

Increases in staff costs:	You may find that certain members of staff become key to the business and that you will feel forced to comply with their requests for pay rises to avoid losing them.
Taxation:	Employer's National Insurance contributions and Corporation Tax are two taxes which are sometimes forgotten in the forecasting process.
Income Tax:	You should not budget for your own salary/drawings from the business simply by considering the amount you plan to 'take home'. Add on to this figure income tax, employee's and employer's National Insurance payable.
Loans for Purchase of Assets:	Whilst you may be able to obtain loans for the purchase of fixed assets, the continued availability of those assets can only be assured if loan repayments are made on time. Therefore it is vital to allow for these repayments as well as the interest cost.

Quantifying the finance required

How much money?

Your cash flow forecast aims to give an indication of the likely minimum cash requirement during the period covered by the forecast. It would be dangerous to have only that minimum level of funds available - there should also be a contingency fund.

Five main uses of cash requirements and resources should be planned for:

- Meeting current day-to-day financial obligations - e.g. purchase of stock, payment of bills and wages. These items of expenditure are unavoidable. An inability to meet these cash outflows is likely to lead to the downfall of the business.
- Repayment of loans. This is also unavoidable expenditure, vital to the survival of the business.
- Purchase of fixed assets. Initial expenditure on fixed assets is unavoidable -production will rely on it. Further upgrades or replacement of fixed assets can, to a certain extent, be timed to coincide with periods of high cash balances, but should not be delayed to such an extent that continuity of production is threatened.

- Giving a cushion against unplanned expenditure. A cushion must be regarded as necessary, to cope with the inevitable unforeseen variances in the assumptions underlying the projections.
- Taking advantage of investment market opportunities. Although your projections are unlikely to highlight many such opportunities, spare cash should be considered a valuable resource, and therefore should be earning a return at all times.

Flexing the forecast

You should be able to rework your model to test how changes in key variables would impact on your forecasts.

Consider changes in:

- Sales forecasts
- Debtor payment patterns
- Material or stock costs
- Other costs such as labour, rent and overheads
- Timings of outflows
- Interest rates, where borrowings are at variable rates

As already suggested, it is far easier to adjust variables if forecasts are prepared on cashflow forecasting software.

For example:

XYZ Limited predicts sales of one unit in month 1, rising by one unit per month

Each unit is sold for £1200 and costs the company £800. Fixed office costs are payable at the rate of £200 per month

In the cash flow forecast, it is predicted that all customers will pay in the month of sale and suppliers will also be paid in the month of sale

The cash flow forecast for the first six months is therefore as follows:

	Mnth 1	Mnth 2	Mnth 3	Mnth 4	Mnth 5	Mnth 6
Receipts from customers	1200	2400	3600	4800	6000	7200
Payments to suppliers	(800)	(1600)	(2400)	(3200)	(4000)	(4800)
Fixed office costs	(200)	(200)	(200)	(200)	(200)	(200)
Cash flow for the month	200	600	1000	1400	1800	2200
Opening balance	-	200	800	1800	3200	5000
Closing balance	200	800	1800	3200	5000	7200

What if the customers actually pay one month after the sale?

	Mnth 1	Mnth 2	Mnth 3	Mnth 4	Mnth 5	Mnth 6
Receipts from customers	-	1200	2400	3600	4800	6000
Payments to suppliers	(800)	(1600)	(2400)	(3200)	(4000)	(4800)
Fixed office costs	(200)	(200)	(200)	(200)	(200)	(200)
Cash flow for the month	(1000)	(600)	(200)	200	600	1000
Opening balance	-	(1000)	(1600)	(1800)	(1600)	(1000)
Closing balance	(1000)	(1600)	(1800)	(1600)	(1000)	-

Changing just one assumption has made an enormous difference to the month end cash balance.

If, in the above example, XYZ Limited has a £1600 overdraft facility, it will be unable to pay its suppliers in month 3 until it has received cash from its customers.

Even then, the company cannot pay its fixed office costs.

This is a simple example of 'flexing' your forecast, allowing for unexpected bad news.

Working capital management

Net working capital is made up of: debtors + stock + cash - creditors

The management of working capital is concerned with the liquidity position of the company. The main aim of working capital management is to have as little cash as possible tied up in your working capital.

In an ideal world, cash receipts from debtors are used to purchase stock and pay off creditors so that the stock can then be sold and money is received, thus returning to the beginning of the cycle. However, you should have a cushion of cash to allow for debtors not paying on time (or at all), creditors requiring payment before debtors pay you, purchase prices increasing suddenly and other unforeseen expenditure.

Monitoring and updating the forecast

To ensure the success of a cash flow/business plan, you must

Action	Reason
Obtain monthly financial information and discuss progress with colleagues	To monitor progress and ascertain whether objectives are being met

Action	Reason
Compare actual results with budget and consider the reasons for variances	To understand the reasons for variances. Future budgets will be more accurate, or future expenditure will be lower
Adjust projections for new assumptions arising from the variance analysis	So that the projections will reflect the most up-to-date knowledge and information
Keep in touch with suppliers and customers	To identify if variables need to be changed - e.g. prices of stock , changes in demand, payment/ credit terms
Update the opening bank balance on the projections to reflect the actual balance	So that the projections are as up-to -date as possible

- Produce the forecast yourself, don't delegate it to your external accountant
- Make realistic assumptions and ensure that all categories of cost are included
- Consult with all areas of the business
- Ask your external accountant to review your forecast
- Ensure that a contingency is available to cover unexpected cash outflows

Tony Perkins, BDO Stoy Hayward

Once a business is under way owner-managers often breathe a sigh of relief believing that forecasts are a thing of the past. How wrong they are. Whilst every business needs luck it can't depend on it. Like a lookout on the bow of a ship, a business should keep a continuous lookout a year or so ahead. Don't wait until the end of one year's forecast to start another, or it could be too late.

Market Research

The Duke of Wellington defined reconnaissance as "the art of knowing what is on the other side of the hill". Market research is the business equivalent of this activity. Unfortunately many business starters are not really aware that there is a hill in the first place. Such people pursue the 'one per cent' syndrome, or the market research cop-out clause. This describes the situation in which the prospective business owner starts a venture on the premise that, "if we only get one per cent of the market we'll be a great success". This argument is then advanced so that no time is wasted in doing any research whatsoever. After all, the business has only to sell to this tiny percentage of possible buyers! This type of thinking leads to many business failures.

If the market is so huge as to make one per cent of it very profitable, then inevitably there are many large and established competitors. For a small firm to try to compete in this situation is little short of suicidal. It can be done, but only if sound research has identified a market niche. And therein lies the rub. The bigger the market, the smaller the entry niche must be to assure success, and the better the research must be to find the target. Please read this chapter with great care.

MARKET RESEARCH

The temptation when starting a new business is to tell friends about it and to be encouraged by their reactions. Be realistic! Their enthusiasm is not enough and it is unlikely, in any case, that you are aiming your product or service at people like them.

All our decisions in life are based on our interpretation of the information available at the time. When you buy a car, you take into account all that you know about its fuel consumption, likely reliability, the cost of spare parts, safety features and so on. The same should be true when you set up a business, and there is a lot more to find out - Who are the competitors? Who are the customers to attract? What is the demand? What is the best way to publicise your product or service? What is the most powerful selling message?

"Knowledge is power" wrote Francis Bacon in the seventeenth century and his words have never been more true than today. The more you know about what people want, the more you know about what your competitors already provide, the stronger your position and the better your chance of success.

The information you will need depends very much on the nature of the business you are starting and who the customers will be - other businesses or the general public. The key to success is to establish:

- Exactly where the target market lies
- Who makes decisions on which suppliers to use and what matters to them
- How best to reach them

Many other subsidiary questions lie within these. You will need to consider how people define 'good customer service' in your particular market. If you are selling a product, you will need to select the most effective packaging and research the most effective pricing (Would you make more money by increasing the profit margin and selling fewer, or cutting margins and selling more?).

A lot of information is available free of charge in a library or on the

Internet. Searches in business directories will reveal the number and nature of competitors, their geographic location and their market share, and a great deal can be obtained from organisations such as Business Link and the Federation of Small Businesses. You can seek out the facts yourself or employ a market research specialist to do it for you. However, there will always be some questions left unanswered, and this is where you can invest in some research specific to your own requirements.

Market research is the means of obtaining the answers in a systematic way, talking to the appropriate mix of people so that the survey accurately represents the views or records the behaviour of the entire group that is relevant to the client organisation - whether this is the general population, your own customers, people who own PCs, or people who bought Des O'Connor's last album.

The selection of the research sample (the participants) is more important than the number of people included in the survey. They must be chosen to represent the target group in as many ways as possible - for instance the appropriate mix of age groups (in the general public) or categories of business (for a business survey).

There are basically two types of research - qualitative and quantitative. Qualitative collects attitudes and explains behaviour and opinions. A questionnaire would restrict the possible replies. The interview is replaced by an informal discussion of the relevant topics and involves intensive interviewing and analysis by experienced researchers. This makes it expensive, although a great deal of valuable and often creative information is obtained. However, it will not provide facts and figures which depend upon larger numbers of carefully selected participants and a structured questionnaire - i.e. 'quantitative research'.

Decisions need to be made on the way to obtain the information and the number to interview. The larger the number of participants the more accurate the survey results and the greater the scope for identifying differing views according to age group, size of business or other aspects. However, a pragmatic approach is needed to assess value for money, since doubling the number does not double the accuracy. Many aspects have to be taken into account when considering questionnaire design and survey method (face-to-face, telephone or postal) and it is wise to take the advice of an experienced professional.

How to choose a market research supplier:

- Use handbooks published by recognised bodies such as the Market Research Society (0171 490 4911) or BMRA (0181 374 4095). This ensures that the agency personnel are bound by a strict code of conduct and, in the case of BMRA members, to the highest standards of research. The BMRA offers 'Select Line' - a free service that will identify up to six member companies which meet your requirements in terms of speciality, size and location.

- A useful web site for market research is www.mrweb.co.uk and both the MRS (www.marketresearch.org.uk) and BMRA (www.bmra.org.uk) have web sites too.
- Approach two to four agencies that meet your criteria, and ask for their ideas (a research proposal will be free of charge).
- A clear brief is essential to get the best out of your research agency and should give the background to the project, your objectives, whether you want a report or just the data and, ideally, the approximate budget and time available. The research agencies will be happy to advise on the most appropriate methodology.
- You should select your chosen partner, taking into account:
    - Their understanding of the research objectives and suitability of their recommended research approach
    - Evidence of their experience in relevant areas
    - The background and experience of the researchers who will be handling your project, and details of fieldwork, data analysis and reporting standards
    - The fee quoted and what it includes
    - The rapport between you and the people you have dealt with at the research company

Market research will help you make the decisions necessary to start to build your business and can continue to keep you abreast with information that is vital to the company's success.

Measuring:
Facts - how many people buy/read/watch X
Behaviour - how often people buy X
Attitudes - what people think of X compared with Y
Changes in facts, behaviour or attitudes

Understanding:
Behaviour - why people buy X
Attitudes - why they think X is better or worse than Y
Changes in behaviour and attitudes

Testing Out:
New ideas, products and advertising
New markets for existing products and services
Hypotheses (We think young people are deterred by the price, is this true?)

Jill Carter, Abacus Research

Yes, market research is essential, but the amount of research done has to relate to the sums at risk. If a venture calls for a start-up investment of £1000, spending £10,000 on market research will probably give a poor return. So concentrate your efforts on the handful of questions that will determine success or failure, rather than on the many answers it would be nice to know.

Finding Finance

The late Bob Payton understood the problem of raising finance more than most entrepreneurs. Even with a ten year track record in the hospitality business and with a company turning over £10 million and making profits of £1 million he found raising money a constant problem. Getting the £4.5 million needed for his last venture, Stapleford Park, the Leicestershire country house hotel, was as difficult and gut wrenching as trying to raise £35,000 for his first venture, the Chicago Pizza Pie Factory.

So don't expect it to be easy. Financiers need to be convinced you will take as much care of their money as you would of your own. If you don't have money in the first place that can be a very difficult circle to square.

In my experience . . .

From a cartoon strip which we had created for the International Herald Tribune commemorating the Johnnie Walker Ryder Cup we decided to make some limited edition prints. We didn't do any test marketing but rather went with gut feel. In the rush to get things done I agreed to have 200 of each of the first twenty cartoons printed on a sale or return basis from Valderrama, host club for the event in 1997.

It was fortunate that that our break even point was relatively low in terms of sales. If we had sat back and thought about it we would have realised that the key to selling the prints was the players themselves - a Nick Faldo 'Memorable Moment' will always sell better than one of Howard Clark (no disrespect to Howard). We still have 198 prints of Bernhard Langer's missed putt in Kiawah in 1991 - true it was a memorable moment but it certainly didn't sell.

- Always know your worst case scenario
- Always make the time to think through a project fully

Jamie Cunningham, Professional Sports Partnerships Ltd

Bank Financing

The entrepreneur setting up his or her own business is likely to require sources of finance other than his or her own. For small businesses one of the most common sources will be the high street bank. It may provide cash in a variety of forms but will usually require security to protect its own investments.

The bank may provide an overdraft under which borrowing may fluctuate, just like a personal overdraft. The overdraft is intended to provide working capital and aid cash flow, but should not be used for capital expenditure. Interest on the overdraft will be charged at a margin over the bank's base rate but exceeding the overdraft limit can be costly - usually in the form of an increase in the interest rate and a daily fee. An overdraft is repayable 'on demand' by the bank and although banks may be willing to indicate how long they intend the facility to remain available, this should not be treated as any form of commitment.

For capital expenditure, a term loan or an on demand loan may be considered.

A term loan is one where a specified amount is made available to the borrower for a specified period, usually one or more years. It is repaid in fixed instalments, typically monthly or quarterly, whether in equal amounts or otherwise and may include a 'balloon payment' – a payment of all outstanding borrowing at the end of the loan period.

The essential difference between this and an on demand loan is that the bank cannot call in (demand early repayment of) any of the repayment instalments before the due date unless the borrower defaults (i.e. breaches the terms of the documentation or fails to make a payment to the bank). An on demand loan, like an overdraft, can be called in at any time even if the borrower is complying with the terms of its credit and even though it may be adequately servicing its debt. Interest rates on term loans can be fixed or variable and, if variable, will usually be linked to the bank's base rate for smaller loans. On demand loans will generally be subject to a variable rate of interest.

Whatever type of facility is chosen, the borrower will incur extra costs, such as arrangement fees and costs in relation to the loan and the security.

The bank will need to protect itself in the event that the borrower fails to make the repayments. It will take security in the form of fixed charges over land and other fixed assets. The bank's consent will then be needed to sell or otherwise deal with those assets. If the borrower fails to repay the debt the bank may sell the assets to recover its investments. If the borrower is a company, the bank will invariably require a floating charge over the business as a whole. Assets subject to a floating charge (and not subject to a fixed charge) may usually be used and disposed of in the ordinary course of business. However, the bank will be able, in some circumstances, to 'crystallise' the floating charge, i.e., convert it into a fixed charge.

If the borrower is a company (and banks do appear to be more willing to lend to companies) the directors may be asked to provide personal guarantees which may be supported by mortgages over the matrimonial home or assignment of life policies. The willingness of directors to provide guarantees is often viewed as a reflection of their commitment to the future of the business.

Remember, whatever type of facility you choose and whatever security is taken by the bank you should always take professional advice on the terms and conditions of the deal and documentation. These will usually be quite onerous and banks often require quite detailed ongoing information about the business.

Do also remember that, although your first port of call is likely to be your own bank, it is always advisable to 'shop around' for the best deal and to prepare a clear concise business plan to 'sell your story'.

James Taylor and Nicola Maslen-Fincham, Shoosmiths

EQUITY– DIFFERENT KINDS OF SHARES

What is a Share?

According to the Companies Act 1985, it is a 'share in the share capital of the company, and includes stock'. Not very helpful. A better description would be 'a bundle of rights in a company'. What these rights (and obligations) are will depend on the particular class of share.

To discover this, we look to the company's 'constitution' - its Memorandum and Articles of Association - noting that, where no different or separate rights are said to belong to different classes of shares, they are treated as equals.

It is impossible to give a definitive list of different types of shares as, with a few caveats, a company can issue new shares with any rights and obligations that the then shareholders can imagine. The usual differences are in respect of voting rights, right to dividend, return of capital in a winding-up, and transferability. Capital is the nominal value of the shares (the £1 in '£1 shares') and shares will either be fully paid up, partly paid or 'due', depending on how much of the capital money has been paid to the company.

Usually, the shares of a company can be divided into up to six categories:

Ordinary shares:

Every company has ordinary shares ('Class A' shares). If there is only one class of shares they will be ordinary shares. The ordinary share is that which the public associates with 'equity'. These shares usually carry a proportionate entitlement to the dividends of the company, to vote at General Meetings, and to share in any surplus in a winding-up of the company.

Ordinary shareholders usually receive a dividend from their shares, and/or a return of capital on a winding-up. But they are not necessarily entitled to this. For example, the directors recommend to the Annual General Meeting that a dividend be paid, and shareholders can then vote themselves a dividend up to but not exceeding that sum. But the directors need not declare a dividend, even if there are sufficient profits available.

Preference shares:

In contrast to ordinary shareholders, preference shareholders will be given some form of preferential treatment. They are usually entitled to a fixed rate of dividend from the company's distributable profits, in 'preference' (i.e. before) anything is paid to the ordinary shareholders. The trade off is that preference shareholders usually receive no preferential repayment of capital in a winding-up. More generally, whatever rights are given to preference shares, these will be the only rights that those shareholders will enjoy.

Preference shares are usually subdivided as follows:

Participating preference shares: In addition to their preferential right, such as to a dividend, these also have the right to share in any surplus profits available after dividends have been paid to both preference and ordinary shareholders. Preference shares will be non-participating unless otherwise stated.

Cumulative preference shares: These provide the right to an accumulated dividend. If the preferential dividend is not fully paid one year because the company has insufficient profits, that year's entitlement to dividend is carried forward so that the next year all arrears of preferential dividend must be paid before other shareholders get anything. Preference shares will be cumulative unless the contrary is stated.

Redeemable shares:

Shares of any class can be redeemable. This means that the shares will be 'bought back' by the company on whatever terms are specified by the Articles. They will then be cancelled. Broadly, any limited company with existing non-redeemable shares, if authorised by its Articles, can issue redeemable shares, redemption of which can be at the insistence of either the company or the shareholder.

Deferred shares:

These shares are usually those issued to incorporate the company, and their rights (for example, the rights on a winding-up) will be subordinated to those of ordinary shares.

Employees' shares:

Issued in an employees' share scheme to increase employee commitment and to obtain tax advantages, these shares usually contain restrictions on transfer.

Convertible shares:

Any class of share may be 'convertible' if the Articles of the company allow the shareholder to convert it into shares of another class. For this reason alone, it is worth studying the provisions of the Articles – conversion of shares can have a drastic effect on the balance of power amongst shareholders !

Scott Halborg and John Spratt, Shoosmiths

VENTURE CAPITAL - ALL YOU NEED TO KNOW (AT LEAST TO START WITH)

There has never been a greater availability of venture capital for businesses starting up, expanding or looking to undertake a management buy-in or buy-out. A record £4.9 billion was invested in more than 1300 companies in 1998, of which £2.8 billion was invested in UK companies. This raises the total invested since 1983 to almost £28 billion in up to 18,000 companies.

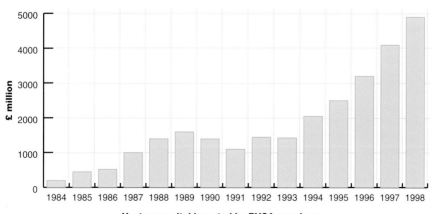

Venture capital invested by BVCA members

95

What is venture capital?

Venture capital, whether from a venture capital firm or a business angel (private investor), is long term and committed. It involves participation in the share capital of your business and seeks to increase the value of the business for all the shareholders without taking control. A conventional lender such as a bank, has a legal right to add interest on a loan and to its repayment, irrespective of your company's success or failure. The venture capital investors' returns on the other hand are dependent on the growth and profitability on your business because they have acquired a stake in it.

The ability to provide long term capital as well as experience and contacts, sets venture capital apart from other sources of business capital. This combination has been demonstrated to grow companies' sales, exports and investment at a faster rate than others. In a recent survey, almost 95 per cent of venture backed companies said they would not have existed, or would have grown less rapidly, without venture capital.

Well known venture capital backed companies

Some companies that are now very well known were formerly venture capital backed companies. For example, Sage Group plc, the sponsor of this book, raised venture capital to help expand its business and this assisted it in becoming the successful company it is today. Venture capital has also helped many others either to achieve independence from their parents, to start up, expand or to turn around their business from receivership. These include companies such as The Denby Group plc, Del Monte Foods (UK), Dunlop Slazenger Group, LDV Ltd (formerly Leyland Daf Vans), and the Tetley Group. To become a successful venture capital backed company you need determination and an experienced and ambitious management team and an excellent company with significant growth prospects.

The type of companies that receive venture capital

The majority of venture capital investments are in established expanding businesses. However, in 1998, an all time investment record was reached in start-up and other early stage companies. Investment in start-ups rose by 91% and in early stage companies by 75% to £111 million and £177 million respectively. The number of both start-up (115) and early stage (126) companies backed rose by 10% overall to the highest level seen in at least seven years, acounting for 21% of all the companies backed in 1998. This is good news for many entrepreneurs, but it still takes considerable determination and ambition to raise venture capital for small start-up situations in particular.

If you are seeking an investment of less than £100,000 there are currently 27 venture capital firms who are members of the British Venture Capital Association who maybe worth approaching, subject to your company meeting their other investment preferences. Business angels are worth considering for smaller amounts of early stage venture capital. They may be contacted by registering with a business angel network, of which there are at least 40 in the UK.

The sources, types and styles of venture capital available vary considerably. It is important to consider the stage of your company's development, the amount of finance you are seeking, and the type of industry in which your business operates. A description of your business and an explanation of its financing requirement should be set out in a detailed business plan, which should have a good executive summary. Only those sources of venture capital whose investment preferences match your requirements should be targeted.

British Venture Capital Association

FINANCING A SMALL BUSINESS

Money is a vital ingredient in any business growth plan but where do you go to get an independent guide to what's available, where from and how much?

One starting point is your local Business Link which has appointed financial management counsellors to meet demand from busy owner-managers pushing for growth and pushed for cash.
This is a brief summary of some of the many options available.

Clearing Banks

Usually the first port of call, either to the manager responsible for your account or perhaps a manager from another bank keen to encourage your custom.

If you're not happy with the help you receive from your bank, consider your options because the banks are certainly investing in winning new business accounts.

Banks will arrange overdrafts usually to meet working capital or short term needs. Business loans are available to cover medium or long term asset finance, and business mortgages can be arranged for property purchase or improvement.

Rates of interest vary although some loans can be taken on a fixed rate basis.

Small Firms Loan Guarantee Scheme

Lack of security and/or absence of a track record may make conventional loans difficult to obtain from a bank. The SFLG Scheme may well be able to assist in such cases. Run by the DTI, the scheme will provide a government guarantee for business loans granted by banks and other financial institutions.

The guarantee covers 70 per cent of the outstanding loan, although this increases to 85 per cent for established businesses that have been trading for two years or more. The minimum amount is £5000 and the maximum is £100,000 although for established businesses the maximum increases to £250,000. Terms of loans in all cases vary between 2 and 10 years. Consult your bank for more details about this scheme.

Finance Houses and Leasing Companies

Hire purchase or leasing arrangements can enable businesses to acquire assets such as plant, machinery and vehicles. These arrangements can ease cash flow and may be tax advantageous.

The range of companies offering hire purchase and leasing is enormous, and Business Link can help you with an objective overview. The tax implications of this form of finance should be investigated thoroughly with your accountant.

Factoring and Invoice Discounting

Factoring improves cash flow by releasing funds tied up in unpaid invoices, and can also maintain a full sales ledger and credit control service for a client business. Ongoing credit checks are carried out to minimise bad debt problems.

Invoice discounting is similar to factoring, but does not include the sales ledger or credit control function which is left in the hands of the client business.

Factoring and invoice discounting are rapidly growing in popularity, and in some cases are tending to replace traditional bank overdraft finance. The factoring companies are beginning of offer 'add on' packages, such as limited stock lending, and foreign trade finance.

Trade Finance

Trade finance may well be able to assist a business which has confirmed orders with creditworthy customers, but is unable to find the additional working capital to finance the sales. This form of finance bridges the gap before and after the sale of finished goods by funding the goods themselves and/or the sales invoice to the end customer.

Usually existing bank facilities are unaffected and charges over the company's equity and directors' guarantees are not required. Usually, no minimum or maximum turnover requirement is set, and the facility can be used on an 'as and when' basis. One-off deals can be accommodated, and the facility is often helpful to seasonal businesses.

Specialist Lending Schemes

In some areas, specialist finance schemes are available, such as those provided by West Midlands Enterprise and British Steel (Industry) Ltd.

The range and availability of these schemes varies from area to area, and the Financial Management Counsellor at your Business Link will be able to guide and assist you.

Local Authority Finance

Many local schemes are in existence, usually on a top-up basis, to supplement mainstream finance sources or grant assistance. Again, the range and availability of these schemes varies from area to area and your local Business Link will be able to guide you.

Venture Capital

Venture capital institutions operate in a specialised marketplace and deal with the provision of risk capital for businesses where there is a higher than average expectation of future growth.

For taking that high level of risk, a higher rate of return is required and an equity investment in the company is made. Often, there is active involvement by the venture capital organisation to support the company's management in its growth strategy.

The venture capital route is not right for every business, and your local Business Link will be able to advise you as to its suitability.

Business Angels

The mainstream venture capital schemes usually apply only to larger businesses and in relatively large amounts. Many small businesses can benefit from equity investment, and increasingly this is taking the shape of an investment made by an individual, or a 'business angel'.

Such informal equity investment, usually up to £100,000, often brings with it the added advantage of the business expertise of the investor, which can make a significant difference to the investee business.

Business angel investment is not a 'quick fix' solution but may well be a route worth considering for your business. Your local Business Link has access to business angel matching services, and will be happy to discuss this with you.

Grants

The area of grant assistance to businesses is large and complex, and there are many unscrupulous operators in the field.

Your local Business Link is equipped to provide you with a list of grant schemes that may be appropriate to your business and particular requirement. Don't hesitate to make use of their expertise.

A main provider of grant assistance is the DTI, under Regional Selective Assistance (RSA). This is available in what are termed 'assisted areas'. RSA is a project grant aimed at the manufacturing and selected service creators which is based on the fixed capital costs of the project and the number of jobs the project is expected to create or safeguard.

Additionally, the DTI operate the SMART Scheme aimed at helping individuals and small and medium sized enterprises to improve their competitiveness by developing new products and processes to the benefit of the national economy. SMART grants are provided on a competitive basis for two distinct types of project - a technical and commercial feasibility study into innovative technology, and development up to preproduction prototype stage of a new product or process which involves a significant technological advance.

Full details of the SMART scheme are available from your local Business Link.

Richard Sharper, Business Link, Wolverhampton

FINDING FINANCE -
A SUMMARY OF THE OPTIONS

You might think that you have already done most of the hard work when you have found the new business opportunity, the niche in the marketplace, or the unique product and the means to produce it and that life will be plain sailing from here.

Unfortunately not. Having convinced yourself of the inevitable success of your business proposition, you now have to persuade someone else to give you the money to move it forward. This sounds like the easy part - after all there is so much money floating around the banks, the City, or locked up in pension funds that all you are looking for is a mere drop in the ocean. But like the needle in the haystack how do you find the money with your name on it?

Naturally, the easiest to find is your own money: your savings, your unmortgaged property, your life - through insurance, and your other assets are all a logical starting point. You may not feel you can put all of your worth behind a business because of the risks involved, but whichever route you go down you will normally be expected to invest some of your own assets. Banks seek personal guarantees, venture capitalists like to see owners taking risks with their own money - why should they risk their clients' money if you will not risk yours? The stock markets too are not keen for all the money raised on a flotation to go into the owner's back pockets.

If you can fund the project from your own resources you should try to do so. Only in this way do all of the rewards of success flow to you. As soon as you bring in other sources of finance they slice off some of the reward, be it interest, share of the value on the sale of the business, or dividends. They may also constrain the business through the use of covenants, borrowing limits, and the placement of financial obligations on the business - potentially not only carving off part of your rewards but also capping them by restricting your operation.

Identify appropriate sources of funding

The first stage in identifying what source of funding is appropriate involves understanding precisely the purpose to which the finance will be put. If your need is short term, then the funding should be short term. Starting out in a contract cleaning business, with a major contract, you need sufficient funds initially to buy the mop and bucket. Six months into the contract they will have been paid for and so there is no point in getting a five year bank loan to cover this, as within a year you will have cash in the bank and a loan with an early redemption penalty!

Conversely, in starting up a manufacturing business, you will be buying machinery to last probably five years, designing your logo and buying stationery, paying the deposit on leasehold premises, buying a van, and investing funds in winning a long term contract. As the profits on this are expected to flow over a number of years, then finance them over a similarly long period of time, either through a bank loan or inviting someone to invest in shares in the company - in other words a long term commitment.

Short term finance

All too often companies utilise an overdraft to acquire long term assets, and that overdraft never seems to disappear, eventually constraining the business. Look at your own credit card balance and you will realise that the new kitchen that you bought last year is still there and is costing you far more than the 'special deal' on finance that was offered to you at the time.

The principal form of short term funding is a bank overdraft, secured by a charge over the assets of the business. The overdraft was originally designed to cover the timing differences of, for example, having to acquire raw materials to manufacture finished goods which are later sold. If your overdraft does ever disappear, then you need to re-examine your financing. Raising bank finance is a question of knowing what your needs are (if you import raw materials can the bank provide you with Letters of Credit, do you have a number of overseas suppliers who prefer settlement in their own currency for which you will need foreign currency checking facilities?) and then meeting with bankers to assess the range of packages on offer.

The use of factoring and invoice discounting is increasing as a form of short term borrowing. Instead of an overdraft, factorers and invoice discounters advance monies against sales invoices as they are raised. The facility that you are able to call on is limited to a percentage of your outstanding debtors at any one time. The main difference between the two is that the outside world is aware of the factorer, but the invoice discounter tends to have a relationship solely with the company. The other side of the equation is that a factorer will undertake the initial debt collection, thus potentially saving on costs.

This form of finance is growing in interest to start-ups. For example, a company with a distribution agreement to a major retailer needs to manufacture the first products a month or so before delivery. It can use the facilities of a factorer to secure an advance at the time of delivery to the customer to meet the supplier's invoices as they fall due.

Longer term finance

Longer term finance is available in two forms - lending and equity. In assessing which is the most appropriate, it is again down to an understanding of your needs and the risks involved that dictate the route to follow.

Lending is on a low cost basis, usually on 'points above base rate' terms and it may be secured. However, someone has taken a view on your business as being low risk - generating cash in a reasonably dependable and secure manner.

Lending may be from banks, or it may be from more risk-conscious lenders such as merchant banks, providers of mezzanine finance - a form of borrowing which gives the lender some shares as well - and high interest lenders such as hire purchase and finance companies. Each of these charge a higher percentage depending upon the risk of potential non-repayment and the ability of the business to generate cash.

It is the gamblers in the finance game who are generally providers of equity. Venture capitalists and others, at first glance, come up with a wealth of different classes of shares - such as 8 per cent convertible or redeemable, cumulative preference shares - sometimes creating complications where none really exist. However, it is done with a purpose. When looking at types of shares it is useful to break them down into their constituent components, or rights. Consider a particular class of share and ask yourself:

- What is its entitlement to dividend – discretionary (if so who decides) or enforced? How many votes is the holder of that class entitled to?
- What percentage of the company does the holder of that class get if the company is sold?
- Is the holder of the share in for the duration (normally an ordinary share) or are you required to repay him like a bank loan (redeemable preference shares)?

- Can the holder of the share interfere in the day-to-day running of the business, through a shareholders agreement or through the appointment of directors to the Board?
- Can the share change its nature, in other words can it convert from, for example, a preference share (with a fixed repayment value) to an ordinary share, with the entitlement to a percentage of proceeds on sale?

The privileges that the other shares are entitled to reduce the overall return you make on your own investment in the business.

Understand the motives of the lender

An essential, although often ignored, point in seeking finance is understanding the motives of the individual or the company providing you with finance. For the right financing arrangement a meeting of minds has to occur, and the final arrangement has to be sensible to both parties.

In short term financing a banker or other lender seeks security of recovery against other debtors or stock. The banker does not want any risk of a bad debt and will offer relatively low percentages against assets you regard as secure. Stock acquired under retention of title clauses (title does not pass until the goods are paid for) may only provide security of below 30 per cent of purchase price, if at all. Similarly a debtors book which has a number of non-blue-chip balances will not be seen as secure. A banker will continually evaluate your balance sheet on the basis of a disaster scenario - will you still be covered if you fail?

A venture capitalist, even though there may not appear to be much venture left, will seek a high degree of return through the sale of the business in a specified time frame. His funds are unsecured, so there will be significant 'interference' in the way the business is run. He is likely to have a director representing his interests and a shareholders' agreement which says you cannot do anything material if it is not in the pre-approved annual budget and often has draconian clauses whereby he can take control of the company in the event that preference shares or loan stock are not paid out on time.

The venture capitalist does this because he is investing pension fund money, funds that the general public has put away to provide comfort in their retirement. He therefore needs to be seen to be protecting that money. His return is likely to be sought through capital growth, realised through a sale of his shares. He may look for returns of 25 per cent to 60 per cent per annum. In cash terms he will look to double his money in three years - a useful benchmark to think about. If the project is riskier, say a start-up or a rescue, then these returns are often higher. This level of return is required because, in a portfolio, some investments will be successful, some will fail, and some will be problem situations from which he cannot engineer a profitable sale. Therefore, the average return on the portfolio is much lower than the return on any one deal.

When individuals are looking to invest, tax breaks can also be a critical driver. They may seek to shelter capital gains, reduce income tax, or invest in a company which will give them tax efficient income or capital gains. Government schemes such as the Enterprise Investment Scheme and its predecessor, the Business Expansion Scheme, were set up to encourage private investment in private companies. Generally these investors are required to be passive under the tax legislation, however finding them can often be harder than one would believe.

You may be steered to one of the securities markets, such as Ofex or AIM. However the fundamentals do not change - this is equity funding and the shareholders will have their own reasons for investing. These again may be tax driven, and any such issues would be undertaken through a professional adviser.

Seeking professional advice

Finding the funds for new business is where the professional comes into play. You need to recognise that there is an army of people in the country who have seen it and done it before. Your bank manager, solicitor or accountant will be able to provide simple guidance on how to find finance. Similarly, the Business Link network and similar organisations are providing guidance to individuals starting out in business. There are a number of obvious places to start.

Banking is reasonably obvious - start with your personal bank manager and work through the organisation. Your bank manager will earn kudos for introducing you to his corporate banking side. For other short term funding such as factoring the Yellow Pages is as good a place as any for contacts. Remember in factoring, though, the charging arrangements can appear complex and it may not be right for every business so it is best to go armed with a professional adviser of some sort.

Equity funding is harder to track down. The British Venture Capital Association publish guides on raising venture capital funding and how to approach venture capitalists. It also advises on which ones focus on which industry, and which are the few who will look at start-ups. It will also provide a guide as to what venture capitalists look for - in essence a good product, with a good market and a management team capable of making it work.

Finding individuals to invest is a dangerous area. There may be several around but gaining access to them is difficult. There are two principal reasons for using a professional adviser in the legal, accounting or banking sectors. First, they may have the contacts to direct you quickly to those individuals seeking to invest in your type of business. Second, they will guide you through the regulatory process relating to raising funds from individuals. In essence, you have to go through a number of legal hoops if you are seeking to advertise - or produce any statement designed to induce someone to invest - and the penalty for breaching this legislation can be a prison sentence. Look at the Sunday personal finance press and see how often the Financial Services Act is referred to!

Finding finance is a question of fundamentals. Matching the funding to the need is critical. It is a matter of evaluating the degree of risk, and then focusing on the sector of the funding market that is most likely to find the risks associated with your proposal to be in accord with their investment guidelines. A successful business is a partnership between the entrepreneur and the financier, built on an understanding of each other's aims, ambitions and abilities.

Tim Berg, Baker Tilly

At the very least after reading this chapter you should appreciate that, whilst all money may have a pound sign in front of it, in the UK at any rate, not all money is the same. The recession in the 1980s saw nearly 60 per cent of small firms in the UK funded exclusively by overdraft. The corresponding figure for Germany was 18 per cent. So when the going got hard the bankers called the shots and clawed back on overdrafts, which are by definition repayable instantly on demand. Those firms with long term loans or, better still, outside equity, could ride out the storm (provided of course their businesses were basically sound) and wait for better times. So the rule is, have a financial strategy, not just an overdraft.

In my experience . . .

In my second year of business I needed to borrow from the bank some additional working capital. With the help of the finance director I put together a reasonably sophisticated budget and cash flow based on a conservative view of sales prospects and therefore a pessimistic view of the level of borrowing required. I felt sure that if I demonstrated that I was being more than cautious the bank would see that the figures did not need to be massaged.

The bank's initial reaction was to turn down my application because only a small profit was forecast for the end of Year 2. This was due in part to the proposed expansion, relocation and new office space in the second half of the year (when the balance was forecast to be in credit). A slight massage of the figures and some simplified explanations of the business plan enabled the bank to agree to the overdraft facility.

- Keep the presentation simple
- The bank manager will discount your projections, so don't do it for him

Dan Hiscocks, Travellerseye

Businesses that prosper have a competitive advantage. But unless you can prevent others from following, that advantage could be short-lived. The most common ways to protect your ideas are: patents, which protect how something works; trademarks, which protect what something is called; design registration, which protects how something looks; and copyright, which protects work on paper, film, record or in electronic form.

This form of protection has been around a long time. For example it was at Thomas Jefferson's insistence that the US Patent Office, now the largest in the world, was set up in 1790. Let the fate of professor Joseph Henry of Princeton be a warning to all who would ignore this field. In 1831, Henry invented the telegraph, a word that had been coined thirty seven years earlier, by a Frenchman named Claude Chappe, for a kind of semaphore system employed during the French Revolution. Henry not only had the idea of transmitting messages as coded electrical impulses through wires, he also worked out all the essentials to make the system feasible. All he didn't do was patent the process. That fell to one Samuel Finley Breese Morse, who then took until 1844 to get sufficient funds to string a wire from Washington to Baltimore and demonstrate 'his' invention. All Morse really invented was the code that bears his name. But it was he and not Henry who became immensely famous and rich.

PROTECTING YOUR PRODUCT

Whatever activities your company pursues, you will need mechanisms and procedures to ensure that the intangible assets are protected in the same way as the real assets are. The value of this intellectual property can be enormous. Even in a small non-manufacturing company there will be valuable assets of this nature - including customer lists, procedures, stationery and promotional material, the company's name and a variety of other assets. More obvious examples of intellectual property that you may own include copyright and design rights in original designs and literature, inventions, a trademark or brand name and anything else that is novel, original and proprietary to the company.

Risks of non-protection : The value of these assets cannot be under-estimated, nor can the risks of failing to ensure that you have systems set up that will enable you to keep control of these assets and know when they are being threatened. The consequences of failing to do so may involve you in costly and time-consuming litigation to prevent infringement and preserve your asset, or the possibility of what is confidential and secret being revealed on the open market, thereby reducing its value.

Registerable rights : Certain intellectual property rights are capable of being registered - potentially worldwide. The benefits of registration are that generally you will obtain a higher level of statutory protection and more clearly defined rights than for unregistered common law rights. You may also, particularly in the case of patents and trademarks, obtain the comfort of knowing that a search has been made into the validity of your claim which has not revealed it either to be infringing someone else's rights or lacking the necessary degree of novelty or originality to be capable of registration. More of this below.

Non-registerable rights : Rights that cannot be registered (at least in the UK) include copyright, your customer and contact lists, and knowhow. The lack of registrability does not prevent you from putting good housekeeping practices into place but may mean that you will have to overcome a higher burden of proof to establish the existence of those rights and your ability to exploit them and prevent others from infringing them.

Insurance : You will already have had to obtain insurance for a variety of risks. You may want to consider obtaining insurance cover to enable you to bring a claim against a third party who infringes your intellectual property rights. Intellectual property litigation is particularly expensive due to its often complex and technical nature. If you do own a portfolio including patents, trademarks and copyright in particular, then it may be worth obtaining a quote for intellectual property insurance in addition to the others mentioned.

Trademark

Trademarks may be either registered or not. If yours is not then you will be reliant on the laws of 'passing off' to protect your rights.

A registered trademark is 'any sign capable of being represented graphically that is capable of distinguishing goods or services from one undertaking from those of another undertaking'. It may comprise words (including names), letters, numbers or even the shape of the goods or packaging. It may feature colours or may be three-dimensional. A trademark is capable of registration if it falls within the statutory definition.

Searching : Before applying for a registered trademark it is often a good idea to carry out a search of the Trademarks Register to ensure that no-one else is already using that mark and that you are not infringing someone else's rights.

The Trademarks Registry, based in Newport, has a number of informative leaflets which it readily makes available to individuals and companies who may be interested in applying for registration. You can do this yourself but it may be easier and more straightforward to instruct a trademark agent to do so on your behalf. A trademark agent is professionally qualified and will be familiar with the rules and guidelines to be followed in obtaining a registered mark.

The process of applying for and obtaining a mark will typically take between 12 and 18 months. Whilst it is relatively straightforward there is always the possibility that someone may object to you registering that particular mark. If a formal objection is lodged then the Trademarks Registry will listen to representations by both parties before making a decision.

Classes: The Trademarks Register is divided into 42 different classes which cover a wide variety of goods and services. When you apply for and obtain a registered trademark it will be in specific classes that cover the goods and services for which you use the mark. This means that an entirely unconnected party may also have a trademark for the same word or logo but in different classes. Both proprietors will be entitled to exploit their own mark exclusively in the classes for which they have protection. More complicated rules apply to particularly well known marks - Coca-Cola for example.

Duration: A registered trademark has a potentially limitless duration. Once granted, the registration is effectively back-dated to the date of the application. The mark is then in force for a period of ten years from the date of application and is renewable for further periods of ten years.

Patents

What is a patent? A patent, once granted, is a state-backed monopoly right to exploit an invention, whether this be a product or a process. The patent lasts for a maximum of 20 years from the date of application and is renewed annually. The owner of a patent is able to prevent others from exploiting that product or process without his permission and also to license third parties to manufacture. A patent can be transferred or jointly owned and may also be security for a loan. It is possible to register a charge over a patent at the Patent Office.

Applying for a patent: This is probably best done with the assistance of a patent agent who will be able to assist you in drafting your application in the correct technical language. This is absolutely essential as failure to draft the application correctly may result in a third party being able to challenge the validity or manufacture a product or exploit a process that is very similar to yours but does not fall within the claims of the patent. Applications should be submitted to the Patent Office in Newport, Gwent.

Is your invention patentable? To obtain a patent the invention must be novel, capable of industrial application and not contrary to certain public policy guidelines. To assess the novelty your patent agent and the Patent Office itself will search the register of previously granted patents and also make enquiries of other publicly available sources of information to check that there is no 'prior art' - which would mean that your invention is not in fact novel and consequently not capable of being patented.

Duration: The maximum period for which a patent can be maintained is 20 years from the date of application. It is renewed on an annual basis with an escalating fee, justified on the basis that if it is still being renewed 19 years after application then it must be worth protecting.

Territory: Virtually every country in the world has its own patent office which will grant protection within its own borders. A European patent extending the territory to certain designated countries within Europe can also be applied for after making an initial application in just one country. The Patent Co-operation Treaty will also enable you to extend the territory in a relatively straightforward way.

Publication: The patent must contain all the information needed to make or manufacture the invention. Once obtained it becomes public knowledge and if not renewed may be exploited by competitors. You may therefore wish to consider the possibility of relying on confidentiality agreements to protect your invention for longer than 20 years. The grave danger of this is that it will be considerably more difficult to enforce your rights if someone copies it and licensing third parties is much harder to exploit effectively.

Copyright

What is copyright? Copyright is perhaps the most common intellectual property right and the one with which people are most familiar. It will exist in original literary, dramatic, musical and artistic works, including computer programs and computer-generated work. It cannot be registered and arises automatically. The owner of a copyright in a work has the right to stop others from reproducing that work without his or her permission. For a work to be copyright protected it must be original, though if two people produce an identical work simultaneously they will both own the copyright in their own work.

How to protect copyright: To best protect copyright in any work (typically lists and databases) certain good housekeeping practices need to be put into place. Ensure that any drawings are dated and signed. Keep records showing when lists are updated and who is responsible. Use the © copyright symbol on anything that is published, together with the company's name and the year of creation. All of these will help if you ever have to establish ownership of copyright in a work.

Duration: Copyright typically lasts for the life of the author or creator plus seventy years. Copyright in computer-generated work will expire seventy years from the end of the calendar year in which the work was made.

Confidentiality

Before you talk to any other organisation about the possibility of entering into some sort of joint venture or licence it is essential that they have confirmed that any information you give them will be kept confidential and not disclosed to anyone else. They must also agree to return on request anything you have provided to them. The best way to ensure confidentiality is to prepare a short agreement or letter to be signed by the other party and returned to you.

Employees and Contractors

Any intellectual property created as a result of work carried out by an employee in the course of his or her employment will generally be the property of the employer. It is nevertheless a good idea to confirm that this is the case in contracts of employment. If an employee creates something after working on a project which is outside his or her normal duties then the resulting intellectual property could be deemed to belong to them. If employees are to be encouraged to be creative then you may wish to set up a formal scheme whereby successful ideas will be rewarded - and the company owns the rights.

These assets are valuable and setting up proper records and routines from the outset may save considerable problems later on. It isn't necessary to keep every piece of paper with jottings on but a trail of the creative process could be invaluable. Make sure your staff are aware of the potential value of the intellectual property and that confidentiality provisions are in place before you talk to another organisation about an idea or a project.

Kate Kelly, Shoosmiths

Protecting yourself against someone else infringing your intellectual property can be a time-consuming and costly business. It took tiny Polaroid nearly 10 years and millions of dollars to block giant Eastman Kodak from pirating its instant photography process. Elias Howe, a young Bostonian, invented and patented the first workable sewing machines in 1846, but couldn't persuade anyone to buy them. Depressed by his failure he spent two years in England in a forlorn search for a more receptive market. On returning to Boston he found that one Isaac Singer had stolen his patent, set up a sewing machine factory and was raking it in.

So don't relax just because you have 'filed your claim'. It may be prudent to take out some patent transgression insurance too.

In my experience . . .

I was advising a computer software company. The company had signed a distribution agreement, the product was on the launch pad and everything looked good. The principals of the company had all come from another (larger) company which suddenly realised that my clients had just run into a product that was not only competitive but now also had a major distribution facility. So they issued a writ claiming breach of copyright - completely erroneous but the legal costs were huge for a small company. It threatened the relationship with the distributor, diverted management time and nearly caused the company to collapse. In the end the claim died, leaving the company with a big legal fee bill but still with a business, which has since gone on to success.

- Hold intellectual copyright in a non-trading company
- Buy legal insurance (but check the small print)
- Keep accurate records, particularly of all meetings
- Send written confirmation and details of any disagreements
- Take advice on procedures before starting them
- Understand that the law does not promise justice - just uncontrollable procedures and costs

David Bailey, David Bailey Enterprises

PREMISES

An interesting study carried out in 1997 by Cranfield School of Management revealed that the fastest growing small firms, in terms of both profits and turnover, were also most likely to be those who were most satisfied with their location. And it's not just retailers who have to worry about where to set up.

Jeff Bezos, who founded Amazon.com, the American Internet bookseller, in 1994 is a good example of using location strategically. He researched the market and set up in Seattle, in part because it was a national hub for book distribution but also because it had software skills in abundance.

By contrast, Darryl Mattocks, Internet Bookshop's founder, stayed at home in Oxford. In 1994 when his first orders came in he walked over to a nearby bookshop, bought the books and walked over to the post office and sent them. Even today, the problems caused by setting up in Oxford costs his customers a day's delay in dispatching.

When Internet Bookshop revised its order system software in May 1997 the entire fulfilment operation shut down for a week. When Amazon.com faced a similar crisis it solved the problem in less than 24 hours. Locating in the centre of a source of key skills paid off handsomely.

By May 1997, Amazon.com was taken public at a valuation of nearly $500 million. This compares with the Oxford-based Internet Bookshop which is listed on Ofex, a small pseudo-market and worth $10 million

Finding Premises - The Legal Issues

Many new small businesses start life on the dining room table – my parent's business certainly did! Whilst this has the advantage of reducing overheads in the early stages, a business run from home may result in a breach of the Town & Country Planning Acts as well as any restrictive or other covenants (e.g. covenants contained in a lease) which affect your home. Equally it may reduce your ability to take tax-free, the whole of any capital gain made when you come to sell the house.

Practical experience suggests that in the early stages at least, if the business is of a type that can be run from home (e.g. one which is clean and high-tech) you will simply just take the risk. Once the business is more established and you come to move out, what are the likely major concerns affecting your choice of premises from a legal point of view?

Key considerations

Whether you purchase premises which are freehold or leasehold, old or new there are certain key considerations which are common to all.
They include:

Position: Are the premises where you want to be and of a suitable type?

Planning permission: Do the premises have planning permission for your proposed use? If not, how long will it take to obtain it and what are the chances of it being granted? If the premises do have planning permission then that permission may well come with conditions controlling the permitted use. Make sure that you could operate the business in compliance with those conditions.

Environmental considerations: Your business may need consents under the Environmental Protection Act 1990 and related legislation, particularly if that business involves heavy manufacturing and/or environmentally unfriendly emissions. Can the premises be simply adapted so as to obtain the necessary consents, if those consents are not already in place?

Fire prevention: Do the premises have a fire certificate at present? If not, will your use require one and how easily could the premises be altered so as to meet the Fire Officer's requirements?

Access: How is access obtained? Is access obtained directly off a publicly adopted highway (over which everyone has rights of way) or will you need to check that the premises have rights of way over the roadways leading to the premises? If this is an issue make sure that your solicitor knows about the point. Check also that there are no road schemes affecting the premises. Highway limitations on lorry routes or the pedestrianisation of precincts, for example, can all have an effect which (depending on your business) may be either beneficial or detrimental.

You will be delighted to know that you can do some of the legwork on these issues yourself by making enquiries direct of the Planning Officer, Environmental Health and their related organisations, the Fire Officer and the Highways Officer. This approach may well save you time and money. However, you must get the information properly checked (e.g. by your solicitor or surveyor) when you decide to buy or lease. One reason for this is, that without proper verification of the information, it is unlikely that any bank will lend you the money required for your new premises.

Leasing premises

If your selected premises are to be held under a lease then before you enter into that lease it does need careful examination. This is a job for a professional and no list of key points can be definitive, but here is a checklist.

- What area is actually comprised in the lease? If you need (say) the factory premises **and** the yard at the back make sure the lease includes both. If it doesn't, then the position needs to be investigated.
- How long is the lease? If you intend to stay put for say 10 years but the lease has only 8 years still to run it may not be suitable.
- What is the current rent? Check that this rent accords with any particulars you may have been given. Check the review pattern of that rent and the date of the next review. Equally consider the basis of review. For example, will the rent only go up at review or is there the prospect that it may go down? Make sure you are clear about the position of alterations and improvements at review. If you do works to the premises at your own expense, will these alterations or improvements be ignored at review or (as occasionally happens) actually be rentalised?
- Check the amount of the other outgoings payable e.g. business rates and service charges under the lease. Remember that service charges may include the cost of external works. You do not want to take the premises and suddenly find that you are liable for a large and unbudgeted bill for, say, a proportionate part of replacing the roof of the whole of the premises.
- Establish who is liable for insuring the premises. Is it to be you or your landlord? If the landlord, check his policy and see if it is possible to have your interest endorsed on the policy or if not endorsed at least noted.
- The lease will state the use to which the premises can be put. Check that this actually allows your use and find out how much flexibility your lease permits to change or expand that use.
- You may need to make alterations to the premises (see the discussion above). What consents do you need, and from whom and how much latitude do you have under the lease to make alterations without making an application for licence for alterations to your landlord?
- Most leases require the tenant to keep the premises in repair. Check the standard demanded by that lease and compare that with the

premises themselves. If (as is almost always the case) the actual state is lower than that demanded by the lease, you may ultimately face a substantial bill for what are known as dilapidations because you will have to put the premises into the state demanded. Consider this aspect as part of your commercial negotiations for the lease at the outset.

- Can you dispose of the lease either by selling it or underletting it? What are the restrictions on these methods of disposal? Establish whether, if you dispose of the lease, you will nevertheless retain liability for it. Remember that (generally) tenants of leases granted after January 1, 1996 do not retain liability for that lease after they have assigned (sold) it. Prior to that date the position is reversed - a fact which has crippled many small businesses because they suddenly found themselves liable for arrears of rent run up by a **subsequent** tenant.

- Establish whether the lease grants the tenant security of tenure at the end of the term. If it does then the tenant may be able to obtain a renewal lease, but if that tenancy has been "excluded" from the security of tenure provisions of Part II of the Landlord and Tenant Act 1954 then that possibility is not available. If the premises in question are (for example) high street retail premises and you intend to put in a lot of hard work generating goodwill in the area, it would be unfortunate if at the point when you were seeing a return for your hard work you were forced to move.

As a rule of thumb, the newer the premises and the higher their specification the greater the chances of the premises complying with the necessary statutory requirements referred to above and being in a good state of repair, but the higher the rent - and vice versa.

Purchasing premises

By contrast, if you decide to purchase freehold premises, you will not need to worry about any restrictions placed in a lease. To that extent you are your own master. When considering premises of this variety, in addition to the general considerations referred to above, your solicitor will need to ensure that you are purchasing a good and marketable title. Make sure, however, that he knows the business you are going to run from the premises so that he can check there are no restrictive covenants or other legal concerns affecting the premises that would prevent your proposed use.

A major advantage of freehold premises over leasehold is that they can comprise an asset for balance sheet purposes. Equally, the cost of mortgage interest taken out for the purposes of purchase may well not exceed the rent payable for equivalent leasehold premises. The disadvantage, to my mind, is that such a purchase may well tie up a great deal of working capital that could be put to other uses.

Graham Bennett, Shoosmiths

Premises For Your Business
- Rent Or Buy ?

With the greater use of new information and communications technologies, the question of where to locate a business should, in theory at least, be almost redundant. Fax, e-mail and videoconferencing permit business to be conducted from any location, whether this be a High Street address or a tele-village in rural Wales.

In reality, however, location remains important. In a recent survey of a large cross-section of the UK corporate community, location was ranked second only to cost as a key criterion in premises selection. This partially reflects the fact that, whilst innovation in the communications sector has never been more rapid, the adoption of new equipment and the changes in work style this fosters is a much slower, more incremental process - evolution, rather than revolution. Face-to-face business remains important, as does access to staffing resources and proximity to clients and suppliers. Even leading academics agree that the sense of place seems to be ingrained within our psyche.

For a new business, location is generally a more important issue than for a large established corporation. Customer service and client retention are critical, as are efficient supply chains and cost-effective delivery mechanisms.

As a property market, the UK is one of the world's most mature and diverse real estate sectors. Access to accommodation is not really a problem even in the smaller provincial towns, and premises come in all shapes and sizes. Many companies place considerable emphasis on the quality and specification of their premises, while for others premises are more a place to house equipment and keep the weather out, making quality and image less important.

The issue of whether to rent or to buy premises is a common conundrum for new companies, especially the comparatively small ones.

Purchasing freehold property has the following advantages:

- Firstly, ownership of premises takes the company out of the open property rental market. Managers are not distracted by ongoing discussions/disputes with a landlord and the company's accounts are not affected by the vagaries of the open market, that typically operates on leases within which rents are reviewed against the open market every five years and only in an upward direction. Subject to the economy and the state of the property market, rental levels can double overnight at rent review and thereby hit hard on the company's overheads.
- Secondly, freehold purchase, like any other investment, is a means of generating a profit on capital. If the property purchased goes up

in value, it can be sold to yield a return which can be fed back into the business. Sale and leaseback, where the company sells its freehold interest to an investor, remains in occupation and takes a lease from its new landlord, is a common method of freeing up fixed capital to fund business expansion. The problem here, however, is risk, as values can go down as well as up. A property purchased at the wrong point in the property cycle or at too high a price may produce a significant capital loss.

The principal disadvantage of buying a property stems from the fact that real estate is a comparatively expensive commodity. Purchase requires either the commitment of substantial capital or exposure to significant borrowing. Most new companies take the view that capital should be directed towards the business itself rather than the premises.

Most new companies therefore lease rather than buy their premises. Why?

- Leasing offers a certain degree of flexibility, which is fundamental to the company's ability to respond and adapt to change. If, for example, a company grows and requires larger accommodation, it is usually much easier to exit a leased building rather than one which is owned. Conversely, if the business contracts to create surplus accommodation, surplus space can be sub-let to another company to produce rental income.
- In addition the management and maintenance of a leased building are usually the responsibility of the landlord, though this is reflected in the rent a company pays. Most companies welcome the reduction in administration time and the ability to focus on the core business which this affords.

Leasing however, is by no means a panacea and can create problems. For instance:

- Every country in the world has a different property market in terms of its leasing system and regulatory mechanisms. Companies with premises in a number of locations are often forced to contend with and understand a number of complex and different markets. This is extremely difficult without professional advice.
- In the UK, the time spans of leases are among the longest in the world. Following the early 1990s recession, the traditional 25-year lease is now rare but lease terms remain at 10, 15 or even 20 years. Even the big multinationals have little or no idea what their business will look like in 10 years time and the premises they will therefore require, let alone a new company venturing forth for the first time. Whilst leasing is more flexible than purchase, the UK leasing system is relatively inflexible in comparison with other markets. Lease interests can be assigned to another organisation, enabling the company to

vacate its premises before the end of its lease, but this requires negotiation and marketing and hence professional advice.

This is one of the principal factors underscoring the recent growth in serviced offices. Specialist operators own and run a serviced office which has a number of tenants on short term leases who are provided with support services and access to shared amenities. This overcomes the issue of flexibility as the company can vacate or increase the space it occupies at short notice – sometimes as little as a month.

Flexibility does however, come at a price. In order to make a reasonable return, serviced office landlords require above average rental income. Rents on serviced accommodation can be as much as 50 per cent higher than those on comparable space in the open market on a per unit area basis.

The property sector is controlled and run by the estate agents and surveyors. The classic property transaction will involve the company negotiating, via its appointed agents, with the landlord, via their appointed agents. While principal-to-principal transactions are increasing, agent-to-agent deals remain the norm.

Unlike most of the rest of the world the UK is adversarial in that the landlord's agents are required to secure the best possible rent or price whilst the company's agent is required to get the cheapest and most flexible arrangements possible. In reality, agents compromise and strike a deal which is satisfactory to both parties. The company's agent takes a commission based on the rental level agreed. The UK agency market is densely populated and highly competitive and this gives considerable flexibility in negotiating commission rates and makes shopping around advisable.

It is possible for a new company to secure premises without appointing their own agents, although in this instance, high quality legal advice is essential. The problem with the 'go it alone' approach is that it can be time-consuming and frustrating and ultimately more costly than appointing an agent and paying a commission.

Overall, the issue of premises is clearly a complex one and there are many potential pitfalls of both leasing and buying. While most companies are entirely happy with their premises, the property market is littered with discontented occupiers and some very expensive mistakes. An inappropriate property strategy can ruin a company and act as a major impediment to business growth. Good advice is therefore essential.

Stephen Mallen, Partner and Head of Research, Knight Frank

Business founders often take it for granted that all investment in premises is a good thing. Hopefully the lessons of the last few lengthy property recessions will sound a few alarm bells. The rule with property is to remember it's there to help you make a profit from your business. Once you start to think of property as an investment in its own right, and taking on more commitment than you need, you are moving into a whole new business area and should ask yourself two questions. Do I have the necessary skills and knowledge? And if property is such a hot proposition why am I bothering with dry-cleaning, or photocopying or whatever else it was that you planned to do.

EMPLOYING PEOPLE

Half of all small firms employ only the founder. However it may just be that for all the pain of employing people there really is some gain. Research suggests that employing people improves your chances of surviving as a business. It also seems that, up to a point, employing people makes you more efficient too. On average, owner-managers working on their own generate only £28,000 worth of sales each year, whilst those employing up to nine people generate more than three times that.

SIZE No. of Employees	Number of Businesses x 000	Total Employed x 000	Turnover £ m ex. VAT	Turnover per employee x £ 000
0	2,600	3,000	84	28
1-9	790	200	242	86
10-99	185	4,600	721	156
100-499	14	2,700	991	397
500+	3	7,500	1,570	209
All	3592	20,600	3,608	175

Source: DTI Statistics for the UK, 1993 - June 1995, p8

But the key to success is to employ the right people, which is what this chapter is all about. The chapter advocates trusting more on job profiling, interview techniques and psychometric testing, than on a firm handshake and an impressive CV.

FINDING THE RIGHT PERSON

When a manager decides to buy a new car, a great deal of time and effort is usually devoted to the task. Brochures are carefully inspected, prospective vehicles are viewed and test-driven, and factors such as performance, reliability and appearance are carefully considered.

Why is it then that when it comes to finding a new person for the business, a much more casual attitude is often adopted? Notions like 'gut feeling', finding someone who can be 'one of us' and recommendations from friends and relations suddenly come into play. This is particularly curious since if the car turns out to be unsuitable, it can easily be replaced - not so with an employee!

The whole process of recruitment can present the small business owner with an enormous task. The person has to be attracted to apply for the job, they have to be interviewed and selected, appointed and inducted, installed and trained - usually all before they reach any stage of productivity.

This makes it doubly important to find the right person. Each person in an organisation is part of the chain that ultimately provides the customer with the goods or services, and each part of that chain is a critical link in getting the end result.

The first step in finding the right person is to outline the demands of the job required, both now and in the future. This is a 'job specification' detailing what the job involves - this may include such things as producing word-processed reports and dealing with customer complaints.

From this, the employer can draw up a 'person specification' which will show that the ideal candidate would have word-processing skills and would, perhaps, be calm under pressure and able to resolve problems quickly. Some of these attributes may be demonstrated by skills or qualifications, others will only be learned from experience. In addition, the person required may have to fit into a team environment, or may have to work unsociable hours. Since it is unlikely that the perfect person you have defined actually exists, the qualities and competencies should be categorised into 'essential' and 'desirable'.

The aim is to attract a pool of people to apply for the vacancy, from whom you can make a choice. The obvious way is to advertise in the local press, but this may not always be the best method. Advertising can be costly and time-consuming. Writing advertising copy is not a job for an amateur and agencies can be expensive. In addition, an advertisement is likely to bring a flood of replies - many unsuitable - from which you have to shortlist, interview, appoint a candidate and then reject the unsuccessful.

Another option for the small firm is to use a recruitment or employment consultancy. A good consultancy may already have a bank of candidates to choose from. If not, they will do the advertising, shortlisting and initial interviewing for you, leaving you with a few suitable candidates for final interview.

Your person specification will almost certainly include skills as well as attributes, and a good consultancy will follow these up too, testing abilities and taking up references.

In choosing a consultancy it is important to select one operating to quality standards and with staff qualified to do the job. The Institute of Employment

Consultants is the only body that supplies qualifications to the industry, so check that the consultancy's staff are qualified IEC members. Similarly, the consultancy itself will usually be a member of FRES, the Federation of Recruitment and Employment Services.

Employing people is part of the growth process of any business and it is very satisfying for an owner-manager to be able to create a job for someone. If the business is to continue to prosper, however, finding the right person is something that should be approached very seriously indeed.

Susan Smith, Chief Executive, The Institute of Employment Consultants

THE LEGAL IMPLICATIONS OF EMPLOYING PEOPLE

The moment you consider employing staff there are legal implications. These begin with your recruitment procedures and you should observe the principle of equality of opportunity. The legislation on discrimination covers job applicants as well as employees. The relevant statutes are:

The Sex Discrimination Act 1975 & 1986
The Race Relations Act 1976
The Disability Discrimination Act 1995
The Trade Union & Labour Relations (Consolidation) Act 1992.

Care must be taken when writing or placing adverts, shortlisting candidates and subsequently interviewing them. Unlimited compensation can be awarded where a claim for unlawful discrimination succeeds at an industrial tribunal.

When taking staff on, there is an important distinction from both a tax and a legal point of view between an employee and an independent contractor. Although both types of individual agree to undertake work in return for payment, an employee does so under a contract of service, whereas an independent contractor does so under a contract for services.

It is a criminal offence to employ someone who does not have the right to stay or work in the UK, so an employer needs to make certain basic checks before taking on new employees. Seeing and copying any of a list of 17 prescribed documents, such as a P45 showing the individual's National Insurance number, provides the employer with a defence.

Having taken on a new employee, there is a legal obligation to supply them, no later than two months of the start of their job, with a statement of the main terms and conditions of their contract of employment. These initial employment particulars must include the:

- Names of the parties
- Date on which the employment began and any period of continuous employment
- Scale or rate of remuneration or method of calculation, together with frequency of payment
- Hours of work, entitlement to holidays, sick leave, sick pay and pensions
- Entitlement of employer and employee to notice of termination
- Job title or brief job description
- Place of work
- The period for which the job is expected to last, if not permanent, or when any fixed term is to end
- Existence of any collective agreements that directly affect the employee's terms and conditions
- Details of the employer's disciplinary rules and grievance procedures (employers with fewer than twenty employees need only give the contact name for raising a grievance)
- Prescribed information where the employee is required to work outside the UK for more than a month.

Regardless of the number of hours an employee works each week, they gain certain important rights, such as:

- The right not to be unfairly dismissed after one year's continuous service
- The right to receive statutory redundancy pay after two year's continuous service.

An employee is eligible to bring a claim for pay parity within the Equal Pay Act 1970 against his or her employer without any qualifying service and all employees are entitled to receive an itemised pay statement from the employer before or each time they are paid. Female employees qualify immediately for eighteen weeks' maternity leave when they are taken on.

All workers, whether employees or not, are protected against unlawful deductions being made from their wages and can claim reimbursement.

Nigel L Baker, Lexicon Employment Law Training

EMPLOYING PEOPLE - THE UPS AND DOWNS

It is safe to say that, other than in exceptional circumstances, your business only grows when you employ people. Businesses are built by employing workers who contribute skills and industry to improve and expand business performance.

What are the implications of employing people?

The law states that every employee must have a contract of employment. This outlines the employee's duties and responsibilities alongside your legal obligations as an employer. Furthermore the contract of employment will contain details of the terms of employment. Often, the formal contract of employment takes the form of a letter of appointment which is sent to a successful applicant and outlines in detail the terms and conditions of the employment.

Employment law in the United Kingdom is relatively interference free, although the adoption of the European Union's social contract may eventually put some further restrictions on employer flexibility. Generally speaking however, you will find little difficulty in observing the legal constraints that surround employment today.

It is important to balance your requirements as an employer with your responsibilities to the employee. Proper hours of work, holiday entitlement, arrangements for sick leave, pensions provision and disputes procedures are just some of the issues that have to be set out and agreed. Your desire to grow your business and to get the best out of your employees must respect employee rights. All successful businesses tend to reflect happy and contented workforces and benefit from high productivity and lower absenteeism and sickness rates. The motivation of employees is the first responsibility of management who have to work hard at it and give it absolute priority.

Who to talk to?

The process of recruitment may be described simply but accurately as matching the right person to the right vacancy. However, that is where the simplicity ends, as the tasks necessary for successful recruitment rely, to a great extent, on human judgment. This is one task where the computer may help but it cannot give you the answer!

Of course, help is at hand. There are a number of ways in which you can get advice, often at no cost to your business. Initially, you have to consider the various elements of recruiting, the first of which is to identify the vacancy and to make your mind up about the specification (what job is on offer and what skills, experience and personality will be necessary to fill it). Armed with this information, you then move on to the next step in the process which is finding the right person. Various different methods are open to you. You could instruct a recruitment agency/consultancy, you could register your requirement at the local Job Centre, you could advertise the position in the press or you could simply employ your brother-in-law! If you are inexperienced in recruiting there is no doubt that a job agency is probably your best bet. They will advise you on candidate availability, salary and wage levels, the need or otherwise to advertise and will work with you through the process to a successful conclusion. For this they will charge a fee only when you successfully employ someone through their efforts. That fee (often negotiable) will probably be based on a percentage of the annual salary cost. The percentage varies but can range from ten to twenty per cent depending on the seniority of the position.

The attraction of using a consultancy/agency is obvious - no fees until success, lots of free no-obligation advice and assistance and, probably most important, the better use of your time in your business. Your management time is not wasted by interminable phone calls and interviews with unsuitable candidates.

Of course the other methods can be successful. Depending on the type of position, it may well be worth registering your vacancy with a government-owned Job Centre, and in certain specific cases direct advertising may be the way forward.

Interview techniques

The interview is still the most common way for employers to make decisions on offering jobs. It is the culmination of a recruitment process which may include curriculum vitae preparation and submission, application form completion or even aptitude or psychometric testing.

The interview is usually seen to be the most nerve-racking element in the recruitment chain and it can be so for the interviewer as well as the interviewee! The trick is, as you would expect, preparation. The interviewer (particularly the inexperienced interviewer) must prepare thoroughly for the event. Interestingly enough, the interviewing skills required to determine a person's suitability to be employed are similar whatever the level of the position on offer. Body language and initial impressions are very important - some experienced interviewers say they make their decision on job offers in the first couple of minutes - and you should assess how comfortable you felt with the candidate's appearance, attitude and approach. Your interview preparation work will have included a list of the personal attributes you require and they can be judged throughout the interview. You should also have selected the interviewee on the basis of their experience and past performance which is always a good predictor for how someone will perform in the future. Go through the past employment record carefully asking relevant questions. Go on to family background and leisure interests and end with discussing future aspirations. You should then describe the job on offer and try to elicit some questions. If the candidate appears, on the face of it, to be a serious contender for the position, go on to discuss the terms and conditions of the position on offer.

At the end of the interview, which should take no longer than one hour and no less than thirty minutes, you should carefully record your impressions and conclusions for future reference. With even the most impressive of candidates, it is not a good idea to make job offers on the spot.

Finally a few standard questions which can tell you more about the candidate than appears on the surface.

- Tell me about yourself.
  You really want to hear them talk and to see what they emphasise or leave out.
- Are you happy with your career to date?
  This can give a good indication of self confidence. Are they a happy and positive person?
- What do you dislike about your current job?
  This may give you an indication of the candidate's suitability for your position.
- What are your strengths?
  This should tell you what they are good at and how that will help you.
- What are your weaknesses?
  This will give you an indication of the risks you will take in employing this candidate.
- Why do you want to leave your present position?
  This should determine whether the candidate is really being pushed.

Temporary and contract staff

In the last ten years the UK has seen a phenomenal growth in the use of contract and temporary staff. Organisations use such staff to perform a whole range of tasks, from daily casual blue collar labour through to senior director level management.

There are no legal restrictions in the UK on the use of this type of labour, but there is a framework of law that controls and regulates the agencies and consultancies who, in the main, supply these workers to their clients. These temps are employed by the recruitment agencies and are usually charged out to their clients at an hourly, weekly or monthly rate. The temp is not part of that client's staff and as a result that client is not responsible for keeping payroll records, deducting PAYE and National Insurance costs, etc. The employing client only pays the agency for the time worked by the temp.

The growth in the use of temps has resulted from a realisation that they can provide an effective, productive and reliable solution to many employment requirements. The most obvious is to cover for increased workload at particularly busy times. The flexibility to expand employee capability on a temporary basis gives significant benefits both in the financial sense and in the non-disruption of normal day-to-day patterns. Similarly the use of temporary staff to cover specific projects is widespread. In recent years the implementation of computer systems – no matter how small or large - has been the undisputed territory of temporary staff. The benefits to the employer are enhanced by the temp's knowledge and experience gained from countless other assignments in the field. Other examples are for credit control and debt collection functions to improve cash flow.

So alongside cover for illness, maternity leave, unfilled permanent positions and long-term holidays, which were once the staple diet for the temp, the market now offers really interesting and important positions. The day of the permanent temp is with us. The employment of someone on a temporary basis is also regarded by many employers as a test period which can and in many cases does lead to a permanent job offer.

The cost of taking people on this basis, when set against the employment costs and obligations for permanent positions, is said by most specialising agencies to be cost-effective. You are of course only paying for the hours worked - no lunch hours, no holidays and no sickness pay - so there can be a significant saving. However, flexibility is probably the key. Workers are available at a moment's notice and the assignment can be terminated immediately on completion of the task.

David Bogg, Group Press Officer, Michael Page International

In my experience . . .

The key tip for saving money on services is to negotiate. You might be surprised at how many organisations are open to negotiation on price:

- Never believe the number of hours a computer specialist tells you things will take - always get a fixed price
- Always negotiate with a bank on their charges (and make sure that all charges are included) - try to get a turnover rate based on the amount of money that goes through the account
- Tell your insurance broker that you want your account rebroked annually and that you expect the bills (as a percentage of income) to go down every year as long as you have established a good record
- Always get more than one price when ordering
- When ordering stationery always ask your supplier if the goods in question are at a special price
- Don't delegate the purchasing task to anyone who is afraid to ask these questions

Robert Inglis, Riordan Eabry & Co

EMPLOYING PART-TIME STAFF

In recent years there has been an increasing incidence in the use of part-time staff by employers. The UK has the highest proportion of its workforce working part-time of all the EU states. One quarter of Britain's workforce works part-time and women account for 84 per cent of that total. Part-time work is the most common form of non-standard working arrangement and can have advantages for both the employer and the worker. There is no statutory definition of part-time work and it can be on a permanent or temporary basis.

From the employer's point of view, part-time workers can provide the organisation with the flexible workforce it requires to meet customer demand, particularly where there are seasonal fluctuations. Part-time workers are also common in clerical and secretarial work, in the hotel, catering, retail and leisure industries, distribution, public services and health care sectors. Part-time employees are now used at all levels within many organisations, including senior management.

The use of part-time staff can enable a new or expanding business to increase its labour costs by degrees and employ some staff to cover peak hours only, thus saving on the costs of employing full-time labour. Part-time workers have no right to receive the same rate of pay as full-time employees and are often not entitled to the same contractual benefits. However, in some cases, an employer may be susceptible to a claim for indirect sex discrimination where part-timers suffer less favourable terms and conditions of employment. The EU Directive on part-time workers' rights must be implemented throughout member states by April 2000, ensuring the equal treatment of part-time workers and full-time workers. Part-time employees in the UK already have equal eligibility for pension schemes and the same statutory protection as full-time employees with regard to unfair dismissal and redundancy pay.

The majority of those who work part-time as opposed to full-time wish to do so. This is particularly relevant in the case of women returners following maternity leave. Part-time working increasingly suits individuals who have other responsibilities and interests in their personal life.

Part-time staff need to be carefully managed by an employer in order to make sure that they work efficiently, are kept fully informed about workplace developments, and are integrated into the business so far as circumstances permit. Motivating part-time employees by offering them the same training, development and promotion opportunities as full-time staff is a worthwhile policy for employers.

Nigel L Baker, Lexicon Employment Law Training

THE NATIONAL MINIMUM WAGE

The national minimum wage establishes a minimum level of wages for workers below which their wages will not fall, subject to certain exceptions. It came into force on 1 April 1999 through the National Minimum Wage Act

1998 ("the Act"). The Act sets out a framework for the national minimum wage, with further details set out in the National Minimum Wage Regulations 1999 ("the Regulations").

The introduction of the national minimum wage, a commitment of the Labour Government's 1997 election manifesto, was controversial and was opposed by the CBI and other employers' organisations fearful of its impact on employers and, in particular, upon small businesses since it applies regardless of the size of the employer's business. The Government set up the independent Low Pay Commission to ensure that the national minimum wage would be introduced sensibly and in accordance with prevailing economic conditions. The Low Pay Commission estimated that about 2 million people would benefit from the Act, 70 per cent of which would be women. The Government accepted the recommendations of the Low Pay Commission as to the initial level at which the national minimum wage would be introduced. As a result, most workers in the UK aged 22 or over must now be paid at least £3.60 per hour. Most workers aged between 18 and 21 must be paid at least £3 per hour (rising to £3.20 in June 2000) and those aged 22 or over starting a new job may be paid £3.20 per hour for the first six months, provided that they are receiving accredited training on at least 26 days during that six month period. In fact, the CBI reported in October 1999 that the minimum wage has not had a significant detrimental effect upon business.

Workers entitled to the national minimum wage

The Act applies to all "workers" which means any individual over compulsory school age who is engaged under a contract to do or perform personally any work or services for another party. The Act therefore covers more than mere employees and adopts a similar definition to that used for the purposes of the statutory provisions in respect of unlawful deductions from wages, in the race, sex and disability discrimination statutes and under the Working Time Regulations 1998. It applies to individuals such as home workers, agency workers (to whom the national minimum wage would normally be paid by the agency responsible for paying the worker rather than its client business), casual labourers, part time workers and workers on full time contracts. It applies whether or not they are employees and whether their contracts are express or implied, written or oral. It also covers pieceworkers who are paid for the items that they produce rather than the hours that they work, and individuals paid wholly or partly by reference to commission rather than a fixed wage or salary. There are no variations according to region or industry sector or the size of the business. Similarly, there are no qualifying periods of service.

The Act does not apply to an individual who is genuinely self-employed (as distinct from someone who describes himself as being self-employed for tax purposes), to workers below age 18 or, for the first year of their apprenticeship, to apprentices aged under 26. Students on higher education "sandwich" courses need not be paid the national minimum wage for the period during which they are placed with an employer, unless they are studying for a post-graduate degree or diploma. Genuine volunteers, including charity workers, who are either unpaid or who receive only reasonable expenses or benefits in kind also fall outside the scope of the Act. Similarly, individuals working and living as part of a family, such as au pairs, will not be entitled to the national minimum wage.

The rate of the national minimum wage

The minimum rates applicable to various categories of worker are set out above, and apply however the worker is paid - whether monthly, weekly, daily, hourly or by session. Employers should ask workers for proof of their age to ensure that payment is made at the correct rate where it is dependent solely upon age.

The initial levels of the national minimum wage will not be increased automatically but will be reviewed subject to the advice of the Low Pay Commission, which has suggested that the standard rate should rise from £3.60 to £3.70 per hour from June 2000.

Calculation of wages

Employers must ensure that remuneration paid to workers matches or exceeds the appropriate minimum rate. The Regulations describe the hours and benefits which employers must take into account.

A worker does not have to be paid the national minimum wage for each hour worked but the average payments made to him over the "pay reference period" must reach the requisite level. The pay reference period will be the interval at which the worker is paid but will be no more than one month. For example, the pay reference period for a monthly paid worker will be one month and for a weekly paid worker will be one week. The hourly rate is calculated by dividing the gross pay received or earned (if attributable to but not received during that pay reference period) by the total number of hours of time work, salaried hours work, output work and unmeasured work (see below) done by the worker in the pay reference period. However, where pay may fluctuate from one pay reference period to another, employers should beware that they will not be able to make up a shortfall in one pay reference period by claiming credit in respect of payments made above the national minimum wage during another pay reference period.

The hours for which the national minimum wage must be paid vary according to the way in which the worker is paid. The Regulations identify four types of work:

- time work
- salaried hours work
- output work
- unmeasured work

Where a worker does different types of work for the same employer, or for different employers, a different hour's calculation will apply for each type of work which the worker does.

Time Work

A time worker is paid according to the hours he works, whether regular or irregular. The national minimum wage is calculated by dividing the total gross pay by the total hours worked over the appropriate pay reference period. Generally, the time worker must be paid not only for the hours which he actually works but also the hours for which he is available for work (e.g on-call or on standby at the workplace and travelling during normal hours). For the purposes of the calculation, the hours worked which are to be taken into account do not include rest breaks, even if they are paid, travelling to and from home, holidays, sick leave or maternity leave or sleeping between duties at the place of work.

Salaried Hours Work

A salaried hours worker is paid for a set basic number of minimum hours each year and receives an annual salary in equal instalments. He is a salaried hours worker even if the actual hours worked vary, provided the regular payments remain the same. The hours which count are as outlined above in respect of time work. The rate paid is calculated by dividing the gross pay for the pay reference period by the basic hours set out in the contract. An individual will be treated as a time worker for overtime for which additional pay is paid.

Output Work

An output worker is paid on a piecework or commission basis - although he is treated as a time worker if his hours are fixed by the employer. Since the national minimum wage is paid by reference to an hourly rate not a piece rate, the employer has the option either to enter into a "fair estimate" agreement with the worker or to pay him the national minimum wage for each hour worked. A fair estimate agreement must be agreed in writing before the start of the pay reference period and state an estimate of the hours to be worked. To be "fair", that estimate must be at least 80% of the number of hours that an average worker would take to complete the task in similar conditions. As a fall-back, the agreement must also give the worker the right to be paid an agreed piece rate or commission rate for each item produced or sold in the pay reference period. It must also require the worker to keep a record of the actual hours output work he does, which he must provide to the employer as soon as possible after the end of the pay reference period. If no "fair estimate" agreement is reached, then the employer must pay the national minimum wage for each hour worked, regardless of the number of items produced or sales achieved.

Where the worker works for more than the "fair estimate" hours, the employer need only pay him the national minimum wage for the "fair estimate" hours. However, the worker is entitled to the piece rate set out in his contract for product or sales achieved in those additional hours. When the worker works less than the "fair estimate" hours, he must be paid the national minimum wage for the hours actually worked.

Unmeasured Work

Unmeasured work is a residual category which does not constitute time work, salaried hours work, or output work, but includes work where there are certain tasks to be done but no specified hours or time when they must be done. The employer typically requires the worker to work when he is needed or when work is available. This category may include live-in workers such as pub managers and care workers.

The employer has the option to either reach a "daily average" agreement of hours to be worked or to pay the national minimum wage for every hour actually worked. A "daily average" agreement must be made in writing before the start of the pay reference period which it covers and must set out the realistic daily average number of hours which the worker is to work. The burden of proof rests upon the employer to demonstrate, if challenged, that the daily average is realistic.Unless a "daily average" agreement is reached, then the employer must pay the national minimum wage for each hour worked.

Payments

The Regulations state which payments or benefits are to be taken into account when calculating whether the national minimum wage has been paid. The starting point is gross pay, but which excludes certain specific payments such as any loan, advance of wages, pension, redundancy or lump sum retirement payment. In addition to basic pay, any incentive pay, bonuses or tips (but only tips paid through payroll) will count towards the national minimum wage. However, the premium element of any overtime or shift premium rates will not count. Similarly, any allowances paid to a worker to compensate him for working in dangerous conditions or unsocial hours or for working in a particular area (e.g. London weighting) do not count towards the national minimum wage unless they are consolidated in standard pay. Where an employer provides accommodation to a worker, he is entitled to deduct an amount from the worker's pay or can charge the worker for that accommodation. However, there is a limit to the permissible amount of that deduction or charge which can count towards the national minimum wage and any excess will not count. Apart from accommodation, no benefits in kind, including meals, count towards the national minimum wage.

Records

All employers must keep "sufficient" records to establish that they are paying their workers at least the national minimum wage. The burden of proof will rest upon the employer to prove to any worker, enforcement officer, tribunal or court that the national minimum wage has been paid. What may be "sufficient" will vary amongst employers and amongst workers. For example, existing pay records may be adequate to demonstrate that a worker paid well above the national minimum wage is in fact receiving that sum. In practice, the closer the worker's gross pay is to the national minimum wage, the greater the risk and the amount of detail which the employer should maintain to demonstrate both the fact that the worker receives the requisite amount and how that sum is calculated. An employer who has a "fair estimate" agreement or a "daily average" agreement or a "training agreement" must keep copies of those documents.

The records need not be retained in any particular form and can be held on computer. However, the employer should be able to produce them upon request in a single document. The records must be kept for three years following the pay period to which they relate.

Enforcement and Remedies

Parties cannot contract out of the Act, since any provision in an agreement which purports to do so is void.The enforcement agency for the national minimum wage is the Inland Revenue. It is entitled to investigate workers' complaints, check employers' records and interview employers. If an enforcement officer believes an employer has failed to pay the national minimum wage to a worker, then he may serve an enforcement notice requiring compliance. Subject to the right of appeal, an employer who fails to comply will then be served with a penalty notice imposing a fine of £7.20 in respect of each worker for each continuing day of non-compliance. If that sanction does not succeed, then an enforcement officer may encourage the worker to bring a claim before the Employment Tribunal, pursue that case on behalf of the worker or pursue a criminal prosecution against the employer.

Criminal offences of failure to comply with the Act may be punishable by fines of up to £5,000 for each offence. Potential offences include refusal or wilful neglect to pay the national minimum wage, falsifying or failing to keep records, intentionally obstructing an enforcement officer and refusing or neglecting to give information to an enforcement officer. Where the breach is committed by a limited company, then it is not only the company which may be liable but also its directors and any manager, secretary or other similar officers if the offences have been carried out with their consent or connivance or neglect. There is, however, a defence where any person charged with a criminal offence can show that he "exercised all due diligence and took all reasonable precautions" to ensure compliance with the Act and the Regulations.

A worker paid less than the national minimum wage to which he is entitled has a right under his contract to receive the amount of the underpayment.

A worker who believes he is entitled to the national minimum wage can make a written request to his employer to inspect and copy the records which the employer is obliged to keep. The employer must produce those records within 14 days of the request. If the employer refuses, the worker can make a complaint to the Employment Tribunal which may require the employer to pay 80 times the level of the national minimum wage - currently £288.

If the worker is an employee, then if the principal reason for his dismissal or selection for redundancy is that he asserted, in good faith, any right under the Act (such as the right to the national minimum wage or access to records) then the dismissal will be automatically unfair. The normal qualifying service period of one year will not apply. If the worker is not an employee and the detriment he suffers is the termination of his contract, then the amount of compensation awarded must not exceed the amount which he would have received had he been an employee who was unfairly dismissed.

A worker also has the right not to be subjected to any detriment by an employer because he does or might qualify for the national minimum wage or because he has taken any step to enforce or benefit from any rights under the Act, or because he has done something which leads to the employer being prosecuted for a breach of the Act. In cases of detriment which fall short of dismissal, the tribunal will make a declaration as to the fact of a breach of the Act and has discretion to award such compensation as it considers just and equitable. In exercising that discretion, the tribunal will take into account the nature of the infringement and the losses or expenses incurred by the worker as a result of that breach, the duty of the worker to mitigate his losses and the extent of any contribution by him.

Other than in exceptional circumstances, any claim in the Employment Tribunal must be commenced within three months of the date of the alleged act or deliberate omission of the employer in breach of the Act.

Trevor Bettany, Partner, Speechly Bircham

DISCRIMINATION LAW - THE PITFALLS

Discrimination Law applies to all aspects of the employment relationship from recruitment to termination. However, unlike other employment claims:

- There is no upper limit on the compensation that can be awarded to employees.
- Employees are entitled to claim damages for injury to feelings (which

in themselves can be substantial).

- Employees do not have to have been employed for a particular period of time before being able to issue a claim in the Employment Tribunal.
- Employers can be held to be vicariously liable for the acts of their other employees which may be discriminatory, and in certain circumstances, the acts of third parties towards their employees.

Employers therefore need to know what constitutes unlawful discrimination and how to avoid it.

Disability Discrimination

The Disability Discrimination Act 1995 applies to all employers who employ 15 or more employees and makes it unlawful to treat an employee less favourably because of their disability where such less favourable treatment cannot be justified by the employer. A disability has been defined as a physical or mental impairment which has a substantial or long term adverse effect on an employee's ability to carry out normal day to day activities. It has been held that certain types of work-related stress or clinical depression can constitute a disability. In addition an employer has a legal duty to make reasonable adjustments to enable disabled applicants to have access to the employer or a disabled employee's working environment in order to enable the employee to carry out their work. However this duty is not owed to disabled applicants or employees unless the employer knows, or could reasonably be expected to know, that they have a disability and as a result they are placed at a substantial disadvantage by the employer's work arrangements or premises.

Age Discrimination

In February 1999, the United Kingdom Government issued a voluntary code of practice on Age Discrimination. While employees do not currently have a right to claim on the grounds of Age Discrimination, it could be possible to formulate a claim under the Race Relations Act 1976 or the Sex Discrimination Act 1975. This is because an age requirement could amount to sex or race discrimination. For example, in the case of James -v- Eastleigh Borough Council 1990 Mr James successfully claimed he had been discriminated against when he was charged 75p to enter a swimming pool and his wife was not - the council having adopted a charging policy of free entrance to those who had reached state pensionable age 60 for women and 65 for men. This was held to be direct sex discrimination.

Race/Sex Discrimination

The Race Relations Act 1976 and the Sex Discrimination Act 1975 make it unlawful to treat an employee less favourably on the grounds of their race, sex or marital status. The law recognises three types of discrimination, namely direct discrimination, indirect discrimination and victimisation.

The Sex Discrimination Act applies equally to the treatment of men and women, with the exception of special treatment that is afforded to women in connection with pregnancy or childbirth.

With regard to pay, if for example, women engage in like work or work rated as equal to that of a man, or work of equal value to that of a man, women can claim under the Equal Pay Act 1970 and the Sex Discrimination Act that she should in fact be paid the equivalent of her male counterpart.

The provisions of the Race Relations Act 1976 is similar to the Sex Discrimination Act. What amounts to discrimination on racial grounds is defined as less favourable treatment because of an individual's colour, race, nationality, ethnicity or national origins.

There is rarely direct evidence for an Employment Tribunal to establish if there has been less favourable treatment on the grounds of race or sex and therefore the Tribunal has to draw inferences from the evidence that is available.

Harassment and Bullying

It has been held that harassment or bullying can amount to Sex, or Race, or Disability Discrimination. Substantial awards have been made for injury to feelings for harassment or bullying. In Armitage, Marsden and HM Prison Service & Others-v-Johnson (1997) which was a racial harassment case, the Employment Appeal Tribunal awarded £20,000 for injury to feelings and £7,500 aggravated damages on the basis that the Employer carried out an inadequate investigation of the Employee's complaints.

Employers cannot therefore afford to ignore allegations that discrimination is taking place in their workplace.

Ranjit Dhindsa, Shoosmiths

TRAINING AND DEVELOPMENT

People are a company's most valuable asset - they can and do make all the difference between success or failure.Training is about the development of people within and for the organisation. Training has to be an ongoing process and a natural part of a 'learning for life' attitude within a company.

It also has to fit into the organisational framework. It is not an isolated activity - the benefits of the right kind of training will influence the development of the business and shape each individual's contribution to the overall business effort. A training and development plan - detailing the type of people to be recruited and how they should be trained to meet the needs of the growing business - is therefore an essential part of an organisation's business plan.

The key to effective training is to identify practical approaches to developing people's skills, knowledge, understanding, qualities and creative talents, based on a real understanding of their needs and those of the business.

In deciding what kind of training, if any, is required, the initial questions to address are:

- What is this business and how is it going to be developed over time?
- What skills/knowledge/qualities/creative talent etc are needed now, or will be needed for the future, to match the desired and anticipated growth and development of the business?

It is also essential to ensure that employees perceive training as a positive experience. Reactions to training are highly personal and linked to an individual's experience of early education, on-the-job training and/or specific training courses. The reactions are sometimes positive, more often very critical and bordering on negative:

"That was a total waste of time: I didn't learn anything"
"Not another training course? I hope it's more interesting than the last one"
"I was given lots of hand outs"
"I fell asleep: it was so boring"
"Most of it wasn't relevant"
"I couldn't understand what he was talking about, but it made a change from work"

Make sure training is a positive worthwhile experience

Effective training should contribute to an individual's professional and personal development. Above all, it should:

- Have a clear purpose, which is relevant to the individual's specific needs
- Be interesting and challenging
- Be worthwhile in terms of time, effort and cost.

The basic purpose of training is to fill a gap in existing knowledge, understanding and/or skills, so that an individual has the ability to perform a task or set of tasks, and to improve performance.

For the purpose of training, the mechanics of a specific task - that is the precise steps involved in completing the task - can be broken down and simplified. However, if you think of learning to drive a car, it soon becomes apparent that the mastering of the basic mechanical operations - starting the engine, using the brake, clutch and accelerator, moving off, changing gear, etc - are not in themselves enough to equip the learner for the reality of driving. Competent driving includes the interaction of a range of highly complex skills - observation, spatial awareness, thinking ahead, timely anticipation of others' reactions, risk assessment, confidence - the list is endless!

As with learning to drive, knowledge, understanding and skills are the basic training requirement. The application of these in real-life situations to gain experience, combined with the development of more personal aspects or qualities, make up the total picture.

Identifying training needs

To identify training needs, senior managers must have a clear overview of employees' strengths, weaknesses and capabilities. A useful approach is to determine the desired and the actual levels of performance. The gap between the two identifies a need for training.

To determine what should be happening we need to ask?

- What production/operational/service/other targets/goals have been set for the individual/team/department? i.e. What is the desired level of performance for maximum efficiency and effectiveness?
- What precisely is expected of the individual/team/department, in order to meet their targets?
- What therefore is required of them, in terms of knowledge, understanding, skills, attitude, experience etc. . . ?

Answers to these questions will give a picture of what should be happening. The next stage is to examine what is actually happening to see whether there is a gap between desired and actual levels of performance. Are targets being met satisfactorily? If not, what is the reason for the gap in performance? Is it due to a lack of skills/knowledge/experience? Would training help? Would other forms of support, guidance or assistance be helpful?

Having identified a training need, the first step is to set a target for the training. These targets pinpoint the reason for the training and can be used to check that the training was useful and achieved the right results. Good targets come from asking the right questions, e.g.:

Question. What skill does the employee need to learn?
Target. To teach the employee to operate the lathe safely and efficiently.

Question. What knowledge and understanding does the employee need to acquire?
Target. To ensure the employee is familiar with the procedures for processing complaints.

Question. What quality does the employee need to develop?
Target. To improve the employee's ability to communicate verbally with potential customers.

Training methods

Once the target is identified the next step is to select the right training method from the many available.

- Internal on-the-job training. Organisations can design their own training programme, with emphasis on the development of specific skills or attributes for a given task - customer service, telephone answering, machine operating, production tasks etc.
- Learning by observation. Individuals can learn from a colleague or supervisor, by seeing how a job is carried out and by picking up inside information. This method of learning is often undervalued.
- Learning through one-to-one instruction. A colleague or supervisor spending time with an individual can pass on invaluable hints or tips about how to improve performance.
- Qualification-linked training. This is a more formal approach. Currently, for example, National Vocational Qualifications (NVQs) offer a comprehensive means of gaining qualifications in the workplace. NVQs are very relevant to the organisation's and individual's needs: they are of a practical nature and allow employees to develop capabilities at different levels.

However, the company does not have to rely only on its own training resources. Training providers are many and varied. A good way of finding the best help available is to contact the local Training and Enterprise Council (TEC) or Business Link offices. Expert guidance and support are to be found through either of these two sources. Both receive government funding, which keeps costs reasonable. They also have a special interest in helping small companies, so that the help given is practical and suited to the particular needs of the organisation.

Whatever the method chosen, all training needs regular evaluation to check that targets identified earlier have been met.

Needs must be re-examined on a regular basis to see what has changed, how well people are doing and what else needs to be done. This is very much a matter of creating the right atmosphere in the company and the right attitude to learning - the 'learning for life' attitude. Learning needs to be seen as part and parcel of everyday life inside and outside the workplace, not as a special one-off event.

The right atmosphere and the right attitude to learning can and do give companies better chances for success in an increasingly competitive world.

Training strategy

 Identify future development and needs of the business and its people

 Ask how well business and people should be performing

 Check whether there is sufficient progress against targets set

 If there is a gap between achieved and desired performance consider if training is required

Specify the type of training required, then set targets

Seek outside help if required

Carry out training

Check that targets have been met

Paulette Lockington and Stephen Winder

Having found the right person many small businesses then set about putting their new employee in conditions that are almost bound to lead to underperformance, if not outright failure. For every pound spent on equipment for the average UK worker, Britain's main competitors spend two. More than one in three small firms invest one day or less each year in training their employees. Owners often think that product knowledge and company systems will be soaked up by a process of osmosis. A few minutes on the phone to many businesses will quickly dispel that myth. Disorder and ignorance are the norm which only systems and training can overcome.

Practicalities

If quality is hard to measure, in a small firm the consequences of poor quality are all too easy to recognise. Repeat business drops and rejects rise. According to one former chief executive of the National Westminster Bank, basic mistakes by employees account for between 25 and 40 per cent of the total cost of any service business - presumably he included his own in that statistic. Read this chapter to see how you can achieve business excellence from the outset and in any event insure against failures.

THE BUSINESS EXCELLENCE MODEL/EFQM EXCELLENCE MODEL

Most new businesses seek to become excellent but to achieve excellence needs a systematic approach - it doesn't happen by chance, nor will it develop overnight. There is, however, a management framework that is rapidly becoming the accepted methodology for keeping your business on track and encouraging continuous improvement, providing the competitive stance that you need to succeed.

The Model has a robust pedigree, having been developed after extensive research into companies that, according to peer review, demonstrate excellence. Initially developed by the European Foundation for Quality Management as the basis upon which to judge applicants for the European Quality Award it is now implemented across sixteen European countries. In the UK it is promoted by the British Quality Foundation (BQF) by providing products and services to help organisations of all sizes and sectors to strive towards excellence.

What is it?

©1999 EFQM. The Model is a registered trademark of EFQM

The Model identifies, at a high level, the major factors that influence organisational performance. It includes the five main areas of good management practice:

- Leadership - the ability to motivate and drive the organisation forward
- Managing people - developing their potential and creating a learning culture
- Managing resources - ensuring cost-effective utilisation of all resources
- Policy making - how to link strategic planning to business objectives
- Processes - cross-functional process management that is customer focused

Addressing these areas will enable you to maximise your efficiency. The guidelines provided by the BQF describe the behaviour and characteristics exhibited by excellent companies so you can see at a glance how you compare under each heading. All these factors are linked within the Model to emphasise that they need to be considered together, not in isolation. For example, you may start up your business with sophisticated IT systems but unless you calculate the financial implications correctly, develop processes based upon computerised procedures and train your people to use the systems efficiently you are unlikely to realise your aims.

The second part of the Model addresses the variety of results that you should monitor which come from managing the inputs to your business. Note that excellent companies look at more than just the financial results - the effect you have on your customers, your staff and the local community, all deserve attention.

The success of any business relies upon your ability to balance what you put in, how effectively you manage those elements, what you seek to get out and how sustainable those results are. The Model provides the prompts, from which you select those that are appropriate to your business - i.e., you tailor it to meet your own requirements.

Using the Model

The power of the Model is its ability to reflect the needs of any organisation. It is not a prescriptive standard like ISO 9000 that dictates what should be done to achieve a specified level of performance. Behind each of the nine boxes is a series of prompts that address a wide range of issues, constantly reminding you to check how effective you are at managing your business.

Any business needs to improve its performance constantly. You cannot afford to stand still, but must anticipate changes in the needs of your customers, suppliers and stakeholders.

One of the key factors therefore in striving for success is the ability to measure your performance, to recognise what you are doing well and what needs to improve. The Model provides the framework for you to assess where you are now and to measure your progress. Self-assessment against the Model gives a score out of a 1000 points and highlights the areas where improvements can be made so that your action plans are prioritised to key areas. The assessment process requires you to analyse your activities and to give a percentage score against 32 sub criteria linked to the nine boxes, with 50 per cent of the overall score going to Enablers and 50 per cent to Results.

By using self-assessment as part of your planning process you can ensure that decisions to go for perhaps an Investors In People programme or an ISO 9000 certificate are made after consideration of the needs of the whole business, not just as a response to a one-off observation or the status of the competition.

Managing for excellence

The Model is a representation of your business and an awareness of the prompts that underpin it can help you in many ways including:

- Self assessment - to track progress over time and against benchmarks
- Implementation review - to assess how well established projects are managed
- Recruitment criteria - by identifying the types of skills that are required

- Training programmes - to ensure that skills develop in line with the business
- Decision-making - to ensure that all items are systematically addressed
- Restructuring - making sure that all the elements come together effectively
- Appraisal - reviewing the key aspects of personal performance

Becoming an excellent business needs hard work and commitment. The Model is helping thousands of organisations across the UK and Europe to meet the challenges that a modern business faces.

Eileen Murray, The British Quality Foundation

Unfortunately, unlike the ideas advanced above, few small firms have continuous improvement as one of their goals. Often they rely on the maxim "If it's not broken don't fix it." But unfortunately customers are usually the first people to find out when things are broken and they rarely come back for more duff goods.

A better maxim would be that of Julian Richer, the founder of the Richer Sounds hi-fi chain. He sets out to maximise his customers' opportunities to complain. From the ship's type bell which shoppers are invited to ring if they get great service in one of his shops, through to the post-purchase questionnaire in the top of each box, he seeks out customer feedback at every opportunity.

FINANCING BUSINESS PURCHASES

Choosing the best way of financing assets is a vital feature of running any business. You may know your own requirements and what you have to spend, but do the two factors add up and, if so, what is the best way to finance the asset to suit your present and future business needs?

The Finance & Leasing Association's members fund over a third of all UK fixed investment through a number of different finance schemes and have formulated a number of business finance options that may be applicable to your particular business:

Outright purchase Paying cash is generally the easiest and least expensive option. It does, however, carry quite a high risk with the possibility of encountering cash flow problems in the long term. It could also be the case that your money may be more profitably employed elsewhere in your business. Due to high administration costs, finance houses tend not to consider financing anything under £2000 - £3000 thus limiting the choice available.

Pros: The transaction is interest free if you fund out of reserves. Bank or finance house borrowing will incur interest

You can sell the asset at any time
You can claim back VAT

Cons: It could cause you cash flow problems
Maintenance costs require budgeting and can be expensive
Your capital could be put to other uses

Hire purchase Hire or lease purchase is the only option, except outright purchase, that will eventually result in you owning the asset. It is, therefore, important that you ascertain the value of the asset at the end of the agreement.

Pros: You can claim back the VAT on the capital - up front
Interest is allowable against profits
Your working capital remains intact
You eventually own the goods

Cons: You take most of the risks of ownership

Finance lease Although finance lease is similar in economic effect to hire purchase, the ownership of the asset remains with the leasing company. The finance lease agreement can consist of two periods, the primary and secondary. The primary period is the lease period that was initially agreed upon and during which the rentals, consisting of capital and interest, are repaid. If the asset turns out to have a longer working life than expected the agreement may enter a secondary period at nominal cost.

Pros: You will not have any ownership worries
Rental charges are allowable against profits
VAT can often be reclaimed on the full amounts of the rentals
You may be able to decide when and if the asset is sold
If sold you may get a rebate in rentals from the proceeds
Cons: It is the leasing company which claims capital allowances - you cannot claim them

Operating lease/Contract hire This is basically a long term hire agreement where the asset remains owned by the leasing company. Rentals are paid over an agreed period. In the case of an operating lease, rentals only cover the depreciation on the asset and the finance charge. With contract hire the agreement will also include maintenance. These agreements are usually more common with assets which have a strong second-hand value and market as well as a determinable working life.

Pros: You do not have ownership worries
You do not have to dip into your working capital
You don't usually have to worry about resale values on the asset

You can set rentals against profits

The agreements are classed as 'off balance sheet'

Cons: Equipment needs to be well maintained as this is linked to residual value

It is the leasing company that claims capital allowances - you cannot claim them

Once you have investigated which finance option best suits your needs, remember to make the following checks before entering into any agreement:

Is the finance house or leasing company reputable? Does it belong to an organisation such as the FLA who operate a Code of Practice to which all its members adhere?

Have you chosen a finance house/leasing company which can offer the best deal on your requirements, as some specialise more in particular asset types?

Is the agreement flexible to account for any future changes in your business requirements?

Does the length of the agreement realistically match the life of the asset?

Do you understand your responsibilities and those of the finance house/leasing company for any maintenance contracts?

Only when you are completely satisfied that these points are covered, should you go ahead and sign the financing deal.

Ian Hagg, Finance & Leasing Association

Obligations

Paradoxically, the government is a major source of help and encouragement when it comes to setting up in business, but they are also the principal instrument of closing many down. Through the Business Links and the TECs, the government provides help with training, quality initiatives, the first steps in exporting, introducing new technology and so forth. But the Inland Revenue and Customs and Excise are in the forefront, ahead of the banks and other creditors, in blowing the whistle on the failing or sometimes only floundering enterprises. Some bosses are tempted to treat the VAT (value added tax) they have collected from customers and the tax they have deducted from employees' wages as a part of their own cash flow. To compound this transgression, such imprudent (if not actually criminal) proprietors often view their ultimate tax liability on profits as being such an unlikely event as to be safely ignored and so not provided for. This attitude is usually brought about because owner-managers cannot easily see the value of paying money over to government departments whilst they themselves have more pressing needs for the funds. While this may be the case, it's a crazy approach. If there are problems it often helps to discuss them with the Revenue - don't avoid the issue. If you're upfront and honest, more often than not these government institutions, particularly the Inland Revenue, are prepared to help. To ignore them, however, is folly.

STATUTORY OBLIGATIONS ON SETTING UP A BUSINESS

The statutory obligations for setting up a business vary depending upon the type of business being set up.

Sole trader Apart from the obligation to register with the Inland Revenue as being self-employed, there is no specific statute governing setting up a business as a sole trader.

Partnership This is established from the moment two or more persons start to carry on a business with a view to making profit. If there is no partnership agreement then the Partnership Act 1890 sets out the terms that will govern the partnership relationship. However, it is recommended that partners define their roles and responsibilities in a tailor-made written partnership agreement.

Company This will not come into legal existence until it has been registered at Companies House and a Certificate of Incorporation has been issued. The Companies Act 1985 requires certain forms to be filed at Companies House along with the company's constitution and a fee. As a time saving device, 'off-the-shelf' companies can be purchased. These are companies which have been incorporated but have not yet traded. However, off-the-shelf companies will not cater for specific requirements.

Naming a business

Sole trader/partnership If the name of the business consists of the sole trader/partners' surnames with certain permitted additions then no restrictions apply. Approval is occasionally required, for instance for a name that is similar to the name of a government department. The sole trader/partners' names must also be shown on business documents.

Company A company must have a corporate name which is registered with the Registrar of Companies. It cannot be the same as any other company's name. The company name, registered office and registered number must be featured on letters and business documents. Its registered name must be displayed outside places where business is conducted.

Taxation

There are obligations to pay tax and keep records when setting up and running a business. It is important to check with an accountant what obligations are imposed and whether or not to register for VAT.

Insurance

An insurance broker should be used to take out general business insurance covering (as appropriate) public, product and employers' liability. Businesses operating from home may find that home insurance is affected.

Licences/Registration

Certain businesses require special licences to trade (such as employment agencies and children's nurseries).

General

These are the principal statutory obligations, but there may be additional statutory requirements depending on the type of business being set up. It is therefore important to check with a solicitor which statutory obligations must be complied with in each individual case.

Keith Lewington and Rachel Ellwood, Shoosmiths

What's in a name?

Choosing the right trading name or names for your company is crucially important. The name is the first thing your customers and suppliers will come across, and will be said every time the telephone is picked up. But how do you make sure you get it right? The name has to perform a number of functions - it should be memorable and distinctive, make you stand out in the market and ensure that you are not confused with competitors. Whilst it may be helpful to include a description of what you do or where you are based, this may prevent you from applying for a registered trademark if the name does not distinguish your goods and services.

It also needs to be legal. The Companies Act contains certain requirements that the company name must meet, including the need for 'Limited', or the Welsh equivalent at the end, not offensive (in the opinion of the Secretary of State), nor too similar to a name that already appears in the register of names. Other factors to bear in mind are that names that suggest a connection with the Crown or a local authority are not permitted without the approval of the Secretary of State, as is the case for a fairly lengthy list of words including 'British', 'International', 'Sheffield' and 'Trust'. Do some research in your field of business to make sure that the name you want to use isn't too similar to that of an existing organisation - otherwise you could find yourself having to make changes before you have really got started.

If you pick the right name you will be able to start to develop your reputation right from the first day of trading. If you get the wrong name you could find yourselves having to change your stationery and starting again.

Kate Kelly, Shoosmiths

Handling Your Tax, VAT and Other Obligations

When you set up your own business you obviously expect to make a profit. Of course as soon as the profits start appearing, so do the tax bills. A little time spent at the beginning thinking about your tax position can save you a lot of time and money later on.

There are two main things that you need to consider: how are you going to deal with tax administration and how can you make sure that you do not pay any more tax than you have to.

Administration

The procedures for notifying the Inland Revenue that you need to follow when you set up your business depend on whether you decide to act as a sole trader, in partnership, or trade through a company.

If you are a sole trader or in partnership, then you do not have to notify the Inland Revenue immediately. Your previous tax office may get in touch to find out what you are doing. Even if they do not, you have to tell the Inland Revenue that you have set up the business by 5th October following the tax year in which the business started trading. Tax years run from 6th April one year to 5th April in the next.

If you set up a company, there is also usually no need to notify the Inland Revenue - they will get in touch with you. They will be told automatically when the company is created, and you will probably receive a new company enquiry form.

If you are a sole trader or partner, your tax return will normally be sent to you shortly after the end of the tax year. You can get the Inland Revenue to calculate your tax liability for you, but then the completed form has to be returned by 30th September. You have until 31st January if you or your accountant are going to calculate the liability.

Companies have to send copies of their tax computations and accounts to the Inland Revenue within twelve months of the end of each accounting period.

You can deal with all of your tax affairs yourself, but for most people running a business this can be very time-consuming and potentially expensive. Tax is highly complex, with lots of areas where mistakes can be made. You will probably find it simpler to use an accountant. To make this easier, you can sign an authority for the Inland Revenue to send copies of tax assessments and other correspondence directly to your accountant. This will allow him to deal directly with the tax authorities on your behalf.

For an unincorporated business, you have to make a payment of tax on account on 31st January during the tax year, and 31st July after the end of the tax year. Any balancing payment must be made by 31st January after the end of the tax year. This final payment will include taxation of capital gains, but the payments on account will only cover your trading profits, and any other sources of income you may have outside your business.

Companies have to pay tax nine months after the end of each tax accounting period. This is usually the same as the period you choose for preparing accounts, but cannot be more than twelve months. This may mean that you have to pay tax before your accounts are finalised, particularly if you have a long accounting period.

It is vital to meet statutory deadlines for notification of liabilities, payment of tax and submission of returns. There are cash penalties for failure to comply - some are fixed and automatic, others are discretionary and depend on the amount of tax involved.

Even before you have started in business you should consider how tax will affect you. Whichever form your business takes, the taxable profit will differ from the profit shown in your accounts because:

- Certain expenses which may be included in your accounts, such as entertaining, will not be allowed as a deduction for tax purposes
- Tax allowances for some costs are given only when payment is made, rather than when the liability arises (normally used for accounting purposes)
- The depreciation charge in your accounts is ignored, and instead you receive capital allowances. These are often calculated on a very different basis from depreciation.

If you are a sole trader or a partner you will be charged tax on your profits, not on the money you take out of the business. Therefore you may end up paying tax, even though you have reinvested the profits that you have made and have seen very little of the cash.

The taxation of company profits is carried out under a very different system to that of sole traders and partnerships. Companies pay corporation tax on their profits, after deducting expenses which include directors' salaries. Dividends paid by a company are also subject to tax, but this can usually be offset against corporation tax at a later date.

When you start your business you may make a loss in the first few years. If you are a sole trader or partner you may be able to offset any such losses against other personal income, including that from a previous occupation. This option is not available if you set up a company.

National Insurance

The rates of National Insurance contributions are higher for companies and their directors and employees than for sole traders and partners.

As a director of a company you will pay Class 1 contributions. The level of contribution is a percentage of your gross earnings to an overall annual limit, although there is no liability if earnings fall below a lower limit. In addition, the company has a liability to pay contributions, with no upper limit.

As a partner or sole trader you would be liable for Class 2 and Class 4 contributions. Class 2 contributions are at a flat rate. There is no liability if your profits are low, but this needs to be agreed before the liability is cancelled. Class 4 contributions are based on your taxable profits, and subject to upper and lower limits.

Although more expensive, Class 1 contributions entitle you to unemployment benefit and certain other benefits which are not available to those who pay Class 2 contributions.

It may be possible to mitigate Class 1 contributions by the use of 'non cash' benefits, but the most popular benefits, company cars and mobile phones, are now caught by Class 1A, at similar rates.

VAT

Unlike other taxes, VAT is based on your turnover and costs, rather than your profits. As such, the sums involved may be much larger than your income tax or corporation tax. It is a tax on consumption which is paid by the ultimate consumer. Most businesses simply act as collector, but the volume of legislation means that this is a far from easy task. Making sure that you account for VAT correctly is essential for any business, and neglect may result in very significant penalties.

When starting a business, professional advice on when to register is important. If the value of your taxable sales or services is likely to exceed or has exceeded the registration limit, you must register within a very tight deadline.

Once registered, a separate VAT account must be kept to record amounts of VAT added to your sales and VAT charged to you for business supplies. At regular intervals, normally quarterly, details must be included in your VAT return.

There are a number of important points to remember:

- VAT cannot be reclaimed on a supply unless supported by an invoice giving certain details, including the supplier's VAT registration number and a description of the goods or services
- A surcharge arises if VAT returns or payments are submitted late
- VAT cannot be reclaimed for goods or services not used in the business

If your business is registered for VAT, all your invoices and credit notes must contain specified information, such as the date of supply and your VAT registration number.

Customs and Excise normally visit a new business within eighteen months of registration. This inspection of your records is to ensure that VAT is being properly accounted for.

Businesses with a small annual turnover can use the Cash Accounting Scheme for VAT. Under this scheme, you can account for VAT by reference to the dates of receipts and payments, rather than the dates of invoices. This may be beneficial if you offer credit.

Capital Taxes

Capital taxes are often forgotten when setting up a business, as they generally apply only if you die or give away the business (inheritance tax) or when a business or asset is sold (capital gains tax).

However, legislation provides a number of reliefs from these taxes. In order to take full advantage of these reliefs it is important to consider planning for these taxes early in the life of your business.

Employing others

For your business to get off the ground or expand, you may need to take on staff, whether full or part-time.

Income tax, in the form of pay-as-you-earn (PAYE), must then be deducted from your employees' pay. Inform your tax office if you intend to employ other people in your business. They will then issue the various forms and records that must be maintained, together with guides on how to complete them. The easiest way of getting in touch with the appropriate tax inspector is to phone up any local tax office.

There is also a statutory duty to deduct National Insurance contributions which must be paid together with the employer's contributions and PAYE.

Payroll records should be carefully maintained, because errors may result in additional tax liabilities and penalties. You should be alert to the danger areas, particularly fringe benefits and payments to those claiming to be self-employed. Special procedures are required for casual labour.

David Chopping, Partner, Moore Stephens, London

Don't make the mistake of believing that just because you are trading as a limited liability company you as a director are not personally liable for the company not discharging its obligations. The shelter of limited liability is now a pale shadow of what it was in 1895 when the Companies Act rendered it no longer necessary to have an Act of Parliament or a Royal Charter to set up a company. In the past two decades the notion that limited liability is a privilege rather than a right has gained a strong legal hold. Firstly fraudulent directors were stripped of protection from their creditors and now merely incompetent ones can find themselves personally responsible for the liabilities of the business. Directors found unfit to manage can be disqualified from holding office elsewhere.

Such events are no longer unusual. Each year over 600 directors of mostly small firms find themselves barred from office or facing large charges against personal assets, which they naively felt were sheltered from 'plunder'.

STAKEHOLDER PENSIONS & NEW REQUIREMENTS FOR EMPLOYERS

The Government are implementing a major pension reform programme aimed at getting more people to make private pension provision. These reforms will have a direct impact on the majority of small businesses.

There are three main elements to the proposed new legislation:

- First, a new product will be available called a Stakeholder Pension from April 2001
- Second, new requirements on all employers in respect of workplace access which will enforced from April 2002
- Thirdly, a new integrated tax regime for personal pensions and Stakeholder pensions

A New Product: Stakeholder Pension

Stakeholder Pension will be very similar to a personal pension scheme and will probably replace group personal pensions as the choice of many small businesses when setting up a scheme for employees.

The two main differences between a group personal pension and a stakeholder pension are compulsory minimum standards and the member protection requirements.

Both measures are intended to give employers and employees greater confidence in making private pension provision.

First, Compulsory Minimum Standards. Stakeholder Pensions must comply with the following minimum standards:-

- There must be complete contribution flexibility without penalty, such as stopping contributions and transferring money out into another pensions
- The minimum an individual can put in must be £10
- The individual must receive an annual statement of the value of their pension
- The only charge can be an annual management charge and this must be set no higher than 1% per annum

The annual management charge must cover all basic scheme set up-costs, administration and investment management, plus the cost of providing basic information and advice.

Second, the Member protection, otherwise known as the Governance, Requirements. These are intended to ensure a stakeholder pension scheme protects member's interests and complies with the minimum standards. It means that a scheme either is established under a trust or has a Stakeholder Pensions Manager who will have contractual duties towards the employees.

The Tax Regime

The proposals are that there will be two pension tax regimes (as at present) :-

- the existing occupational pension tax regime
- a new integrated simple regime for both personal pension and stakeholder pensions

The Personal pension & Stakeholder pension regime will have the following main features :-

- an individual can contribute to both stakeholder and PPP at the same time
- The contribution limit will be £3,600 or the age related limits for PPPs if higher
- Contributions are paid net of tax, higher rate relief reclaimed through tax return
- Contributions can be continued for 5 years after earnings have ceased

Employer Access Requirements

These new requirements will impact on the vast majority of small firms in one way or another. All employers will be required, by April 2002, for all employees to :-

- identify & facilitate access to a designated stakeholder pensions scheme
- provide payroll deduction to employees who wish to contribute into the designated scheme
- consult with employees on which designated scheme they will offer
- inform employees of the existence of the stakeholder pension scheme

Employers are not to provide advice to employees on the suitability of the scheme for them as individuals but merely to designate at least one stakeholder pension scheme which the employee can have access to.

Furthermore, employers are not obliged to contribute to the stakeholder pension scheme.

Employers will be exempt from these requirements if there is:

- an occupational pension scheme available to all employees, or
- an equivalent group personal pension scheme available to all employees, or
- there are no employees earning more than national insurance lower earnings limit

With the pension options available to small businesses already complex and the new legislation from April 2001, it will be vital that small employers seek professional pensions advice at an early stage.

The most appropriate sources for advice will be employee benefit consultants and independent financial advisers who are not tied to any particular pension company or pension scheme arrangement.

Stephen Ingledew, Head of Corporate Pensions, NPI

INSURING THE HEALTH OF YOUR BUSINESS

A well insured business stands a much better chance of surviving a disaster than its under or uninsured counterpart. Every year, hundreds of small and medium sized firms close down as a result of financial losses too big for them to survive without insurance cover.

So there is no argument about the need for insurance. But, just as important as the decision to buy insurance is the need to analyse your requirements carefully so that you end up buying the right type and amount of cover. Many businesses find the help of an intermediary or broker invaluable when making these decisions. Others are happy to deal direct with insurance companies.

Dealing direct can have advantages. You avoid paying commission, and so may find your premiums cost less. But the big drawback is that you are probably not an insurance expert! So, without the right advice and support, you may not track down the best value and policy for your business, and end up paying more for your insurance than if you had used an intermediary. Commercial insurances are often more complex than personal policies, and often need to be tailored to the requirements of your business, with human resources given as high a priority as your property or equipment.

But, however you choose to buy your cover, please remember that your insurance needs are not fixed. Like your business, they will change from year to year. It is vital to review your requirements each time you renew your policy, and remember to bear in mind insurance whenever you make any changes to your operations. New equipment, an increase in staff numbers, changes to your premises or in the vehicles you use, could all have an impact on your insurance arrangements. You will not always need extra cover as a result of changes like these, but you should keep your insurance company informed about them, either directly or through your broker.

Whichever types of cover you choose, remember that there are two compulsory classes of insurance :

 Third Party Motor Insurance. By law you must insure your legal liability for injury to others, and damage to their property arising from the use of vehicles on the road. Most commercial motor policies would have more cover than this legal minimum: either third party, fire and theft, or comprehensive cover. If you own more than five vehicles you can arrange a fleet policy, with claims experience of your 'fleet' being the main factor upon which premiums will be based.

 Employer's Liability. Unless your employees are close relatives, you must insure yourself against any legal liability you may incur for their injury, disease or death, arising out of, or in the course of, their employment with you.

All other non-life insurances, with a few exceptions relating to very specific areas of business, are optional, and that is why it is so important to consider and plan your insurance arrangements carefully. Too little cover could close your business down. Too much is an unnecessary drain on your precious, and possibly limited, resources.

INSURANCE ADVICE FOR SMALL BUSINESSES

If you are in business you will need insurance; without it your livelihood is at risk. An unexpected loss could cause financial hardship and destroy years of hard work. By law, some types of insurance are compulsory.

Your insurance needs

Property

Buildings and contents can be insured against fire, lightning, explosion of gas and boilers used for domestic purposes; with or without the addition of 'special perils' such as explosion, riot, malicious damage, storm, flood, impact by aircraft, rail or road vehicles, escape of water from tanks or pipes and sprinkler damage.

'All risks' insurance gives wider cover including any accidental damage or loss not specifically excluded. However 'all risks' will not cover wear and tear, electrical or mechanical breakdown and gradual deterioration, which will be specifically stated in the policy document.

To what value should they be covered?

- **Buildings.** The business premises should be insured for their full rebuilding cost (including professional fees and the cost of clearing the site) and not the market value. You may need expert advice to calculate the rebuilding cost which often differs significantly from market value.

- **Contents.** Your stock should be insured for its cost price without any addition for profit. Provision can be made for seasonal fluctuations (Christmas or Easter). Plant and business equipment can be insured on either a 'replacement as new' or an 'indemnity' basis. If indemnity is chosen, wear and tear will be taken into account when settling any claims.

Engineering

Engineering insurance provides cover against electrical or mechanical breakdown for most machinery, including computers. By law, many items such as boilers, lifts and lifting machinery must be inspected regularly by a qualified person. Insurers can arrange to provide this service.

Theft

Contents are usually covered against theft providing there has been forcible and violent entry or exit from the premises. Damage to the building resulting from theft or attempted theft will also normally be covered. Theft by employees is usually not covered - cover against employee dishonesty can be arranged by a fidelity guarantee policy if required.

Money

Money insurance is on an 'all risk' basis and covers cash, cheques, postage stamps and certain negotiable documents.

Different limits will apply to money on the premises in and out of business hours, in safes, at homes of directors or employees and in transit. There may be requirements in the policy relating to the safe keys and the method of transit.

Personal assault cover may be included which will provide compensation for you or your employees following injury during theft or attempted theft of money.

Goods in transit

Goods in transit insurance covers goods against loss or damage while in your vehicle or when sent by carrier. The sum insured may be a limit for each vehicle or any one consignment.

Business interruption

Even minor damage to your property could seriously disrupt your business leading to loss of income and extra expenses.

Business interruption insurance will compensate for the shortfall in gross profit together with paying any increased working costs and extra accountant's fees incurred.

When arranging this insurance you will need to estimate the maximum time needed to get your business working normally following the most serious damage. The insurers will ask for an estimate of your anticipated gross profit. If an auditor later certifies an actual figure materially lower than this estimate a return of premium is normally given.

Motor vehicles

By law you must insure your legal liability for the injury to others and damage to their property arising from the use of vehicles on the road - third party insurance.

Most business policies are either comprehensive or third party, fire and theft. Comprehensive cover includes damage to your own vehicle. The third party section of a commercial vehicle policy is usually limited up to £1,000,000 - with private cars it is unlimited.

Your insurers will require full details of types of vehicle and their usage, details of goods and samples carried, details of drivers and, where applicable, the maximum number of fare-paying customers.
If you own more than five vehicles a fleet policy may be arranged. The claims experience of your fleet will be the main rating factor in assessing the cost of your policy.

Legal expenses

The cost of taking or defending legal action could place a considerable financial strain on your business. Legal expenses insurance covers legal costs such as solicitors' fees and expenses, the cost of barristers and expert witnesses, court cases and opponent's costs if awarded against you in civil cases.

Types of dispute normally covered include contractual and employment matters, for example claims for unfair dismissal, racial or sexual discrimination, the recovery of bad debts, and disputes with a landlord other than those relating to rent or service charge (particularly relevant for small businesses when dealing with a large corporation or local authority landlord).

The policy cover will also include the cost of employing specialist accountants and lawyers to protect your rights, for example if your business is subject to investigations on tax or VAT matters. Most policies will offer a confidential telephone legal advisory service to answer commercial legal enquiries.

Other risks

The following insurances may be provided under a 'package' business policy or separate individual policies can also be issued:

- Credit Insurance Cover against the risk of debtors becoming insolvent and unable to pay
- Book Debts Cover against loss of money arising from accidental damage or theft of books of account
- Fidelity Guarantee Cover against loss of money or stock arising from dishonesty by your employees
- Frozen Food Cover against loss of frozen food in deep freeze units caused by breakdown or damage to the unit or failure of the electricity supply
- Glass Cover for the replacement of glass following malicious or accidental damage
- Travel Insurance. Individual or group travel insurance policies can be arranged providing cover during business journeys abroad which includes medical and legal expenses, personal accident and loss of baggage
- Key Person insurance to protect your business on the death of a 'key' employee who has special skills or expertise on which your business relies

Your legal liabilities

Running your business creates considerable legal responsibilities towards your employees, the public and customers. Injury to your employees and members of the public could result in you being legally liable to pay damages if you or your employees have been negligent.

Liability insurance will pay the amounts of any court awards or damages, claimants' costs and expenses where you or your employees are held legally liable, subject to any policy limits.

The main liabilities that you face in business are:

Employers' Liability

By law, all employers must insure against their legal liability for injury, disease or death to employees sustained by them and arising from their employment.

Employees will normally include, in addition to those under a contract of employment, apprentices and other trainees and those hired from another employer. The only exception is where all your employees are close relatives and you should check if you think that this may apply to you.

You are legally required to insure for at least £2,000,000 but in practice most policies offer £10,000,000 liability. The law also requires that you exhibit a certificate of employers' liability insurance at each place of work.

Public Liability

Public liability insurance covers your legal liability to pay damages to members of the public for death, bodily injury or damage to their property which occurs as a result of your business activities. It also covers legal fees, costs and expenses such as representation at any coroner's inquest, fatal accident enquiry or other court hearing because of an accident.

When deciding on how much cover to buy, you should carefully consider the maximum claim that could be made against you. Awards for injury can exceed £1,000,000. Certain businesses, where there is a spreading fire risk or possibility of multiple personal injuries, could face claims for damages far exceeding this figure. The limit of indemnity will apply to claims arising from a single incident.

Motor Vehicle Liability

By law you must insure your legal liability arising from the use of vehicles on the road as described in the section earlier.

Product Liability

If you make, repair or sell products, you could be held legally liable for damage or injury arising from defects in their design or manufacture even if you have not been negligent. Product liability insurance covers you in these circumstances up to a maximum amount each year.

The Consumer Protection Act 1987 makes it a criminal offence to supply unsafe consumer goods.

Employee Benefits

You should not overlook the advantages of insurance in providing benefits to your employees. For example, group pension, private medical insurance and income protection schemes can be arranged. These not only benefit your employees (who increasingly are seeing these policies as a valuable part of the employment package) but can benefit your business by providing employees with 'peace of mind' and, in the case of medical insurance, help them return to work quickly if they need medical treatment.

Buying insurance

Having identified your insurance needs, how can you arrange cover? Package or combined policies are available to provide cover against many of the risks described in the previous section in a single policy document. These policies can be tailored to the requirements of your business. Some businesses may find individual policies more appropriate.

Insurance Companies

An insurance company may transact all kinds of insurance business or may specialise in certain types. Insurance companies may sell to the public direct or through insurance brokers, intermediaries or agents. Many companies have a network of branch offices from which quotations and advice can be obtained.

Lloyd's

Lloyd's is an insurance market where individuals join together to form syndicates and carry out insurance business. Lloyd's syndicates do not deal direct with the public and enquiries must be made through a Lloyd's broker.

Insurance Brokers

Insurance brokers and intermediaries are specialists offering advice and help in arranging insurance cover. They can advise on the types of cover your business should have and can arrange the insurance for yours. Your accountant may also be able to help in giving insurance advice.

Malcolm Tarling, Assistant Media Manager, Association of British Insurers

HEALTH AND SAFETY FOR SMALL BUSINESSES

Whatever the type of business, there is always the possibility of an accident or damage to someone's health. All work exposes people to hazards - manual handling of goods, dangerous machinery, toxic substances, electricity, working with display screen equipment, or psychological hazards such as stress.

The reason there are not even more accidents and diseases caused by work is that systems of prevention are in place which have been built up over many decades. Safety does not come about by accident: most accidents happen because they have not been prevented. Yet despite all the precautions that are taken in the UK, there are still 1.06 million workplace injuries every year as well as 2.1 million cases of ill health caused or increased by work. This costs Britain up to £16 billion per annum or nearly 3 per cent of our Gross Domestic Product.

Even small businesses have accidents

For example, if you are a small manufacturing company employing 25 people, you might have an accident leading to a reportable (over three day absence) accident about every other year - but, in the same period, you might have at least two significant injuries which required first aid, and over 120 potentially costly 'damage only' accidents.

Attention to health and safety is not just about being socially responsible. It also makes good business sense and you should regard it as just as important as any other key business objective. On the face of it there do seem to be a lot of regulations and there is a lot of supporting guidance, but the underlying principles are really quite straightforward.

Essentially you have to ensure absence of risk to safety and health of employees and others 'so far as is reasonably practicable':

 You have to have a system with people and procedures in place to manage health and safety. If you employ more than five people, you must set this out in a written health and safety policy statement

 You need to be able to show how you plan, organise, control, monitor and review preventative measures

 You need to appoint a competent person to help you to comply with your legal obligations

 You have to identify your main hazards, assess your risks and again, if you employ more than five, record the result of your assessment

 You have to make sure that your risk control measures are adequate and that they are used and maintained and they continue to work

You have to put in place any back-up measures that may be needed like health surveillance or emergency procedures

You also have to inform, train and supervise employees

The law sets out certain health and safety goals to be achieved and indicates appropriate benchmarks to help you work out whether your controls are up to 'reasonably practicable' standards. There is an underlying requirement to reduce or eliminate hazards at source, or isolate people from them, for example by guarding machinery, before using other forms of control. Relying on the use of personal protective equipment - like respirators or protective footwear - is a last resort and is only acceptable when all other options have failed. Besides goal setting duties, the law also sets down some 'must do's', e.g. having sanitary and welfare facilities, first aid provision, reporting and recording accidents, displaying the statutory HSE poster, and so on.

If all this is new to you, where do you start?

First of all, you need to get a good overview of the subject. Start with some basic reading such as HSE leaflets (you can get a menu on autofax by dialling 00839 06 06 06) or get hold of a copy of HSE's **'Essentials of Health and Safety at Work'** from HSE Books, Tel 01787 881165. Contact RoSPA (Tel 0121 248 2000) and consider going on a basic training course. You can also access much useful information, including guidance on hazards, on HSE's website [www.open.gov.uk/hse/hsehome.htm] or by telephoning HSE's Infoline on 0541 54500 (charged at national call rate). RoSPA can also help with its Health and Safety Review services for smaller businesses which can provide a comprehensive diagnosis of strengths and weaknesses in your management of health and safety. You might also consider becoming an 'occupation' member of RoSPA and joining a local RoSPA affiliated health and safety group.

Armed with this knowledge, try to answer the following questions: 'When it comes to health and safety, where are we now as a company? ' and 'Where do we want to be this time next year?'

 Start by looking at your firm's health and safety policy statement. It should be the basis of your firm's health and safety plan.

 Ask yourself whether you have an effective health and safety management system in place - in other words, a planned way of tackling problems.

 Have you got clear policies and objectives for health and safety? Have you organised key people to achieve them? What training do they need?

Are you monitoring progress - for example, by inspecting the workplace regularly or investigating accidents and 'near misses' - to learn from your mistakes?

Risk assessment is the key to working out what needs to be done - but don't make it over-complicated. Remember, although you have to do it by law, it is really only any use if it can be used as a working tool to help you understand how, when and to whom harm can occur, how bad it could be and whether your existing control measures are adequate or you need to do more, and also which are the biggest problems that you should be tackling first of all.

If you are the person in overall control of your business 'the buck stops with you', but you cannot achieve a safe and healthy working environment on your own. It has to be a team effort and you need to consult your employees and, where appointed, their safety representatives. You need to get proper health and safety coordination going with other businesses with which you come into contact such as clients, customers, suppliers or contractors. You need to build awareness of and commitment to safety throughout your workforce.

Above all, you need to remember that besides protecting people and the environment, action on health and safety can also make a major contribution to business success. Not only will it help stop accidents and work-related ill health among your staff, but it will reduce your accident losses, improve your profit and loss statement and help you become more efficient. If you think saftey is expensive, try having an accident!

Roger Bibbings, Occupational Safety Adviser, Royal Society for the Prevention of Accidents

COMPETITION LAW

Businesses ranging from the single trader to the largest corporate group are affected by UK Competition Law which changes dramatically with effect from 1st March 2000. UK Law is now broadly consistent with European Law in this area.

Statutory Control

UK Law now outlaws any agreements, business practices and conduct which have a damaging effect on competition in the United Kingdom. More specifically the legislation prohibits:

* Anti-competitive Agreements,
* The abuse by a dominant business of its position in the market.

Generally the prohibition on anti-competitive agreements only applies where the parties to an agreement enjoy a combined market share of 25% or more of the relevant market. However, new businesses should be aware that in some cases the competition authorities can take action irrespective of the size of the businesses concerned. So, for example, businesses found to have engaged in price fixing activity (see below) could be challenged, however small they may be. Also, niche products may find they fall under the scrutiny of the competition authorities even when the business itself may be small.

Examples of anti-competitive agreements include:

* price fixing (e.g. a company forces its distributors to resell its products at a set price)
* market sharing (e.g. a joint venture agreement between "competitors" who impose on each other non-compete clauses in different parts of their market place)
* discrimination (e.g. members of a trade association keep a newcomer out of their market)

Dominance of the market may be found to exist where a business has a market share of 40% or more.

Examples of abuse of a dominant position:

* predatory pricing (the dominant company offers its products for sale at artificially low prices to drive competitors out of business)
* refusal to supply goods or services where the motive of the supplier or the effect of its conduct is to limit the ability of third parties to compete with it
* tying customers to use ancillary products of the supplier where there is no real justification for taking away the customers' freedom of choice

The implications for breaching Competition Law are serious. There are wide powers of investigation. Officials can enter business premises and review documentation without notice. Third parties could claim damages for lost profits due to breach. Also the penalties can be severe and include fines of up to 30% of turnover (not profits) and suspension of offending activities.

Common Law Rules

Certain other Competition Law rules not embodied in statute can also have an impact on commercial dealings. This body of rules is known as the doctrine of restraint of trade. The most common applications of these rules are found in two situations. The first is where an employee accepts restrictions on future conduct on leaving employment. The second situation relates to the sale of businesses where the seller may agree to restrictions on its liberty to maintain a similar business in the future. In both of these situations contract terms are not enforceable unless the restraints protect a legitimate business interest and go no further than is necessary to protect that interest

Andrew Pickin, Shoosmiths

BUSINESS OWNERS - SOME FOOD FOR THOUGHT . . .

The age of owner-managers is spread from the 18-25 age group to the over 65s. Owner-managers aged between 41 to 60 years accounted for 61% of the total.

The survey showed that almost all small firms use external financial services. Less than one in two use external sub-contractors and nearly two-thirds use external legal services.

When asked from whom work is received we found that the distribution of customers for small firms is fairly even across small businesses (57.5%), medium sized businesses (56.3%), large businesses (53.8%), and the general public (57.5%).

Contacting customers and suppliers in the future

When asked about contacting customers and suppliers in the future it was interesting that over a third expected to use e-mail more in future to contact suppliers, and just under a third expected to use e-mail more in the future to contact customers. It was also significant that small firms are more conscious about face-to-face contact with customers than suppliers.

Method of contacting customers and suppliers in the future. The Personal Profile of a Potential Innovator

- **Aged between 36 to 60** - 14% of owner-managers questioned were aged between 36 to 40; 36% between 41 to 50 and 25% between 51 to 60. "Innovation" is seen as particularly important to owner-managers aged between 41 to 60.

- **Potentially work an average week of between 41 to 60 hours** (58% of the sample) with 15% working in excess of 71 hours.

- **Main motivation for starting up a business** for these owner-managers was the **financial incentive** and **being your own boss**, particularly among those respondents aged between 41 to 60. 50% of respondents identified ' being your own boss' as the most important factor in starting up a business, followed by 33% who viewed the financial incentives as most important.

- **Main motivation for being in business now remains the same** - financial incentives (30%) and being your own boss (27.5%). Interestingly, although 'building up a family business' was not seen as a particularly important consideration in starting up a business, it is the third most important factor for being in business now.

Extracts from Durham University Business School Small Business Research commissioned by Sage Group plc

In my experience . . .

As a young and very inexperienced Sales Engineer I was most anxious to broaden my knowledge and increase my personal efficiency. As a move towards this end I decided to practice the art of remembering names and facts by association of ideas.

I can remember sitting in the reception area of a large and very well known manufacturing company in the north of England waiting to be called to the office of the Chief Engineer, a gentleman I had met on one previous occasion, and then only briefly.

I was summoned to the inner sanctum and armed with my newly acquired expertise in remembering names I confidently strode into his office and with outstretched hand and announced "Good afternoon Mr Oldfield, I'm pleased to meet you again". "Oldacre" he retorted rather tersely "Yes!" I exclaimed, "I knew it was something to do with farming!!"

Syd Mathews, Partner, Precision 82

Administration, Production and Communication

Chapter Five

Finance, Book-keeping and Administration

The single most common cause of small business failure is poor financial controls. Owner-managers frequently leave all financial issues to their auditors to sort out at the year end, They have the mistaken belief that keeping the books is an activity quite divorced from the 'real' task of getting customers or making products.

By the time the first set of annual accounts are prepared many small firms are already too far down the road to financial failure to be saved. The final year-end accounts become all too final and yet another promising venture has been ruined by financial illiteracy.

Pacioli, the Venetian monk credited with devising the basics of modern accounting in 1493, said "Frequent accounting makes for long friendships". He could easily have made the same claim for the likely longevity of the business.

MANAGING YOUR BUSINESS RECORDS

A company needs constant financial management to ensure that it is maintaining its progress in its marketplace, staying within the margins set by its management and is generally heading in the direction laid down for the business. Without such control a company can drift off course into unprofitable work using slack costing procedures, materials that are too expensive, taking too long to produce goods, not delivering on time, failing to collect its money on time and a variety of other commercial crimes.

A well run company will have available to its senior management on a regular and timely basis, accurate and realistic financial information that helps the management in controlling the business and making decisions for the future. The word 'timely' is possibly the most important aspect of this and it is vital to the well being of the business that the records are written up regularly and kept up to date. No business should be making decisions based on information that is several months old.

How much information to produce is a very important question, because too much information, or produced too often, can be worse than too little information. Too much information can be difficult to take in; figures produced too often have a tendency to be ignored. Each business needs to decide exactly what information it requires and how often this is to be done. It must also, importantly, decide to whom it should be distributed.

The amount of reporting may also change throughout a year, particularly with a seasonal business. This may also vary between divisions in a business where different products or services are involved, as the requirements of these differing types of business may indicate that different levels of financial information are necessary.

Cash book

The company's cash book does not, as the name suggests, record only cash transactions. The cash book normally records a company's bank transactions principally, but may also record some aspects of cash dealings. It can consist of a separate book for each bank account, particularly where the accounts are used for specific purposes, or it can be designed to record several accounts in a columnar form.

It will record the amounts received by the company, showing the date, the customer or other party paying, the amount received, and some details of the reason for the payment (sales, insurance claim, refund, loan etc.). It also records, for example, into which bank account the monies are deposited.

By accumulating totals of these types of receipt to provide a total of sales invoices paid, the company can keep a track of its outstanding debtors and other aspects of its bankings. The receipts record is written up from the paying-in book and also picking up details of transfers, direct credits etc. from the bank statements.

The cash book will also record the payments made, showing in a similar sort of way, the date of payment, the payee, the type of payment (cheque, standing order, direct debit, cash), the cheque number or reference, the amount of the payment, and some description of the payment. One payment may cover a number of items - for example an automated bank payment to a number of suppliers - and the cash book must record sufficient detail to enable the company's records to be completed. It is important to know which suppliers are being paid and how much is paid to each.

The cash book (payments) is written up from the cheque stubs of the company and also details of standing orders, direct debits, transfers and bank charges etc. These latter items will be picked up from the bank statements.

Information on bank payments is also recorded by the bank, so could be reconstructed from their records if the company's records were to be destroyed. Some records are not duplicated in this sort of way, and cash payment records in particular would not be recorded by anyone outside the company. It is important, therefore, that records are maintained in sufficient detail and with adequate security or copies made for back-up purposes.

A cash book may also record an analysis of types of expenditure such as purchases, wages and salaries, office costs, hire purchase payments and rent and rates in as much analysis as is useful for the business.

This is the sort of information that can be very useful in preparing regular management information.

Using computer systems to do this can ensure that the records are arithmetically accurate and that the analysis is complete. This makes the analysis much easier to maintain and more flexible to changing business situations.

Perhaps the most important figure in the cash book is the balance (in hand or overdrawn). This is produced by finding the difference between the total receipts and the total payments. (The balance must be brought forward to each month - an amount in hand is brought forward as a receipt, an overdraft is brought forward as a payment.) The balance should be calculated on a regular basis and, in many businesses, a running record is kept of the balance to assist in managing the cash resources of the business.

Example - Bank cash book

		1	2	3	4
Date	Details	Total	Credit Sales	Cash Sales	Other Receipts
		£	£	£	£
03-05-98	Cheques	22494.50	22494.50		
	Cash	1825.00		1825.00	
04-05-98	VAT Refund	1569.00			1569.00
	Cheques	18947.00	18947.00		
05-05-98	Cash	1898.00		1898.00	
06-05-98	Cheques and Cash	9524.00	8273.00	1251.00	
	Insurance Claim	4725.00			4725.00

'Total' records the amounts to be paid into the bank while columns 2 to 4 break this down so that totals of each type are easily available at the end of the month. (The total on each line, or each page, of column 1 must equal the sum of the equivalent totals in columns 2,3 and 4.) The records can show separate bankings for cheques and cash (as on May 3rd and 4th) or a total banking covering both (as on 6th May).

Any items not relating to sales would be analysed into column 4 with sufficient information shown either in the 'detail' column or in an additional column (say between 3 and 4).

Example - Payments

Again 'Total' records the full amount being paid out, whether by cheque, standing order, direct debit or other type of bank payment.

Date	Payee	Cheque No.	Total	Purchases	Wages / Salaries	PAYE NIC	Standing Orders	Cash	Other Payments
			1	**2**	**3**	**4**	**5**	**6**	**7**
03-05-98	Material Supplies Ltd	421.00	4,530.00	4,530.00					
	AB Carriers	422.00	527.80	527.80					
	Salaries	BACS	12,473.40		12,473.40				
04-05-98	Hire Purchase	SO	537.00				537.00		
	Cash	423.00	200.00					200.00	
	HM Customs & Excise	424.00	5,101.00						5,101.00
05-05-98	Insurance	SO	441.00				441.00		
	CD Leasing	DD	587.50	587.50					
	Inland Revenue	425.00	6,201.25			6,201.25			
	Transfer to Deposit Account	Tfr	15,000.00						15,000.00

The amount in 'Purchases' should relate to payments only for those items whose invoices are recorded in the purchase day book. (These are principally those items subject to VAT, whether they are purchases of materials, goods for resale, or services and suppliers.) This should include any lease payments, for example, or other items where VAT is involved.

'Wages/Salaries' and 'PAYE/NIC' record payments for those items only - net wages paid and total paid to the Inland Revenue respectively.

'Standing Orders' should be used to record those regular bank payments which do not involve VAT. These can include hire purchase, insurance, rates etc.

'Cash' records the amount of cash drawn out of the bank - not the amount of cash spent.

'Other' relates to items not falling into the specific columns, and again should show sufficient information in either the 'Payee' column or in an extra column of narrative.

Purchase day book

The purchase day book records the cost of goods purchased by the business.

The book should provide the basic information of date of invoice, invoice number, supplier, type of goods or services, cost of goods etc., VAT amount, total amount. It can also show a reference to an order number, which will help in checking back to other records.

The analysis provided by this record should be designed with a view to any departmental analysis required by the business, or the analysis between types of product supplied by the company.

The record should ideally be created to record purchases in date order, although this is not essential. However, a company will normally want monthly totals of the various types of purchases, so it is important that the invoices are entered in the correct month, even if not exactly in the completely correct time order.

The types of analysis will depend on the nature of the business and could include, for example:

Materials, goods for resale, packaging, transport costs, delivery, contract costs, printing and stationery, telephone, advertising, promotion costs, insurance, leasing, repairs.

The monthly totals of these costs can be used by the managers of a business to provide a very quick glance at the direction the business is taking. However, they should obviously bear in mind that the cost of materials for production will be affected by changes in the levels of stocks held by the company. A low monthly figure may not mean the business is more efficient in production - it may just mean that stocks are going down at the same time. However, it can be a useful first indication of problems.

The purchase day book is also the starting point for preparing the purchase ledger, which records the amounts owed to each supplier. This is achieved by recording, on a page for each supplier, the invoices received for goods or services on one side and the payments made to suppliers on the other. The difference between these two totals is the amount still outstanding. (Credit notes and purchase refunds also need to be included, where appropriate.)

Example - Purchase day book

Date	Supplier	Invoice Number	Total	VAT	Goods	Materials	Telephone	Printing	Repairs	Rent	Advertising

The columns should be chosen to reflect those items recurring often enough to warrant a separate column. A 'miscellaneous' column should include other items.

Sales day book

The sales day book records each sale invoiced by the business, preferably in the order that each sale is invoiced to make it easier to check back through the records and to extract daily, weekly or monthly totals for managers.

The book also records the date, the customer, invoice number, selling price of the goods, VAT amount and total amount of the invoice. It may also record details of the type of goods sold or the department raising the invoice. This enables departmental sales figures to be collated or totals of different types of goods, depending on how the book is set up.

A business survives on its sales, and a regular knowledge of the amounts sold is vital to the managers controlling the business. They must have a budget figure for sales per day/week/month against which to chart their actual progress. With no budget they are in uncharted territory and have no insight into how much they need to sell in order to survive, break even or make a profit.

The sales day book is used as the starting point for preparing the sales ledger, recording the amount owed by each customer. This is very similar in nature to the purchase ledger.

The sales day book's other use is as a prime source of information for completion of the 'output' side of the business's VAT returns. For this reason it is one of the prime records that will be scrutinised on an inspection by Customs and Excise.

As with the other record books described, the sales day book must be written up regularly, completely and on a timely basis in order to be of any use. Whether the name derives from 'a book to record the day's sales' or 'a book of sales to be written up every day' may be open to debate, but the first shows the information produced when the second occurs.

Example - Sales day book

Date	Customer	Invoice Number	VAT	Total	Sales Type 1	Sales Type 2

Sales types are set to identify the categories relevant to the particular business.

Petty cash book

The petty cash book is used to record cash expenditure, usually quite small amounts on items such as postage, stationery, office sundries such as tea and milk, travelling costs etc.

The book can be set out in a similar form to the payments section of the cash book, with columns for date, details, voucher number, total, VAT element, and analysis columns headed for the various types of expenditure.

The petty cash book will also record the amount of cash drawn from the bank to pay for this expenditure, and by comparing the amount drawn with the amount spent, the amount 'in hand' shown by the records can be calculated. This should be compared with the actual cash 'in the tin' on a regular basis, or by spot checks.

Example - Petty cash book

Date	Details	Voucher Number	Total	VAT	Stationery	Travelling

As with purchases and sales, the headings will depend on which items are regularly paid in cash.

Bank reconciliation

The bank reconciliation is the means of ensuring that the company's bank records are complete and accurate by comparing them with the bank's records of its dealings with the company.

The process is to start with the balance as shown on the bank statement at a particular date and to account for items which have not yet 'hit' the bank account, to eventually come back to the figure shown as the bank balance in the cash book.

Start with the bank balance, add on any bankings up to date which have not yet appeared on the statement and deduct any cheques sent out which have not yet gone through the account.

This assumes that all 'direct' bank payments and receipts have been completely recorded in the cash book. Reconciling the bank statement often highlights items of this type that still need to be entered in the cash book.

Example:

Balance per bank statement		£11,720.42
Add:Uncredited bankings	£4274.33	
	1049.12	5323.45
		17,043.87
Unpresented cheques:	1000.00	
	2435.03	
	427.50	
	342.40	
	70.50	
	1250.00	
	443.26	5968.69
		£11,075.18
Cash Book: Receipts	147,574.21	
Payments	136,499.03	
	£11,075.18	

All the books described can be kept in a variety of different formats, depending on the individual preference of the people using the records. They can be in the form of bound book, pre-printed with column headings, or blank columns for more flexible use. They can be in loose leaf form to be even more flexible, and enable one period to be removed once completed. (The auditors can have the relevant period without holding up the current period's record keeping.) If a loose leaf system is used it is important that pages are not lost or mislaid, and that pages 'borrowed' or extracted are replaced.

P J Sudell, Turnbulls Chartered Accountants, member of the UK 200 Group

USING YOUR FINANCIAL INFORMATION

No-one sets off on an important journey through a new area, unknown to them, without some sort of guide or map. So it is with a business starting off - it should have a clear plan of its way ahead from various aspects, including financial, production, marketing as well as others.

The financial plans should be set out in a way that enables the progress to be monitored easily and effectively. The plans should take into account any known fluctuations - seasonal or other - in expected turnover and also fluctuations in costs, particularly where prices are dependent on predictable variations.

The plan should be set up to cover a sequence of regular periods, normally a month (or in some cases, a week) and must be framed simply enough to make the figures easily accessible. The overall length of the plan will probably be a year in monthly segments and then perhaps four further years in annual figures. A business may also need to monitor separate departments or branches, or individual product lines, and this must also be built into budget plans.

To be able to compare the actual results with the plans, regular management accounts are needed, and must be prepared promptly after each period to make any comparison with budget worthwhile. To go back to the map metaphor, it is little use finding that you took the wrong turn three miles ago. It is far more effective to compare the route and the road as you go! It is also important that someone has the task of navigator and checks progress against the budget on a regular basis.

Specific items to be considered in making the comparisons are:

 Turnover

 Cost of sales and margin

 Main overheads - wages, property costs, distribution, finance costs etc.

The same eventual budgeted profit can be achieved by a much higher turnover at a lower margin, but wouldn't it be useful to know whether that lower margin could be improved without reducing turnover? This could have an enormous upward effect on the profit! This is where computers can be useful - in testing the "what ifs" of the budget.

Management reports may need to cover other aspects as well as accounts - for example, the number of production hours achieved, or days lost through machine breakdown, or details of types of stock held to ensure that production can continue.

The other matters included will vary quite significantly from business to business and need to be specific not only to the type of trade but also to the management, the geographical area and other aspects. Management reports must be easily readable and understandable, and trends through the year are a useful extra piece of information. If they are not easy to read, they will be ignored and that is worse than not having reports in the first place. Trends can be shown graphically as well as in tables of figures, and this style is probably easier to grasp, with quite sufficient accuracy for decision-making. Graphs, pie charts and bar charts can also make the whole report look more interesting!

The management accounts should be set out in broadly the same format as the annual accounts so that like is being compared with like from previous years. Management reports should be available to all senior management to show the company's progress, so that they can take corrective action as soon as necessary and can plan further developments and progress in the light of the company's achievements. The reports may also be distributed selectively to other department supervisors so that they are aware of their own section's results and, again, of any problems that need attention.

Reports should be prepared and distributed on a regular basis - usually monthly - but it may be beneficial to do fuller reports less frequently - every quarter for example. Abbreviated reports for shorter periods - e.g. weekly - could highlight a specified brief list of topics such as turnover, stock levels, debtors, cash collection and orders in hand.

In reviewing the management reports, there will always be discussion about various means of maximising profits. Increasing turnover is always an option, but it may be difficult to achieve in a restrictive market. Cuts in overhead costs or cost of sales can also increase profit. And while a cut of £1000 in overheads or costs goes straight to the bottom line, an increase of £1000 in sales may only add £200 to the profit. These are difficult decisions. There is a limit to how much cost cutting can be done before efficiency suffers, and increased sales may involve higher marketing or promotion expenses so that the effort may have very little impact on short term profit.

Overall, a new business may well be compared to a minefield, with numerous traps and hidden pitfalls for the unwary, but success can be achieved with a good map and plan for the progress of the business, updated regularly for the changing situations the business encounters and the developing markets in which it is working. Don't let this put you off trying!

Paul J Sudell, Turnbulls, Chartered Accountants - Member of the UK 200 Group

COMPUTERISING YOUR ACCOUNTS

Every business needs to keep accounts and records of its finances. Computerising your accounts system will make keeping the books much easier, give your business a more professional image, improve your efficiency, and give you timely access to accurate information that would take hours to extract from manual records.

Everyone sets out on their quest to find an accounts system for their business with the very best intentions but often with only a sketchy idea of what these systems are capable of doing. All too often, a system is selected and installed before anyone realises that it does not have enough functionality, or is inflexible and unable to grow with the business.

Reasons for computerising

There are many different reasons for putting your accounts system onto a computer. Routine tasks such as filling in the VAT returns take minutes instead of days, statements and other regular correspondence can be mail-merged and personalised and up-to-date balances included. If your business is growing, a computerised accounting system will make life much easier when you take on new staff, when you increase your spending and when you have more invoices to chase.

A computerised system does all of the hard work associated with routine tasks for you. It ensures that VAT returns are accurate and fully reconciled, that invoices are not missed out of the return at the end of the business period and figures are not transposed.

Furthermore, the clearly presented, accurate invoices and statements the accounts system produces can only enhance the reputation of your business, making it look more professional to your suppliers, to your bankers and accountants, and to your customers.

Further to this, once the information is recorded it can be used to give you a snapshot of the business performance at any time by running out a Trial Balance and Profit and Loss statement.

Although what lies behind the system is basically a traditional double-entry book-keeping system, the difference is that only one entry is needed for the entire system to be updated. The accounts system is thus a powerful aid to decision-making.

Keeping the money coming in

Everyone in business understands the importance of chasing up outstanding bills and getting them paid. But few companies take steps to ensure that their customers will be capable and willing to pay once the goods or services have been supplied. Debt chasing and credit checking are particularly important if you are dealing with a large number of new customers on a regular basis but can be time-consuming and difficult.

With a computerised accounts system, invoices will always be accurate. And will be printed in a clear, easy-to-read format. Statements can be issued regularly and they will always be up-to-date. You'll be able to print out a list of debtors whenever you want to and see at a glance which invoices are outstanding for 30 days, 60 days, and 90 days or more. If it looks as though a bill may not be paid, you can spot it earlier then take whatever action you deem necessary.

Most accounting packages can also produce debt-chasing letters for you if bills remain unpaid for a certain period of time. The accounting software will prepare a letter for any debt that needs to be chased, automatically inserting the customer details, the amount overdue, and the length of time outstanding.

Dealing with the VAT man

As you use the system - as you post invoices or purchase orders - the software automatically records how much VAT you've charged on your sales, and how much VAT you've paid on your order. The system will know if anything is exempt or can't be reclaimed under Customs and Excise rules. It will know when the return is due and, when the time comes, it will calculate and print the VAT return for you.

If you are exporting products to EC countries or importing supplies from the EC, some accounting software will also calculate and print out the Intrastat report you are required to submit. And it's not just big businesses with hundreds or thousands of transactions every quarter that can benefit. Most systems can deal with cash accounting so even small businesses can save just as much time and effort.

If the VAT man ever has any queries the computer system will allow you to check into the books and give you a list of any relevant invoices or purchase orders, so any mistakes or queries can be identified immediately.

Finding the right stock level

Many businesses are chiefly concerned with the buying and selling of products, and for those that are, it is vital to know which products are selling faster and which slower, which are profitable and which not, or when stock levels need replenishing. Keeping tabs on what you buy and what you sell, what you paid and will be paid for those products is also critical in calculating how much working capital you will need to employ and in managing cash flow.

Perhaps even more critical to trading businesses, is the need to find out quickly if too much stock is hanging around for too long. Having cash tied up in stock that is not moving is bad news. It is vital that any business dependent on keeping its stock moving can identify slow moving lines easily.

The computerised accounts system with an integrated stock control module can help you do this by keeping track of exactly how much stock you have in your warehouse, when it came in, how much it cost, what its present value is and how much money in total it is tying up. Detailed reports on stock movements can, in time, give you a clear picture of trends in stock movements enabling you to plan ahead, place and call off orders in a timely fashion, and make optimum use of the capital available.

In my experience . . .

I had just started my own business. I had done it on a shoestring and finances were tight so I decided to do my own accounts to save money. Over the next four years the business expanded and I had been sending my accounts to the Revenue on time, paying what I thought was the right amount of tax. In my fifth year of trading I decided to buy the house that I was living in and had been renting. I applied for a mortgage and was promptly turned down. I applied to a second lender and the same happened again.

When I finally got to the bottom of what was happening it turned out that I had failed to pay the right amount of tax to the Revenue and I had a County Court judgement outstanding against me. This had happened because I was doing the accounts - a job I was clearly not suited to.

- Get an accountant as soon as you start your business
- Make sure the Revenue comes first on your list of creditors
- Do what you are good at - not what you think you are good at

Geoff Andrews

Checking on profitability

One of the most obvious advantages of a computerised accounts system is its ability to show you if you are profitable or not at any time. Because you enter all your overheads, purchases and sales onto the system, as long as it is up to date, it can produce accurate Trial Balance and Profit and Loss statements at any time.

In addition to these key indicators, with many accounting systems it is also possible to produce simple management reports that your accountant would probably have had to calculate and present to you otherwise.

Providing information for management

The accounting system is the heart of any business operation and, by linking it up with other business applications such as spreadsheets, databases and contact management systems, your computerised accounts system can become the focal point of your IT system, using the same set of data, customer and supplies information to run not only your accounts system, but also your office administration and sales and marketing operations.

It is very easy in most systems to compare, for example, actual figures against those budgeted over a year, month, or even a week - or over a series of products, branches or cost centres. You can see how different product lines, regions, even individual salespeople are performing. You can examine, in fine detail, where you spend your money as well as where you make it. If there are any weak spots in your system, you can identify them at an early stage and take steps to put them right. Subsequently, you can use the information to ensure that the measures you have taken are having the desired effect.

Much of this information can be made available through reports printed directly from the accounting package but it is also possible with many systems to read the information into a spreadsheet where it can be manipulated in any number of ways or included in cash flow forecasts, budget projections and other managerial reports.

With this information at its fingertips, management will be in a much better position to make strategic decisions about the employment of capital, purchasing, pricing and sales strategy.

Looking after your suppliers

Just as you might expect the customers who value your services to pay you within a reasonable time frame, you will want to pay those businesses and individuals that supply products to you on a timely basis. You will also want to be fair and consistent about payment, and keep careful control on the outflow of funds from the business.

If you buy many different products or services from one particular supplier, you will be able to see the total amount owed to that supplier and, when suppliers ring up chasing bills, you will be able to access the information immediately and give them an accurate idea of when an invoice is likely to be cleared.

Keeping tabs on orders

If you are in any business that does not always supply the products or service as soon as the order is placed, you need some way of managing orders. Once the order is placed, the onus is normally on the supplier to come up with the goods when they are required and you'll need some way of checking how an order is progressing. If you are waiting for new stock to arrive, you will be able to find out when the goods are expected and, with this information stored, you should be able to tell how long it will take to do the work and fulfil the order. You may also be able to send out acknowledgements of orders. This not only looks professional, but also ensures that the customer is clear about what has been ordered and corrects mistakes before a lot of time and money is wasted.

When you use the order processing part of an accounting software package, you start to appreciate the usefulness of having the whole system integrated. Not only does the system help you keep track of orders, it also makes sure that you are in a position to fulfil them as quickly as possible. If component stock levels are getting low, the system will tell you and once a delivery has been made, the information can be passed on from order processing to sales invoicing and an accurate bill produced and sent to the customer right away.

Streamlining the year end audit

Subject to turnover, at the end of every financial year, your accountant will need to audit your records and, with a manual system, this can take a long time. Not only is it an expensive exercise for you, it is probably one job most accountants could do without.

If you have a computerised system, the year-end audit is made much simpler for you and your accountant. In fact, with some accounting software, you can do much of the work for the accountant before he sets foot on your premises. You can, for example, produce reports which all auditors will require, such as the trial balance. Some packages have utilities which enable the auditor to run random checks on the transactions and postings and some have facilities for the pre-production of debtors' confirmation letters. Auditors will normally send those out to debtors to check that the transaction did take place.

In this way, the auditor's life is made much simpler and, hopefully, it will take less time to conduct the audit, your personnel will be free to carry on with their work sooner, there will be a smaller fee for you to pay and, if you require it, your accountant can get on with some work that will benefit the business further.

Administering Payroll, Tax and National Insurance

For many companies, administering a payroll and National Insurance contributions can be a nightmare but using a computerised system can save immense amounts of time and effort.

The tables, forms and numerous documents normally used to calculate and keep track of the payroll can all be discarded and the headaches and heartaches of calculating the figures and keeping everything up to date become a thing of the past. An automated payroll system will calculate wages, tax and National Insurance as well as printing the payslips for you. It will deal with year-end procedures producing P11, P14 and P60 forms as required. It will calculate Statutory Sick Pay, make arrangements for holiday pay and maternity allowances, calculate the National Insurance due on car and fuel benefits, and much more.

The payroll software is usually provided separately from the accounts software but in some systems the two can be linked. If you have any doubts about using a computerised accounts system, you should not allow yourself to be put off the idea of using an automated payroll. The benefits are enormous.

Having said that, systems that can be integrated with accounting ledgers are very useful indeed, because the adjustments in payments being made to staff will be transferred to the accounting ledgers automatically. This means that it won't be necessary to re-enter any information into the ledgers, saving time all round.

Deciding which system to buy

The purchasing decision should be made with great care because you will effectively be running your business on the accounting system.

These days, some 'packaged' accounting software can be tailored to suit your business. For a while, it was true that most products you simply bought off the shelf and apart from a few parameters it was not possible to adjust the way the system worked to suit the way you do business. It was either that or, at massive expense, have a system entirely designed from scratch. Today, many best-selling products can be configured to match the way you do business already.

The price of accounting software can be used as a very rough guide to the flexibility of a system. The lowest cost products (some of the basic book-keeping packages now only cost around £99) are very simple, but inflexible. In products that cost between £200 and £500, you may be able to adjust some of the screens and data fields, and for most businesses this will provide an adequate degree of flexibility. All accounting systems conform to the fundamental rules of double entry book-keeping.

Companies with specific requirements often find that a standard package meets 80 per cent of their requirements, but simply can't cope without that other crucial 20 per cent. If you find this is the case with your business, don't worry, you are not alone and there are plenty of experienced dealers and systems houses out there who will be trying to address your exact needs. Indeed, they may have already written some software that is geared to specific vertical markets and comes somewhere close to meeting your needs while integrating with a standard accounting system.

Whatever your particular needs, you will still need the control that the core accounting system gives you and if the additional functionality can be tailored to fit and then integrated with the central system, you will have the complete system that meets your every requirement, as well as those of your accountants, the Inland Revenue and Customs and Excise.

Planning for the future

Hopefully, your business will continue to grow over the coming years. An accounting system will help you cope with that growth but you must take care to choose a system that is capable of growing with you for some time because the pain of changing it later, while you are still growing, will be considerable.

It is tempting (particularly if you are a smaller business, trying to keep a tight rein on overheads) to go for a good, simple and inexpensive option. But while such a package might suit your purpose in the short term, when you start dealing with two or three times as many customers and start taking on more staff, the limitations of the package will soon reveal themselves.

Of course, it is hard to envisage what might happen and difficult to justify the expenditure required to buy a system that is powerful and flexible enough to meet needs that you might have in the future. You simply don't know yet what those needs will be.

But if you can't invest in a bigger system than you can afford right away, you can guard against outgrowing the system by purchasing a product that can be upgraded easily. In other words, buy your entry-level system from a company that can demonstrate a clear and established upgrade path to a bigger, more flexible and powerful accounting software package.

The software houses that supply more than one package will always make sure that it is possible for you to upgrade from one version of their software to another. But do ensure that you can take your data with you when you upgrade to a more comprehensive accounts system. Otherwise you will have to use a lot of time and effort re-keying data and setting up control accounts.

Selecting a supplier

The person or company that supplies the system will play as big a part in its success as the system itself. It needs to be someone that will supply a complete solution for your business, not just one part of the system.

Unless you are buying the most basic of packages, the accounting system you choose will have a profound effect on the way your business is run and, potentially, on the way it is managed. By working with an experienced supplier of business accounting solutions, you can make virtually certain that you will get it right first time. A good dealer will also carry the authorisation of well established accounting software vendors and have plenty of other customers already using their products.

It is usually best to try to buy the entire solution - the PC or system unit, printer, accounting and any other software, from a single source. That way, you will always know where to turn when advice or help is needed.

Choosing products from a well established manufacturer and, buying your system from a reliable, respected and professional reseller, should help you make your computerised accounting system a real success.

Do's and don'ts

Don't

Walk into a shop or dealership and buy the cheapest thing on offer. Remember, it is not the PC that does the real work, it is the software and if you buy a system that is not suited to your business it could cost you a lot of time, effort and money later on.

Do

Define what it is that you need your accounting software package to do. Do you want to run your whole system on it or just do some sales invoicing? Will you need to automate just the main ledgers or would you like to put sales order processing, purchase order processing and stock control onto the computer? Do you have any special procedures or requirements you must stick to, whatever the system? Do you need an integrated payroll system and will you want to extract management information for the use in decision-making? Only when you have answered these questions can you begin your search in earnest.

Start to collect some information on accounting software products and PCs and read some of the reviews published in computer magazines.

Talk to your accountant, who may be able to advise you about some packages. Information may also be available from professional bodies such as the Institute of Chartered Accountants.

Graham Parker, Customer Services Director, Sagesoft Ltd.

Anyone who does not computerise their accounts from the outset of launching a new business should ask themselves why they have taken such a short-sighted decision. Once your accounts are on the computer, not only will you have timely information but you will be able to analyse your figures in ways that are impossible on manual systems. In seconds you can see, for example, how many orders of £1000 and more you have received in the four weeks since you introduced that special discount scheme. Or how often and when a particular customer buys from you, and how much they spend. You can see average weekly sales at the push of a button (or two) and see how those compare with last week, month or year. In that way you can spot trends and seasonal patterns at a glance, which is invaluable both for analysis and as an aid to planning ahead.

In my experience . . .

Some Useful Business Jargon - With Translations

The cheque is in the post	You can whistle for it
To be completely honest. . .	I'm going to lie through my teeth
Never in a million years. . .	Not since the last time
He's an old mate and I just want a favour. . .	I saw his name in the paper and I'm just trying it on

Eddie Hoare, Elegant Days

Production

The average small business struggles hard to make eight or ten percentage points of profit. The other ninety per cent or so is consumed in costs of one sort or another. The purpose of production is to ensure that customers get what they want when they want it, but using the least amount of labour and material, bought at the keenest prices possible in the process. Neither should so much material be held or processed so as to fill up warehouses, which have to be paid for in their own turn and the stock within them financed. Many small firms could double their profits on the same amount of sales if the 'production' process were better managed.

PLANNING PRODUCTION

Production budgets

Yearly production budgets are based on the quantities in the sales budgets managers believe customers will buy.

They are affected by:

- The quantities of product it is economical to make
- Seasonal patterns of demand
- Production capacity

It is important to make sure that:

- Sales budgets only include what can be made
- Production budgets do not include what cannot be sold

Production schedules

What is actually made cannot be governed by the yearly budget. Each month, or each week, what is to be made must be planned, based on actual sales orders or the most recent estimate of what can be sold.

Economic quantities

Production planning is affected by:

- Economic batch sizes based on the trade-off between plant set-up costs and stock holding costs
- Economic order quantities which bring together delivery lead times, quantity discounts and stock holding costs

Both increase stock holdings, often at considerable cost, resulting in a risk of obsolescence and customer dissatisfaction.

Where possible, production and purchasing should move to just-in-time approaches where only what is needed is manufactured or bought. In such cases, the quantity to include in the production budget is what the customer is expected to want - the monthly sales budget quantities - so that stock levels are kept to a minimum.

Seasonal patterns

In many trades demand is not constant over the year. To even out production the business builds up stocks in advance of demand. This affects production budgets and schedules, budgets for stocks and cash flow forecasts.

Production capacity

Capacity is represented by different kinds of people and plant. These, or a section of them, can form a bottleneck, limiting the quantity that can be made.

Even though demand may be high, the production budget can only include what can be made, not what can be sold. The best way to set production quantities is to focus on those products that offer the highest contributions. The choice then is either to allow those production figures to constrain the sales budget or to take steps to remove the limitations. This means increasing capacity to obtain more of the scarce resource by:

- Employing more workers with the skills required
- Training the lower skilled people

- Expanding the hours existing plant is available by instituting shift working
- Contracting out part of production to other manufacturers
- Investing in more plant

All these options have costs and risks which must be set against the profit contribution lost by capacity being below demand.

Cash

From all the budgets, including the production budget, a forecast of how much cash will be needed month by month must be made. This gives early warning of the need to seek additional funds.

The routine of producing cash flow forecasts should not be just a once-a-year exercise. It must be repeated regularly, using the most recent estimates, including the production schedules and the costs and stocks they create.

Jake Claret, Deputy Secretary, The Chartered Institute of Management Accountants

SELECTING AND WORKING WITH SUPPLIERS

Anyone in business who believes that a supplier is a company or individual to be screwed into the ground is on a hiding to nothing. In this day and age a supplier needs to be considered as a partner in your business. Anything short of this means that you are not making the most of your opportunities.

You may not want to believe me, so let me quote you from David Brown, Chairman of Motorola UK, who says "Motorola treats its suppliers as part of its extended family. If we are prepared to train our own staff, we should and we do extend that training where required to our suppliers."

He said this in the presence of the Minister for Small Businesses, Mrs Barbara Roche. She questioned his motives and he replied "Of course, while the sentiments are right, it is also right for the bottom line."

So there you have it - if you want a successful business you must be sure to select your suppliers well and deal with them properly.

How to select a supplier

Contrary to popular belief there are a lot of suppliers who choose themselves. And what is more these account for a fairly large percentage of your outgoings. For all utilities - gas, water, electricity, telephone - you will probably find only one source of supply. The best advice here is to meet them in your office, be absolutely sure you get on the right tariff and be even more sure that you pay by the cheapest route - whether that be direct debit or even up front.

The second category of suppliers are those for one-off purchases or capital items - the office furniture, the computer system, the cars. They are very different from utility suppliers. In this case you know precisely what you want and there is a multiplicity of suppliers - not forgetting that many of these items can be bought second-hand. This is when it is really worth shopping around. Before spending money it is only sensible to take advice to ensure that you are selecting the product that best meets your needs at a price that best meets your budget. To help you in this, at the one end of the spectrum are the "Which" type magazines and at the other the expensive consultant. If you do use the expensive consultant, do try wherever possible to pay on a results basis.

The next issue is often the most difficult. You will find that you spend a disproportionate amount of your budget on a myriad of small items - pencils, photocopying paper, general stationery and so on. It is tempting to leave these purchases to an office junior - but don't! Calculate how much money you are spending, group the items together and go to a local supplier, who will probably be an owner-managed business of your size. Draw up a contract with a promise from the supplier that he will sell to you at prices cheaper than you could buy anywhere else, on the understanding that you will buy all these products from him alone.

I have saved the most important suppliers to last. These are the people that make a significant contribution to your product or service. For the central heating installer this is probably the central heating boiler or the control system, for the furniture maker it will be the supplier of timber, and so on. Your customers will probably judge you as much on the quality of these key suppliers as on the work you do for them, so choose them very, very carefully. Be more concerned about quality than price. Be more concerned about continuity of supply and delivery than price.

Now we come to the general round-up. Assuming you are in business and have been for some time profitably, visit your key suppliers and ask them two simple questions: (1) Are my orders profitable work for you? And (2) What percentage of your total turnover is made up by my orders? It may take a few visits to get to the truth but it really is worthwhile to know these things. If your work is not profitable to your supplier he will not be looking to research and find better products and services for you - neither will he be in business very long. Also, if you make up too large a percentage of your supplier's order book you are vulnerable to his success or failure. You will be amazed the effect it has simply to ask these questions and the improvement in performance that can be generated simply by treating your supplier as a partner in your business.

Lastly, in all of your purchasing decisions it is essential to realise that price is not the only, nor the paramount consideration. Quality, certainty of supply, actual delivery dates and terms of payment may all be more important than price at different times. You may consider that you have made an excellent deal by cutting the price to the bone, only to discover that you are your supplier's worst (least profitable) customer and are dealt with accordingly.

In conclusion, it is fashionable to talk about marketing - how to sell, company image, vision and long term objectives - but if you don't have the right working relationship with your suppliers all of your marketing efforts may come to naught, because at the end of the day every business relies on its suppliers for its own success.

Stan Mendham, Chief Executive, The Forum of Private Business

LEGAL SAFEGUARDS TO ENSURE PRODUCTS, GOODS AND SERVICES ARE WHAT YOU WANT

Every business needs to limit its risk whether it is buying or selling. A good starting point is to use standard terms of business which have been professionally drafted to meet your specific needs. These standard terms manage the transaction and minimise time and cost of negotiation. They also limit your liability (if selling) and extend your rights (if buying).

When you are selling

Price

- Does it include VAT, packaging, delivery, insurance?
- How long do quotes remain open?
- Can you vary the price if list prices change between order and delivery?

Payment

- Specify method, time, instalments and interest on late payment
- Consider securing payment by deposits/retention of title clause

Delivery

- Where does delivery take place?
- Limit liability for late delivery/damage in transit to the extent legally permitted
- Reserve the right to suspend deliveries and cancel the contract if you become concerned about the solvency of your buyer

Warranties

- Specify what warranties/guarantees are included, exclude terms implied by law

- Warranties given by you should not extend beyond those given to you by suppliers

Exclusion clauses

- Exclude liability for damage/breach of contract for defective goods or services to fullest extent permitted by law
- Consider interaction with your insurance cover

Obviously opposite considerations will apply where you are a buyer but the following additional points should be considered:

When you are buying

- Include a specification and a statement that goods will conform
- Look for a fixed inclusive price
- Negotiate discounts for prompt payment
- Include a clause whereby seller pays you £X for each day delivery is late
- Specify a quantity and state that any variation is a breach
- Specify a time and place for delivery

Product liability

- Obtain warranties that you can pass on to your customers
- Require seller to supply safe goods that comply with relevant regulations
- Oblige seller to implement quality control procedures and keep records
- Reserve right to inspect production and make changes
- Seller should insure against product liability and your interest should be noted on the policy
- An indemnity if seller's product causes you (or a consumer) loss
- Consider parent company guarantees

Well drafted terms of business incorporated into the contract can minimise business risk but whether you are able to impose your terms will depend on the commercial clout that you have. You must however try to avoid the 'battle of the forms' when both seller and buyer send their terms of business to each other saying that they are dealing on their terms as you may not know whose terms apply until you get to court.

Karen Harrison, Shoosmiths

THE BRITISH STANDARDS INSTITUTION

The British Standards Institution (BSI) is now the world's leading standards and quality services organisation. Formed in 1901 and incorporated under Royal Charter in 1929, BSI is the oldest national standards making body in the world.

Independent of government, industry and trade associations, BSI is a non-profit distributing organisation. BSI is globally recognised as an independent and impartial body serving both the private and public sectors.

BSI works with manufacturing and service industries, businesses and governments to facilitate the production of British, European and International standards. As well as facilitating the writing of British standards, BSI is one of the world's leading standards authorities representing UK interests across the full scope of European and International standards committees.

CE Marking

To make the trading of products with EU countries easier and cheaper, a single product mark called the CE mark was introduced. By displaying the CE mark a manufacturer has made a declaration that their product conforms to the minimum legal requirements for health and safety as outlined in European Directives.

The Directives require manufacturers to display the CE mark on the packaging and accompanying literature of their product and therefore the mark often acts as a visual guide to consumers that the product they are buying meets the specified minimum standards.

Where a New Approach Directive is in force, it is (with few exceptions) an offence to place a product on the market without CE marking. The manufacturer is legally responsible for ensuring that the product conforms to the requirements of the Directive and for applying CE marking.

The steps to CE mark your product

- Identify the Directive(s) relevant to your product,
- Identify the entry route of your product into the EC,
- Determine the dates by which action must be taken,
- Identify if there are relevant Harmonized European Standards,
- Determine that the product complies with the essential requirements of the Directive(s). Take appropriate measures to comply or identify existing data and test reports,
- Identify whether independent assessment of your conformity, or some aspects of it, is required from a Notified Body,
- Evaluate and control the costs of any new test and assessment measures required,

- Prepare the Declaration of Conformity and the required supporting evidence,
- Maintain Technical Files and any other reports required by the Directive(s),
- Check that no other purely national requirements still exist in countries where the product may be sold,
- Apply CE mark correctly on the product and/or its packaging and accompanying literature.

Where can you obtain the CE mark

Many European Directives require products to be independently certified. To do this a manufacturer needs to contact a notified body. This is an organisation that has been nominated by a Member Government and has been notified by the European Commission.

BSI is a notified body for many European Directives and is able to offer all of the services required for CE marking a product. These services include:

- Product testing
- Quality system assessment
- Type examination certificate issue
- Technical file and design dossier evaluation
- Surveillance of product and quality system
- Identification of standards

Key Points:

 CE marking on a product is a manufacturer's declaration that the product complies with the essential requirements of the relevant Directive(s)

 CE marking indicates to officials that a product may be legally offered for sale in their country

 CE marking requirements are not uniform between, and even within, Directives

The Kitemark

The Kitemark is the British Standards Institution's own product certification mark recognised by 88% of adults in the United Kingdom. Unlike the CE Mark, the Kitemark is a voluntary mark and therefore not a legal requirement.

In business terms the Kitemark is one of the most recognised and respected product certification marks; it is visible proof that a product conforms to a published specification and meets the highest possible quality and safety standards through regular independent and testing by BSI.

Samples of products are tested against the performance criteria within the appropriate published specification. In addition, management systems will be assessed against BS EN ISO 9000.

If a product meets the requirements of the specification and the management system is acceptable then a business will be awarded a licence to use the Kitemark trademark.

Samples of the product will be tested at regular intervals throughout the year, and management systems will be subject to further assessments. It is this ongoing process of audit testing and assessment that makes the Kitemark so highly regarded and sought after by manufacturers. Furthermore the Kitemark acts as a highly visible, voluntary commitment from a manufacturer to the quality and safety of their product and provides the final consumer with added reassurance that the product is fit for purpose.

Distribution

A can of beans may cost just a penny or two at the factory gate. But by the time it reaches your late night, open seven days a week corner shop, its selling price will have risen anything from four to eight times. In other words there is more value in the distribution chain than in the product itself. Which if you think about it, makes sense. After all, a tin of beans in a factory warehouse in Glasgow is of little value to a hungry person in Ealing at 8pm on a Sunday evening.

MAKING THE BEST DISTRIBUTION CHOICE

If a tree falls down in a forest when nobody is around, does it make a sound? Armchair and pub philosophers have debated this type of conundrum until fists fly or the landlord throws them out. Harmless it may be, but this particular problem is applicable to many businesses and especially new ones. If a firm offers a superlative product but is unable to deliver it when the customer wants it, what is the point?

Transport, logistics, distribution - whatever the movement of goods is called - is recognised increasingly as an important aspect of business for a variety of reasons. For low value products transportation can account for a high proportion of the total cost. For example, it represents around 40 per cent of the typical cost of aggregates. For some manufacturers it is important because transport is tied into production: modern motor manufacturers, for instance, have parts delivered in the exact order they will be used on the productionline.

It's all very well looking at success stories, but how does a new or expanding company ensure that it finds the right distribution solution? Anyone who has bought a mobile phone will be familiar with the general principle. Work out exactly what the needs are and remember to be generous to allow for growth or problems, and then choose whichever package fits best.

There are certain short cuts, many of which do not cost very much. Probably the best and cheapest is to join a trade association, such as the Freight Transport Association, which can supply cost information and advice on the legal niceties that must be complied with. Read specialist trade magazines, such as Commercial Motor and Motor Transport, which often carry cost tables and advice.

Once the needs are established the fun can really begin. Will it be best to use a courier/haulier, a distribution company or buy a vehicle? Couriers/hauliers can be the best option if there is an insufficient volume of product and deliveries to justify finding a logistics partner or buying a vehicle. They leave the client with real flexibility but the downside is less control and higher unit costs.

Distribution partnerships are becoming increasingly popular as they allow the client to concentrate on the core business while offering lower unit costs than hauliers and giving more control and service. When choosing a partner, service quality is as important as price.

Finally, a firm can buy a vehicle and make its own deliveries. This can make sense for many smaller companies where the administrative burden will not be too great. It gives total control, but does mean a driver must be found. If this option is chosen, straight purchase must be weighed up against contract hire and leasing, as the latter can fix costs.

In truth, transport solutions begin with the choice of the location of premises. Where will the customers be? If the answer is nationwide, motorway access could be useful. Then again, where are suppliers situated - and so on. Nobody said it would be easy, but it is easier if you go in with both eyes open and have done the necessary homework.

Geoff Dossetter, Freight Transport Association

One very simple way to manage distribution in a new small business is to restrict the area in which you operate, initially at least. After all, if you are selling office furniture and are based in Putney, why extend your reach beyond the M25. Within that boundary you could grow to £100 million worth of sales a year and still have less than one per cent of the market. Go as far as Aberdeen and you have major problems if something goes wrong (and it will) and you have to visit to recover the product or smooth the client's ruffled feathers. You can't be too careful, he may know the editor of your trade magazine!

Don't feel that 'production' is an issue only for manufacturing companies. Goods and services both involve production and that process can be improved. A shopkeeper can plan stock levels so that customers are never disappointed and yet the back-up stock is at a minimum. A house painter can plan to have the right materials bought at the keenest prices for each job, rather than having to rush back and forth from the local hardware shop two or three times a day. (This may require more cash outlay, but in all probability it will pay dividends.) A designer can take two days rather than three to produce a leaflet - all examples of how production efficiencies can improve the profitability of current operations.

Office Systems and Communication

After the USA and Japan, businesses in the UK are the largest users of computers and other areas of IT (Information Technology) in the developed world. Unfortunately it is mostly large firms that are the main users. Large firms are twice as likely as small firms to be heavy users of computers, according to a survey carried out for the DTI in May 1997. It would also appear that small firms are more likely to use computers for tactical, albeit vital, activities such as accountancy, rather than for strategic areas such as creating customer databases.

The truth of this last point can be easily confirmed by reading any item of mail from one of your suppliers offering a new product or service. Although you are one of their customers, and presumably they know something of your needs and buying history, your supplier will ignore everything that could make their correspondence personal and relevant. You, along with everyone else, will receive the same bland impersonal and usually irrelevant communication, and do much as 98 per cent of other recipients do - bin it. It has to be said large firms are guilty of these crimes too, but whilst they may appear more guilty than small firms, that is only because they make greater use of direct mail.

MANAGING YOUR INFORMATION TECHNOLOGY

It's new, it's IT and it's supposed to revolutionise the way we work. But as recent business surveys show, the very words 'Information Technology' are almost guaranteed to get the pulse rates of most people who run their own business racing with confusion and apprehension. While almost every small business now has a computer system of some kind, relatively few know how to get the most out of it to help make their business more efficient. Unless you are a computer whiz, it might be a good idea to get some expert advice when you set up your business rather than wait until things get even more confusing later on.

No matter what kind of small business you run, there are a growing number of technological tools at your disposal to help you manage and run your operations more effectively. As well as computer systems, many more businesses every day are discovering the benefits of e-mail, data transfer via ISDN links, video and teleconferencing, desk-top publishing and a host of other Information Technology tools.

A few tips for assessing your IT needs:

 Do your homework - more and more articles are being written in industry journals on how IT is being used to help improve efficiency and systems; your industry association may just have a file on them or a staff member who can offer advice

Don't be afraid to ask others in your own business field for advice - chances are you can learn a lot from those who have already gone through the process

Decide what you want new information technologies to do for your business and write a specification

Set yourself a budget and shop around for equipment - make sure there are adequate safeguards such as service contracts and technical support

Ask your supplier for customer references and contact them to see if the promises are fulfilled

The good news is that as demand grows for these products and services in a competitive marketplace, the prices are tumbling and what were expensive sophisticated systems affordable only to larger concerns yesterday are today within the reach of most small businesses with more modest budgets. New technologies though will still represent a serious investment to any small enterprise and the cost of getting things wrong will be even higher.

The bad news is that information technologies are changing so rapidly that even the experts find it difficult to keep pace with the change. Do you buy a new lap-top computer and link it via a modem on your mobile phone today, or should you wait until next month when a more powerful and cheaper model comes on to the market? Who do you turn to to find out?

Who to talk to?

A common problem lies with the equipment or telecommunications service suppliers themselves. Although their sales staff may know a lot about the technical capabilities of the products they are selling, most often they will not know how to explain the benefits these products can bring to a particular business. Technology is one thing and understanding its capabilities, adapting it to meet the needs of your business, and actually getting your staff to use it effectively is an entirely different matter.

Even after-sales technical backup can be a problem with so called Help Desks jammed with enquiries, creating a backlog that can last hours or even days. Meanwhile, your staff will be tearing their hair out in frustration and your business will also be left in a waiting queue - a potentially expensive situation that negates the lower cost of the technology in the first place.

In this situation you may be tempted to turn to your sister-in-law's nephew, who, you have been told, is a prodigy on just such matters. He may well be bright, but would you use this route to have someone figure out your current tax situation? Probably not.

There is some good news though. You can get help and it may not cost you that much money either. There are a growing number of companies, usually small, which can offer some help with your information technology or computer related problems. Some also specialise in areas such as world wide web page design or other Internet applications, or just help sort out other people's computer problems.

The government has also done some serious research into the lack of awareness and understanding that many small businesses have about information technology and computers and there are several programmes about under the small business section of the Information Society Initiative, which comes under the DTI. This is administered through the network of Business Links around the country and offers subsidised consulting to small business on IT related problems. In other words, you can engage some expert advice and help at a fraction of the normal commercial consulting price.

Through these programmes you can get help from consultants who can give impartial advice on any computer or information technology related matter including:

- A review of current operations
- Identification of requirements
- How IT can best be employed in operations

Many small companies realise they need the advantage of computer-based systems in meeting their business goals but they either don't get the best use out of the equipment they have, or don't know where to turn to get impartial advice on new or upgraded systems. Independent consultants who aren't tied to any particular product or service can help them review their needs, advise on the best way to organise and maintain their data or help with specific problems such as data security, networking their computers, or even how the end of the millennium will affect their computer systems.

In the long run, it may be a small price to pay for getting the most out of your IT resources.

Kevin Curran, Partner, TNL

A software company had a good leading edge product. All it needed was distribution but it had no money to build its own distribution group. The only deal on the table diluted the equity massively. Sitting on a plane, the MD fell into conversation with his neighbour who, it turned out, had the week before canned an internal project to develop precisely the product that the software company had just built. His company had wasted several million pounds failing to provide what was regarded as a product crucial to their portfolio. Within four weeks a distribution agreement had been signed, the software company was cash rich and there was no dilution of the equity.

- You have to kiss a lot of frogs to find a prince
- Keep on networking!

David Bailey, David Bailey Enterprises

HOW TO MAKE TECHNOLOGY WORK FOR YOU

You can't escape it. Everywhere you look, there's intense coverage about how new technologies, such as e-business and the Internet, are revolutionising the world we live in.

Many of these changes have been driven by commercial considerations. In fact, e-business - doing business electronically over networks and the Internet - has created a whole new business model. Crucially, it has been new and smaller companies which have been able to capitalise on the much-vaunted 'level playing field' it has created. But what *really* lies behind all the hype?

If you're shouldering the responsibility for a smaller business, you need to be sure technology is really working for you. It's quite a responsibility. After all, one of the characteristics of smaller businesses is that they're unlikely to have the sizeable IT departments found in large corporations. The person in charge of IT may have a number of other responsibilities. They certainly can't waste time leafing through endless brochures, articles and manuals.

It's clear that getting the right advice early on is a good first step. But IT companies have an (often deserved) reputation for speaking their own language, not yours. It can be disheartening to find yourself faced with a barrage of technical information, mystifying jargon and details of products obviously intended for companies that have nothing in common with your own.

Actually, experience shows it is not all the fault of the IT vendors. New and smaller enterprises are just as guilty of asking the wrong questions - and having unrealistic expectations. That's often due to the way IT is presented as a panacea for all ills. It can lead people in smaller companies to assume that an IT solution can solve all their problems outright.

This can lead to problems. Rather than looking at the efficiency of existing business processes, for example, they simply automate them. This can mean just adding IT to an inefficient process, rather than tackling the process and the IT requirement together.

So the key is to ask the right questions. Start at the beginning - with the fundamentals of your business and the strategic issues that need to be addressed. Then apply IT as a means to a business end, not an end in itself - and make sure your IT vendor does the same.

Having a vendor who is prepared to be a partner, rather than just a supplier, means you can exploit their IT expertise to make up for what your company lacks (because it doesn't employ dozens of IT specialists). A recent DTI report showed that some 60 per cent of SME IT projects fail because of lack of IT knowledge and project management skills. That's a lot of wasted time and money. Time and money that could be better spent on getting specialist help from a company that's already invested in the tools, the skills and the expertise.

It's also vital to choose an IT vendor who can provide the right level of support. Most new and smaller businesses depend on stable cash flow - so big ad hoc charges for repairing crucial systems (that always seem to go down at the worst possible time) can be crippling. Taking practical steps, like getting a solid support and maintenance contract means you're not at the mercy of systems failure, and you can budget properly against any mishaps. A disaster recovery contract can also insure you against Acts of God. So, for instance, if your building is flooded, you can get your systems recovered and carry on doing business as fast as possible. On a day-to-day level it's also reassuring to know there is an efficient help desk available when you need help.

On a different note (but one that's also fundamentally to do with cash flow), when preparing to make an investment in IT, it's worth taking a look at the finance deals that are available. They can take the sting out of a big investment - and there are dozens of IT resellers springing up who have all-in-one deals designed specifically for SMEs.

So, used properly, IT can help you exploit its inbuilt advantages more effectively. It lets you capitalise on the fact that you don't have big overheads, allowing you to do business in virtual environments - through Web sites and over the Net - at low cost. It allows SMEs to get more from a smaller workforce by helping people communicate and work in a team more effectively. And it enables them to forge stronger relationships with the suppliers, business partners and customers they rely on.

So, asking the right questions of your own business and of your IT vendor is essential. Careful examination of the business problems you expect IT to help with will pay dividends. As can exploiting the expertise and specialist advice of your IT vendor (whose core activity is IT after all) rather than trying to do everything yourself. Then you'll find you're in great shape to see your IT really living up to all those big promises.

It's true. IT can empower your business.

Drew Crawford, Business Development Manager, IBM (United Kingdom) Ltd.

IT In Your Business - Looking Ahead

The first thing to remember is that the needs of the business come first so look at your business and analyse its processes. Find out how the various activities interlink, take a view of the whole that already exists and plan for eighteen months, three years and five years ahead. The detail will decrease over the longer periods and the guesswork will increase. However, it will give you a perspective to start from and a vision to work towards. The processes you analyse will be drawn directly from the business and therefore will be intimately part of your overall business plan.

The best way to do the analysis is to draw a simple diagram with boxes for processes and lines to show links. Putting descriptions in boxes and on the lines helps greatly. One client put up three long sheets of plain wallpaper in the staff kitchen and attached felt-tip pens. Everyone was then invited to add their thoughts by way of drawing on the existing diagrams. (One sheet was for Sales, one for Accounts and one for Operations.)

The advantage of this method of modelling the business is that it is easy to understand, gives a visual focus for discussions and is very flexible. Therefore as the business develops and the business plan changes so too can the process diagram. Some clients have even used the diagrams they have drawn (tidied up) as discussion aids for use with potential IT suppliers to provide an insight into their business processes.

This latter point about drawing suppliers into a close understanding of the business processes is key to long-term success. Drawing up a detailed list of requirements for a system to fulfil and then giving this to a potential supplier does not give them any real opportunity to understand you and your business. The IT suppliers have skills and perspectives that could be useful to you, therefore do not try to limit their involvement by giving them a closed list but expand it by providing a model that is open for discussion. They will gain a good understanding of where you are starting from and what your vision for the future of the business is.

Videoconferencing

Videoconferencing offers the opportunity for face-to-face meetings between people, without the need for long distance travel. Current systems allow application sharing so documents, drawings etc. can be displayed on-screen whilst being discussed. Also multi-point conferences are becoming more common, where more than just two locations are involved in the meeting.

As a minimum, at present, videoconferencing systems require at least two channel ISDN telephone lines. Therefore if a business in the UK wants to talk to a business in the USA they will each need an ISDN line at their site. The costs of such lines are decreasing but the overall costs are still worthy of close examination. Also, although the technologies are rapidly improving, the cost of the additional equipment needed for commercial use is still quite high.

Perhaps the most overlooked aspect of videoconferencing use is that many people do not like to be 'on camera'. They need to be gently introduced to the idea and made to feel comfortable before being placed in the position of having to use the technology in a commercially active role. Too many times videoconferences look like bad television soap operas, because everyone involved has tensed up and become very wooden.

However, despite these issues, using videoconferencing as part of the overall communication strategy of a business can make real savings by reducing travel and accommodation costs. Videoconferencing will never replace the person to person meeting but it helps make such meetings more effective when they do take place.

The Internet for SMEs

The importance of the Internet for SMEs is growing but only when they realise it is a communication medium and should be utilised as a part of their overall business process model like any other application or tool. The question to be asked is whether such and such a process can be matched by application X. Then looking at the future needs (from the business process model) ask if use of the Internet technologies could provide benefits?

Some advantages of Internet connectivity lie in inexpensive communications from any location worldwide. Another is the ability to appear to be available 24 hours a day 365 days a year. Yet another possibility is to design your own presence on the Internet in such a way that your company looks much larger than it may really be. (This is of particular advantage to the very small business that has large competitors.) Customer service opportunities abound and the ability to provide up-to-date, accurate information to your customer base has never been cheaper or easier.

Use of the Internet only for advertising is short term and unlikely to provide large returns for many businesses. The tools to allow full commercial interaction are available now and will link into existing systems. This is the challenge - meet the paradigm change that the Internet brings to the supply chain whilst keeping your business growing to plan.

Groupware

Electronic mail or (e-mail) is a means for individuals to communicate directly with one another. The communication is point to point since one person sends and the other person reads. Although the message may be sent to more than one person by the sender, the readers still read it individually. Groupware takes this starting point and expands it into a powerful tool for business use. Typically groupware will make diaries available with lists of tasks to be done, but in a shared environment where groups of people can see and act upon the information. (Hence the term 'group'ware.) However, this is not the limit of the possibilities. Some systems then go on to use the same principles to make discussion areas available so that conversations can take place between groups of people who may be spread geographically and functionally. The essential difference from e-mail, is that in groupware the users start to co-operate in their use of information. There are a few systems that go even further than this and also permit companies to design their own solutions from the existing building blocks of the groupware system.

Unfortunately there are a number of systems that claim to be groupware which are not. Others go part way to the solution but come up short. This is the major problem that faces SMEs - selection of the solution which matches their needs - and is not only tied up in the usual IT terminology but also clouded by truths and half-truths. As the technology matures this sort of problem will lessen but for now expert advice is essential.

Business Link, Gloucestershire

THE INTERNET

Most small businesses acquire a computer when they start up or shortly afterwards. One of the most effective ways of using that computer is in accessing the wealth of information available on the Internet which provides access to sources of information and companies throughout the world.

Benefits of the Internet for small businesses

Communication Electronic mail is a means of sending messages from one computer to another on a local, regional, national and international basis for the cost of a local telephone call. It is particularly effective if you want to share documents in electronic format.

Presence and marketing Internet marketing is becoming popular involving both research and the active outflow of information. The Internet can give businesses the opportunity to publicise their activities to other businesses who might otherwise never hear about them. Businesses may take out 'pages' (which function like advertisements or articles in the press) on the World Wide Web describing their product or service and soliciting market response.

An Internet presence allows even the smallest firm to be seen and compete alongside major players as small firms can potentially get the same exposure as a multi-national company.

Access to information and expertise The Internet contains a vast amount of free information produced by governments, businesses, academic institutions, enterprise agencies, individuals etc. which can be useful for businesses - information that costs money to create or is charged for elsewhere. This includes, for example, market research reports and databases which are unlikely to be freely available, but the Internet can also be used to access subscription services. Information in relevant fields can be located using either one of the search engines or by typing in the URL (Uniform Resource Locator) if the Internet address is known. Once relevant information has been located it can either be printed out or downloaded.

Useful sites

http://pne.org/cobweb Set up and operated by Project North East, a local enterprise and economic development agency, this site provides useful information to start-ups, small businesses and their advisers. The site includes a considerable amount of free information including names and addresses of all the enterprise agencies in membership of the Federation of Enterprise Agencies. It also acts as a gateway to a low cost subscription service which provides almost everything that you will ever want to know about starting your business.

http://www.microsoft.com The home page of Microsoft provides information about its software products, including those for the Internet and web page creation. In addition there is also a very popular small business section.

http://open.gov.uk This site provides links to the home pages of government departments, local authorities, etc.

http://www.businesslink.co.uk This site provides information about Business Links, which help start-ups and existing businesses, and their services.

Tracey Mellor, Project North East

HOW IT CAN HELP YOU PUNCH ABOVE YOUR WEIGHT

Does size matter? Not on the Internet it doesn't, because new technology can give your business more clout.

The Internet is a great leveller. Someone looking at an attractive, professional Web site need have no idea about the size of the company behind it. All they'll see is a businesslike window on the world.

And perhaps more importantly, it's as easy for a potential customer to find your site as that of your biggest rival.

In fact, a new or smaller business could mean you have a striking advantage over your larger, more established competitors. Although big companies have massive budgets for sales and marketing, they're also saddled with having to invest millions in bricks and mortar, for offices, warehouses, and retail outlets.

Being small gives you the flexibility to use IT cleverly. You can use 'network computing' to punch above your weight and market your products at an incredibly low cost. And also it's easy now to do real, secure, business over the internet and the other computer networks. At IBM we call this e-business. As an example, one bakery I know of generates £6000 of business yearly through Web advertising. The cost? A mere £60 per annum. The numbers speak for themselves.

So why isn't every small business rushing to get on the Web? Well, there are several inhibitors - some very real, others more imaginary.

To begin with - there's cost. Many people imagine that the initial investment involved in getting on the Web must be prohibitive, and the costs unpredictable. Yet in fact, it's possible to let an IT vendor design and host your Web presence for you - and for a fixed fee. They make all the investments in hardware, software, support and so on. You just reap the benefits - and pay a regular amount that's easy on your cash flow.

A big fear is that the technology is just too complex to get to grips with. For companies with a small (or non-existent) IT department, the prospect of building the right IT infrastructure from scratch is daunting. The good news is that IT vendors are beginning to wake up to the needs of new and smaller businesses. You can now buy a low-cost server pre-loaded with everything you need to build a fully functioning web site. This will include online advice and support. There are dozens of resellers who specialise in providing packaged solutions - often aimed specifically at smaller businesses and niche markets.

But it is security that's the most persistent worry. After all, establishing trust is vital to the conduct of any business. You need to ensure absolute protection against fraud. It also means protecting yourself at all costs against hackers, unscrupulous competitors and viruses. The good news is, the IT industry has focussed its efforts in the last couple of years on providing this kind of protection. Not only can you now specify levels of security on your web site (so your business partners can view data that the public can't), you can now guarantee secure financial transactions over the Net. The recently introduced Secure Electronic Transaction (SET) protocol ensures a standard for making critical transactions safe. e-business is now safer than ever.

Finally, some people ask themselves a perfectly reasonable business question. Will a fancy web presence turn out to be an expensive white elephant? One of the costly lessons learnt by bigger companies is that Web technology isn't an end in itself. It has to be carefully thought through and applied to deliver real business value. Few SMEs can afford the extravagance of an attractive but purely informative web presence. From the outset, Web sites must be well designed with doing business in mind. This doesn't just mean marketing and selling products direct to customers. It can also mean doing business with partners and suppliers more effectively, and at low cost - for instance by letting them view the status of an order, or see if certain goods are in stock.

Network computing and e-business are already drastically shaking up the markets - but only if SMEs really begin to exploit the potential. By delivering the market reach and sales opportunities previously only open to the big guns, technology is promising to alter the balance of power forever between SMEs and their bigger rivals.

But the key to your success is to seize this opportunity now. The first step is to talk to IT vendors, and find out just what the opportunities are. Be sure that the IT vendors understand they must speak the language of the smaller business and can understand your priorities. Then you can really start to punch above your weight - and keep winning.

Drew Crawford, Business Development Manager, IBM

COMMUNICATIONS IN THE OFFICE

In the modern office, businesses can choose how they communicate depending on the type of information they are sending. Telephones, faxes and e-mail co-exist, giving businesses a range of flexible communication tools.

However, as the first impression is often the one that lasts, effective communication skills are as essential to business success as investing in new technology or equipment.

Telephone techniques for success

Everyone knows how to use the telephone but not everyone knows how to use it effectively.

Research by the Henley Centre shows that nearly 90 per cent of customers are prepared to take their business elsewhere if the first point of contact is handled badly.

To create the right first impression, the following basic rules should become second nature when you pick up the phone:

- Create a positive image of your company by answering the phone promptly, within three or four rings, with a cheerful voice
- Establish clarity by greeting each call with "good morning/afternoon/ evening" and stating your name, company or department
- Identify the caller by taking a note of their name, title and company
- Ensure you are putting a call through to the correct person or department by pinpointing the purpose of the call
- Concentrate, don't do two things at once

Using the telephone as a sales tool

The thought of having to sell anything over the telephone fills most people with an intense dread and yet each year businesses in the UK spend over £1 billion on telemarketing. By following a few simple rules, everyone can conduct a professional sales call:

- Always plan what you are going say
- Find out the full name and title of the decision-maker and ask to speak to them
- Make clear notes of everything that is said
- Sell the sizzle, not the sausage - emphasise the benefits of your product
- Ask open ended questions such as 'Why, When, Where, Who and How'
- Establish that the customer needs your product or service
- Find out how the product or service is intended to be used and how it fits with what they have already
- Establish which other products may interest the customer
- Confirm if the customer is interested in placing an order and if so, close the sale by taking the order

Having your calls accepted

There remains, of course, the fear that you may never get through to the 'decision maker' in the first place. Remember that everyone at sometime has left messages that have gone unanswered or has been unable to get through to an important contact. A few simple tips may help your calls be accepted:

- If your call is urgent, leave a polite, clear message explaining why it is urgent
- If you are caught in 'voice-mail jail', try a different route by obtaining the general switchboard number and ask to speak to the department secretary
- If your contact is out or in a meeting, ask when they are next available and make a firm arrangement to call them back at that time
- If someone is hard to get hold of try calling them at an unusual time, perhaps when their secretary has left for the evening

- If you are making an introductory call, leave a message explaining who you are and why you are calling

Working from home

If you work from home you will find that, as well as being a vital link with the outside world and an essential business tool, the telephone can be a major distraction.

The following tips should help you make better use of the telephone:

- Schedule a regular time to take calls and advise people that this is the best time to reach you
- Family and friends calling for a chat should be gently reminded that you are working - offer to call back after business hours
- Unsolicited sales calls should be dealt with decisively and politely - if you know you don't want a product or service, do not agree to be called back or put on a list
- If you use a messaging service, test it regularly by leaving a message for yourself
- Make sure that the whole family learns to answer the telephone and take messages in a professional way
- Use an answerphone in the evening to handle all business related calls - you need time to relax

Audio conferencing

Whether you are working from home or for a large company, business travel is often an essential part of working life. Every year people travel thousands of miles on their quest to communicate in business. As well as being expensive, business travel is also time-consuming and not always necessary.

Audio conferencing is an increasingly popular technology which allows people in three or more locations, nationally or worldwide, to hold a meeting via the telephone.

It helps reduce the costs involved in maintaining regular contact with colleagues and clients, as well as being flexible enough to be arranged in under 10 minutes. Key decision makers can therefore 'get together' to discuss urgent matters, even if they are located in other parts of the country or in different countries.

For effective audio conference meetings, the following tips should come in useful:

Before the call:

- Notify all participants of the time and date of the meeting
- If participants are calling into the meeting, ensure that everyone is given the dial-in telephone number
- If a conference co-ordinator is calling out to participants, ascertain where each person will be at the time of the meeting and forward a list of contact numbers to the co-ordinator
- Elect a chairman to direct and control the meeting
- Work from an agreed agenda outlining the subjects/topics to be discussed

Beginning the call:

- Use a phone where you will not be disturbed
- Conduct a roll-call to check that participants are present and the lines are clear. The call co-ordinator can carry out this task

During the call:

- Speak clearly
- Always state your name when joining the conversation
- Direct your questions to a named participant
- Acknowledge all questions directed to you, even though you may not have an immediate answer
- Do not interrupt other speakers, wait until they are finished
- Summarise key points of meeting and agree actions before ending the call
- Keep background noise to a minimum

Communications on the move

While audio conferencing and videoconferencing are revolutionising the way we work and reducing the need for business travel, there are still many instances when face-to-face meetings are essential, which inevitably means spending time out of the office.

It is important to keep in touch when you are on the move and the latest advances in technology are designed to ensure you never miss a call. Invest in one of the following ways to stay in contact:

Mobile phones:

Keeping in touch using a mobile phone is now even easier as many have messaging services and some have the facility to send and receive faxes and e-mails, which means documents can be sent to you wherever you are.

Call management services:

With a call management service, you can route incoming calls and faxes to anywhere in the world. If you are unsure of your movements on any particular day, a 'hunt' facility will try various numbers to track you down.

These services can be updated according to your daily schedule from any tone phone, including mobile phones.

Calling cards:

If you need to phone clients or colleagues and do not have any spare change or do not want to incur expensive hotel surcharges, calling cards allow you to make cash-free calls from the majority of phones worldwide. They are a particularly useful way of staying in touch when you are travelling overseas.

Communications for the future

We are already experiencing changes in the way we communicate, with the arrival of new technology like e-mail and video conferencing. As technology rapidly advances, so too will our choice of communications tools and how we use them.

The key word is 'convergence' - bringing computing, electronic media and telecommunications together into a single package that uses media like the Internet to connect you with everyone with whom you wish to speak.

In transforming how businesses receive and exchange information, convergence is just as beneficial to SMEs as it is to large, multi-national organisations.

It creates powerful applications that allow smaller organisations to have access to the same facilities as large organisations, without incurring expensive investment costs. It can help SMEs to use resources more effectively, market and sell products in new ways, target customers more accurately, even to adopt more flexible working methods.

The trend for more flexible working practices, particularly amongst SMEs who may not have a conventional office-based structure, is being furthered by convergence. Technology is facilitating new ways of working, from home, on the move and even in 'virtual organisations' where teams of individuals based in different locations, or even different countries, communicate without barriers.

Clearly, choosing the right communications platform is essential, otherwise you could find yourself missing out on a truly interactive future.

And the winners in this 'connected' future? They will be the people who are not just proficient at using this technology; they will be the skilled communicators who use their 'wired world' to maintain and develop contact with their customers and colleagues.

Luke Broome, Director of Business Support, Cable & Wireless Communications

Information is Power

For any size of business, renting or buying property which can accommodate all the needs of your company is often impossible with storage space being at premium. Almost all companies are faced with this ever increasing dilemma of where to store all the documents and files that they want to keep, or have to keep by law. Some information is important for companies to access on a day to day basis, with fast and easy retrieval of documents being a necessity. Other documents do not have to be accessed for months, if not years.

All this information may just appear as piles of records, but to companies it is their business, and it is an area which needs to be managed properly. Different companies place varying levels of importance on how their records or files are stored; however, it is not until a crisis hits or an important document is needed urgently that people realise the power of proper data management systems.

In addition, consider the amount of our working lives that are conducted from our individual PCs or company networks, giving you the extra problem of backing up your computer system, especially if it is an integral part of your business. I am sure we have all experienced occasions when our work has been lost or files cannot be found on our computers, so you can imagine the disruption to the continuity of your business if your critical data was lost for ever.

Can anyone help?

How to store your information or how to back up your databases needn't be a problem that you have to worry about, or try to deal with on your own. It is a problem that you can outsource. This could not only free up storage space in your premises, but also your time. It can, in many ways, prove to be a worry free solution for you, providing total peace of mind.

What services can be offered?

There are a number of services available to help companies with different kinds of information and data storage problems.

Boxes: Information in the form of letters, legal documents and files can be stored in uniquely referenced boxes at secure off-site premises. Whenever you need a box, all you have to do is order the box by quoting its unique reference number, and it will be delivered directly to your desk. Depending on how your boxes were catalogued or indexed, you can request particular files from different boxes. This means that individual files can be delivered to you, rather than the whole box. After you have finished with the box or file all you have to do is phone to get the box or file collected. If you need your information in a hurry, there is an 'urgent' service you can use which gets your information delivered to you within 2 hours. If you want your files immediately they can be scanned, directly faxed or e-mailed to you in an instant.

Files: If you would prefer your records to be kept within separate files, this can also be done. Each file can be barcoded and then stored. When you need a specific file, you state the unique barcode reference of the requested file when ordering and it will be delivered directly to you. You can also place an 'urgent' order for files as well.

Backing up data: If your business relies on its IT systems to operate effectively, then backing up your data or ensuring your disks are kept safe is a priority. Disks can be collected and delivered in the same way that boxes and files are, and are individually bar coded for instant identification. Systems can also be backed up online if your data changes daily. Your information will not only be stored in temperature controlled conditions, but will also be in a 'Halon' environment, which means your data is totally safe and secure. You have twenty four hour, seven day access to your data - if a crisis strikes, you will get your critical data back within two hours.

Internal Systems: If your filing system has expanded rapidly and you want to keep all your files on site, but have a problem keeping track of where they are, there is a product which can track them for you. A system can be introduced to your offices that tracks records and generates an audit trail of where all your files are. All files and staff are barcoded, so when a member of staff picks a file that they need, they swipe their barcode, then the file's. By scanning the bar codes, you will have instant access to real time desk to desk movements of your files. The system can also track movements of information and assets from one site to another, putting you in complete control.

Confidential Destruction: So what happens when you no longer need your files or information and you do not know what to do with them? Well, you can get your information destroyed confidentially and securely, which means that no information falls into your competitors' hands. To give you added peace of mind, you will also receive a 'Certificate of Destruction' which guarantees that your information has been destroyed.

Businesses are often caught out by their failures, as much as they are by their successes. If you can plan ahead and develop data processes that can grow as your company grows, you will have responsive systems which will make your business more effective and far more efficient. Filing or data storage should never be underestimated, as the contents they hold are your company's competitive edge. Without the information your company would not be able to run. One thing you should remember is, information is power and it is how you utilise that power which makes the difference.

Mark Jackson, Marketing Manager, Hays Information Management

Computers have, in effect, levelled the playing field between large and small competitors. Often small firms find it hard to attract and pay for the very best staff. Landlords are frequently reluctant to take on small and new businesses as tenants, especially for desirable retail sites. Suppliers will rarely offer either credit or favourable terms of trade. Every valuable asset a business needs to make its way in the world becomes more expensive year by year, raising the barrier ever higher between established firms and new entrants. Every asset, that is, except computers. The power of computers doubles every two years whilst the price halves every five, or so it seems.

For barely a thousand pounds a new or small firm can have a computer and the necessary software to allow it to manage its customer base, control the accounts, write letters, prepare leaflets and put together high-level visual presentations for meetings with clients and prospects. For the same outlay you could also have an e-mail address and web sites on the Internet, making your business a player on the world stage from day one. That is not such a fanciful claim as it may sound. Amazon.com, the Internet bookseller set up in 1994, already sells over $10 million worth of books overseas each year, all without a single overseas office or salesperson.

Small business owners like to say: "You work 24 hours a day, but at least you get to choose which 24". That entrepreneurs work hard is not in dispute. But how many work smart as well? That requires building a team, delegating responsibility, communicating goals and objectives, rewarding success and ultimately removing those unable or unwilling to perform.

These are all the tasks of managing people. Unfortunately there is something in the average business founder's make-up, that can render them poor managers. This incapacity has its roots in the belief that many owner-managers have that there is really no such task as management. Sadly nothing could be further from the truth - arguably it is the most important point of business. Don't ignore it - your business depends on it. Such people see the need to manage as evidence of either a failure in recruitment (because after all "surely competent employees are self-managing") or a failure in the education system as a whole which produces too many people with no grasp of what is required of employees in the 'real' world.

Both of these views are dangerous fallacies. All people need managing, if you are to achieve the goals you want to achieve rather than the results they are willing to deliver. The best footballers need managing or they languish far down the league tables and orchestras need conducting, even though presumably all the musicians know the music they are playing. One-man bands rarely achieve much, so to become successful (and hopefully rich) you must become an excellent manager as well as an innovator with new business ideas. There are numerous items to consider, staff review programs (i.e. how are you getting on) incentivising, getting people involved and generally caring. Good recruitment and management of people is gloriously rewarding. Poor care can lead at best to upset and at worst complete ruin.

Managing People

People are a company's most important asset. Although this may be a truism it cannot be repeated too often. It is people - with their individual and collective enterprise, drive, initiative, creative talents, efforts, capabilities, motivation and enthusiasm - who are the backbone of any organisation.

Without people, organisations could not exist or survive. Yet, all too often, these important human resources are taken for granted. In seeking to improve efficiency and effectiveness, some managers, particularly in larger companies, may tend to emphasise productivity or operations, finance or marketing - the functions which are the work of organisations. It is assumed too often that the people who are essential to carrying out these functions, will adapt to fit in with any changes.

Enlightened companies take a very different approach. They realise how crucial people are to every aspect of organisational life. They acknowledge the proven link between satisfied employees and better economic performance. People can make things happen if their working environment is positive and actively encourages them to contribute to the growth and development of the organisation.

Smaller companies are better placed and have greater freedom to create an innovative and continuous learning culture, and to adopt more flexible working practices.

The challenge for management is to aim to develop a management style that is based on:

- Involvement of people in every stage of the business growth and processes of change
- Fair and honest dealings with staff
- Good communications between staff
- Recognition of individual effort, initiative and achievement
- Encouragement of professional and personal growth opportunities for access to training

These and other such characteristics will inspire loyal and motivated staff, and will firmly underpin the future success and prosperity of the organisation.

Paulette Lockington and Stephen Winder

How to Motivate

"Usually when you listen to some statement, you hear it as a kind of echo of yourself. You are actually listening to your own opinion. If it agrees with your opinion you may accept it, but if it does not, you will reject it or you may not ever really hear it." Shunryu Suzuki.

There is one school of management known as the 'mushroom' technique: keep everyone in the dark and feed them rubbish. Then there is the old Eastern Bloc shop floor saying: "They pretend to pay us and we pretend to work". Neither approach can work either today or in the future. The best piece of advice I can give to senior managers is to shut up and listen.

How can managers motivate their people? By listening to them, and by being seen to listen.

Recent Industrial Society research revealed that 'upward communication' is very important - even essential - to organisations' success. Upward communication involves senior managers listening to front line employees. It is acknowledged as vital to success in such prime areas as customer care, employee commitment and creativity.

Yet only a third of organisations train managers in listening or facilitation skills. It is as though we just assume we all know how to listen.

In practice we slip easily into listening for what we agree or disagree with, to confirm what we already know and to apply our own preconceptions. It is a tougher but infinitely more rewarding discipline to learn how to set our subjective opinions aside and make a conscious, creative act of granting our listening to people. This sows the seed of a rich harvest. By listening, we can see what is really at stake, and see new possibilities for achieving results.

John Garnett, a great predecessor of mine at the Society used to say: "The good thing about employees is that with every pair of hands you get a free brain." Let's get our hands and our brains working together!

I've been asked to provide some bullet points under the heading "How to motivate". I have only three:

- Listen
- Listen
- Listen

Tony Morgan, The Industrial Society

THE VALUE OF INDIVIDUALS AND TEAMS

It is almost impossible to get through a management magazine or guru's primer without reading "Your people are your greatest asset". I wonder how well the advocates of that principle live up to it in their own dealings with employees and colleagues.

But even if a principle is not always lived up to, that doesn't make it any less true. Starting up a business does offer the chance to try to find the right people to make a dynamic and productive team - the team of people who are going to be responsible for generating the results you are looking for.

The demands of a changing, competitive world have caused managers to focus attention on the power of teamworking. Effective teams are greater than the sum of the individual parts. To unlock the potential of teams at work we need to take a radical approach to the question of roles and workloads.

Traditionally the process of matching roles and people starts with the role and squeezes the person into it, like a fat man contorting himself into a narrow telephone kiosk.

The more liberating approach is to start with the people, not the jobs. No two people have the same combination of talents, aspirations, strengths and weaknesses. Every one of us is a funny shape, and in addition we can change our shape, like a jelly.

In the perfect company all these funny shapes would add up to the overall shape of the company, i.e. everything the company needed to have done would be done, and, what is more, it would be achieved by totally fulfilled people, each one in a tailor-made, ideal job.

This is not as far-fetched as it may look at first sight. Clearly you cannot move from the 'jobs as boxes' approach to the 'people as jellies' approach overnight. But you can go a considerable way towards it.

If you are starting with a blank piece of paper, take a really bold and radical view of the people you have at your disposal and the tasks you need to be carried out. Don't force people into jobs marked 'X' or 'Y'. Why not hire the kind of person you require, subject of course to key recruitment and selection criteria, and then get the team to gel laterally, with individuals carrying out the tasks best suited to them.

You may be amazed at the exciting results you achieve by taking a more flexible approach to individuals and teams.

Andrew Forrest, The Industrial Society

WHAT THE SECRETS OF YOUR DESK REVEAL ABOUT YOU

When is a desk not a desk? Answer, when it is a key to the personality of the individual who sits behind it. New research commissioned in the UK by Regus, Europe's largest provider of serviced offices with approximately 30,000 workstations worldwide, shows that your desk says more about you than you would suspect. Your boss and your colleagues can see at a glance if you are a team player, hard worker, ambitious or even calculating.

Leading independent psychologist, Donna Dawson, surveyed and analysed hundreds of photographs of desktops from companies all over London in order to reach her conclusions. They show how much people's immediate working environments reflect distinct personality and character traits which provide strong clues to their abilities, preferences, strengths and weaknesses. Says Regus Director, Clive Hammond: "It seems that you cannot successfully hide behind your desk any longer, without your boss and colleagues knowing more about you than you might like." The research identifies six different desktop personalities:

THE BUSINESS-LIKE, ORGANISED DESKTOP

Description: This 'functional' desk, typically in neutral or bland colours, usually features few personal touches, has little paperwork on it and is likely to be dominated by equipment and technology. Every work item is in a fixed place with a space cleared in the middle for a notepad and pen. Most usually, this desk will belong to an accountant or a PA. Personality: This person is good at their job, has little patience and doesn't tolerate fools. Not team players, they like to be left alone to get on with what they do best, focusing on one thing at a time. Their approach is a no-nonsense one, and they are unlikely ever to initiate any social interaction in the office.

THE ORGANISED CHAOS DESKTOP

Description: This desktop, along with the surrounding shelves and floor, will be overflowing with papers and folders; the 'In/Out' tray will be groaning under the weight of more paper; and there will be few personal effects, mainly due to lack of space. Post-it notes, stuck everywhere, will be acting as reminders of deadlines. Personality: Contrary to appearances, this person is not sloppy, just overworked. A hard worker, with unshakeable faith in their own system, he or she will find it hard to say 'No', wanting to be liked. Flexible, hard working and efficient, they will lose time tying to find things and worrying how to get everything done.

THE CREATIVE CHAOS DESKTOP

Description: This desk is also cluttered, featuring a variety of differing projects, often with books, papers, drawings, notes and photos piled on top of each other showing evidence of a lively, agile and creative mind. This person has a lot on the go, and is often out of the office. Time is of the essence to this individual, who is naturally suspicious of technology and not interested in impressing others. They are likely to be in a creative job, such as a journalist, author or PR executive. Personality: Energetic and lively, this person tends to focus on their work. They won't have time to socialise or take breaks and will often lose or misplace things. However, they can improvise and are excellent lateral thinkers because of a creative and independent approach.

THE PERSONALITY EXTENSION DESKTOP

Description: This desk is an extension of the outgoing person who sits behind it, often with loads of personal touches, such as postcards, amusing epigrams, personalised mousemats and posters. The desk is, in effect, a home from home. Through their desk, this person is saying: 'I am an individual, not a cog in the company machine'. Certain jobs, such as advertising and marketing, will encourage this kind of personalised environment. Personality: This individual is a 'people person', on the whole outgoing, sociable and talkative and ready to socialise at a moment's notice. However, this type of personality can get 'down' quite easily, needing lots of praise and encouragement and needing to feel motivated. When they are, they work hard.

THE 'SHOW' DESKTOP

Description: This projects a 'contrived' image of the person behind it. Often large and imposing, it is generally made of good wood, with a leather inset or huge blotter. It will create the illusion of space and control, with very little covering the surface. This could be a boss's desk, or that of a doctor, recruitment consultant, personnel manager or someone who interviews others. A clear space represents power and control, inferring that someone lower on the ladder is dealing with paperwork and detail. Personality: These individuals are often enigmatic, giving little away about themselves and what they think. They may appear calculating and unemotional. The desk is also used to show off personal status and can act as a buffer for a defensive, inadequate or insecure personality. When it is called for, these types can be both intimidating and smooth.

THE TROPHY DESK

Description: A slightly messy desk, this features lots of 'things' which are designed to broadcast how well the owner is doing, either professionally, socially or financially. 'Trophies' may include maps of work-related travel, stuffed animals with expensive logos, company awards or items from successful campaigns. This person is projecting a rugged individuality. There will be a careless air to the desk, as if the occupant would rather be out and about planning and executing big things. It will often belong to a high-powered salesman or media person. Personality: These are friendly, energetic, ambitious and sometimes noisy people. Often pushy and bossy, they make excellent leaders. They love a challenge and think big - 'No' is not a part of their vocabulary when they want something. Able to mix with everyone, except when it comes to material things, they are not too good on detail, leaving that for others to work out.

Clive Hammond and Colin Peck, Regus

DISMISSING PEOPLE

An employer cannot simply dismiss staff on a whim. Even where there appears to be a good reason to dismiss an employee there are legal procedures to follow. An employer must honour the employees' contractual rights regardless of their length of service. Any employee who is dismissed in breach of his contract can claim damages for wrongful dismissal.

One important contractual right is that relating to entitlement to notice. Once an employee has been employed for a period of one month or more but less than two years, they are entitled to at least one week's notice of termination. After this, an employee is entitled by law to receive one week's notice for each complete year of continuous service, up to a maximum of twelve years. The contract of employment can provide for better but not worse notice entitlements. Payment in lieu of due notice is often given to an employee who is being dismissed. An employee who is guilty of gross misconduct forfeits the right to receive notice and can be summarily dismissed. But this does not mean that they can be sacked on the spot without first having had the benefit of a disciplinary hearing.

Employees with at least one year's continuous service have the statutory right not to be unfairly dismissed. An employer can only dismiss an employee for one or more of the five potentially fair reasons as stated in Section 98 of the Employment Rights Act 1996. These are:

- Reasons related to the capability or qualifications of the employee
- Reasons related to the conduct of the employee
- That the employee was redundant
- Because it would be illegal to continue to employ the employee in their job
- Because of 'some other substantial reason' justifying the dismissal of the employee

The employer must also act reasonably in deciding to dismiss the employee, rather than imposing some other form of disciplinary action. What is reasonable depends on all the circumstances and on the size and administrative resources of the employer's business.

An employer must follow a fair disciplinary procedure before actually dismissing an employee. This involves:

- A full investigation into the matter
- Making sure that the employee knows the case against him
- Giving the employee the opportunity to state their case personally or through a representative
- Deciding the case without bias
- Providing the employee with a right of appeal

A potentially fair dismissal can be rendered unfair if the employer fails to follow a fair disciplinary procedure. It is automatically unfair to dismiss an employee for certain reasons and in such cases claimants do not need one year's qualifying service. These include:

- Either being, or not being, a trade union member
- Being pregnant or taking maternity leave
- Taking certain types of action on health and safety grounds
- Seeking to enforce one of their statutory rights
- Reasons connected with the transfer of an undertaking from one employer to another

An employee has three months in which to lodge a claim for unfair dismissal at an employment tribunal. If the claim succeeds, the tribunal can award:

- Re-instatement
- Re-engagement
- Compensation up to a normal maximum of £56,600

Nigel L Baker, Lexicon Employment Law Training

There is a very simple and true maxim that applies to managing people. What gets measured gets done and what gets rewarded gets done again. You could do worse than to start by managing yourself more effectively. If your team see you rushing in every direction with no discernible output, then you should not be too surprised if they do the same. A good example will always attract followers.

In my experience . . .

Two senior managers of a branch office in East Anglia were poached by the opposition and most of the service engineers followed them, leaving the branch all but unmanned. A major national contract depended on all depots being able to call out an engineer and have one there within two hours, so the defection left a hole in the coverage.

The managing director, at his wits end, called the London-based senior staff together and asked for ideas. The north London staff volunteered to cover East Anglia until more staff could be hired and trained - and did so for three months. They worked long hours and drove hundreds of miles - all above and beyond the call of duty. But the contract was saved and the company survived.

- You can't buy loyalty - someone else could always pay a higher price - but you can win it by being upfront with your employees
- Very few problems are insoluble - all it takes is being open to ideas and compromises

Karen Ryan, Ryan Refrigeration Ltd

Managing your Money

You would never seriously consider driving a car without a dashboard full of instruments. At the very least you would expect continuous information on fuel, speed, distance travelled, engine temperature and battery charge state. You need a similar set of controls for your business. Information on sales, money owed to and by you, stock levels, the length of time it takes to collect money, and of course the cash position - these are the firm's equivalent of the dashboard. Then you need to be able to monitor performance against the standards you have set yourself in the budget.

All this information makes it more certain that you will reach your business destination safely and on time.

EFFECTIVE CREDIT MANAGEMENT

Credit management has a huge capacity for being misunderstood by everyone not actually involved. Traditionally controlled by the finance department it also has strong links with the selling process. The skills required to obtain prompt payment are identical to those needed in sales - preparation, communication, persistence and persuasion.

It should be easy for sales and credit management to cooperate - after all they have the same goal of company profitability - but this will happen only if there is a company-wide awareness of the importance of credit management and a clear definition of the credit function's responsibilities. Typically these are:

- Managing the sales ledger, usually the largest asset on the balance sheet - and the business' sole source of cash
- Maximising working capital through fast collections
- Maximising profit by reducing interest payable, again through fast collections
- Minimising the impact of bad debts
- Supporting sales by identifying growing customers and setting maximum, but prudent, credit limits

The average business makes about 4 per cent profit p.a. and pays about 12 per cent interest. In this situation a debt has to be little more than 60 days overdue before all profit is eroded. It is the task of the credit function to prevent this by ensuring:

- Good risk control - assessing credit-worthiness, agreeing payment terms, establishing credit limits and maintaining ongoing accounts.
- Fast cash collection - chasing overdue accounts and suspending delinquent accounts, arbitrating in disputes and in some cases factoring out debt recovery
- Keeping a clean sales ledger - recommending receivables budgets and bad debt and dispute reserves, updating credit policy and procedures, and reporting on delinquent accounts

The best way to codify the responsibilities of the credit function is to produce a credit policy and procedures document, spelling out:

- The scope of the credit function
- A flow chart showing authority for all decisions - acceptance of new customers, status change for existing customers, payment terms and exceptions, credit limits, temporary suspension of accounts, third party enforcement, and regular cash chasing routines
- General selling conditions - interest charges on overdue accounts, unambiguous payment terms

These ground rules remove the potential for internal disagreement and your customers will notice they are dealing with a cohesive and professional organisation that means business!

Risk assessment does not inhibit sales, as some companies seem to fear. Quite the reverse. Setting payment terms and credit limits helps to abolish potential dangers to your relationships with your customers - and protects your investment.

Moreover, most customers recognise that credit is a privilege, not a right. Sending a credit application at the earliest opportunity will demonstrate your professionalism and will also help you to decide on their ability to pay on time.

The form should be tailored to the type of business your customer runs - consumer or trade customer, sole proprietor, partnership, Limited or Plc company.

All forms should include the following:

- Name, home or business address and trading style
- Invoicing/statement address
- Telephone and fax number
- References - bank, finance house, trade, private
- Value and period of credit required

For trade credit add:

- Full names and addresses of proprietors
- Trading address
- Registration number of limited company
- Registered office address
- Length of time business established
- Type of business
- Contact name, job title and telephone/fax numbers
- VAT registration number
- Request for a copy of the company letterhead

For consumer credit add:

- Personal details (age, marital status, dependents)
- How long at present address/previous address
- Tenant/mortgagee, house/flat, (un)furnished
- Employment details (employer, occupation, time in service)
- Current and previous credit transaction details

Always include the following points, with provision for the customer's signed agreement:

- The buyer to accept the seller's general Conditions of Sale
- The buyer to accept the seller's payment terms

Details can be negotiated but the end result must be unambiguous, mutually acceptable and agreed in writing by the customer if problems are to be avoided.

Of course the information provided is useful only if it is properly followed up:

- Do take up references and verify replies
- Use an agency report or balance sheet/ratio analysis for trade credit
- Use an agency report or credit score calculation for consumer credit

Having accepted a credit customer in principle, the next steps are to agree payment terms, method of payment and the credit limit.

Payment terms

Normally your standard terms will apply, but you may reduce your risk by offering specific customers stricter terms including shorter period, up-front deposit, stage payment or any combination of these. But whatever the terms it is essential that they are convincingly agreed. Never rely on the fact that the payment terms are quoted in the Conditions of Sale.

In cases of dispute, legally the supplier's terms take precedence, providing it can be shown that the buyer was aware of and agreed to them when placing the order. So it is worthwhile to set up a simple but specific payment terms agreement when the account is set up, e.g.:

"We shall require payment from you within 30 days from the date of our invoice, no discounts allowed. Please confirm your agreement by having an authorised officer sign below".

If the customer quibbles or substitutes his own terms you may decide not to trade or to negotiate, but make sure that the amended agreement is signed. Unambiguous agreed payment terms minimise collection difficulties, lead to faster cash collection and improve customer relations.

Methods of Payment

Credit periods and payment methods may be varied to account for perceived risks or extended manufacturing and delivery terms. Commonly used methods are:

- Cash with order - i.e. no credit
- Cash on delivery - useful for 'off the shelf' products only
- Credit card - can be costly
- Timed payment - e.g. "30 days from date of invoice"
- Monthly credit - payment for a month's supplies on a specified date in the next month
- Progress payments - periodic payments during an extended contract based on cost to date
- Staged payments - percentage payments geared to specific events during the contract e.g. "25 per cent on delivery of materials to site"
- Retentions - an agreed percentage retained by the buyer to ensure the supplier's attention during a warranty period
- Direct debit - useful for marginal risk and slow accounts and now becoming widespread for consumer accounts - trade accounts are beginning to use Direct Debit because of its risk limiting benefits but also to harness its administrative advantages. . . could be the future
- Certified cheque - useful if there is a doubt in the buyer's financial standing
- BACS - Electronic transfer of funds
- Bills of exchange - signed acceptance entitles the supplier to full payment on an agreed date

Setting a Credit Limit

The credit limit you set should have enough credibility to be divulged to the customer while avoiding the need for continuous updates as sales grow. Some of the options are:

- **Set a limit geared to sales.** For example, monthly sales x 2. Simple, but prone to frequent adjustment as sales vary
- **Set a maximum regardless of sale.** Various formulas have been used, for example "the lesser of 10 per cent of buyer's net worth or 20 per cent of working capital but not to exceed 20 per cent of total of buyer's creditors". Such formulae require analysis of the customer's balance sheet but have the advantage of being suitable for disclosure to the customer
- **Use an agency report.** A Dun & Bradstreet compact report on credit-worthiness will include a suggested credit limit
- **Use a credit insurer** Businesses with credit insurance cover are given a limit on the amount that is covered for any account

The best solution is probably to do your own calculation, based on the most reliable sources available. You might, for example, use a recognised formula to set your own maximum credit limit, for comparison with the Dun and Bradstreet recommended limit. Now you would have a bracket of opinion, you could set your limit within the bracket depending upon the trend of the potential customer's financial strength.

Finalising the Details

Once the details are agreed, it is wise to send the customer a courtesy letter saying how pleased you are the account has been opened, confirming the payment terms and credit limit and advising them of their account number and the name and telephone/fax numbers of their contact in your company's accounts department.

You can then set up a sales ledger account for the new customer. To avoid future problems it is advisable to monitor new accounts carefully for three to six months.

Effective Invoices and Statements

Every communication with a customer about an order is a weapon in your cash chasing armoury. Credit managers should always have a say in their design.

Order acknowledgment/advice notes - give an early opportunity to clarify areas of potential difficulty:

* Always quote the key conditions of sale
* Show the payment terms clearly

Invoices - should show all the detail required for prompt payment:

* Invoice number and date
* Customer order number
* Dispatch method and date
* Quantity and description of goods
* Itemised and total price of goods (VAT and carriage where applicable)
* Payment terms, better still the actual due date

Statements are a convenient vehicle for the first reminder message e.g.. "Of the balance shown XXX is overdue. Please pay now." Show sufficient information on each item to identify it clearly (date, original reference number, customer order number etc).

* Separate out invoices, credit notes, part payment, overpayment and disputed items
* Show the cumulative value

Good cash collectors need the same skills as salesmen. To persuade customers to pay up while keeping them sweet, they need to be:

- Articulate
- Organised
- Politely diplomatic
- Persuasive
- Persistent
- Patient
- Assertive
- Able to listen and question
- Skilled in negotiating

In addition they must be able to finalise payment agreement with a commitment from the customer, and of following this up.

Payment requests may be verbal or written. The more valuable the customer, the more important it is to have direct contact.

- Key accounts warrant personal attention through visits or telephone calls
- Middle range accounts can be dealt with by telephone or routine letters
- Others may require only routine letters

Telephone Reminders

On the telephone your main aim is to use communication skills to make the contact want to pay you before any other. This needs structure, preparation and organisation as well as interpersonal skills.

- **Personalise the call.** Ask for your contact by name, say who you are, the organisation you represent and the reason for the call. Be nice, be polite and never let the call sound robotic or routine
- **Be prepared.** Have with you all the information you may need to respond to the disputes or excuses - account details, chasing history, payment terms, credit limit, overdue invoices and orders on hand
- **Never allow yourself to be fobbed off.** Make it clear you intend to get immediate settlement. Pursuing to higher levels will often solve the matter
- **Confirm the commitment.** Conclude the call with a firm mutually understood and acceptable commitment from the customer. Say 'thank you' for appreciated assistance, and always confirm the agreement

Dealing with Excuses

The most successful collectors are those able to react and deal with excuses for non-payment. These fall into two categories, administrative and cash flow, although administrative excuses are often used when cash flow is the real problem.

Cash flow excuses are more difficult. Any admission of insufficient funds must be taken seriously. You will be only one among many creditors affected so you must get tough.

- Suggest the debtor borrows from his bank
- With a limited company, or plc, imply exposure for wrongful trading. Simply ask if, under the circumstances, they are still trading. They should get the point
- With others, talk tough and get tough. If you don't, someone else will
- Always press for the full amount. Fall back on instalment arrangements only as a last resort

Remember always that you can't get blood from a stone. Watch for warning signs of cash flow problems so that you aren't caught out when a customer goes down.

Written Reminders

Routine letters can be effective if you:

- Are concise - i.e. itemise the debt quoting all relevant details and dates
- Never apologise - Don't use 'get out' clauses like "ignore if paid in last seven days"
- Escalate as needed - Send a sequence of letters one to the original contact in Accounts, the next to the Buyer or Trader contact and the last to the Financial Director. Vary the tone and wording of the letters to reflect the interests of the addressees

Do remember that faxed letters have immediacy. They are also cheaper, faster, more personal and more effective.

Sanctions. Having sent a final demand and followed it up with a telephone call, the matter must be brought to a conclusion or else these outstanding debts will drain your company's profits. The most commonly used sanctions are listed below.

Stop List. Suspend deliveries of all goods and services. Warn the debtor of pending suspension and do not lift it until all overdue accounts have been cleared.

You can also ask sales to nominate accounts where early warning of suspension would be useful. Advise these customers they should be 'on stop' now but you are giving them some days' grace to put things right.

Legal Action. This is the last resort because it usually means the end of the relationship. Before taking legal action you need to be sure that all disputes are resolved, that you have a good proof of your claim and that the debtor can afford to pay.

- Solicitor's Letter - Avoids expensive court action. A good third party stimulus
- County Court - For claims less than £50,000, but seldom used for the higher end of the spectrum as the High Court is considered more effective
- High Court - For debts in excess of £50,000 but often used for lower amounts
- Winding up Petition - Through both High Court and County Court. This really is the last gasp when pursuing a debt as it can put the debtor into liquidation. Be sure to appoint a reputable agency

Debt Collection Agency This means you have signalled your seriousness publicly - the debt is no longer a game. But do make sure you place a reputable and efficient agency on the account.

The golden rule is never to issue a sanction threat unless you are prepared to carry it out. Don't be classified as a bluffer.

SIGNPOSTS OF INSOLVENCY

Insolvency in a customer usually means a total loss for unsecured creditors. But bad debts rarely occur without warning. Good credit managers will be on the lookout for

- Slow paying with lame excuses
- External reports of payment problems
- Unguarded comments by customer's staff
- County court judgments
- Bounced cheques or direct debits
- Adverse press comment
- Late lodging of accounts
- Qualification of accounts by auditors
- Worsening ratios in accounts
- Bank and trade references amended downwards.

The pragmatic approach is to accept that not all customers are blue chip but while several will be risky they still have the potential to provide profitable sales. So accept their business, but with strict contracts and be on continuous watch for the signals listed above for signs of trouble.

The above is a digest of the booklet Effective Credit Management by M G Dixon issued by Dun & Bradstreet International in cooperation with the Sage Group PLC. In addition to more detail on the above the booklet outlines systems for setting credit management targets, marketing performance and reporting to management. It also includes useful sample letters and credit control conversations as well as illustrations of how Sage financial management software can simplify the management task.

Richard Selmon, Dun & Bradstreet Ltd

It often takes small firms a long time to learn just how important having effective control is. Look at the table below.

	£0.5m-£1m	£1m-£5m	£5m-£10m
Debtors Days	57	50	47
Annual Stock Turn	9	10	12

These figures come from a Cranfield study in 1996 on how effective small firms are at controlling their working capital. The smaller firms (£0.5 m - £1m) took 57 days to get their money in from customers and turned their stock over nine times each year. The larger firms in the study had much better control. Their debtors paid in 47 days and their stock turned over twelve times. The evidence supports the hypothesis that very small firms often have few controls so actually don't know what is going on - often until it is too late.

WOOLF - A NEW LITIGATION REGIME

Ensuring debts are paid on time is an important part of keeping a healthy cash flow. However, all businesses will be confronted with contractual disputes and bad debts from time to time. This may well necessitate action being taken to recover money due to them through the Courts.

The rules of procedure governing the British Civil Justice System have been radically overhauled recently by the "Woolf reforms" which came into effect in April 1999. The aim of the new system is to encourage a more co-operative and consensual approach to dispute resolution. The emphasis of the Courts is to ensure that cases are dealt with "justly".

The underlying desire of the reforms is to make the litigation process quicker and cheaper. To achieve this the new system has made a number of significant changes.

Court's Role

The Court will take a much more "hands-on" approach to the way in which cases are run. They will adopt the role of case managers. This will ensure that matters do not simply drift.

The Judge will now encourage you to co-operate with the other side and encourage you to identify relevant issues at an early stage. The Courts will no longer tolerate parties who use the system as a tool to pressure their opponent. The Judge will also fix timetables for the matter to be heard. This timetable will be strictly enforced and severe penalties will be handed out to those who do not conduct their case in a manner that ensures adherence.

The Court will allocate all claims to one of three categories:

- Small Claims Track. Claims which have a financial value of up to £5,000.
- Fast Track. Claims which have a financial value of between £5,000 and £15,000.
- Multi Track. Claims of over £15,000.

These "tracks" will effect you in the following ways:

- Small claims track does not allow recovery of costs, although the Court has a discretion to award expenses up to £200, depending on how you have conducted the case.
- Fast track claims proceed very quickly, with a maximum of 30 weeks until trial. Solicitor's costs will be recoverable but they will be severely limited.
- Multi track claims will see the Court taking a very hands on approach. Case management conferences will be set up where the Judge will review all the steps taken by both parties in the case. The emphasis will again be on speed and resolving the dispute.

Penalties for non compliance

You must be aware that if you miss deadlines or cause delay in the case the Court will impose strict and severe penalties upon you. If you miss deadlines set by the Court you face the following sanctions:

- Costs penalties
- Dismissal of your case by the Court

Nick Worthington and Andrew Betteridge, Shoosmiths

In my experience . . .

1. Don't go looking for new customers at the expense of neglecting your existing ones.

2. Deal with everything once and efficiently

Michael Hockley, M & H Tapestry and Craft

The Internet

Chapter Seven

The way business is done is set to change forever and we should regard ourselves as fortunate to be living through such an exciting time of transformation. There are more business opportunities now than there have ever been and, whether ready or not, sooner or later your business will be affected by electronic methods of trading i.e. e-business.

There is no great mystery to doing business electronically. It is simply a means of using technology cheaply and quickly, giving you the flexibility to improve your competitive stance and ultimately to make your business more profitable.

Each business will have a different timescale which they are working towards when they are thinking about their company's approach to e-business. At the beginning of the designated time frame there is "getting access" and at the end is "e-business" and in between are a series of steps that your business needs to take in order to get there.

All of these steps are covered in the following chapter but in brief comprise: getting access; setting up a web site; marketing your web site; maintaining and developing web site complexity; embracing e-commerce (i.e. developing an online shop); and then enabling your whole business to be electronically integrated with both suppliers and customers (i.e. e-business).

There is absolutely no need to be daunted by e-business as it is entirely your choice as to the pace at which you approach and take each step.

GETTING ACCESS

For most small businesses it is no longer a question of should they connect to the Internet but rather how best to do it. The Internet offers a wealth of information, a quick and cheap means of communication and an exciting new way to do business. The question still facing most businesses, therefore, is how best to get access to this brave new world.

What you need is a simple guide to the technology and the terminology so that the process of going online is a series of informed decisions rather than a leap in the dark. You need to know what hardware and software you should buy, how you connect your machine to the Internet and who is the most suitable Internet Service Provider for you.

Three Reasons why you should connect to the Internet

A small business should connect to the Internet to find information, to communicate and to do business online:

To find information - The range of information available through the Internet means that no small business can afford to be without access.

Businesses, Research Institutes, Universities, Local Authorities, Development Agencies all post a wide range of information on the Internet. As the majority of this information is free, it is too good an opportunity to miss!

To communicate - Using e-mail you can communicate with other businesses and customers. E-mail allows you to transfer electronic information across the world for the price of a local phone call. This both reduces communication costs and improves communication effectiveness.

To do business online - You can use the Internet as a means of promoting your business, selling products and services online and dealing with suppliers and customers. This will increase your business efficiency, extend your markets and allow you to reach new customers. This can all contribute to the profitability of your business.

The first step before purchasing any equipment is to examine why you want to connect to the Internet so you should consider the following:

* Will you be accessing the Internet regularly?
* What type of Information will you be searching for?
* What will be the main use of the Internet?
* How many people in your business require Internet Access?
* Do you intend to sell your products on the Internet?
* How much money have you got to spend?

The more benefits you can see from the Internet the more money you will be willing to spend. If you require one person to access the Internet infrequently to search for text information the equipment you will need to purchase will be very different from a business that needs multiple people to use the Internet all of the time and wants to set up a trading web site.

The Resources you will need to connect to the Internet

There are three key resources any business needs to connect to the Internet: a computer, a connection and an Internet Service Provider (ISP).

What type of Computer will I need?

Before you start buying the specialist equipment you think you need, have a look at your current computer. The chances are that if you have purchased a computer in the last year it will be capable of connecting to the Internet without the need for any new equipment. You will have purchased an 'Internet-Ready' machine. Even with an old computer you can get connected at a minimal cost by adding some new memory or a faster processor.

If you are buying a new Windows PC make sure that, as a minimum specification, it has a Pentium or AMD 400 MHz central processing unit (CPU) and 64 Mb of RAM

If you are considering an Apple Macintosh machine, all of the newer PowerPC CPU equipped models are fully internet capable. As with the Windows PCs, ensure that there is at least 64 Mb of RAM fitted, the more the better.

The CPU is the 'brain' of your computer and carries out the majority of calculations and information retrieval from the memory. The MHz rating shows how fast the computer can perform these tasks and so a 400 MHz machine is faster than a 350 which is faster than a 300 and so on, although this figure can be misleading when comparing an Apple machine with a PC.

RAM (random access memory) refers to the amount of memory available in the computer. The more RAM your computer has the more easily it will cope with large amounts of information and complex programs. If you are thinking of designing your own web site and want to use a graphics package to do this then you will need to have sufficient RAM.

What type of connection will I need?

As important as the type of computer that you use, is your method of connecting to the Internet. This determines not only how quickly you can access information but also the type of information you can access.

There are several methods of connection including modem, ISDN and leased line. One of the main differentiating factors is the speed of connection. Modems are slower than ISDN which in turn is usually slower than a leased connection. Connectivity is measured in kilobits per second (Kbps). The higher the Kbps figure, the faster your connection to the Internet. The absolute minimum connection speed is 14.4 Kbps. At this speed the Internet appears very slow and patience is a virtue. If you have only ever seen the Internet through a 14.4 connection you might wonder what all the excitement is about. You will have difficulty in downloading anything other than text and simple graphics in an acceptable time. Today, speeds of 56.6 Kbps and above are now quite common and at that rate you will be able to enjoy graphically-rich, interactive sites that may well include video, animation and sound.

Modems connect through an ordinary telephone line. They can be fitted inside a computer or as an external piece of hardware. Older modems may be only capable of speeds up to 14.4 Kbps but most modern computers come with a 56K modem as standard and this can be plugged directly into a telephone socket. This is by far the easiest method of connecting to the Internet and is suitable if only one machine needs access. You can use this type of connection if you do not regularly need to access or send large amounts of information over the Internet. On the negative side, because of the relatively slow connection speed, there will be some Internet applications that this connection is not suitable for, such as viewing certain types of multimedia clips.

The next step up from the 56K modem is to use an ISDN (Integrated Services Digital Network) connection. This can connect you to the Internet at speeds of 128Kbps and more. This method requires the installation of additional hardware to your computer in the form of an ISDN Terminal Adapter and the installation of an ISDN Line from the local telephone exchange to your place of work. The costs for these can vary but are not excessive and once the system is installed the costs of using ISDN are very similar to those of using a 56K modem.

The advantages of using ISDN are threefold. Firstly, ISDN is much less susceptible to line noise than traditional modems, meaning that there is less chance of the Internet connection breaking. Secondly, ISDN allows the user to connect to the Internet in under 5 seconds, saving time for those businesses who connect regularly. Finally, because of the increased speed and connection reliability, ISDN allows the user to access many types of multimedia such as audio and short video clips. This type of connection is ideal for those businesses wishing to transfer large amounts of information whilst minimising expenditure. Once the ISDN lines are in place, it is possible to have several computers in the building with direct access to the Internet through a router. A router will allow a number of computers to access the Internet through a single connection.

Some businesses require very quick 24-hour dedicated connectivity between their offices and the Internet. The solution for these businesses is to use a leased line connection. Connection speeds can vary from 64K upwards. This type of dedicated access has cost implications both in terms of the equipment needed to access the Internet and the ongoing running costs of the system.

Having a leased line connection means that multiple machines in the office can be connected to the Internet and large amounts of information can be transferred very quickly. This type of system is ideal for companies who require constant access and have large amounts of information to transfer.

Which Internet Service Provider should I use?

You will need to access the Internet through an Internet Service Provider (ISP). An ISP will give you the software you need to connect to the Internet. They should also provide you with technical help to get your business online. There are now hundreds of ISPs, all offering very similar products but at varying costs. Your choice of service provider will depend largely on how you intend to use the Internet and you should consider the following when selecting an ISP:

Access and Performance - Can the ISP guarantee that you will connect easily to the Internet or will their line often be busy? Who are their other customers? Using an ISP who has a large number of non-business clients may mean that you share the service with millions of people, rather than hundreds of businesses. Does the ISP provide access via the type of connection you require? Many ISP's still do not support ISDN connections. How quickly will they deliver your e-mail? How long do web pages take to download?

Technical Support - Do they provide 24 hour technical support? Is the customer service team friendly and knowledgeable? What is the cost of the technical support? How long will you need to wait before receiving support?

E-mail and Web Pages - Does the ISP provide you with an e-mail account and the ability to post a web site on their server? How much does this cost or is it included in the initial price?

Cost - Many ISP's now offer free access to the Internet, others charge a monthly subscription fee. What are you getting for your money? When considering which ISP to use consider all of these factors as well as any special features that are being offered.

ISP's tend to fall into three categories, those that provide free access for the general public, those that provide general services to both the public and businesses usually via a monthly charge and those that are set up to provide professional services to the business community.

Freeserve, Bun, Zoom and Tesconet all provide Free Internet Access to the general public except for the cost of the telephone calls. If you chose to use one of these ISPs to provide your connection to the Internet then all you need to do is look in the shops, newspapers and even your own letter box for the software they provide free of charge to help you connect to the Internet.

Sage.com is a specialist ISP that caters for the users of Sage software products. It has all of the benefits of a free ISP, is tailored for the small business community, and comes with free support from Sage's technical support team.

If you have decided that you would rather use an ISP who provides a higher level of service and customer support then you may wish to consider providers such as Netcom, Compuserve, Pipex or Demon. To discover more about these businesses and the services you can expect try looking in the specialist Internet Magazines. It will be an important exercise to work out whether the additional costs incurred through this type of ISP are worth the quicker access. Prices vary depending on the number of hours the system will be used. All ISP's will provide you with software to connect to the Internet. This will normally come in the form of a CD-ROM.

The highest level of service is offered by providers such as Rapidsite and Virtual Internet. These companies cater for businesses who require full web site capabilities including domain name registration, large reserved storage space, interactive web elements, high capacity e-mail and e-commerce facilities. Charges are levied depending on the capacity and facilities required. Generally, these companies do not offer dial-up access which would need to be obtained via either a free access or charged access provider.

As part of their service most ISP's provide their users with e-mail accounts. This means that you can send and receive e-mail. This is one of the most widely used aspects of the Internet and can reduce a business's costs dramatically. Most ISP's provide their customers with an e-mail address such as fred.smith@smithsigns.freeISP.com. The e-mail address is your postal address on the Internet and is what your customers and suppliers will need from you if they want to send you an electronic document. E-mail addresses issued by your ISP tend to be very long and promote the ISP rather than your business.

In order to personalise your e-mail address you will need to register a domain name. A domain name is your business's unique address on the Internet, and can refer specifically to your company, products or areas of business. A domain name is used not only as your e-mail address (fred.smith@smithsigns.co.uk) but also as the address of your web site (www.smithsigns.co.uk). There are several advantages to having a domain name:

* An e-mail address can reflect the nature or name of your business without advertising your Internet Service Provider
* Even small businesses look big with their own domain name
* People will find it easier to remember
* You can change your ISP while still keeping the same e-mail address and personalised domain name

When choosing a domain name for your business you must consider whether to have a .com or a .co.uk. There are no hard and fast rules but a .co.uk is the usual choice for those businesses who only trade in this country while .com is often the choice of those businesses that trade internationally. Often your choice is restricted if the name has already been registered by someone else. If this has happened you may have to register a variation on your name. So for example if smithsigns.co.uk had already been registered then Fred Smith may have to settle for smith-signs.co.uk as his domain name. There are several specialist companies such as DomainNames.com, NetNames and Netbenefit who register domain names and will be able to offer advice on choosing the best domain name for your business. You can also register through your ISP such as Freeserve or Sage.com.

An additional service to domain name registration is to have e-mail forwarding. This allows you to use a number of e-mail addresses that are then directed into your e-mail post box. For example Fred Smith may choose to have sales@smith-signs.co.uk, info@smith-signs.co.uk as well as Fred.Smith@smith-signs.co.uk. This is useful in making a small business appear to have many more departments than it does in reality.

What can I do with the Web Space my ISP has given me?

Many ISPs provide web space as well as connectivity to the Internet. This can be used to develop your own presence on the Internet in the form of a web site.

Some businesses decide to design their own Internet site using software packages such as Microsoft Front Page. Many, however, decide to use a professional web design agency to develop the web site for them. If you choose to develop your own web site this can reduce cost but often the end-results do not provide a very good impression of your business, making it look amateur compared to those competitors with a professionally designed web site. Consider it this way, you would not design and produce your own brochures so why design and produce your own web site? There are literally thousands of Internet Design Agencies who you can use to develop your web site. Prices vary depending on experience, professionalism and the amount of work you require.

How to Choose an Internet Design Agency

* Prepare a clear brief. This should cover your goals and objectives, target audiences, specific areas for inclusion, budget and time scale, as well as background information on your business.

* Speak to other businesses that have worked with Internet design agencies. Word of mouth is a good way of discovering the good and bad businesses to work with.

* Approach three or four Internet Agencies that meet your criteria and arrange to discuss your project with them. Listen to their ideas and ask how they would approach the task.

* When making the decision on which agency to work with you should look at their understanding of your business, their background and existing clients, any designs they have produced for you and the price they have quoted you.

Getting access to the Internet could be one of the best business decisions you have ever made. As well as helping you to find lots of useful information and communicate better using e-mail, it could provide you with a new and exciting way to develop your business and sell in markets that were previously out of your reach. You may discover that your business already has most if not all of the technology it requires to take advantage of this exciting new medium, so why not give it a go?

James Bunting, Leighton

BUSINESS AND THE INTERNET

An awful lot has been written about doing business via the Internet. Today, the question is not "Should I get on the Net?" it is "How do I move on to the next level and use the power of the Internet to expand my business and make it more competitive?"

IBM's own e-business transformation is moving apace: we've web-enabled many of our core business processes to increase efficiency and profitability. By the end of this year, we will have purchased $12 billion worth of goods and services over the Net - saving $240 million this year. IBM Business Partners will soon be able to buy 1800 - that's nearly all - IBM products on the Web. We anticipate revenues of more than $10 billion via Web sales in '99.

We are convinced that the magic e-business can work for large organisations like IBM can drive huge benefits for small business too. Lugton Breweries, a four person Scottish cooperative, went global through the Net using IBM's Home Page Creator. Sales increased nearly 1000 per cent in 12 months. Hawaiian Greenhouse, a small family firm, used IBM's Lotus Domino Merchant software to move from a wholesale to a retail distribution model. Within 10 months, their retail revenues were double their original wholesale business. They expect to double their retail turnover again in the coming 12 months. Using the Internet, small business can appear - and become - very large, quickly.

It is disappointing, as the Government's Performance and Innovation Unit's Report "e-commerce@its.best.uk" highlighted, that "Small and micro companies are falling badly behind" in exploiting e-commerce, with the UK's "micro" companies near the bottom of the international league table in terms of Web presence. This inertia is baffling, particularly when very small business has been such an engine of growth for the UK economy.

The first step is always the hardest to take, but if you are running a small business today, you need to act with urgency: make it a small step - get on the Web, then perhaps make a move into buying and selling over the Web. But take that step now, and do not lose sight of how powerfully the Internet can transform the way in which your organisation operates.

Carl G Symon, Chairman & CEO, IBM UK Ltd

Planning your Web site

What does web site-planning entail?

Your web site should be planned with two main considerations at the forefront of your mind:

Who is/are my target audience(s)? and
What do I want to achieve?

It is fundamental for your business to understand that, unlike normal communications channels, the web is a fluid medium. To get the best out of it requires a dynamic approach to its evolution and this needs to be incorporated into the planning process.

This is particularly relevant when you consider who your different target markets will be. In the short term you may decide that your primary target will be local customers who have a similar profile to your existing customer base. However, even as you launch your web site you may find that your customer base rapidly evolves to include a new set of clientele on the other side of the world.

Your planning process must, therefore, take account of this potential and rapid change. In addition, because of this diverse customer base, you will need to consider the complexity of factors that drive and motivate different segments of the market to purchase.

Put in simple terms, you must plan for the mindset of your customers.

- Who are your customers?
- Will they include suppliers as well as buyers?
- What will they expect from your web site?
- What should they be able to do in your web site?
- What information do you want to provide them with and how will this information vary between customer groups?
- What are your competition doing for them?

Taking just one potential element of your web site - online shopping - one of the questions you will need to ask yourself is "are my customers ready to purchase online immediately?" If so, you will need to incorporate an e-commerce enabled "shop" (see e-trading) at the outset. Alternatively, they may not be ready to purchase immediately but in 6 month's time they will be. You will, therefore, have to decide whether to build in a shop from the outset or whether to master the other elements of your web site first and then look to incorporate the "shop" at a later stage.

Arguments exist for both options. For example you could argue that the shop should be there from the outset so that clients know that they can purchase from your web site when they are ready to do so. Alternatively, you could maintain that the shop shouldn't be there because it may worry customers who are primarily seeking reassurance and are information gathering.

The contents for your web site development plan:

1. The target market(s)
2. The competition
3. Setting the goals
4. Allocation of resource
5. Plan the implementation
6. Collect the content
7. Design the site
8. Prepare the PR and marketing plan
9. Test
10. Launch
11. Act on feedback
12. Deal with demand
13. Add the Internet to overall strategic business planning

1. The target market(s)

Target markets differ according to the nature of your business, your geographical spread and your ambitions. When planning for your target audiences, you should consider both who they are in the short term and also who and where you would like them to come from in the medium to long term.

It is likely that your web site will need to answer the requirements of a range of audiences. Identified below are three target markets that you may want to consider when setting up your web site. You may decide that your web site needs to cater for other audiences in which case you should work through the same logical process for each.

The customers

Ultimately, any marketing and communication you undertake for your business is about driving in more revenue. Therefore, getting more from your existing customers and attracting new customers has to be one of your primary objectives.

Even if you think your customer base is very local and unlikely to come from anywhere else in the world, there is still plenty of opportunity to use your web site to both enhance your service to existing customers and to convert more customers, albeit local, via the web.

For all customers you should think about using your web site to enhance the service you provide online. For each question, identified below, you need to work out the answers as they relate to you, your business and your customers. These considerations should then be incorporated into your web site strategy. For each customer group identified you should think about the following:

- Do your customers expect you to be online?
- How will you use the site to enhance service delivery?
- Will your customers expect and be prepared to buy online?
- How will you offer reassurances about your business and its security policies for your customers?
- What level of commitment will you offer them e.g. on delivery times etc.?
- Should you give discounts if customers buy online because you save on administration costs?

The suppliers

You should consider how you can use your web site to aid the relationship you have with your suppliers. Identify who currently supplies your business and then negotiate with them to see if, by using your web site, both you and your suppliers can save on administration time and costs.

In particular, you should consider how you could use the web to aid stock control and, thereby, ease any cashflow issues you may have.

For example, you could allow supplier access to your database or set up a dedicated password-protected (see glossary) area of the web site. Through this avenue you could regularly update your stock levels, agree re-order points and leave your supplier to check your web site and distribute orders at the appropriate times.

Not only will this free some of your administration time but it will also ensure that you do not have surplus stock delivered before you are ready. If you can build administration discounts into this model too then this is better still.

Don't forget that you can always use your web site to publish competitive tenders. In this way you encourage suppliers to come to you rather than spending your time searching for them.

The investors

If you start your business with the help of investors or if at some point you come to incorporate them, then it is important that they can see what is happening to their investment. Many investors now expect to see detailed financial information on web pages so that they can retain their confidence in their initial investment decision.

If investors are important to you and your business, then this is definitely something you need to consider when setting up your web pages. You may want to consider publishing both your annual accounts and business plan online. You could use the web as your only means for publishing this information (assuming you have no legal requirement to publish elsewhere), thus saving considerable print and production costs and giving you a platform that you can easily and frequently update. If you want this information to be exclusively published online and only accessible to your investors, then it's possible to create a "password-protected" area of the web site in order to do this. In this way, you can distribute the password to your investors, publish confidential information online, and rest certain in the knowledge that no one else will be able to gain access to it.

2. The Competition

In order to make an informed decision about how you approach your web site design, you will need to be aware of what your competition is up to. For example, if you are late entering the web market place there is no point starting your web design several stages behind that offered by your competition. Similarly, if your competition are not online yet, but you anticipate that they soon will be, then you will need to make some predictions about what you believe their web site will contain.

It is always worthwhile searching the web for similar industry web sites, even where there may be no geographical conflict. In this way, you will be able to judge for yourself who has used the web to best effect. You will need to bear in mind, however, that there could be web applications that you are not privy to and which could give substantial enhancement to customer/supplier relationships i.e. password-protected areas.

Once you have assessed what the competition are up to and have made some assumptions about their future progression, you will then need to judge this against your own set of objectives.

The great advantage of the web is that even small businesses can compete with the larger ones if the product and customer mix is correct. Competition in the electronic world can be completely different from the offline world. If, for example, you are able to supply your products world wide, you could find yourself competing against a bigger company with an established brand in the UK but also looking to break into the global market place. In this scenario, as far as the new customers are concerned, both companies start from a position of equality in the online world. These potential customers then make their decisions by a different set of criteria such as - is the web site professional? Does it reassure me? Is their product range extensive and competitively priced? What is their delivery commitment?

Some companies have set up as "web only" concerns and have created successful online businesses without having any traditional "high street" presence, the most obvious example being www.amazon.com - the leading online bookseller. Many of these businesses operate out of low cost premises and keep their overheads to a minimum. To the online world they are smooth, slick, large operations because of the web site and supporting service they have created. They demonstrate that it is possible to compete in the global market place in a way that they would be unable to elsewhere.

3. Setting The Goals

Having established who your target audiences are and what the competition are planning or have implemented, it is then possible for you to set some goals for your web site.

The most important consideration for any goals that you set is that they are realistic and achievable - so start simple and add on as you grow in confidence. If you fail to do this, then you could end up demotivating yourself and any others that work for you on the project. The danger will then be that you discard the web as part of your overall business strategy and then find yourself revisiting it several months down the line when your competition have subsequently overtaken you.

What will you do with your web site?

These are some examples of the goals you may wish to set yourself and your business.

- Improve corporate/brand image - having a web site says something about the company you are. It tells the world that your business is innovative and a market leader
- Find new prospects - you could discover new customers round the corner or on the other side of the world. Having a web site opens up a range of new opportunities.
- Perform transactions - you may want to use the web to sell things, in fact your whole business could be geared exclusively to the web.
- Improve customer service - your customers may expect you to be online. You could use the web to enhance the service you are able to offer with quicker response times. Also, administrative cost savings could result in customers benefiting from online price reductions.
- Reduce costs - Having a web site can often reduce other business-related costs. For example, the supply chain can be shortened because you can talk directly to the customer without the intervention of any third parties. In addition, promotion and communication online is often cheaper than traditional forms of advertising.
- Attract future employees - The web is becoming increasingly important for recruitment. This is particularly true for graduates and IT professionals. If these people or other web users are important to your business then it is worthwhile setting this as a goal.

- Satisfy investor relations - as previously mentioned, it may be important to your business to have a site that successfully satisfies your investors.

4. Allocation of resource

Having established that you need a web site and what you need one for, it is then time to consider what resource will be allocated to it. The issues that you will need to plan for are not solely related to finance but perhaps more importantly, time. Not only will you need to set aside some time at the outset, but in order to make best use of your site you will also need to make an on-going commitment to ensure that it is constantly updated. In addition, you will need to ensure that all responses are monitored and that when dealing with customer comments and online purchases a swift commitment is made.

5. Plan the implementation

Just as important as planning the resource you will need to allocate is the need to consider how this will impact on the rest of your business. Inevitably, you will, at some point, turn to an external party to handle some part of the physical implementation - whether this is using a "free" provider or whether you decide to use a specialist agency. However, you will need to consider the implications that your web site will have on the running of your business. For example, if you are selling directly online you will need to consider how you will handle: credit card transactions, international taxation issues, internal legal questions, and distribution - all of which will have implications with regard to how they integrate with the rest of your business activities.

6. Collect the content

You will also need to plan for the practicalities involved in setting up a web site. These include collecting all the content you require for your web pages and rewriting much of the copy so that it is suitable for on-screen reading. The basic guideline for this is to keep all copy short and sharp and where possible no more than one screen full. In addition, you will also need to collect any photographs, graphics or product images you require and where necessary arrange for new images to be taken. In particular, you will need to be aware of any copyright issues you may confront when publicising images and copy across the web.

7. Design and Hosting of the site

How you approach site design is handled later in this chapter. However, you will need to consider it in the planning process and it is worth mentioning some of the issues here. Not least of which is whether you will design the site yourself using free web templates such as those offered by Sage, or whether you will need to employ a specialist web design agency.

In both cases you will need to think about how the design reflects the needs of your different target audiences. This will have particular relevance for any navigation issues that arise i.e. how you lay out the information and web links to ensure that customers can find their way around the site with ease. Before sitting down to do any form of web design it is important that you clearly work out what information you will put under what titles so that the web pages link together in a coherent fashion.

So, for example, if you had a section on recruitment you may title it either "Recruitment" or "Jobs" depending on the tone you wish to set. Underneath this title could be links to:

Current jobs;
- Speculative CVs (gives candidates a chance to market themselves to you, even when no current vacancy exists);
- Apply online (you could either get candidates to send in their CVs against specific jobs or you could ask them to complete an online application form);
- Add your name to our mailing list (you could regularly update your vacancies and choose to e-mail these to potential candidates and thereby offer a value-added service).

How you prioritise these links and the tone you set will be crucial to how your customers will navigate your site. If it is important to you that customers visit a particular page then it is worthwhile considering how you would prioritise these in order to achieve your specific goals.

You will also need to make a decision as to who will actually "host" your web site (see previous section). This decision will be determined by: cost, reliability and speed of access. All these factors will affect how your target audiences perceive your web presence.

8. Prepare the Marketing and PR Plan

It is imperative to plan all your communications initiatives in conjunction with your web plans so that you have a cohesive approach to your target audiences. This relates to all the points previously mentioned, and in practical terms means that if you have simply lifted your corporate brochure and created it as a web site and someone responds to your web site and asks for more information what are you going to send them? Equally, if you publish your web address on your brochure and someone takes the trouble to visit your web site what will they see that is any different from what they have seen already?

One of the best forms of marketing for your web site is, of course, the web itself. The web's greatest advantage over other forms of communication channel is that everyone who uses the web is actively searching for information.

Your primary objective will be to ensure that all your potential target audiences find your web site during their searching process. Having found a reference to your web site, the next objective is to get them to visit it.

Considering how much information is published on the web, it is actually quite well organised. Individual web sites can be registered and indexed with "search engine sites" so that everyone can find them. There are many search engine sites on the web, some reference every single web site available, others break down references by country, and some by a particular subject or group of subjects. Others are designed not only to reference useful web sites but also to give you a range of comprehensive and related information themselves.

The major world wide search engines include:
www.yahoo.com
www.altavista.com
www.excite.com
alltheweb.com
www.hotbot.com
www.infoseek.com
www.lycos.co.uk
www.askjeeves.com

When you arrive at these search engine sites you need to select the option to register your site. In most cases you will find the link from their home page.

So what does registration of your web site involve? Registration is generally free and works by indexing every web site's unique address - URL (Uniform Resource Locator). If you have purchased your own domain name your web site address will normally be written as either "http://www.yourcompany.co.uk/" or simply as "www.yourcompany.co.uk". If you haven't purchased your own domain name, then your address will be written as follows: "http://www.yourcompany.hostname.co.uk".

Each search engine has its own requirements for web site registration. For example, if you submit your site to www.yahoo.com (probably the largest online search engine) you will need to give them:

- Your company's unique web address
- 20 key words (i.e. you must try to guess what your potential customers will search for)
- A 200 character description of your business

Other search engines use all the words in your web site and give them a hierarchy according to where in the site they appear and others still use words written in the programming language called META tags. You may find you need some technical help when you get into this level of sign-posting sophistication but it is worth considering at the outset.

Each country, each region and often each town have their own search engine. Needless to say, it would be in your best interest to get your web site registered in as many different search engines as possible. In particular, if your web site is primarily aimed at local audiences then the local directories, of which there are growing numbers, could be of particular importance, especially at the outset.

Whilst you can buy software to do a large part of the registration automatically, in the initial stages it would be worthwhile spending some time exploring the web yourself in order to try to determine where you might like to register your web site. This process is both revealing and rewarding because it often leads to relationship building with other online businesses where you agree on reciprocal web links because of complementary business objectives.

The other form of online marketing to consider is "Banner Advertising". This is a paid for service but gives you a chance to advertise your web site on other web sites and search engines. Once you have decided where you would like to advertise you should then agree a rate. Some web sites set a fixed fee for advertising, others calculate the fee on the basis of the number of people that use it to "click through" to your web site. In both cases, you will need to get your banner advertisement designed for the web so will probably need to agree a fee for this with a design agency. Many companies regard banner advertising as one of the most effective forms of advertising in comparison to other both on and off line methods.

Of course, you should publish your web address in all your traditional marketing materials. This includes letterheads, fax headers and business cards, as well as brochures and adverts.

Once you are ready to launch your web site, you should think about a publicity launch or a press release announcing it. However, you will need to make sure that what you have done is newsworthy and that there is a significant story for the press to get their teeth into.

9. Test

Once your web site is near completion, it is a good idea to get it checked by some of your existing customers to ensure that it satisfies their needs and more importantly that it all works properly.

You can put the web site on the internet and arrange for whoever is going to host/design the site to keep a password on it until you are ready for the world to view it. You can give this password to a select number of customers and suppliers etc. and collect their comments and make any necessary amendments before you launch it.

10. Launch

Once you are happy with your web site you should remove the passwords and start registering it with all the search engines.

If you are going to take part in a major launch event, be careful that its timing does not conflict with other major events in your industry or area that will deflect focus from its launch.

11. Act on Feedback

Not only will you be able to determine customer opinion from the number of relevant orders or enquiries you receive, but you should also be able to track visitor information electronically too.

When you get your web site hosted, you should also ask about free tracking software. This tracks where your web site customers have come from (countries of origin), what days and times they have visited and which pages were viewed most frequently. Even at a very basic level this information will tell you a lot about your target audience(s) and what they find the most interesting. It will also help you plan how you will improve the site as you go along. For example, if you find some pages in the site are much more frequently visited than others you could either decide to increase this section of the web site or make sure that the other sections of the web site were improved to match it.

The main point to note is that you should consider all feedback you receive and plan how you will act on this in the short to medium term.

12. Deal with demand

Looking on the optimistic side, you need to determine whether your business is ready to deal with the demand. For example, are your systems set up to handle the increased order processing and distribution? Have you determined who, within the business, will be responsible for online customer relations?

Unless best case scenarios are anticipated at the outset, you may find worst case scenarios developing fairly rapidly.

13. Add the Internet to overall strategic business planning

Finally, once you have set all your web site plans in place, you will need to ensure that these plans are added to the overall strategic development of your business.

Having realised the importance of operating a web site and properly planning its instigation, it is imperative that you keep up with the rapid pace of online development.

The best approach to making your move online is to ensure that you plan properly. Time spent in forward planning will avoid subsequent need for major changes.

The web is not something to be daunted by. Having a web site will add value to everything else you do in your daily business life, you just need to plan for it.

Dawn Baker, Sage Software Limited

PREPARING FOR AN INTERNET SITE

Now that you have a computer, an Internet connection and some web space, you may decide to design your own Internet site. This may be simply as an experiment or because at this stage you cannot justify spending the money on using a professional Internet Agency. Either way, as the site will be representing your company and will be many people's first contact with your business, it is important that the site creates a good impression.

The first step on the road to success is to get the correct software for editing images and creating web pages. There are several packages on the market such as Microsoft Frontpage, Macromedia Dreamweaver and Sausage Software's Hotdog. All have their strengths and weaknesses and vary substantially in cost but they do take the pain out of HTML programming.

Having a piece of packaged software does not guarantee a good site. You have to realise that the web site has to be well designed and functional. Remember, good design whispers but bad design shouts out. So, what factors should you take into consideration when designing your site?

Begin by asking yourself the following questions: What is the site trying to achieve and who is your target audience? The design you would use to sell toys to 12 year olds will be very different to the design you would use to try to persuade a business to use your services. In both cases your objectives and target audience will dictate the design.

Secondly, consider the impact of technology on how your site will be seen. If your users are mainly home-based then they would be most likely to be using slow dial-up connections. If that is the case then reduce the graphical content of your site and make sure that all picture file sizes are optimised. As a general rule try to keep graphical content on each page to a maximum of 50K, this will ensure that visitors to your site do not have to spend a great deal of time waiting for the site to load.

Don't try to be too clever. The failure of many sites is that they try to include every new technology that is available: real audio, java, scripting - in fact, everything including the kitchen sink. This is a common failure of web sites, and an area that even professional internet agencies get wrong! Some of the best and most effective web sites only use text and graphics. The rule to remember is only use what you need to use.

Awareness of how the audience will read your page is crucial as this tells you where to put your most interesting information. Visitors to your site will almost certainly begin by looking in the top left-hand corner, so this is where you should position your company's logo. The key to good Internet design is to lead the eye to the content.

When considering which colours to use on the site, you'll again need to be aware of your target audience and what you are trying to achieve with the web site. A business's web site will usually make use of the company's corporate colours. The colours are very important in terms of supporting the message that your business is trying to portray, and the text should read well on the background colour that is chosen.

Creating a good web site is not just about designing the site but also about the content. What you say about your business is always very important, but never more so than on your Internet site. Remember, unlike your corporate brochure, you don't know who is going to see your web site. Provide information that visitors will want to read, don't just copy your brochure onto your Internet site. The information should be dynamic and change regularly encouraging visitors to return to the web site and build a relationship with your business.

Taking the above factors into account by no means ensures a successful web site, but it will help you develop a site that creates a positive image of your organisation at very little cost.

James Bunting, Leighton Internet

DESIGNING A WEB SITE

A web site can be as simple as your company name and address or as complex as a clever shop that tells you what others, with the same tastes as you, are buying. What web sites do have in common is that they communicate with others and once on the web this communication is worldwide, twenty-four hours a day and seven days a week.

Keep navigation simple

An untidy, disorganised, illogical and overly complex site is certain to deter your present customers and your potential ones. A logical and simple structure is essential, along with self-explanatory, clearly labelled buttons, so that a visitor can go directly to a product or service. Screens should include an option to return directly to the top level, or home page at the very least, and many also include a toolbar on every page that shows the major sections of the web site itself. For larger sites a readily accessible site map is invaluable.

Tip: Beware of too many links embedded in the text itself. These have the disadvantage of being difficult to maintain because they are often overlooked. And do you really want the reader to leave the page half way through a paragraph? Jumps do lure people away but they may not come back and then your message will be lost!

Keep it fast

You can have the most beautiful site in the world, but if your customers have time to make a cup of coffee while your graphics download, they won't come back. Graphics are pretty, but slow. Text is rather boring, but fast. Compromise - use graphics sparingly to promote your site. Some sites cleverly use the background colour in table cells to enhance the visual appeal. These can be very fast loading and bring life to otherwise plain textual pages. However, any background images that interfere with the readability of the text are simply barriers to communication and are sneered at by those that know!

Tip: Be sure to use the lowest jpeg resolution you can without degrading the image too much. There is a happy balance between beauty and the beast! Use GIFs for logos and line art.

Make it appealing

Content is king! Your web site is your company's shop window - so it is worth investing on the quality of the content. And check the spelling habitually before publication and double check telephone and fax numbers.

Make it topical

Update the contents of your site promptly whenever necessary to ensure that sales and product and service information is always up-to-date. Once users lose confidence in whether or not the data is current then they will stop relying on your site and telephone anyway.

Tip: Give ownership to the sources of the information. For example make the sale manager responsible for keeping the sales prices up to date. Don't shoot the messenger!

Constructing your web pages

Once you have decided on the general appearance and content of your web pages comes the task of actually constructing the pages.

What is a web site made up of?

All web pages are made up of text files which can be created using very basic text editors such as Notepad, Simpletext or even Edit in MS-DOS. For the text itself to be a web page it needs to contain specialist tags that can be recognised and then displayed by a web browser such as Internet Explorer or Netscape.

These tags are part of an agreed set of instructions that go to make up the HTML language which was invented for electronic display of documents.

Just to prove this works, here is your first web page:

```
==========
<HTML>
<HEAD>
<TITLE>Page title  <! --this will appear in the title bar of your browser-->
</TITLE>
</HEAD>
<BODY>
This is the web page text that will appear in the main browser window.
</BODY>
</HTML>
=================
```

Just a few years ago, most web pages were constructed by HTML programmers who would create web pages by manually entering HTML code tags around the text provided (as illustrated above). Creating pages that worked well and looked good could not only be complex but very time-consuming. And worse still, difficult for others to change to keep up to date.

Today we have a whole range of WYSIWYG editors that automatically enter the HTML code for you behind the scenes. The advantages are obvious and you don't have to be familiar with HTML code to create very well presented pages quickly and easily. And of course changing existing pages (including spell checking!) is so easy. Today creating web pages is very similar to typesetting and is within easy reach of those that are able to use normal word processors. Of course, very complex web pages can be constructed which need expert attention, but for the most part these are not necessary.

There are many web page creation tools available and the two I would certainly take a look at are Microsoft Frontpage and Macromedia Dreamweaver.

These web page editors are really used for putting together the components of a web page and maintaining existing web pages. The components themselves may need separate treatment as discussed below.

Working with text

The text you use can be typed directly into your web page editor or copied from your word processor if the words already exist in a document elsewhere. HTML allows you to specify the size, colour, style and even the typeface of the text you use. However, one thing to remember is that any font you specify will only be used if the font exists on the viewer's computer. This is why it is best to keep to the common standards such as Times or Helvetica. If you specify an unusual font such as "Stone Serif" the chances are that most viewers will not benefit from your sophisticated choice as the browser will substitute this with a common font anyway!

Working with photographs, logos and other images

To add images to your web pages you first need to prepare these by digitising the images into special types of computer files. Photographs, drawings and logos can be scanned or digital cameras can download the digital photos directly.

For use on the web, image files need to be saved into either .jpg or .gif format which are specially formulated to be as small (in byte size) as possible. This means that these can be much more easily transported about the internet and displayed in the browser with the minimum delay. Better known image formats such as .bmp or .tif are simply too big to be of any use on the web.

Jpg or gif, which one to use? A general rule of thumb is that you should use jpgs for photographs or paintings and use gifs for logos and graphic art. The reason for this is that gifs support a smaller colour range and compress well when large areas of the same colour are in the picture. This is rarely the case in photographs but common on logos.

Jpgs

When you come to save a picture as a jpg you will be asked about the quality you require. This is where you must compromise between the quality displayed on your web site and the speed it takes to appear on the screen. You will, however, be amazed at how much you can compress the file and still retain a good image. And your viewers will thank you for taking the trouble!

Gifs

Gifs also have the ability to have parts of the image see-through (or invisible) so you can see the background behind the image. This can be very useful for logos in particular because you may want your logo on lots of pages that have different colour backgrounds. If your graphic will only appear on one or two pages then in many cases it is quicker and easier to make the background of the gif the same colour as the page background.

Pngs

The png (portable network graphic) is a relatively new type of image file which was developed when Compuserve threatened to charge developers a licence fee for the use of the gif format. Supported in versions 5 or later of the popular browsers it provides for very small file sizes, a larger colour range than gif and allows see through areas as with gif. Not to be used unless you are sure that your audience will be using up to date browser software but is set to become increasingly popular in the near future.

There are excellent software tools for manipulating digital images readily available from the professional levels of Adobe Photoshop to easy to use shareware packages such as PaintShop. Increasingly, all image editing tools are adding special effects specifically for web image work such as the ability to add drop-shadows and bevels which can add an effective 3D look to a web page.

Working with page layouts

Having a standard template for your page design that you can use and modify for the whole site will save you a great deal of time. Good web page editors allow you to create these template pages or you could simply save a skeleton page that you keep renaming when you are finished building the page. Web pages, though, are not quite like word processing documents because they are designed for screen display and not for printing on paper. And screen resolutions can differ considerably.

Most PCs in use today are set to display at 800 x 600 pixels by default but can be changed at any time to 640 x 480 or increased to as much as 1600 x 1200! What this means is that you, as the web designer, can only guess at what display your viewers are using and if you are not careful a web page that looks beautiful at 800 x 600 can look appalling at any other size!

To get around this problem there are some options commonly used:

- **Do nothing.** Simply allow the text and images to move to the maximum width allowed in the browser window. For very simple web pages this is perfectly OK. But it is always harder to read wide thin paragraphs than narrow deep ones and they do tend to look thin and weak on the page.

- **Use Tables.** Every page on the web site is bounded by a hidden HTML Table that is set to be a fixed width of 600 pixels wide so that, no matter how many pixels the monitor is set to show, the web page will look the same. The advantage of this method is that by confining all contents of a web page within the cells of a table you can be sure that the images and text will not move in relation to each other and therefore will be faithful to the original design. This is by far and away the most common method in use today. But things change!

- **Use Frames.** Web pages made up of Frames are technically much more difficult to create and maintain but can be very effective in skilled hands. Frames can be used to keep information in the correct position on the screen and are particularly useful for keeping navigation panels in the same place on every page of your web site. The added degree of difficulty that frames bring is normally enough to outweigh the advantages and they are less commonly used than they used to be.

- **Use spacer graphics.** A useful but advanced device is to use very small images that are invisible to the viewer but grab and protect space around images, text and table cells. Here is a useful example that you may want to try yourself. Create a transparent gif image 1 pixel high and 1 wide and call this spacer.gif. For your web page create a single table with 1 row and 3 columns. Give the two outside columns a specific width of 150 pixels but leave the centre column without a width setting. Now preview in the browser. You will see that if you expand the browser the centre column stretches but the outside columns remain the same width. However, if you shrink the browser, the outside columns compress too and therefore your careful design may suffer. To protect these outside columns from changing in width use the spacer.gif. Insert the image at the top of each outside column and specify a width of 150 pixels and a height of 1 pixel to the image itself. Now preview in your browser and see what happens; you've protected the column width and you can be sure of your design. This is only one example of a device that is very commonly used - but little seen!

Working with Links

Web page links are a vital component to a good web site and easy navigation between your pages will encourage viewers to stay and explore. Where you put your links on the page is the first choice. Do you have a toolbar of links on every page at the top (or bottom) or do you embed the links in the text itself or both? In many web sites the links are down the left hand side like a simple contents list. On very large sites every page carries a toolbar of top level sections and the links within the sections themselves are on the left of the page. As with everything else in web page design there is always a compromise between the prominence of links and the actual content of the page. After all it is the contents of the page we want viewers to be influenced by and not links to other pages. Yet we want them to find what they are looking for quickly and easily too. It can be hard to get it just right.

A good rule to stick to, however, is that a link should obviously look like a link! The accepted convention is that links are underlined. This should only be overruled where the links are obviously buttons or in a toolbar or in a set of menu options. The converse is true as well - never use underline in your web pages unless they are links!

It really isn't necessary to write click here but it is not totally without merit if you expect your audience to be new to the internet.

Making the Most of your web site

In order to get the most from your web site, you need to be able to attract your target audiences, get them to view as many of your web pages as possible, get them to respond and then encourage them to return on a regular basis.

In the initial stages, the best way to keep someone in your web site is to deliver relevant information in a form that is easy to digest and of real value. Make sure that visitors can easily get the answers to the questions they have about your products or services. An effective web site is one that has anticipated the questions and provided the answers within a maximum of three page clicks. If you're selling on the site, ensure that your visitors are directed to selling opportunities before they leave your site and that products are clearly displayed (see e-trading).

Whilst your natural inclination might be to enhance your web site by incorporating lots of animation and graphics, you need to bear in mind that, even though they may look good, they slow down the user's experience and can lack substance. Therefore, you should use them sparingly.

So how can you ensure that your customers:

* Index your web site in their list of favourites?
* Return to your site on a regular basis?
* Respond to the information you are providing

Customer Retention

A web site, like any other aspect of your business, needs attention and management in order to ensure that your customers respond and keep coming back.

Change the content

The first and most obvious way of ensuring visitors return to your web site is to regularly change the content and keep adding value to it. There is nothing worse than finding a web site that was once very interesting, adding it to your bookmarks, returning 6 months later and finding that absolutely nothing has changed!

There are no rules about frequency of change but try and keep it in line with what you anticipate your customers will want.

For example, if you are sell clothes, then you should try and follow the high street pattern. There are four seasonal stock changes and at least two sales. Whilst the web is unique, there are areas of cross-over with the off line world which you should accommodate in your plans.

Special Offers

You should think about running a succession of special offers on your web site. If customers see that you do this, they are much more likely to bookmark your web site in their "favourites" list and return on a regular basis.

Generally, the special offers should be of genuine worth and should be time limited so that you drive customers back within a given time frame.

You could incorporate notification of these special offers in your e-newsletter or, indeed, use it as a hook to get people to register in the first place (see e-newsletters below).

Competitions

You should think about running regular competitions on your web site as another means of attracting visitors to your web site and then moving them through various web pages. By doing so you ensure that your messages are more easily absorbed and you pick up relevant information from their entry forms.

You need to make sure that the prizes justify the effort you expect the entrant to make. So, for example, if your competition is a virtual treasure hunt with the answers to the questions hidden within your web pages, you should make the prize worthy of the amount of pages your visitors will have to read in order to find the answers. No one is going to trawl through your web pages for a bar of chocolate but they might do so for a year's supply!

In addition, prizes should relate to your products and services and, where possible, you should make them tangible and memorable. For example, if you are going to send out keepsakes, you should make sure your web address, e-mail, telephone number and company name or brand are all highly visible but do so without decreasing the value of the prize.

Reward points

If you are trading online, you may like to think about giving reward points for those customers that place repeat orders or make multiple purchases on your web site.

In your e-commerce solution (see e-trading) you could build your software to take account of this and allocate customers an unique number or password for their purchases. In this way you can keep track of who is buying what and reward them appropriately. If customers think that they will be rewarded when visiting your site they are more likely to return to it when they are ready to buy again.

Introduction of a reward points scheme is quite a complex issue and one that needs very careful management. Ideally, at this stage you should talk to a specialist consultancy about your exact requirements.

Building the Relationship - collecting information

In order to enhance your online relationship with your customers, you need to find out who they are and what they want and expect from your web site. The best way to do this would be to ask them to tell you. If only life was that simple! The only way that online customers will part with personal information is if they think that they will gain from doing so.

For example, some of the UK newspapers ask customers to pre-register before they can even gain access to their web sites. They can get away with this because they are giving free access to most of the content of their newspapers.

However, it is very unlikely that your business will be able to ask people to pre-register at your web site, especially if you want large numbers of visitors. The last thing you should do is create a barrier before they even enter your site.

So how else can you get the information you want from your customers? You should think about the simple things you can do first and then work your way up.

The Response Form

Your web site will, no doubt, include a response form which enables customers to fill in details and make an enquiry. Some of these enquiries might be quite general and others could be very specific. In both cases you should try and elicit a bit more information from your customers than the standard name and address. If they are at the stage of actively asking for information from you, then they are showing an interest in your products and services. Since they are asking you for something, you can quite legitimately ask them for something in return and this should be a couple of extra questions. For example, if you are targeting consumers you might want to find out their age range and their nationality. If you are targeting business buyers then you will probably want to find out who the key decision-makers are, the company's main activity and its annual turnover.

The payment form

If you are selling goods and services online and take online payments, then you will capture customer information by default. However, whilst this will give you some details, i.e. name and address, it will not necessarily give you the information that would aid your business. Therefore, you should try and put in another couple of relevant questions such as those identified above.

At the very least, you should ask your customers for their e-mail address so that you can mail them confirmation when you have despatched their goods. Customers will realise that you are probably going to use this to send them information at a later stage. Therefore, you should assure them that you are only collecting their e-mail address for legitimate purposes and give them the option not to provide it if they are uncomfortable doing so. The assumption that you can e-mail customers without first asking their permission will very quickly reveal irate customers with genuine recourse for complaint.

Register for e-news

One of the best things to set up on your web site is a registration section so that customers can receive your free newsletters (see below). The link for this should be on the home page so that both new users and repeat visitors can find it quickly. It proves that you are in the business of providing information and thereby adding value to your web site. Not only will you capture the information that you want but it will also be willingly provided.

Pre-registration

You will occasionally see some web sites that, prior to launch, invite customers to pre-register their e-mail address so that they can be notified as soon as the web site goes live. This service tries to prevent customers from becoming frustrated with the fact that having found the site in the search engines and having clicked through, they are then presented with a dead end.

However, you should bear in mind, that this type of facility will only be used by individuals if what you are supplying is either very well known or unique.

As a general rule, you should not launch and register your web site with search engines until it is complete. There is nothing worse for web users than to find a site that has so many areas under construction as to be practically worthless. Many people argue that it is much harder to get a customer to come back to a web site if they have already been and failed to see anything of interest, than it is to get them there in the first place.

E-newsletters - delivering a valuable service

Once you have captured an e-mail address and asked permission to use it in the future, you then need to decide what you will send and how often. Don't just use the opportunity to blast sales messages at your customers, this will only result in them never wanting to hear from you again.

Like other aspects of your web site strategy you should think about how you can use e-mail to add value to your customers' working lives, whilst simultaneously driving more sales into your business.

One of the best ways of doing this is to send regular e-newsletters to your customers on relevant business subjects. To do this effectively, you should start thinking about grouping all your e-mail addresses according to your own definition of common characteristics.

For example, you could have collected information on the age of your customers. You could then group customer e-mails by broad age bands. Obviously, your 14 to 18 year old customers will have a different idea of what makes a good e-newsletter to that of your 25 to 30 year olds. So, you should then tailor the news and product plugs within the e-newsletters accordingly.

If you supply products to business customers you should think about setting up industry specific e-newsletters. Therefore, you should split your e-mail addresses according to whether a customer was in manufacturing or retail etc.

Whilst you are only collecting and dealing with a handful of e-mail addresses, it is possible to manage these groupings yourself. However, when you start collecting large numbers of addresses you will then need to talk to your ISP (see glossary) or your preferred Internet consultancy, about managing addresses electronically.

In all cases you should allow for the fact that your customers may want to subscribe to more than one of your e-newsletters or, indeed, unsubscribe from all of them. You should make it as easy as possible for your customers to do this. By doing so, you show a confidence in your e-newsletters and the quality of the service you provide which will result in only small numbers of customers wishing to unsubscribe and a great number subscribing to more than one.

Your e-newsletter content has to be good, strong, punchy advice. You should provide links to further information wherever possible, ideally within your own web site. You shouldn't write reams of copy but keep it to a few salient and relevant points. In between the business advice you can let customers know about new products for sale or further additions to applications and information on your web site.

Lastly, if your e-newsletters are good then they will be forwarded to many different people. Word of mouth on the Internet is a fantastic means of extending your reach very rapidly because everyone else is doing your sales job for you. So, within your e-mail you should say something along the lines of "if you are reading someone else's copy of this e-newsletter and want to get your own direct to your desk, then click here (give web address link) and register online".

E-COMMERCE - TRADING ON THE NET

A legal perspective

If you are not already involved in e-commerce you soon will be! The buying and selling of goods and services over the Internet is increasing at a phenomenal rate and at the time of writing this article it is roughly estimated that 96% of the total server requirement which will be needed 5 years from now has yet to be supplied. Increasingly, e-commerce is being used for business to business transactions in the exchange of purchase orders, invoices, and other electronic documents. As a new business media, e-commerce is becoming "the norm", however; there are a number of risks associated with this media as there are with any others, where businesses need to evaluate and act to minimise those risks.

In my experience there are four main areas which give rise to concern, those being: uncertainty (as to which laws or regulations apply and as to the point at which a contract is made); security (of data and systems); payment methods; and web site content.

Uncertainty

Traditionally, under English Law, a contract is formed at the point of acceptance of a contractual offer, with acceptance occurring when it is communicated to the offer maker. However, technology is moving rather faster than the legislative process and at the time of writing (with the electronic communications bill and European directive on electronic commerce both in draft), it is not yet clear what contract formation rules will be applied to e-commerce contracts. Naturally, risk could be minimised by avoiding using the Internet for contract formation, but often this defeats the object of using the Internet at all for business. Until now, the current view under English Law has been that it is "probably possible" to achieve an enforceable contract by a click wrap structure. That is, the customer reads the supplier's contractual terms on the web site and must accept these by clicking on an icon before the supplier will fulfil the contract. Ideally, the supplier's web site should provide that the customer can make an offer to buy only on the terms set out on the web site, which are accepted by delivery of the products.

Security

"Firewall" software can assist in preventing unauthorised access to information, but is not an absolute and its effectiveness depends on how well it has been set up. As an alternative, if information is highly sensitive then the risk can be minimised by simply not making it available on PC's.

Ideally, systems should prevent introduction of unauthorised software on to the network. It is advisable to put e-mail policies and disciplinary procedures in place to deal with employees' misuse of the Internet. However, to enforce such a policy the technology must also have back up and tracking facilities. Employers may take the view that employees should simply not be allowed to use the Internet for personal use, but only for business purposes.

Whilst firewalls can help improve security and there are criminal sanctions under the Computer Misuse Act 1990 for hacking, a business may still have liability to its customers and others if systems go down or data is lost or corrupted. Pass-wording and back-up/disaster recovery measures may need to be put in place, as well as insurance.

Payment

Although payment is often identified as an area of concern, the use of credit cards to make payments on the Internet is common and increasing. The problem for the supplier is if funds are "not there", so software must obtain adequate authorisation to deal with clearing payments. Paper audit trails, passwords, PINS, encryption (using a shared secret key) and private networks may be used to improve security.

Payment of VAT may be an issue where parties are trading cross-border. Not the least of practical problems here is knowing where the customer is located. The issue of "presence" in a particular tax jurisdiction also has implications since a "tax nexus" has to be established for the purposes of application of direct tax.

Web-site content

One risk of using the Internet to contract is that the supplier will be advertising itself to the world and may inadvertently breach foreign legislation in doing so. Where suppliers are dealing with customers in the EU, then a choice of law and jurisdiction clause should be upheld in business to business contracts (although this is not necessarily so for consumers). Other methods which suppliers use to limit risk, include insistence upon a UK address or setting up alternative web pages for different jurisdictions.

In advertising on the Internet, you should avoid using false or misleading trade descriptions, misleading price indications and misrepresentations to minimise the chances of breaching English legislation. Other countries' legislation and codes of practice can also limit your activities!

Nicki Martienssen, Partner - Shoosmiths

TRADING ON THE WEB

Every day we hear of another well-known retail outlet launching their online "shopping" experience. At the same time, hundreds of less well-known businesses are doing the same thing. All are experiencing various levels of success. This success seems to be directly proportionate to how well they have planned their e-commerce strategy and how competent they are at fulfilling customer demand.

The cumulative result of this drive to "e-commerce" is the opening of hundreds of new web shops each month. There is no need to be alarmed, however, as there is still plenty of opportunity to capitalise on the lessons learnt by these online shopping pioneers. In addition, the growth in the number of web users is still happening at a phenomenal rate so there is an ever-growing pool of potential customers that you can tap into.

True, the early converts to online "shopping" have spent a great deal of time and money learning from costly mistakes and gaining valuable lessons all of which have enabled them to build a loyal web customer base. However, when you make your move to e-commerce you will be better informed than they ever were and also it will now cost you significantly less money and hopefully less time.

Like all elements of your move online, you must plan carefully for how you want to embrace online trading. You must learn to be both something of a psychologist - in your approach to your customers' buying behaviour - and also something of a scientist - in the way you position and display your goods to make best use of your web space. All of your best plans will be laid to waste, however, if you fail to consider the logistical implications of your move online (see below).

As a new business you will already find your time severely pressured, so the first thing you need to consider is how you can use the web to improve what you are already doing elsewhere. In addition, you should then decide whether you want to select a few items from your product range as a test or whether you want to place all items online simultaneously from the outset. These decisions will be largely guided by whether you can handle the logistical implications and whether the web is the appropriate medium to do this.

In terms of the actual system design, the best recommendation is to look at what is available and test what suits both you and your customers best. The main considerations are: is there a system already available or will I have to pay for a tailor-made solution? And how can I find/create a system that is truly flexible (i.e. can you make rapid changes to prices, number of items displayed, VAT calculations etc.)?

The planning process

1. What are you going to sell?
2. Who are you going to sell to?
3. Is the market already established? (see planning your web site)
4. Who are your competitors and what are they doing? (see planning your web site)
5. How much will you charge?
6. What software options do you have?
7. How will you cope with demand?
8. Test
9. Launch

What do you want to sell?

Your decisions about e-commerce will largely be determined by what it is that you want to sell and to whom. Not only will product range and suitability play a role in determining how you approach your e-trading strategy but also market resistance across different borders and cultural diversity.

The considerations for single, stand-alone products such as sports goods for example, are different from perishable items, such as cakes and fudge. Whilst the former is relatively straightforward, the latter will rely much more on logistical implications (packaging and despatch so that your goods remain "fresh") and how you offer words of reassurance to your customers. You may even need to consider guaranteed delivery dates etc.

Equally, there are unique considerations for items that you can download directly off the web such as "news items" or "mailing lists" and software. These items will need to be priced and paid for before the download is completed and in some cases small unit costs calculated and billed using a fast secure system (see software options below).

Within some product ranges there are so many variables that this will have a direct impact on the type of operating system chosen (see software options below). For example, selling clothes online is not simply a question of posting one image for one item. You will need to think about the variables such as choice of colour/texture and sizing options. Therefore, you could have one dress in 5 different patterns, each in five different colours, all in 3 different lengths, and before you know it you have 75 different item combinations that your database and e-commerce software must deal with.

Given the nature of the various products you will want to sell, you will also want to decide how you are going to display them online. In recent years, traditional retail display has become something of a science, with customer psychology at the forefront of shop layout design ideas. In the same way, when thinking about web design for e-commerce enabled sites you should think about the way products are displayed, described and positioned on the web page to make best use of space and more importantly download times.

You will have a number of decisions to make about the appearance and usability of your online shop. You should think about whether you will need photographs for all items, or whether a description will suffice. You should also think about whether colour swatches would aid the customer's decision and if so, how you can represent these most effectively. You will also need to decide how much use, if any, you want to make of audio or video clips - for example, if you are selling CDs should you incorporate audio clips of the band in question or should you rely on your customers' prior knowledge?

There are plenty of e-commerce enabled software solutions in the market place to deal with all your web requirements. In some of the more complicated cases this will require a bespoke programme. However, if you do get to this point, it is also worth considering that in most cases the system can be built to integrate with your existing or preferred database programme, thus making your web site dynamic and easy to update (see later in this chapter for e-commerce software options).

Who are your customers?

On the web, businesses looking at opening new markets compete on an equal footing. Even when a brand name is a household name in its country of origin, it may not necessarily be known elsewhere in the world. Therefore, within new markets, customers make their judgement on the basis of the web site alone.

Equally, even when a brand name is well known, web customers will still shop around and compare these products with less well-known ones.

Web customers make their choices on a different set of criteria to those applied to their traditional shopping routines. If you get your web shop right, they are much more likely to give your online business more credibility than perhaps they would do in the offline world. This is primarily because they are looking for a good deal or more choice so are prepared to consider everyone's offering.

Getting your online shop right is, therefore, imperative. You stand to compete equally online where you may not have a chance of doing so in the traditional market place. You should design your online "shop" with trust at the forefront of your mind. Constantly ask yourself - would I give my credit card details to my web site if I came across it online?

You should also clarify in your own mind who it is that you want to sell your goods to and whether you have the appropriate products in stock. As you cross international boundaries this is even more important as you begin to consider how your products will be received in the international market place. Don't dismiss your products because you consider them to be too mundane. Something you regard as very ordinary here could be considered a luxury item somewhere else.

You will need to investigate, online or otherwise, something about the mentality and attitude of those international audiences you want to target. This will also help you when it comes to displaying and describing your products and services.

In particular, you will need to think about any cultural or religious considerations. Don't offend your audience by any references that could have different cultural meanings elsewhere or by remarks that could be regarded as blasphemous. For example, in Japan, white is the colour signifying death and mourning, not weddings or innocence as it does in the UK.

Of course, there is language to consider too. Whilst English is the recognised language of the web, you may need to consider carefully the words you are using to describe specific items. Take one example - you have a clothes shop and you want to sell "trousers" but your main target market is America and their word for "trousers" is "pants" - but "pants" means a very different thing to the British - what do you do?

You will also need to consider the technology available to your audiences in different countries. Whilst it is a huge generalisation, it is fair to say that Internet connectivity in countries in Eastern Europe is not as fast or as reliable as it is in the USA. Therefore, if your target audience is primarily within Eastern Europe, this should have a major bearing on the way you design your online shop. You will need to consider more carefully the number of images and graphics you use to illustrate your products and services because each one you add to your web site increases the length of time the page takes to download.

Careful planning and research will help you identify all your potential audiences and their relative considerations. Being aware of all the implications for your web site at the outset will save you a great deal of time, money and frustration as you make your move into trading online.

Price versus customer service?

There is a common assumption that when you begin to trade online you should heavily discount your products and services and compete on price alone. Whilst it is true that web customers shop around to look for the best deal, it is also fair to say that price is not the only or indeed their major consideration.

Much more importantly, your online shop should offer good "value for money" and guarantee good and reliable customer service. If, using your bulk-buying power you can also offer a discounted price then all the better, but this should not be your main consideration.

You may want to use your web site to sell quality products or look at discounts for customers who buy more than one product. Many customers offer web buying loyalty points that work in the same way as those operated by the major UK supermarkets. You could choose to make redemption of these points web exclusive or you could make your web sales complementary to your offline sales so that customers see a continuity between your "shops".

Rather than straight discounts, you should consider time-restricted special offers and discounts on repeat orders. In this way, not only do you get the first order but you also drive customers back into your web site and build up a loyalty and commitment between you and your customers.

Within your pricing structure, you will also need to consider how you build in delivery and freight costs. Whilst this seems straightforward it can actually become quite difficult, especially as you need to balance both price and service. You will find that many of the specialist despatch companies vary their charges not only according to what country you are sending to but also what town (see The Logistics section below). Therefore, it is very difficult to set a standard delivery charge before knowing all the likely destinations - this you can only guess at.

When crossing international boundaries your other consideration should be currency and how you will translate prices for your international customers so that they understand more clearly what they are paying for and how that relates to the currency that they understand. You could incorporate a currency converter in your web site design or you could link to another site to do this for you. However, if you choose the latter route, there is always a danger that if you send your customer to another web site to look up information, you will never get them back again!

Payment

As well as thinking about pricing, you should also look at what payment options you want to give your customers. The most obvious choice you will need to make is whether you will accept online credit card payments and if so how these will be processed. There are two options currently available:

You can handle each order manually once you receive the secured e-mail at your office - this will involve someone entering the credit card orders in the same way as you do via other ordering channels.

The other option, and one that many companies are rapidly adopting, is the use of secure electronic transactions. In other words, you work with your chosen bank to ensure that once a credit card order has been placed, this is sent to the bank electronically to confirm that the customer has the funds available to buy. The money gets deducted from the customer's credit card and deposited in your bank account automatically. The customer receives confirmation that the goods are on the way and you receive the order telling you to despatch the relevant goods.

Your customers will probably raise the question of security (see below) and may, initially, prefer to ring or fax through their credit card orders rather than type them online so you should give them this option too. Ironically, it's probably more secure for your customers to enter their details online rather than faxing or phoning with their details since, in the latter cases, the customer has no idea who is listening to or processing their order.

So what about the other payment alternatives such as: cheques, bank transfers, cash on delivery and invoicing? Are you prepared to accept these forms of payments?

Ultimately, you should give your customers as many choices as possible. As with all aspects of web site and e-commerce delivery, it is all about what the customer is ready and prepared to do both at present and over the coming months.

As with all transactions there are associated costs, so you will need to consider how you will build these into the price of the goods you sell online. In addition to shipping costs (see later), there will also be the cost of banking international cheques - if you decided to accept them and also credit card fees. You should discuss credit card fees with your bank and arrange the appropriate handling fees in advance. Some banks raise their handling fees once they know that you are trading online because of their perception of enhanced "risks". You could find that web transactions are charged at 8-9%. Although, in an increasingly competitive and growing market place, these figures are bound to drop in the coming months.

Your e-commerce software options - security

There are two main e-commerce software options available. The first is to buy a pre-built "shopping cart" system - there are many readily available in the market place and they usually cost a few hundred pounds. The second is to have a software programme specially designed and written - these can be designed to your exact requirements but usually start from a few thousand pounds. You can find out about both options either by checking out the web (enter key search words such as "e-commerce", "shopping+software" and "shopping carts") or referring to any of the Internet related publications (your local newsagents should have a selection). You should then shortlist your options and speak to the relevant suppliers to see exactly what they can do for your business.

Both systems are secure. The difference is all in a little "s" character. When you have your own system written you will link into a secure server, register and use your own certificate. Your web address (URL) will then be written https:// instead of http://. That "s" means that your browser is now communicating with the secure server using a protocol called SSL (Secure Socket Layer) and anything sent in either direction is encrypted and secure.

The pre-built "shopping carts" are determined by the way the security programme is written. These use a special programming language called Java which does its own encryption and which runs via any server but only encrypts the data it is sending.

Like all other aspects of your e-commerce strategy, whilst price is obviously going to be one of your major considerations, ultimately your decision should rest with what your customers feel most comfortable with. It is their confidence in your web site that you will rely on for their purchase decision.

In addition, you will need to take into consideration how it all links into your own stock control systems. You should also think about the medium to long term efficiency of your business as well as your short-term financial considerations. If you buy a system that is inadequate to start with, ultimately it will cost you more in the longer term and could have a detrimental impact on your relationship with your online customers when you fail to make deliveries on time because you have lost the relevant information.

Whichever system you choose, you must be sure that you can update the information easily so you can add and delete items as you go along and that this is seamless for the customer.

The Logistics - Handling, Shipping, and VAT returns

Once you have your online order, you then need to fulfil it. You will need to decide at the outset who will be responsible for picking the item, packing it, updating your system and controlling the stock. This goes hand in hand with ensuring that your suppliers can anticipate the demand from your customers and making sure that you have a suitable internet connection to handle the traffic anticipated (see Getting Access on page 234).

Even before the goods are ready to be shipped, you should have arranged who will carry your goods. This may involve setting up different arrangements with different carriage companies, dependent on what services they specialise in. This variety of arrangements can be reflected in the choice you give your customer and what they opt to pay for, e.g. special overnight delivery, first class, second class etc.

It may be worth your while setting up an arrangement with an export shipper so that they can handle all the customs documentation, clearance and taxes and duties on your behalf. Even the smallest and cheapest items will need to go through customs so it is worth anticipating this in advance.

Whatever arrangements you make with your shipping companies will need to be reflected in the costs you hand on to your customers and the way you can update your system. You may opt to spread all shipping costs evenly across all orders or you may choose to charge a premium for the heaviest and bulkiest goods. Regardless, you should be looking to keep costs down and negotiate the best deal for you and your customers.

Last but by no means least you will need to think about VAT and international taxation issues. The same principles apply online as they do off, but are complicated by the export considerations. You should discuss all VAT issues with the VAT office or your accountant. Whilst it is impossible to cover every scenario here, some of the issues that will need to be taken into account are:

- Are you VAT registered in the UK?
- Are you VAT registered in other countries?
- Are your customers VAT registered?
- Are your customers exempt from VAT?
- Do you need to pay local Taxes in your customer's country?
- Can your system cope if VAT rates are changed?

Before you begin to trade online it is imperative that you discuss the financial and legal (see later) implications of doing so.

Whilst there is plenty to think about as you make your move to e-trading, you should not be daunted by these considerations. If you take all these points into account at the outset and incorporate them, then you will be able to truly compete in the global marketplace.

Dawn Baker, Sage Software Limited

THE PATH TO E-BUSINESS - A SUMMARY

- Get the appropriate hardware and software and get your business connected to the Internet
- Start using e-mail to communicate with your customers and suppliers
- Search the Web yourself to get a feel for what is good and relevant to your business
- Start planning your online presence
- Start planning the incorporation of e-commerce
- Talk to the relevant authorities about the implications of e-business on you and your company e.g. VAT office, Lawyers, Accountant and Export Advisors
- Consider whether you want to use some of the free web templates available or whether you want to pay for a bespoke design
- Start collecting the content - photographs, text etc.
- Make sure your business is geared up for the demand

- Get some of your existing customers to test your site
- Think about your marketing and PR strategy
- Act on Feedback
- Launch

INTERNET GLOSSARY

Bookmark your browser provides a facility for you to add favourite sites to its memory so that you can refer to them again at a later stage without having to remember the exact URL.

Browser software generally supplied free, that enables you to search and view information on the Web. Netscape Navigator and Microsoft Internet Explorer are the most popular browsers.

CGI common gateway interface - special programs which reside on your ISP's server allowing interactive operations such as forms, calculations and e-commerce operations.

Cookies are small files which reside on a user's computer allowing web sites to store personalised information about the user. Enables facilities such as allowing users to customise what they see when visiting sites and stores information such as how many times a user has visited a site or the last page viewed. There is a myth that cookies are somehow malicious and are a tool used by 'Big Brother' to violate privacy. This is not true.

CPU central processing unit - the 'brains' of your computer. The electronic microchip which handles the data and runs the programs.

Domain Name the part of a web address that specifies on which computer the information is held and whether it is part of a commercial (.co.uk or .com); government (.gov); not for profit (.org) or academic (.ac or .edu) site. Makes a unique reference to a set of information on a particular computer. Companies often register their trade or product names to ensure continuity of their brand identity.

Encryption/Encrypted a means of coding information so that it cannot be accessed by anyone except the authorised person.

Flash a highly efficient file format increasingly used for animated web page elements but requires a special 'plug in' to be installed on the user's computer. Recent research indicates that over 80% of current web users now have this plug in installed (see Shockwave also).

Frames this is a means by which a web site can be divided so that parts of the web page can be moved (or not) independently of one another. Used by designers as a means of showing a constant and fixed navigation bar within the Web Site.

FTP file transfer protocal - a method by which files can be uploaded from or downloaded to user's machines via the Internet. You will need FTP software to place your web pages and graphics on your ISP's server.

Home page the main page of a Web Site (see below) and the one which tells the user straight away what the Web Site is all about.

HTML hypertext markup language - the language understood by browser software which describes and controls the layout of web pages.

http hypertext transfer protocol - the universally acknowledged means of transferring HTML documents across the internet and often appears as http:// at the beginning of a web address.

https the secured version of http. This means that the transference of documents uses a secure server.

ISP Internet Service Provider - a Company that provides access, i.e. physical connection, to the Internet.

Java programming language which enables more sophisticated applications to be incorporated in your web site.

Javascript a programming language resembling Java which can be incorporated into HTML web pages allowing interactive elements such as 'roll over' buttons, forms and automatic window opening.

Password protected an area of the web site that it is only possible to access when the user puts in a pre-set username and password.

Pixels the number of dots on your computer monitor that make up a page or images on a page. Monitors come in various sizes and resolutions which dictate the quality of the image viewed.

Quicktime a highly compressed file format which allows movies and sounds to be encorporated into web pages. Requires a 'plug in' to be installed on the user's computer.

RAM random access memory - the fast access memory chips which temporarily hold data and programs as they are run on a computer.

Response Form - a web page that is set up as a form with pre-determined fields in which you enter personal details or company details. These forms are written using a special web programming language or script. Users click on a submit or send button and they are sent to a predetermined e-mail address to be dealt with.

Search engine a means of searching for information (as web pages), across the Internet. It works in accordance with the words that a user enters for the programme to search on.

Server a computer that has direct and permanent access to the Internet and is capable of moving files around it.

Sherlock a search utility on Apple Macintosh computers which allows comprehensive web searching using multiple search engines simultaneously.

Shockwave a compressed file format for web animations and games which requires a special web browser 'plug in' (see Flash also)

URL Uniform Resource Locator - the standard way to write the address of a web site so that every page and every site have a unique reference.

The Web shortened version of World Wide Web (WWW). The Web is a vast collection of text, photographs, graphics etc. arranged in pages so that everyone can view them.

Web site a collection of pages that have a common theme, arranged under a common domain.

Web Page an individual page within a web site.

WWW World Wide Web see The Web.

W3C the World Wide Web Consortium, a group of internet software and hardware developers, which controls the international standards for the web. For those interested in internet developments and issues, the W3C web site www.w3c.org is an excellent reference.

WYSIWYG What You See Is What You Get - design tools which allow the designer to see things exactly as they will appear in the printed document or published web page.

Marketing the Business

Chapter Eight

If you can't be positive about marketing it will be difficult to really prosper in business. The idea that marketing is all about 'building a better mousetrap' is as much a fallacy as the quotation itself. What Ralph Waldo Emerson actually said circa 1840 was, "If a man has good corn, or wood or boards or pigs to sell, or can make better chairs or knives, crucibles or church organs than anybody else, you will find a broad hard-beaten road to his house, though it be through the woods".

Unfortunately even this extended axiom has not stood the test of time. No, marketing is about much more than making better products, although it certainly helps if your goods and services do what you claim they can do. So what is marketing? That question will be answered in as many ways as there are businesses but some constants apply to all. Marketing begins with an understanding of your market and thereafter the positioning of your product or service within it. This is achieved by numerous devices including pricing, styling, and refining products to create an appeal and a subsequent demand for them. Having established this market it is then about protecting your name, growing the market by trying new initiatives, and developing your brand image as your business grows.

Advertising

American newspapers and magazines began carrying advertisements in the early 1770s. The world's first advertising agency, NW Ayers, had been established to help clients with creative campaigns. (It wasn't until 1812 that the UK's oldest public relations agency, Charles Barker, started up.)

From about this time advertising became a key component of marketing strategy. George Eastman, who founded the Eastman Dry Plate and Film Company in Rochester, New York, later to become the giant Eastman Kodak, spent a staggering $750,000 on advertising in 1899 alone.

But what made Eastman's advertising so effective was that it was an integral part of his whole marketing activity, not just an announcement of what he had to sell. In 1888 he changed the name of his camera to 'Kodak'. The word meant nothing but he chose it, according to his trademark application, because it was short, not capable of mispronunciation and it was unlike any other word in existence at the time. The name also had the advantage of being onomatopoeic. He also developed a slogan, "You press the button - we do the rest". These simple messages were ideal for advertising as they were easy for readers to understand and remember - two vital attributes if people are to buy your product rather than someone else's.

INTRODUCTION TO MARKETING

Marketing is probably the most misunderstood area of modern business. Ask ten business people what's meant by marketing and they'll come up with ten different answers. The textbooks suggest that marketing is "everything from conception to consumption". While this is arguably true, it is not very helpful. I prefer my own definition! "Marketing encompasses those activities which encourage a potential customer for goods or services to become an actual customer and which encourage existing customers to remain customers and spend more with you".

Note here the word "encourage". A salesperson might "encourage" a customer to buy, but that's not the salesperson's job. The sales job is to make them buy through eliminating all objections. Unfortunately marketing cannot, generally, do this.

Product development should be a marketing-led function. It rarely is, however, because customer research seldom throws up anything truly innovative - nothing worthwhile was ever invented by a committee! So, for our purposes here, I shall define marketing in terms that exclude product development and sales.

But, what about Direct Marketing? Good question. Currently, direct marketing in all its forms accounts for about 3 per cent of total retail sales. Now that's not chicken feed for sure - but I think most people would rather focus on the other 97 per cent!

First things first then. I'm a great Kipling fan. In particular the following quotation stays constantly in my mind:

I keep six honest serving-men,
(they taught me all I knew).
Their names are What and Why and When
and How and Where and Who

Of the six serving men, personally I find 'Why' the most interesting. My clients often come to me asking for an advertising campaign or a mailshot and when I ask them why they want to do it, most blink a few times but cannot give me a considered reply. So, let's try to answer the six questions - starting with Why.

Why do "marketing?"

If you're in business there is only one reason to undertake any marketing activity and that is to increase your profits. Note, this is not turnover but profit. Gaining market share is of no value unless it leads to increased profits. Generating higher market awareness is futile unless it increases the money flowing into the till. So, first principles first. Always ask yourself the question "Will this activity lead to an increase in profitable sales?" If you are already 'doing marketing' then you have to ask yourself whether what you are currently doing is leading to an increase in profitable sales. If you cannot answer this question then stop right there. Unless you can establish that what you are currently doing is working and to what degree, it is pointless continuing.

Many advertising agencies will tell you that it is difficult to measure the results of advertising. This is rubbish put out by agencies who fear being measured against results. There are measures that can be applied in any business. Work out what measures are relevant for your business, ones that you can actually monitor. For example, the number of enquiries you get, or the level of customer traffic in your shop if you're a retailer. It could also be the average order value, the conversion from enquiry to sale - or all of these. Once you know what your baseline is you can then monitor for any change when you 'do marketing'.

Strategy

Next we can start refining our strategy. There are all sorts of ways that marketing can boost profitable sales. The question here is really what your short to medium term objective is. What you're trying to achieve. Marketing can be aimed at gaining sales from new customers or it can be aimed at gaining more sales from existing customers. The two are not mutually exclusive as objectives - but the marketing tools you would apply are different. For example promotions, generally, draw more sales from people who are already customers, as new customers tend to distrust promotions. While advertising will generally draw new sales from new customers, existing customers already know who you are, what you do, what your products are and how good they are - so advertising tells them little.

Timing in business is everything. Before deciding on any marketing activity you need to be sure of two things. First that now is a good time for demand for your product. For example, if you are a perfume company you'll spend 80 per cent of your TV budget in the four weeks leading up to Christmas. On the other hand, if you make garden furniture December will probably be a bad time. However, you can be innovative. For example, take automobile anti-freeze. You won't sell much anti-freeze in July. But call it 'coolant' and watch sales soar!

The second timing issue relates to your own resources. Running a promotional campaign in July is not smart if your sales staff are on holiday in August.

The options for spending money on marketing are truly spectacular - TV, posters, direct mail, sponsorship, incentives, promotions, point of sale, catalogues - the list goes on and on. So where do you put your budget? Well, there are a number of useful rules to follow:

Rule 1 - Pioneers end up with arrows in their backs. So, unless you've got money to burn never go into any 'new media opportunity'. It's best to wait and see.

Rule 2 - Follow the herd. Your competitors will be 'doing marketing'. Find out what they do, then do it better.

Rule 3 - Ask your customers what they read, what programmes they watch, do they 'surf the net' for example.

Who are your customers? Most people think they know who their present and potential customers are - but they don't. Mistake number one is that most businesses make little or no effort to gather the names and addresses of customers. Even in business-to-business you find companies who think they know who their customers are, when in fact all they have is the name of the purchasing manager - who may not be the real customer at all. If you don't know who you are currently selling to, you cannot develop strategies to find more customers like them or even different customers. Once you know who your customers are you can then find out much more about them and what makes them buy from you in the first place.

How do you do it? Seek advice. Many people think marketing is easy, which is why so much marketing is patently poor. It is as much a business specialisation as accountancy and no-one would have someone unqualified do their accounts. When Gerald Ratner tried to do his own marketing on national prime-time television, he single-handedly brought his jewellery retailing company to its knees. If you are seeking advice, find companies that specialise in your business area. But beware. An advertising agency will always recommend advertising, a PR agency public relations because that is what they are selling. Make them justify what they're claiming. Make them face up to Kipling's serving men. And if they can't, walk away - fast.

Tim Beadle, PCMC Marketing Services

Advertising

Effective customer communication is an essential part of any business. Properly used, advertising can contribute to development and growth. Badly used, it can prove to be a costly mistake.

Advertising is a key part of the sales process. Its role is to bring together people selling a product with those who may be interested in buying it. It is important to remember that potential customers are careful with their hard-earned money. Rarely will they buy something they don't want. Research consistently reinforces the fact that people don't feel tricked by advertising. In fact they find it a useful source of information, much of which is entertaining. This explains why over £14 billion is spent on advertising in the UK every year.

Advertising does not work in the same way as the salesperson. Very little advertising tries to persuade anyone to buy immediately. Your customers rarely come across advertising at the same time as they are in a position to buy. Advertising, therefore, has to motivate them to take further action, such as making a telephone call or visiting your premises.

So, before deciding to advertise you must think carefully about your business. What are you selling? Who are your competitors? Who are your potential customers and what do they need to know? You must then choose the most appropriate method of communicating the benefits offered by your goods or services and be sure that you can afford to plan and carry out your advertising with maximum effect.

Should you advertise ?

You must begin by asking yourself "What do I want my advertising to achieve?"

The first step is to analyse the benefits to your business that could be gained by advertising. Only when the objectives of the business are clear can the objectives of advertising be established.

For example, try to classify the goods or services you offer and set growth targets within each area over a fixed time period. Then categorise your audience within each of these areas into existing customers and potential new customers. By completing even this simple exercise, you will be in a better position to begin compiling a marketing and advertising plan.

Knowing your customer

Thousands of new products from large companies are launched every single year. Many of them have advertising budgets running into millions of pounds. Significantly, a number of these products fail because nobody wanted them or was persuaded to try them. The huge sums spent on their development, manufacture, distribution and, ultimately, advertising could have been saved if only the initial idea had been tested using careful market research.

Careful and accurate market research is essential to any business. It can provide vital information, all of which will help you:

- Identify customers
- Increase sales
- Improve products and services in line with customer requirements

Market research options

Desk research is the study of existing information. There is a wealth of literature available, from a range of sources, much of which is either inexpensive or available free. Alternatively a morning spent in a good reference library can give many a good idea and set the imagination racing.

Field research involves obtaining your own information, through direct contact with your chosen audience. This service is most effectively carried out by a market research consultancy for which fees would be charged. However, there is no substitute for high quality information.

If you cannot afford specialists, you can easily carry out valuable field research yourself. For example, to find out why existing or new customers buy from you

- Ask telephone enquirers how they heard of your business
- Telephone your customers and ask them for their opinions
- Enclose a simple questionnaire and an sae with their bill
- Arrange a customer open evening and use it to gather information

Always ask direct questions

People do not respond effectively to open-ended questions like "Do you have any comments?" Think of exactly what you want to know and ask it outright.

Consider offering incentives

You want as many people to respond as possible, because the more information you have the more accurate your conclusions will be. Consider prize draw entries or modest discounts for customers who return the information you request.

Involve your team

Encourage your staff to let you know what customers say to them, good or bad. Arrange a regular meeting to do this or provide them with a book to log customer comments.

Where to advertise

Once you have identified your target audiences, you need to communicate with them either directly (verbally or in writing) or indirectly through an advertising medium.

When choosing where to advertise, you must identify those publications, broadcast media or other methods which offer the best 'fit' with your target audiences. It may be appropriate to use different media and different messages. However, before you decide, you must understand what is available.

Direct marketing

Direct marketing is one of the most accountable forms of advertising media, since both costs and results can be measured precisely. It also assists with customer relations by building a two-way dialogue, thereby helping you to understand customer needs and expectations.

Direct marketing includes such disciplines as direct mail, mail order, direct response advertising, i.e. television, radio and press advertising which invites an immediate telephonic or written response, and telemarketing, where existing or potential customers are contacted by telephone.

The Press

In the UK and Europe the press, by which we mean newspapers, magazines and periodicals, is the most widely used advertising medium, accounting for around 55 per cent of all advertising expenditure. One of the reasons for this volume is that the press is so diverse, including all the following and more:

- National daily newspapers
- National Sunday newspapers
- Regional daily newspapers
- Regional weekly newspapers
- Local free distribution newspapers
- General interest magazines
- Special interest magazines
- Trade, technical and professional magazines
- House magazines
- Yearbooks and reference journals

Publications will provide information on circulation and readership, but only an ABC (Audit Bureau of Circulations) rating guarantees that circulation figures are independently audited. For readership figures in the national press and some other titles, the NRS (National Readership Survey) is the source, and for free newspapers it is VFD (Verified Free Distribution).

Why use Press Advertising?

Flexibility The press offers such variety and scope that it is possible to target specific groups of readers on a national, local or special interest basis. You can segment your audience by sex, age, income group, business or hobby.

Advertisements can be purchased and designed at very short notice. It is possible to use colour illustrations or photographs to enhance your message and reply coupons can usually be incorporated within the design. In the daily press you can even relate an advertisement to a current news story.

Also advertisements can be booked to appear in a given issue, in a given place within the title, such as opposite the television page or within the new products section.

These options naturally all have different prices. Special positions and full colour or spot colour insertions all carry premium charges.

If you don't mind where your advertisement appears, it will be placed on runoff paper, which means anywhere available. This costs less but you have no control over where it appears and remember a good position can make all the difference.

The power of the written word A press advertisement can be used to convey a broad message or to contain very precise and detailed information. The space is available to tell a story, build up an image and present your case to your customer. Once you have booked your space, you have complete control over what is said, how it is said, and, if you choose a special position, where it is said.

Cost-effectiveness If you identify the right titles for your business, with the lowest levels of 'wastage' in the readership (readers who would not be interested in your product/service), press advertising can prove to be a highly efficient method of reaching your audience at what is a comparatively low cost per prospect.

One key consideration when using the press is the measurement of readership, as well as circulation. Readership figures are higher than circulation figures, as they relate to the number of people who see the publication, rather than the number of copies bought (circulation). These figures need to be identified when possible. The National Readership Survey can help.

Measurable response Because you can include response coupons and/or telephone hotlines within your advertisement designs, it is possible accurately to judge the success of each publication. This not only helps you process today's responses, it also enables you to plan your future advertising based upon proven performance data.

Radio

Commercial radio is available to advertisers on a local and national basis either through the national sales houses or your local station. It is a source of information, entertainment and companionship to millions of people, typically providing a backdrop to other activities for lengthy periods, e.g. driving or domestic tasks.

Radio is most popular outside peak television viewing hours, the periods of heaviest listening being breakfast time (6 am to 9 am) and evening drive time (5 pm to 6 pm).

The use of radio depends very much on the overall objectives of the advertising campaign. Radio is an excellent medium for those wishing to build familiarity, accessibility and involvement with the product or service. The loyalty with the medium is subconsciously transferred to the advertiser. There is also the option of sponsorship of programmes.

Why use radio advertising?

The impact of sound The human voice is a powerful selling aid. It can convey emotion and authority and, when backed by music, can attract attention or create atmosphere. The one-to-one nature of the medium, reinforced by its local content, makes it intensely personal for the listener. A good radio station mirrors its audience and the moods conveyed by sound can prove very memorable.

Local radio stations are part of the community and, as such, benefit from being extremely close to their listeners.

Flexibility A radio is portable and can be listened to anywhere and whilst doing other things.

Programming is designed to target distinct audiences. Pop music shows appeal to a high proportion of younger people, whilst chat shows may reach a slightly older, more predominantly female audience, and sports coverage tends to increase the male listening figures. Your advertising can be broadcast to coincide with, and capitalise upon, these variations.

Radio advertising is usually quick and easy to produce. This, coupled with the fact that radio is live, immediate and topical, allows you to add urgency and importance to your message.

Low cost Radio advertising space, known in the business as air time, can be purchased in packages which offer a relatively inexpensive option. The cost of writing and recording advertisements can also be attractive and stations will often incorporate this within their package deals.

Commercial messages can benefit from this intimacy and trust. However, creativity is essential. Radio advertisements are short and the listener's attention is immediately drawn to the next item. Likewise, there is no visual support for your message. The script must therefore be catchy, strong and, above all, memorable. If all these factors are addressed, the radio can be a highly successful advertising medium.

Television

Television is regarded by many as the single most powerful advertising medium available.

Why use television advertising?

The benefits of television advertising are clear from these figures. The audience is massive and captive. By repeating advertisements many times, known in the business as frequency, it is possible further to increase this audience and secure more effective total coverage.

Television can be used tactically - e.g. locally, regionally or nationally - and effectively targeted. Sophisticated data on the habits of viewers is available enabling the advertiser to identify the particular audience profile.

In production terms, the medium offers moving pictures and high quality sound, enabling exceptional creativity to be brought into play by advertisers. Messages can be presented extremely powerfully.

Television advertising is extremely cost-effective for the right type of advertisers, but this does not mean it is inexpensive. Thirty seconds of prime time costs many thousands of pounds. However, given the millions of people watching, the relative cost of reaching each one of them is low. In addition, production costs can be substantial. The most effective method of securing value for money is to produce an advertisement of such quality and longevity that it is used many times over many months or years.

Directories

Directories are a useful advertising medium because they are so highly focused. There are over 4000 directories in the UK, approximately 50 per cent of which are industrial and commercial titles, aimed at specific sectors and well used by them.

Consumer titles, such as Thomson's local directories, are also highly defined but in a geographical sense, making it easy to target customers within given localities.

Industrial and commercial directories are almost totally used by those who are predisposed to purchase. They invariably have a long shelf life, (typically a full year) and are almost always seen by potential buyers only when they are ready to buy. Directories are reference publications and not reading matter for the casual browser.

Directory advertising is not seen as an overt sales pitch. The publication provides information not promotion, and is vital to the customer who is actively seeking the advertiser. For this reason, they are an ideal support medium, providing relevant details to an already captive audience.

Outdoor advertising

Outdoor advertising appears in many shapes and sizes. Some of the more popular forms are listed below:

Poster advertising Ranging from the massive 48-sheet sites on roadsides, to small, wall-mounted 4-sheet sites at the ends of bus shelters

Station advertising Posters appearing in airports, train stations and bus terminals

On board advertising Smaller posters appearing on trains, underground trains, buses and in taxis

Sides and supersides Posters and even individual paintwork appearing on buses and taxis

Mobile advertising Lorries and trucks which are specifically built to carry mobile poster sites

Why use outdoor advertising?

Posters are normally sited in high traffic areas, which can be mobile or pedestrian. Therefore, each individual poster has a high opportunity to see (OTS) rating. Poster sites can be cost-effectively purchased locally, regionally or nationally.

Poster advertising provides an excellent trigger at or near the point of purchase - e.g. in a busy shopping centre or high street. It can therefore be used to make very specific announcements, such as OPENING SOON ON THIS SITE.

By its nature, poster advertising cannot be acted upon immediately. People see posters as they pass by. This means the messages have to be very short and easy to digest. Their most effective use is therefore as a reminder, keeping a product or service in the mind. For this reason, poster advertising is universally accepted as being a highly effective support medium, reminding the audience of other forms of advertising for the same product/service - e.g. press or television campaigns.

Creative advertising

The quality of each advertising message obviously plays a key role in its success. Creative advertising offers many benefits and helps you to meet your overall objectives, by:

- Gaining the attention of the audience
- Capturing their imagination
- Opening their minds to your sales messages
- Differentiating your products and services from all others
- Giving them a reason to choose you
- Adding value to your products and services
- Helping the audience to remember

Being creative is one of the most difficult areas of advertising. You must accept that one man's meat is another man's poison, which brings us back to knowing your customers.

Fortunately, the preparation of creative and effective advertising is an area where you can get lots of help. The experts have developed some tips which you can use when compiling your own ads:

 Match your medium to your audience - People who see your advertising must be interested in what you have to sell.

 Play for position - When advertising in the press, convention has it that early pages are best (with the exception of outside covers and specific special positions). It is also believed that right hand pages receive more attention. The point is, think about where you want to be and make sure you're there.

 Size *does* matter - People are more likely to see your advertisements if they are large.

 All things bright and beautiful - Research shows that people not only notice colour advertising, they are also more likely to read something that is bright and eye-catching.

 Every picture tells a story - Psychologists have proved that people have an almost unlimited capacity for remembering visual images. Pictures show things as they truly are.

 Hit the headlines - Take your key statement and turn it into a concise headline. It doesn't have to be witty, but it must never be clumsy or unclear.

 Watch your words - Make one or two strong claims and support them with evidence. Give your audience a reason to buy, visit, call or try.

 Sign off with style - Summarise your philosophy and your offer in one, concise line. 'We care because you do' says it all for Boots.

 Make yourself easy to choose - Always include your name, address, telephone number and, if appropriate, brief directions and hours of business.

> **ABOVE ALL, MAKE SURE YOUR ADVERTISING STANDS OUT FROM THE CROWD!**

The Advertising Agency

Advertising agencies specialise in the planning, design, production and media buying of campaigns on behalf of client companies who advertise. They provide in-depth knowledge of the disciplines involved in marketing and advertising, together with the creative inspiration required to develop effective ideas.

As with all business services, such as legal advice or accountancy, their expertise costs money. Fees vary depending upon type and volume of work and the calibre of personnel involved. However, if they achieve measurable results, their fees will be outweighed by the additional income they generate.

Choosing an advertising agency

As in most areas of business, initial meetings are free. Agencies will gladly provide a credentials presentation, during which they will guide you through work carried out for existing clients. At this stage, you should ask about costs and whether the agency works on a fixed fee, an ad hoc fee, or a commission basis. Having met them, how impressed you are with what you see and hear will help you decide how impressed your audience might be with the work they do for you.

If you cannot decide on this basis, you should invite a selection of agencies (usually no more than three) to compete for your business. This is known as a pitch.

You must prepare and issue a brief, specifying what you wish to achieve and inviting them to present a strategy and creative ideas for your business. Remember to insist that each agency outlines how they plan to monitor advertising effectiveness. Once appointed, they have to be prepared to be judged on the basis of results. Finally, you should specify a budget, as this has a major impact upon the approaches recommended.

Some agencies will not present ideas without receiving a pitching fee. You should not discriminate against them because of this basis, as it means they are unwilling to increase their overheads to existing clients by seeking new work for themselves. If you become their client, you will appreciate this loyal approach.

Extracted from 'Advertising Means Business', The Advertising Association

In my experience . . .

As a small businessman I am constantly looking for ways of increasing sales. When I first started the thought of paying for advertising filled me with horror. However, a close friend suggested that it might be possible to 'target market' for a very small outlay. By designing my own A5 leaflet and getting friends and family to look at it critically, I had created a cheap and effective way of bringing my product to the notice of a large number of people. My local newsagent delivered the leaflets with the newspapers to new housing estates in my area - my target market. For a total outlay of under £100 I increased my profits by more than £2000 - a very significant return on investment.

- Advertise, advertise, advertise - but in the early years do it cheaply
- Use local distributors
- Know your target market and focus on it

Geoff Andrews

The first commercial radio broadcast took place in 1922 and the first television commercial was shown in July 1941. But for the small business the world of advertising is centred much more on leaflets, brochures, catalogues, yellow pages, directory entries, letter headings, the shop window or, more recently, the web site.

Before you spend anything on advertising ask yourself:

What do I want this advertisement to achieve?
How much is that worth to me?
What message will get the desired result?
What medium will be seen by those I want to reach?
How will I measure the results?

The answers to those questions can halve your advertising expense and double its effectiveness. That may be the best return you will ever get for reading thirty-nine words.

Getting Publicity and Promoting your Product

Not all messages a business sends are equally well received. If a salesperson knocks on your door or phones you, you generally expect them to have their firm's interests at heart rather than your own. You will be on your guard and on the lookout for pitfalls. On the other hand if a close friend in much the same line of work, who you also recognise as being something of an authority on, say, computers, recommends that you look at a particular piece of software, you will be much more open.

This is exactly the role that public relations seeks to assume. Getting your message relayed through the editorial channel of, say, a newspaper, rather than through the advertising channel, can increase its effectiveness more than tenfold. People tend to believe what they read in articles and question what they read in advertisements. "Well they would say that, wouldn't they" is a sentiment always close to the surface when you read an advertisement.

COMMUNICATING WITH YOUR MARKET

There are a myriad definitions floating around regarding the practice of public relations - not all of them accurate! Public relations professionals define the practice as 'the discipline that looks after reputation with the aim of earning understanding and support and influencing opinion and behaviour'.

Public relations is an extremely professional and disciplined practice and more than ever it constitutes a valuable part of the marketing mix for businesses, from SMEs to multinationals.

Good public relations do not just happen overnight. They are often hard earned and require constant monitoring and maintenance - messages need to be updated and communicated effectively.

An effective public relations strategy can ensure that business objectives are met. It can influence shareholders, change legislation, raise issues, increase profitability and improve staff morale. It can also encourage higher prices for products and services. It can make a company stand out from its competitors. Effective public relations has the power to influence perceptions in a way that advertising cannot. Positive media coverage lends an air of almost 'official' endorsement to a company's products or services.

When considering its public relations strategy, the first action of a business is to decide what it wants people to think of it. Does it provide the quickest service? The lowest prices? The latest product range? If any business is not sure what its strengths are and what it does best, how can its customers be expected to know? Every organisation needs to be clear on what its audiences or publics are - existing and potential customers, investors and employees spring readily to mind, but there are many others, depending on the nature of the business.

Public relations frequently involves changing negative or apathetic attitudes into positive and favourable opinion. It starts with a detailed knowledge at the outset of how the public regards an organisation. This might involve conducting market research in some situations, but may just mean starting an honest dialogue with key customers, suppliers or the company's workforce.

Properly planned and implemented, public relations is a two-way process, feeding back reactions and opinions from all audiences so that strategies can be redefined. Public relations is not about spreading good news. It is about understanding the whole business and making sure that the right people have the right information to correct misunderstandings and enable them to contribute to the company's success.

In practical terms, public relations covers many techniques, from newsletters, exhibitions, meetings and letter writing, to lobbying, customer care programmes, media relations, employee communications and investor relations. This diversity means that public relations can convey messages more effectively than other communications media.

A 1996 Royal Society of Arts report entitled 'Tomorrow's Company' clearly identifies the important role that communications plays in business practice. It suggested that those companies with a solid communications programme would be the ones to succeed in the next millennium as there would be an increasing demand for more information by all publics. It is also vital that, in a world where businesses are more accountable to a wider range of publics than ever before, the information given out is clear and 100% accurate, with no leeway for misinterpretation. Companies can no longer hold back information as perhaps they might have done in the past.

People increasingly care about the values of those behind the products and services that they use or may be thinking about using - just witness the numerous media reports of organisations fighting to defend their reputation. In many markets, there is such a wide range of similar products that the only differentiating factor between competing brands is the image or perceived corporate values of that brand. Thus it is important that a business has in place a sound public relations strategy to help give the brand that elusive competitive edge.

Reputations are too important to be left to their own devices. All major organisations use public relations extensively and continuously. Fortunately, public relations techniques are not just for the lucky few or the biggest organisations. Small businesses or individual traders can also benefit considerably (and economically) from using some or all of them in their daily work. By following a few basic guidelines any company can start initiating good public relations:

 Define the public, understand their views and why they think and do what they do

 Be clear on what you, as a company, would like them to think about you

 Make sure employees know why they are working for the organisation, what the organisation wishes to achieve and how they can help

 Convey the company messages in a way that suits the audiences

See the media as a way of achieving the company objectives

 Create an atmosphere of sharing and trusting as the background to your communications. Don't just tell people what you want them to think

 Be clear about company objectives and measure progress throughout the project adjusting the programme and redirecting resources as the results suggest

Do not leave your company image and reputation to fate. Plan ahead and see improving communications as a continuous process, involving everyone who is concerned with or dependent on its success. For further information visit the IPR web site at www.ipr.org.uk

Institute of Public Relations

MAKING THE MOST OF PRESS RELEASES

There is the story of a man trapped in the ruins of a collapsed building. When, after some hours, rescuers reach him, they ask why he did not cry for help. He replies: "It's company policy - at times of crisis we always cut out the public relations".

Amusing as it may seem, there is a grain of truth in this story. In the modern-day world, where we are continually bombarded with information, only those who shout are heard.

For the new business owner trying to sell products and services, this can be a problem. Most forms of promotion, from advertising to events, from sponsorship to product placement, require the budget and imagination of Richard Branson and the organisational skills of Mission Control - both rarely in evidence in the new, small firm.

There is, however, another way, and that is press (or media) relations. In the UK today we have 22 national newspapers, around 90 regional dailies, some 430 paid-for weekly papers and, staggeringly, an estimated 12,000 special interest journals. The British are among the world's most avid consumers of glossy magazines. A brief look along the shelves of the local newsagents indicates just how many titles there are, covering every known hobby, interest, sector or occupation.

In addition there is a thriving and growing radio and television industry, broadcasting, in many cases, 24 hours a day.

All of these media outlets have one thing in common - they need news. A perishable commodity, news is consumed quickly and must always move on.

News is obtained from a wide variety of sources but one of the largest sources of news lies in press releases in these multi-media days more correctly called news releases. A number of surveys have indicated that around half of all news carried by the media originates from news releases.

So how can the small business owner tap into this well of publicity? There are basically three steps:

 Define what is news in your organisation

 Convert it into a usable form such as a news release

 Send it to the appropriate media

At first glance business owners may think they have little to shout about. But take a moment to consider everything about the business:

- Have you opened/converted new premises?
- Have you created local jobs?
- Is the new owner interesting, or had an unusual previous career?
- Is the product or service innovative and if so, in what way?
- Are there any new orders to announce?
- Are there any unusual jobs, in unusual places?

Having decided what stories there are - and in 15 years in PR, I've yet to find a business that has no story to tell - they then have to be written according to a few basic rules:

 Start with an attention-grabbing title

 Make the first paragraph the most interesting or the journalist may not read beyond it

 Make sure you include what is happening, why it is happening, when, where, and who is involved

 Put a date on it

 Include a contact name and telephone number; also include one for outside office hours as the world of news gathering works 24 hours a day

With the news release written, check that you haven't said anything inaccurate or incorrect. If you're not sure, change it or take it out. The purpose of this exercise is to get publicity, not writs.

Now you must decide where to send the news release and this will depend largely on the story. If it is a local story, then the local media will be interested. Look in the local paper and take note who writes about this kind of thing. Listen to the radio and decide who might be interested. Send the release to all of them.

If the story is about your new type of floorboard, you will undoubtedly know the relevant publications to send the release to. If your release is about a motoring product, ring the newspapers and find out the name of the motoring correspondent, if it's about a new service, ask for the consumer editor, and so on.

Having sent out the news release, remember that it might even be sufficiently interesting to make the journalist call you! It's worth devoting a few minutes before this happens to considering what might be asked and what the response should be. It's also never a bad idea to follow it up to make sure it has arrived - this may provide an opportunity to discuss your story . . . but don't bank on it.

Lastly, keep an eye on the press to see where your publicity appears, or if the budget allows employ one of the many monitoring agencies who will pick up your cuttings for you.

Sue Baker, Lexicon Public Relations Ltd

There are few days when Richard Branson is not in the public eye. More often than not as a result of the efforts of his public relations advisers. But you don't need to either be as big as Virgin, or to have outside advisers to get lots of PR. Chantal Coady, who started out with a small chocolate shop in London's Kings Road and built it into a £2 million-a-year business, used PR almost exclusively. She sought out ways of presenting her products that would appeal to a press as diverse as Vogue and the Financial Times. Each year she generated free press coverage that would otherwise have cost hundreds of thousands of pounds. Even if she had bought that advertising the results could never have matched the endorsement her business received by virtue of where its message was presented.

Creating a Brand

The intangible elements of many goods are often what people pay the most for. A pair of jeans without the magic 'Levi' name on them may not be worth anything like as much. Levi Strauss invented the hard-wearing canvas trousers by accident. He set off with a load of canvas following the Californian gold rush in the 1850s hoping to make tents, but found that what people wanted most were trousers. He didn't call them jeans - that didn't come about until the turn of the century. By the 1940s they were known as Levis, and the rest, as they say, is history.

CREATING A BRAND ASSET

It's impossible to escape the influence of brands these days. Walk down a high street, turn on the television, open a newspaper or magazine and we are bombarded by all kinds of brands and brand messages. Every day, businesses are bought and sold for their brands. Politicians discuss the 'branding of Britain'. Celebrities such as OJ Simpson and Tiger Woods are referred to as 'brands'.

Where has all this interest in brands come from and what does it mean for the small, owner-managed business?

Well, quite a lot actually. Branding is certainly big business. All kinds of companies, from manufacturers and retailers to industrial and service businesses, are embracing branding as a key competitive tool. But branding is also of huge importance for small, growing businesses, struggling to be heard in an ever more crowded and competitive marketplace. There are lessons to be learned from the earliest days of branding combined with best practice picked up from recent developments.

Brands were first developed as a means to distinguish one person's product from another (literally, by branding cattle, for example). They developed into 'marks of quality', offering a reassurance of consistency and hence facilitating consumer choice. In recent decades distinctive attitudes, values and even whole experiences have been built into brands, giving them enormous emotional pull and considerable social and financial power.

Initially creating a brand will help a new business to present itself clearly to the outside world (customer, suppliers and investors). Through the registration of trademarks, the brand owner can protect a brand name, visual style, unique shape and even a sound or smell! Developing a distinctive brand culture will help the brand owner to attract and enthuse staff and bind customers to the goals, culture and personality of the business. Careful management of the brand over time will ensure that the products and services, communications and behaviour of the business remain coherent and stand out from the clutter and competitive 'noise'. Branding can help build a more promising and secure future for a small business and may also result in higher margins.

If branding is taken seriously and practised carefully over time, then valuable brand assets can be created. The value of the goodwill created in a small business (its reputation, esteem and ultimately its future sales) will be captured in a single asset - the brand. So, from the start, the brand should be taken as seriously as the other key assets of the business - whether they are premises, machinery or people.

Finally, don't think that branding is all about multi-million pound advertising campaigns, expensive logo designs and legions of brand consultants! Some of today's most distinctive brands were created more by vision, focus and determination than by huge investment. Phileas Fogg and The Body Shop have managed to become household names with relatively little communications spend. The now omnipresent Nike 'swoosh' logo was designed in Seattle for $35!

At its heart, branding is about communicating difference to build involvement. For the small owner-managed business this must be a key strategic goal. Creating a distinctive, legally protectable brand property at the start of a business can ultimately result in a valuable brand asset and key business tool.

Interbrand Newell and Sorrell

Whether you go in for branding or not, at least try to make sure you have a business name that informs the market rather than confuses it. A small firm that calls itself 'Jetwash' and generates three-quarters of its business from the sale of pig pens, is likely to provide for some obscure directory entries, and some very frustrating initial phone calls. (This is a real example, circa October 1997.) Moreover, consider from the outset the value of getting it right. All owners of brands would share the view of John Stuart, Chairman of Quaker, when he said: "If this business were to be split up, I would be glad to take the brands, trademarks and goodwill and you could have all the bricks and mortar - and I would fare better than you".

In my experience . . .

Distinct, innovative packaging clearly helps a new consumer brand to stand out from the crowd, but how does one develop a distinct, innovative beer bottle? The answer proved to be to copy an oval beer bottle of around 1770 from Philadelphia.

After months of mould development and mould manufacture the first 24 bottles arrived by courier. I was so excited I could not wait to show my new bottle to a retail buyer so on the spur of the moment I called the beer buyer at Britain's largest supermarket chain and bullied him into seeing me that same afternoon. The result? He was as excited as me and undertook to stock my new brand nationally as soon as it became available.

- Differentiate your product - give it shelf appeal and make sure it stands out from the crowd
- When you have such a differentiated product don't be scared to show it to the leading buyers - after all, they want interesting, differentiated products too

John Murphy, St Peter's Brewery

DESIGNING FOR PROSPERITY

No longer confined to the style sections of the Sunday supplements, concerned purely with wacky new products or interior decor, design is becoming a critical weapon in the armoury of the forward looking, successful business.

More and more companies, large and small, are beginning to appreciate that good design gives them that extra competitive edge in an increasingly fierce marketplace.

Management expert Tom Peters has pointed out that with "a billion new, talented workers from Asia, Latin America and Central Europe coming online in the next half dozen years", high quality products are going to be available around the globe. The question will be, how do we continue to differentiate ourselves? The answer, more than ever, is through investment in design.

Research by the Design Council has revealed that, on average, 90 per cent of products developed with the help of professional designers are commercially successful. The same study found that the initial cost of that design work was, in most cases, recouped within the first 15 months of the product being launched. Further research on 'business angels' - private investors who invest money in a new product or service - has established the increasing value of design.

Design, in particular the aesthetic value placed on particular products, has come to the fore in recent times because consumption has come to mean more than simply the transaction of commodities. Indeed, the image of material goods has in many cases become the primary reason for their consumption - and this is not just confined to manufactured products.

Not surprisingly, those putting money into a product are concerned with this aspect as a major factor behind any decision to proceed - or not proceed - with their investment. One prospective investor quoted in Design Council research commented, "There are stacks of people making this sort of thing. The problem here is that it's competitive. How well can they get their costs down and how good are their design people at producing yet more and more?"

Investors are also looking for the 'trading formula' - what makes the products and services superior in the market. And more often than not the USP is a matter of design.

Turned on its head, this is probably the best definition of a design strategy. And in this day and age it is quite clear that although design often needs to prove its worth, the wisest investors will want to know how it fits into the overall strategy of the business. One investor, rejecting a proposal, said "I think the business is wrong. They don't have a design strategy. They've got a product, but no design strategy as to what the product is going to do and where it is going to go and how they are going to develop it".

Not all proposals fail through poor design but many more flourish by taking it as a serious part of their business planning.

Luke Blair, Media Relations Manager, Design Council

In our first few months of existence, one major project involved a national newspaper and a ladies golf promotion. I had spent two months researching the needs of female golfers and had arranged golf days at various prestigious venues around the UK. These days were to be sponsored by a major credit card company in association with Cobra Golf Equipment, with the newspaper as host.

The credit card contact - who had claimed to have power of attorney over their golf activities - turned out not to be a decision-maker. The company pulled out, and when the newspaper editor heard this she decided she no longer wanted to be involved - to this day I don't know exactly why. However, Cobra kept their confidence in the project and agreed to fund it. Even when things were not 100 per cent perfect they kept faith with the idea because it was essentially a good one. Today the Lady Cobra Golf Days are the biggest ladies golf promotion in the UK, so what could have been an expensive disaster turned out well for those who stayed with the project.

- Never count your chickens before they hatch
- Always be wary of someone who claims to represent a company's sole interest - there are some that do, but too many that don't
- If you work with the media, always get your agreement in writing

Jamie Cunningham, Professional Sports Partnerships Ltd

Selling

Selling is seen as the hard edge of marketing. It is thought of as either a 'foot in the door' activity or the domain of those with the 'gift of the gab'. There are two important truths about selling. The first is that the better you are at marketing the less energy you have to expend in selling. So if you research your market, target a specific customer group, make your product or service different and better than what is on offer elsewhere, find out what your customers read, listen to or watch, then the business of selling is already more than half done. The second truth will make more sense once you have read this chapter.

INTRODUCTION TO SELLING

All business is about selling. Even the brain surgeon has to sell his skills to the hospital that employs him and if he does not meet his customers' needs then he is no longer in business.

Whether you are selling goods or services you must have a structured approach to selling and carefully monitor results. As Mr Micawber said:

"Annual income £20, annual expenditure £19 19s 6d, result happiness. Annual income £20, annual expenditure £20 and sixpence, result disaster." Selling is your only source of business income.

The first and not always obvious task is to define exactly who your customer is. If you are selling a service such as training, for example, is your customer the company that employs you to train its staff or the individual staff members you are interfacing with? This would apply to a university who will employ a lecturer to deliver a specific curriculum. If the lecturer performs his task well and the customers of the university, the students, are satisfied, then the university gets new customers and the lecturer can use his success on his CV to 'sell' himself for promotion.

Secondly, having identified your customers you must find out exactly what these customers want. Not what you want to give them but what they actually want themselves. Do this by conducting market research, either by simply asking friends or colleagues what they would want or by using companies to provide an independent research service. Once you know what they want, then imagine yourself in their shoes and try to think of some 'added value' extra that will give your product a unique selling point over all your competitors.

Remember that customers buy benefits not features. Helena Rubenstein did not sell make-up, she sold 'hope'. Coca-Cola does not sell fizzy drink, it sells 'friendship and fun'. B&Q doesn't sell 2mm drills, it sells '2mm holes'. Carefully work out what benefits your company can provide for your customers and start producing promotional literature with all these benefits listed. Literature need not be expensive. A one sheet flyer can be produced by your local print shop for a few pence each copy. There are also some grants available for business start-ups to assist with printing costs. Find out about them from your local business shop or Chamber of Commerce.

Once you have a clear picture of your customer, his needs and the benefits you can provide, you are ready to start making sales. If you are in a start-up situation you will probably be your own salesperson. Even if you intend to employ a professionally trained salesperson, it is always best to go through each process yourself. The most successful business people are the ones who can do it all, and can turn their hand to any job in their organisation.

When making sales remember the tip that you have two ears and one mouth, so listen. By listening carefully to what your customer wants you can tailor your product to meet his needs. Objections can always be overcome if you have listened carefully to what he really wants. Always ask questions that begin with 'who', 'where', 'what', 'when', or 'how'. These are called open questions. A yes or no response is no use to you. Remember you are finding the solution your customer wants.

Always close the sale on a positive note. Never expect your customer to ask to buy. Be ready with an order form and close by saying something like "I shall just fill out this order form now and you can decide whether you want delivery this week or next. I'm sure you will be delighted with your purchase".

Help is always at hand from business colleagues. Go to meetings and conferences and hear how others are successful. Read books on the subject and network through clubs and societies. Take advantage of all the help on offer through government schemes and learn to be a good salesperson.

Successful selling is the key to your business success, so never underestimate the importance of sales. If you are employing a sales team then get the best you can afford and be able to do it yourself in order to command respect from the rest of the team.

Marilyn Orcharton, The Small Business Bureau

USING YOUR CUSTOMER DATABASE

When businesses call for marketing advice, it is usually because their sales are declining or at the very least not growing at the desired rate. "We need more business" is the perennial cry. Should we increase our advertising, put pressure on the sales force, or change our brochure?

While such steps may ultimately prove necessary, efforts to retain and develop existing customers may provide a more cost-effective and more assured route to success than looking for new ones.

It is not just a question of delivering the right product, on time and at the right place. We need to know more about our customers' needs and wants, their aspirations and lifestyle. We must in short anticipate their every need and exceed their expectations.

A tall order! Maintaining a good customer contact management system and fully utilising your customer database takes some of the pain out of this exercise, but there is no substitute for actively staying close to your customers. This is not just the preserve of the salesforce or front line staff but should be practised by everyone in the organisation. Customer focus may be your only competitive advantage in fast changing global markets.

A customer database is only as useful as the information stored in it, and therefore it is important that the data entered is accurate and relevant and is regularly updated. Customers like to be consulted - it makes them feel needed - but there is a fine line to be drawn between canvassing opinion and being a nuisance by inundating customers with questionnaires.

Finding new customers and new markets is a different ball game requiring different skills and resources. It is a longer term strategy. The timescale for acquiring new business from new customers should never be underestimated. Developing such contacts can take a long time, particularly in the business to business environment.

It is important to quantify how much new business you need to sustain manageable growth in your company and the number of new customers needed to generate that business. If a few large scale customers will satisfy your immediate aims, a personal approach is best. If your average customer order value is low and you need a large number of them, you may need to resort to other forms of mass communication.

Either way, there is no substitute for knowing your customers and your database is key to this.

Do

- Identify the real cause of declining sales or profitability
- Look at the costs and benefits of retaining existing customers and acquiring new customers
- Review all aspects of your business, not just marketing
- Re-evaluate your overall marketing strategy
- Target your resources where they will have the most impact

Don't

- Cut budgets without identifying what is the real problem
- Just increase advertising spend and hope that sales will increase
- Copy competitors because it works for them - it may not work for you
- Try to sell to an untargeted market
- Expect overnight success.

Liz Thomas , Business Link, Leicestershire

DIRECT MARKETING

There's not many a business plan that will get past the bank manager without a strategic section called 'marketing'. But how can a business best justify its expenditure on promoting its goods and services?

Direct marketing is one form of advertising that is not only totally accountable, but is often the most cost-effective technique.

All direct marketing establishes a direct one to one dialogue with the customer. Most media can be employed - telephone, press, inserts, door drops, radio and TV - but the cornerstone of the direct marketing industry is direct mail.

The medium can be used very effectively for gaining new business. When properly targeted it is a vehicle for reaching a discrete audience with a specific and tailored message.

In addition, direct marketing is a most cost-effective way of developing an ongoing relationship with your customers - to maximise their loyalty, value and consequently profitability over time. The key benefits of direct marketing - in particular direct mail - for new businesses are that it is a responsive, measurable and accountable form of advertising.

Direct mail allows you the freedom to be totally selective as you can pick and choose your target audience, for example, selecting customers by date of last purchase, or prospects by post code. When the targeting is right the recipient welcomes direct mail and the information it contains, and is therefore more likely to respond.

Unlike mass marketing, mailing can be targeted so different audiences receive tailored messages - for example you may want to highlight specific benefits to certain people. You can choose when exactly your customer receives your message and talk on a one to one basis.

Your direct mail campaign can only produce good results when you have the right list. If you are targeting existing clients then the effectiveness of your efforts will be dependent on the most valuable asset of your business - up-to-date, relevant information about your customers. You may also find that you have to supplement this data from external sources.

To reach new prospects, you may decide to buy or rent a list from a specialist list broker. To obtain the list that is right for your business you must give a clear brief to your list broker, detailing as much as you can about the target audience and the required volume/percentage of responses. Share with your broker exactly how the communication will look and what it will offer. Let them know anything you know about the profile of your ideal customer in terms of demographics and lifestyle.

It is also essential that you are clear about how you are going to measure the success of the campaign from the very beginning. This may be driven by cost per response, cost per order or return on investment and is dependent on the business you are in and what your objectives are.

To successfully drive a direct mail campaign you need to be single minded about your goal:

- Be clear what your proposition is
- Identify the most important thing you want your customers to take from the mailing
- Produce a strong offer relevant to your customers that will encourage them to respond
- Think clearly about how you want your customers to respond

Communication of these messages is possibly best left to the experts. Most businesses will look for professional help to ensure that the mailing conveys the offers, is consistent with your brand image, prompts a response and is within budget.

Direct marketing offers businesses greater control over their marketing and advertising budgets. Being a precise and accountable medium, it often proves to be the most cost-effective marketing tool available. Get the elements right, measure the results, fine tune, measure again and direct mail will take on a whole new meaning in your marketing armoury.

Rick Mills, Client Services Director, WWAV Rapp Collins

LOYALTY

Why is it important ?

It used to be thought that a good product backed with good service would automatically lead to repeat sales. Nowadays, research tells us that those customers who pronounce themselves satisfied are often the most fickle when it comes to brand loyalty.

"In business 67% of customers go elsewhere because no one keeps in touch"

That's why it pays to communicate with your customers - to build relationships with them. Just because a customer has bought something from you once doesn't mean they'll buy from you again. There are dozens of reasons why customers might not buy from you again, and only really two why they would.

The first is a negative reason. He or she can't be bothered to look elsewhere (but they might well in the future). The second reason for staying with you is positive. You give the customer a reason to stay loyal. Not just by selling a good product or service, but by initiating a relationship, by taking the trouble to communicate, and by finding out what he or she wants and then offering it.

'A rise of as little as 5% in customer retention could result in an 80% increase in profit'
Source: Datamonitor

"Most companies lose 45 to 50% of their customers every five years."
Source: Marketing Direct article, April '99

Loyalty is a Journey

Why not make it your policy to write to customers every couple of months or so? If you set up an easily adaptable computer template, you'll find it won't take long and is very cost-effective. The more you keep in touch with someone, the more you're likely to be at the forefront of their minds, and the less likely they are to look elsewhere. Good news when it comes to repeat orders.

How much loyalty you show can depend on how much loyalty you're shown. What, however, if those repeat orders are slow to materialise - or in the case of some customers, non-existent? Is it worth staying in touch with customers who don't appear keen to make further purchases? The answer has to be a qualified 'yes'.

Customer relationships have been compared to the relationships we have in everyday life. For instance, there are the 'happily married', who show true loyalty to your company and products, and are keen to know of new developments so are pleased to receive communications from you. There are customers who are 'steady but single' - they may not make frequent purchases, but direct mail sustains the relationship with them. Then there are the 'unrequited', who bought once, but whose interest has waned. Yet even this last group can be worth writing to once or twice - if you have a particularly good offer or piece of news to tell them about.

How you can promote it

Tell Them All Your News

If you're going to keep in touch with your customers regularly, you're going to need something to write about. An obvious starting point is to inform them of new products or services.

"Customers expect regular dialogue as part of a good business relationship"

In fact, not passing on good news could be bad news for you. A recent survey* found that: '57% of customers said it was unfavourable if companies did not inform them of new products or services they might be interested in.' Dentists send out reminders to their patients every six months to remind them that they need a check-up. The same principle could easily be applied by many other companies with new upgrades, products or services to offer. If you've no new products or services in the offing, how about a special offer or a discount or two. You could invite customers to special discount shopping days, store openings or private views.
Source: Office of Consumer Affairs

Questions Could Be The Answer

Questionnaires are not just a fine way of keeping in touch, they're also an excellent source of information for you. (After all, if you really want a long term relationship with someone, it makes sense to get to know them well.) In addition, questionnaires make your customers feel they are in a two way relationship, and that their views count. How do they rate you for service? For staff friendliness? For price? For delivery times?

You can ask customers' opinions on any number of areas. You may only get a small proportion who respond, but many more will welcome the fact that they've been asked. And if those who do respond get a follow-up 'thank you' letter, they'll certainly be appreciative.

If you've got nothing to say, think of something.

So you've got no new products or services in the offing. No special discounts to announce. No seasonal offers with which to bring good cheer. No questionnaires to send out. Never mind, there are still plenty of ways of staying in regular touch with your customers:

- Long-standing customers could be rewarded with a free gift and a 'thank you' note.
- A simple thank you letter to a customer who has just made a big purchase could even persuade them to make another one soon.
- Seen something in the press of relevance to your customers or their business? Send them a copy of the relevant article.
- Even news of news can be good news. Minor changes like improved car parking, new personnel, service efficiencies and so on can still be of interest and benefit to your customers.
- If you are a large company with a large customer base, you could consider producing a regular newsletter or magazine.
- Send your most important customers birthday cards or Christmas cards (preferably just before Christmas). If some of your customers don't celebrate Christmas, consider sending them cards to celebrate other religious festivals as appropriate.
- If a customer changes address or name (i.e. gets married), send them a special moving house or 'wedding present' offer.

Loyalty is a Two Way Process

If customers are important to get, they're even more important to keep. Quite simply, repeat customers are also cheaper customers.

"It costs six times more to get a new customer than it does to maintain an existing one!"
Source: Office of Consumer Affairs

The longer customers stay with you, the more they're likely to spend proportionally on your products or services.
Source: 'Profitable Customers', Charles Wilson 1998.

Why not? They've grown to trust you. In fact it's been estimated that the top 10% of customers commonly account for 65% of sales and virtually all the profits.

Satisfied customers will create new customers too. A single satisfied customer tells on average 10 different people about their positive experience with the company in question. Just help them to remember you by staying in touch.

'When a company consistently delivers superior value and wins customer loyalty, market share goes up and the cost of acquiring customers goes down.'
Source: Loyalty Based management, F.F. Reichheld, Harvard Business Review, March - April 1993.

Direct Mail - The Ins and Outs

Although this section is essentially concerned with using direct mail to create loyalty, it is, of course, also very effective at directly generating revenue. In fact, it's estimated that direct mail generates over £16 billion worth of business for UK companies a year.

In addition, direct mail is actually the most responded to of all media - 61% of all consumers have responded at some time to direct mail, 43% of them in the last twelve months.
Source: DMIS

That's why direct mail is not just worth doing, it's also worth doing well. If you would like a step by step guide on how to plan, create, and produce a mailshot then try the Royal Mail web site (www.royalmail.co.uk).

'Where a purchase results from a direct mail campaign, our willingness to buy again from the same company rises to over 90% - customer loyalty that would be the envy of any retailer.'
Source: Direct Mail Information Service.

Where Can You See The Benefits?

The Royal Mail Customer Loyalty Study

Did you know that over 50% of customers surveyed had bought a product or service directly via direct mail. Or that 74% of those surveyed welcomed receiving direct mail about their areas of interest.

Those were just a couple of the findings from our extensive Customer Loyalty Study. For more information on loyalty from the customer's point of view, and a look at the full results of the survey, visit the Royal Mail web site at www.royalmail.co.uk.

CARING FOR YOUR CUSTOMERS

Customer care and service tell the customer as much about the company as they tell the company about the customer. Customer care and service really does mean understanding, caring for and serving the needs of the customer. It is worth remembering that without customers there would not be any business. But we should also recognise that customer care and service are important marketing tools.

Firstly, and probably most importantly, the way customers are treated affects their view of the company. The staff - the company's front line representatives - can encourage either satisfaction or dissatisfaction, and this can either produce repeat business or the reverse.

Much of this is governed by the way the organisation treats its employees. Disgruntled staff are often preoccupied with their own concerns, which means that the customer ranks low on their list of priorities.

We have all seen instances of the customer being ignored; where the employee prefers instead to chatter with a colleague or friend on the telephone; where the employee is attending to other tasks that could be set aside; where the employee sees the customer arrive and immediately walks away; or where managers or other colleagues interrupt an employee who is in the process of dealing with a customer, as though that customer were invisible.

These are all signs of a company that cares as little for its customers as it does for its employees - a company that is missing a major marketing opportunity.

A second benefit of customer care is that it produces ready-made opportunities for market research. What does the customer think of the product/service? Are their needs understood and being properly met? If not, what improvements could be made?

Some larger companies make the most of these opportunities - every comment or complaint must be written down and sent to head office. They also have tricks for making free use of customer information for their own marketing purposes. Their motive is a lesson to smaller companies, but their methods can backfire and leave customers feeling even more annoyed.

It is important too to understand that marketing is not a completely separate function from the rest of the business. Several major companies make this mistake. Marketing is not some secret activity between the marketing department and the customers. Effective marketing should go hand in hand with every other operation of the business.

The Customer is King

So how should customers be treated to capitalise on these marketing opportunities? The old-fashioned idea that 'the customer is always right' can be patronising and come across as a kind of false sales patter. The concept that the customer is King/Queen is, however, not that far off the mark. The customer should therefore be treated with courtesy and respect. Quite simply this means listening to the customer - it is their perception that counts - encouraging communication and then responding promptly. It also means checking to see whether the customer is happy with the response. Here is an opportunity for the company to show that it values every one of its customers and that it intends to put matters right. If further action is required, it should be made clear at the outset who else will be involved, what will happen next and how long this will take.

Many organisations will have a special phone number, section or whole department for customer service. But if the customer gets a repeated engaged signal, gets put through to the wrong department, is told to call back after lunch because nobody is available, we cannot call this customer service. Customer service is most definitely not about putting the customer through needless hurdles of time, added inconvenience and expense on behalf of your organisation.

It is about putting matters right promptly and sensibly, not about creating a whole new set of problems where previously none existed. This can result in a meaningless record of customer's complaints about how the initial issue was not handled properly. This is no myth - complaints about the mishandling of complaints are on the increase.

There is an art to good customer care and service. It is a far more complex interactive process between the customer and the company than people realise. It is difficult to teach and it is interesting to note that some large companies tend to employ more mature and experienced people for this job because of the type of skills needed.

The art of customer service

Some do's and don'ts of customer service and care reflect the varied, significant and sensitive nature of the role and the personal characteristics required in developing the art.

Don't

- Ignore the customer
- Stop speaking to, turn away from or leave the customer without explanation
- Be rude to the customer
- Shout at the customer
- Dismiss the customer's comments
- Criticise the customer
- Suggest that the customer has a problem and nothing better to do with their time because they have complained in the first place
- Act superior
- Treat the customer as though they are stupid, unreasonable or unbelievable
- Pretend to have knowledge about a product
- Complain to the customer about how the organisation treats them
- Tell the customer they are wasting their time
- Ask the customer what they would like to happen, and then say that something cannot be done because it is not company policy
- Leave the customer feeling more dissatisfied

Do

- Understand the meaning, importance and significance of good customer care
- Have the interpersonal skills required to be able to handle a variety of people and situations
- Have a thorough if basic knowledge of the company, its products and services
- Work closely and in harmony with management and know when and how to refer comments of the customers to the company
- Be alert to the implications of information received
- Take prompt, effective action if a comment warrants serious attention
- Know how to manage stress and defuse tension so that situations do not get out of hand
- Give the customer an honest explanation and a genuine apology if necessary

Rather than dreading negative comments or criticism, managers should set an example to staff by meeting and enjoying the challenge of providing good customer care and service. Turning a disgruntled customer into one who is impressed by the way the company puts things right requires real effort and expertise, but the benefits are well worthwhile - enduring customer loyalty and customer recommendations that lead to repeat and new business.

Paulette Lockington

DIRECT SELLING

Home shopping is big business in the UK, with sales of £9.6 billion in 1996. Selling goods and services to consumers in their homes, or at least away from normal retail stores, can be done through mail order catalogues, direct mail, TV and Internet and direct selling. It is in direct selling, where annual sales now exceed £1.4 billion, that there is the widest range of opportunities for entrepreneurs to start a business of their own, with the minimum of capital and risk.

Direct selling of consumer goods is largely based on impulse sales and the average transaction value is low - under £20. It is not a distribution method that is suited to every type of product. It is, however, ideally suited to personal and household products, for which there is a demand in every home, and where novelty, the opportunity for demonstration and good service can be provided through home delivery.

For entrepreneurs in direct selling, there are two alternatives: participate in an established direct selling business or start your own. For someone without any previous experience it is usually best to start off with an established business. With an established business you will be self-employed and usually have the opportunity to build a business of your own, at your own pace, in a way that is similar to that offered in franchises. The big difference, in direct selling, is that the initial investment required is modest, rarely more than £200. As the business grows there will rarely be any need to invest any further capital. For that reason, many of the most successful direct sellers, are never tempted to start a new direct selling enterprise. However, for anyone who does wish to take that step, then the following is a useful checklist:

Product selection. Select a product that appeals to you. A personal enthusiasm for the product by both the promoter of a direct selling business and by all direct sellers is a vital ingredient for success. Enthusiasm and personal endorsement for a product goes a long way to overcome the need for selling skills.

Pricing. Select a product that offers a realistic profit margin from cost price to retail selling price. A direct selling business will not succeed if the retail selling price is unrealistically high - no matter how large the commissions and bonuses offered to direct sellers. As a general rule the promoter of a direct selling business needs to buy goods at around 25 per cent of the retail selling price. This is much the same margin as that used in the distribution of similar goods supplied through retail stores.

Selling method. The choice is between person to person or selling to a group, commonly known as party plan selling. Party plan sales work best for products that require demonstration. However, party sales require that demonstrators are particularly well trained and are sufficiently self-confident to organise parties that are enjoyed by all the guests who attend.

Choice of organisation or structure. Many direct selling businesses are now organised on a network marketing, or MLM basis. In an MLM business every participant, from the day they start, has the opportunity to sell goods and to build their own group of other direct sellers - and to benefit from their sales. For such a system to work well, it is vital that the product has a universal appeal. This enables participants to promote the product and the business opportunity to everyone they meet.

Legal compliance. Direct selling businesses have to meet the same legal requirements as any other retailer. However, network marketing businesses also have to comply with the Trading Schemes Regulations 1997 and all direct selling businesses have to comply with special consumer protection law and with the special rules for the collection of VAT.

Code compliance. Most of the substantial direct selling businesses in the UK are members of the Direct Selling Association whose Consumer Code of Practice is supported by the Office of Fair Trading. All direct selling businesses, whether or not they are DSA members, are encouraged to comply with this code.

Richard Berry, Direct Selling Association

In my experience . . .

Our business is a marketing consultancy working in the golf industry. Various clients were gained in the first few years of business - solid accounts but nothing too exciting. Then a golden opportunity presented itself - the chance to work closely with a major sports figure and his management company. The project was speculative in that it was dependent on the successful acquisition of a large property. A lot of time and effort were expended in the pre-contract stage - indeed so much that some of the bread and butter clients were not being properly looked after. Months passed and then, for reasons beyond the company's control, the property acquisition fell through. . . meanwhile the 'solid but not too exciting' clients had found another consultant.

This created short term difficulties - indeed threatened the future of the company. But the hard work did ultimately pay off. The star sportsman's management company was later introduced to a different and, in fact, far better property which it did successfully acquire . . and it has chosen to retain our consultancy company offering it an even greater involvement than was originally anticipated. The 'solid' and 'never forgotten' smaller clients are being rediscovered and, touch wood, business is thriving.

- However tempting or glamorous a prospective new project may appear, never forget your bread and butter clients.

- Do not leave yourself exposed by putting all your eggs (or hopes) in one basket.
- The phrase, "Nothing ventured, nothing gained" applies to all walks of life.
- Bad experiences can be turned around - provided that lessons are learned.

Nick Edmund, Global Golf Links

SUCCESSFUL EXHIBITING

There are many factors to consider in planning for an exhibition:

Which show?

First and foremost selecting the right show is paramount to your success level. Ask yourself questions about your anticipated audience, such as "who do you want to reach at the show," and "what do you want to have happen?" With such questions in mind then you have to match your exhibiting objectives with the right target audiences and have the ability to show and demonstrate your products or services.

It is important to do your homework, gathering background information on the show by looking at show statistics for example, and speaking to past exhibitors and attendees. It may also pay to visit the show prior to exhibiting to assess its value and perhaps to plan your space with regard to the position of other attractions, competitors, entrances and exits.

Other things to take into consideration include your distribution area and target audience, hence the geographical location of the show becomes important. As a rule, usually 40-60% of attendees come from within a 200-mile radius.

Why exhibit?

Having decided on what shows you will exhibit at, there are certain acknowledged secrets to trade show planning and preparation. Firstly, you have to think about what you want out of a show and how it can strengthen your present marketing strategy. Do you want to increase existing or introduce new products or services into existing markets? Or do you want to introduce existing and new products or services into new markets? Having decided this, it is wise to set measurable and realistic goals that portray the right image for your company. A display that is durable, flexible and versatile is ideal, especially if it fits your budget which must include exhibition space; the accessories and graphics that complement the display; show services such as shipping, set-up and dismantling; transportation and promotions and special events, to name but a few. Money can be saved by planning your transportation needs well in advance of the show. It is recommended that you choose a carrier that specialises in trade show transportation and will give you the service you need.

It is highly beneficial to develop an overall message or theme in your display. By keeping this in mind while developing your promotional plan, advertising, special events and media relations, you will help to reinforce your message to prospects as well as enable them to better recall who you are. Similarly, graphics are used to create interest, focus attention and tell visitors about your product or service. Graphics are often the first impression an attendee has of an exhibitor, and in just three to five seconds, they need to communicate who you are, what you do and how customers can benefit.

Preshow planning

Cost is obviously a factor when exhibiting, but there are ways of saving money without scrimping on quality.

Proper planning is essential. You can save on expensive last minute charges by planning ahead and establishing a list of key dates and activities. In addition, another tip is to push due dates back a month so that you always meet your deadlines. If you are really organised then producing all of your pre-show mailings at the same time to save on printing expenses, rather than printing several times a year is a good cost-cutting exercise.

The cost of your actual display can vary enormously, especially when it comes to transportation. Look into one that packs compactly to save on storage, is lightweight to save on shipping, portable to transport by car, courier or as airline baggage, can be quickly and easily set-up to save costs, and adapts easily to different spaces by adding or removing components. Consolidating materials into one tub or shrink wrapping individual items onto one pallet can all reduce costs in the transportation process. The more time you have to plan, the better able you are to organise the best transportation options for your specific needs. Your four main choices are common carrier, van line, air freight or courier service, but remember, leaving transportation to the last minute will reduce your options and raise your costs. Graphics too, can be designed and produced ahead of time to avoid overtime or rush charges, while getting your literature proofread avoids change charges. It is advisable to take only enough literature to distribute to highly qualified leads. Offer to send attendees literature so that it is on their desk when they return from the show, thus saving on cartage and production costs.

Other tips for effective cost-cutting include bringing your own "show box" containing handy items such as scissors, pens, paper, tape, extension cords etc. Pre-order show services at least ten to thirty days prior to the show - phones, cleaning services etc. thereby avoiding the floor prices which are often 10-20% higher. Setting up during normal hours keeps the cost down as you are avoiding having to pay personnel for weekends and overtime. Finally, travelling to the show can be costly depending on where you have come from. If flying, it is wise to investigate reduced rates or special deals with airlines, similarly hotels will probably have some special corporate rates available.

As already mentioned, the graphic display has to be strong to draw the attendee's attention, making them stop and look at your product or service. You only have one chance to make the right statement about your company and to demonstrate how it differs from the competition. There are several ways to ensure your graphics are as show-stopping as possible. In most cases bigger is almost always better when you want to attract attention and it is recommended that your graphics should be able to be viewed at a distance of two to five metres or more. For greater memorability, use colour rather than black and white and where possible use photographs over illustrations as they attract the eye, are more believable and better remembered. The pictures should tell a story and people rarely want to be confronted with great walls of type on a graphic panel, so limit your amount of copy and use simple language with short sentences and paragraphs.

Creating strong impressions can also mean using live presentations as an integral part of your marketing plan to appropriately communicate your company or product message. This, for example, can take the form of a theatrical skit, magician, game show, video, audio or singers. It is important to remember not to get carried away with an idea and lose sight of both your audience and the objective of your presentation. You can spend as much or as little on your presentation, but it always pays to be professional as your corporate image is being scrutinised by everyone. If you don't feel up to this task, it is worth hiring a professional company to help with the conceptual ideas and implementation.

Communicating and involving your staff is another way to project the right image by letting them know exactly what you expect from them at each show. A motivated and knowledgeable staff guarantees fantastic trade show results, so select people who want to be there and leave behind sales people who have negative attitudes. It is management's responsibility to create a positive, fun and reinforcing environment and to realise that it takes more than an incentive to succeed. Rewards and personal recognition provide an effective way of encouraging higher levels of performance. Ultimately, everyone should be working together as a team, helping each other out whenever and wherever necessary - this is the formula of a successful display at any show.

Planning is the key to the success of your pre-show direct mail campaign. Your direct mail campaign should be used in conjunction with other pre-show promotional activities such as advertising, telemarketing, press relations, etc. It is important to establish objectives for your promotion and make sure that they tie into your established show objectives and marketing strategy. Also, think about the response you want as well as the result you can realistically hope to achieve. Target the people you want to respond to your mailing, thinking about their interests and concerns. Consider tailoring your message to the appropriate audience if you are promoting to different markets, where you often have to reach multiple buying influences within each company. It therefore follows that who you mail to is equally, if not more, important than what you mail, and to achieve the best possible results, your best mailing list will be made up of your current and past customers and interested prospects. Once you have identified your audience, there are several measures that can improve your success rate. Firstly, you want a threefold goal: to get your piece opened, to get it read and to get the reader to take action. Certain gimmicks and attention-grabbing headlines all get your piece noticed and it is worth producing the letter in colour, too. Successful copy focuses on one key message; highlight your uniqueness and competitive advantage stressing the benefit that is most important to your customer in easy-to-read headlines and create an incentive to entice attendees to your stand. For example, devise a two part premium item the first half of which is sent prior to the show, if the person wants the second half, they will need to collect it at your stand. The best way to measure your mailing success is to establish a tracking system.Use a code on each mailing and, as part of your incentive offer, encourage visitors to bring the mailing to your display in exchange for a gift.

If you decide to give away gifts then they should be designed to communicate, motivate, promote or increase recognition and memorability; ultimately the premium and the message should make an impact. So the item, apart from reflecting your company image, must also be one that best suits your purpose and meets your objective as well as complementing your marketing message. Finally, if you make your premium work for you, ie. considering ideas that will help generate frequent visits to customers and prospects such as calling you for free refills, your money will be well invested.

International Exhibiting

When it comes to international exhibiting, it is very important to know your audience as there will inevitably be different forms of business etiquette to observe. Everything from greeting and addressing your prospects to building relationships should be carried out with formality and respect at the forefront. With different cultures in mind, it is prudent to do your research and be sensitive to things like the meanings of colour and symbols in different countries. Black, white, yellow and purple, for example, are often associated with funerals in Japan (purple in Brazil and yellow in Mexico) while red and yellow are considered lucky in China.

On a more practical level make sure you assess the suitability of your product or service in foreign markets and decide if, for example, modifications such as, size, design, electrical and other standards, colour or special packaging requirements, are necessary. Be prepared to have an interpreter available for foreign visitors and for translating copy or business communication, preferably a native speaker with technical knowledge of your products or industry. To move your product overseas, it is best to hire a custom house broker or a freight forwarder as they are extremely knowledgeable about import duties, documentation, credit transactions, crating services, insurance and bonding.

It takes time to build relationships through personal contact. It may take several appearances at trade shows, however, before your company is taken seriously, but informing yourself on areas like the decision-making process and how it differs between various countries will give you a better understanding of your audience.

As mentioned earlier, it always pays to be organised about the type of transportation you are going to use. The method may depend on a lot of factors including the packaging needs of the shipment; the origin and destination of the shipment; the amount of time set aside for transportation; and pick-up and delivery requirements. Check what help the carrier will give you with customs, documentation procedures, temporary import bonds, warehousing and consolidation. It would be in your best interests to select a carrier that has a dedicated exhibition service, 24-hour tracking capability and drivers who have experience delivering to show sites, or even find out from show management whether they have an official carrier for the event. A recommended carrier is likely to offer special prices as an incentive to use its services. It is important to sort out your insurance and there are several options available for your exhibit: corporate insurance policies, common carrier/van line insurance and extended liability coverage. Remember that every reputable carrier is insured against loss or delay so ask for specifics, that is reimbursements for loss and specific guarantees concerning inclement weather or natural disasters. It may seem obvious, but remember to label every box, carton or crate with the show name and booth number that you are shipping and take pre-printed labels with the return address to replace in-bound ones.

Dealing with show services is probably one of the least attractive aspects of exhibiting, yet it is a real necessity. You should start off by reading the exhibitor service manual which is the official guide to everything the exhibitor needs to know about the show. This includes all the relevant information, rules and regulations, service forms, contractor and shipping information. By making sure that you know which products you are planning to demonstrate and display, and what utilities are required so that you can make decisions on carpeting, furniture, colour schemes, cleaning and security services, you can cut out any unnecessary costs that are incurred when services are ordered on the show floor, which can be up to 50% extra. Being organised, such as calling the electrical department to find out how much power to order and where the utility ports are located in relation to your space, will ensure your display will perform at its optimum level. Similarly, it is possible to cut costs on drayage (which involves delivering your display materials to the assigned space at the show and back), by consolidating shipments and by shipping only once.

Ultimately, show services representatives can make your life a lot easier as they often have the answers to many of your questions or problems, and remember, their job is to help you. Bring along copies of all relevant paperwork, especially plans, service orders, tracking numbers for all shipments, etc., as well as important contact names, phone and fax numbers.

Meeting People

Once you have attracted the attendees to your display it is then time to ask leading questions that will engage prospects and reveal their needs. It is important to find out who you are dealing with first of all, then establishing their main objectives for attending the show and what they actually do. Once the ice is broken, you should move to more probing, business-specific questions to create the fuel for your ultimate sale. Ask them about the product or service they are currently using and what they would like to change about it, or maybe what specific information they are looking for. It is also important to keep the attendee involved and interested during your demonstration by asking questions like "What do you think of this product's performance and how does it compare with what you are currently using?" or, "What specific concerns do you have regarding our products, services, and doing business with us?" To help produce appropriate follow-up action, some well prepared questions can be the key to success; ask the attendee how their company decides which vendors to work with, and what else would be important for them to know and see as the next step.

After the show is equally as important, and a prompt follow-up within three to five days is advisable. There are several good lead management software applications on the market that will fit most needs - or consider designing your own (but the simpler the better). Decide what kind of questions you will receive and how to respond to them. It is a good idea to consider tailoring different follow-up methods to the various types of visitor, for example prospects with an immediate need, to prospects interested in buying in the next six months and finally for prospects who are only partially interested.

In conclusion, it is fair to say that one of the most crucial aspects of any event is its people. The personnel you choose to represent you are your ambassadors and they have the responsibility of making or breaking future relationships with attendees, prospects and customers. Invest time in training them so they know what to do and how to best represent your company. It is important not to get into a routine of visiting shows just for the sake of it, you should continually re-evaluate the reasons why you select a show and ensure that they continue to attract your target audience and achieve results.

Nomadic Display

However you sell, be it direct, using agents or with your own sales team, selling is always something of a numbers game. This is the second universal truth about selling. The more of the right sort of contacts you make the more business you will do. So you need to measure sales activity as well as sales results. The number of phone calls or visits made, the volume and value of quotations sent out, all need to be set as objectives and then monitored.

If your sales are too low but your products (or services) are right for the market and the level of sales activity is high enough, then you have the wrong people doing the selling for you.

In my experience . . .

When I opened a subsidiary in the US, I hired a local businessman to run it. I trained him in the UK and in the first couple of years made frequent trips to support him. The early years were great - steady growth, nice profits and a lot of fun. Indeed things looked so good that I gave him a substantial share of both the UK and US businesses.

Then things started to go wrong - sales slumped and profits collapsed. At first I believed the story I was told "Times are hard and competition is growing", and refused to accept that my managing director had set up his own business in competition and that he was also busily syphoning off all the cash. The result - a costly lawsuit and a two year struggle to re-establish the business.

- Always insist on full operating accounts - investigate them in depth and never be put off
- If you do give stock, always have 'give back' and 'buy back' provisions

John Murphy

Importing from Abroad

The reason for importing must be either because the product is not available in your home market, or because the import is cheaper or better, or at any rate seen as being better. Sometimes the imprint of a particular country can lend certain types of product additional credibility. Health care products and watches are associated with Switzerland and good engineering with Germany.

A Guide to Importing

The activity of importing (and indeed exporting) is fraught with potential pitfalls for the unwary, but the determined can develop a profitable business or aspect of their business if they are willing to do the groundwork.

Research

Product Apart from basic market research, prospective importers must look at some additional elements at the research stage. One of the most important of these is the classification of the product you intend to import under the UK customs 'Tariff'. The aim is to arrive at the correct classification code for your product alongside which will lie key information indicating whether there are any restrictions on importing the product and what these are, and what VAT and duty rates will be levied on the product at importation.

The Tariff can be consulted at most local Customs and Excise advice centres and at many good reference libraries. Having established the correct code you will then be in a position to quote this to the DTI-ILB on Tel: 01642 364333 Fax: 01642 533557 to check that it is legal to import the product concerned into the UK and whether or not an import licence will be necessary.

It is important that you know your product and the regulatory framework within which it is to be marketed. Therefore it is particularly important for you to check at this early stage for any specific EU and or UK regulations that may affect your product. Attention should be paid to compliance with consumer law and product regulations, health and safety issues, packaging and labelling, and to any inherent risk in the product that might give rise to future product liability claims. Help in this area can be sought from the government sponsored Business Link and TEC networks and local authority trading standards offices and enterprise agencies, as well as the DTI Consumer Safety Unit on Tel: 0171 215 0369 Fax: 0171 215 0357.

Country After your product, research on the country you intend to source from is the next thing to consider. You will need to put together a reasonably comprehensive profile of the country concerned. A wide range of inexpensive information can be picked up from the travel sections of good bookshops, from foreign embassies and trade promotion bodies in London, supplements to the Financial Times and Economist newspapers and DTI country desks.

Among the criteria for assessing whether to do business with a particular country or not are: the closeness of its trading relationship with UK and EU; its trade and customs regulations; its political and economic stability; the cost and quality of its production; the quality of its communications infrastructure; and the international standing of the country.

Supplier The final, but no less important, aspect of this research phase is deciding which suppliers to buy from. When assessing a potential supplier abroad, among the more important criteria to use are: whether or not the supplier can meet your product specification at the right price; whether you are able to visit their premises; whether they can manufacture to objective quality standards (BSI, ISO); whether there are any potential intellectual property right complications; the company size and date of establishment; the availability or otherwise of customer references; the markets currently being traded with; the quality of output and staff; and their financial status and production capacity.

Having conducted this research you should be in a position to evaluate the viability of your proposed venture more accurately. You will have an idea of your supplier's ex- works price for the product you intend to import and you will know what duties and taxes will be levied on your product at import. The only significant cost element not accounted for thus far is that of transport and related costs.

The proportion of transport and ancillary charges paid by the importer depends upon what has been agreed with the supplier-i.e. what Incoterm has been agreed - e.g. FOB (free on board) CIF (cost, insurance freight) FCA (freight and carriage to a named point). The main cost elements are freight, terminal handling, insurance, customs clearance and onward delivery.

At this stage you may feel that, all things considered, you may be better off buying from a UK based wholesaler, import merchant, distributor or agent, rather than importing the product yourself. Often the cost-effectiveness of importing boils down to the volume of business you represent to the supplier. His prices will reflect this, the best prices going to volume buyers. You must also consider whether or not your business can cope with the extra work and knowledge acquisition needed to become a successful importer.

The Purchase Contract

When making arrangements to buy goods abroad in the form of a contract, it is always advisable to have those arrangements set down for the benefit of both parties. This should always be done in consultation with an appropriately experienced and qualified solicitor. Information on UK law practices able to assist you in this regard is available from the Law Society on Tel: 0171 242 1222 Fax: 0171 320 5964 and from the Chambers guide.

Normally one would expect any such contract to cover the following:

- Product specification, the more precise the better (refer to quality standards if applicable)
- Ordering and shipment procedures - here you must be careful to examine the scheduling of your buying activity to ensure that the 'lead time' (that time between placement of your initial order and receipt of final delivery) meets your requirements and more importantly, those of your customers
- Insurance and freight - care should be taken to use only standard trade terms (FOB,CIF,DDP etc) known as 'Incoterms' ('Incoterms 1990' is available from ICC on Tel: 0171 823 2811 Fax: 0171 235 5447).
- Packaging and labelling
- Price and payment terms
- Passing of property
- Passing of risk (of loss or damage)
- Right to reject goods
- Testing and inspection
- Product liability, (supplier indemnity)
- Product regulations, (supplier indemnity)
- Intellectual property, (supplier indemnity)
- Documentation-specify all documents required of the supplier
- Duration of the agreement
- Dispute settlement
- The law governing the contract

It should be recognised that the exact terms and conditions of any purchase agreement are usually a compromise between the parties. They will reflect whether or not it is a buyer's or seller's market, as well as the commercial strength and the negotiating skill of the importer in relation to that of the supplier.

The International Movement of Goods

Upon investigation, you will quickly realise that there is a bewildering range of transport services available to you when considering how to move your goods. The basic approach to selecting the routing of your goods is to be open minded in evaluating all the available options, so as to ensure that the most cost-effective method is chosen. In making your choice you will need to balance the main criteria of freight costs, transit time and security. Your decision will ultimately be a compromise and will reflect your own priorities. It should however be noted that the best routing is not necessarily the obvious one. Your goods will move either by surface or by air and the principal modes of transport are road, rail, sea freight and air freight. In practice any movement is more likely to involve more than one mode of transport - i.e. multi-modal.

What factors should influence an importer's choice of transport method?

- Geography
- The nature of the goods - e.g. are they hazardous or perishable?
- Transit time needed
- The value to density ratio of the goods
- Comparative costing of transport modes
- Ease of product handling
- Insurance and security considerations
- Transport infrastructure in the countries concerned
- Cost

You are well advised to use the services of a transport specialist to arrange the movement of your goods. One category of specialists is known as 'freight forwarders', although there are many other transport companies who offer similar services. I would recommend the use of freight forwarders in most instances, especially for low volume movements, mainly because of the variety of value-added services the best forwarders offer these days.

Traditionally the freight forwarder is a company or person acting as an agent on behalf of importers and exporters in arranging international cargo movements and dealing with the associated documentation and procedures - a middleman, making a margin on the difference between the freight rates he buys wholesale from the carrier and the freight rates he 'retails' to the importer/exporter.

Today the role of the freight forwarder has evolved from its traditional freight brokerage origins into a more sophisticated one of providing clients with value-added services, often tailored to individual client need. For further information on freight forwarders, you are advised to refer to the current Freight Services Directory published by the British International Freight Association (BIFA). Contact BIFA on Tel: 0181 844 2266 Fax: 0181 890 5546; or consult the trade press - Lloyds Loading List for surface freight and Herefords Directory for air freight. When choosing a forwarder to handle your business you are advised to deal only with companies that are fully paid up members of BIFA.

Before selecting a forwarder, get to know as much about the company and the quality of its services as possible. It is also important that you clearly define your requirements in terms of what is necessary to meet your own customers' needs, bearing in mind that international logistics is always a series of cost and service tradeoffs. Look for a forwarder who is prepared to understand your business, your needs and those of your clients, and one that will represent your interests to carriers.

It is all about you taking control of your route to your market through your transport agent. Never buy freight services on price alone. Evaluate the total offer - cheap rates are likely to prove false economy in a sector where you tend to get what you pay for. You should look for competitive rates in a service package that, overall, represents value for money.

What transport documents does an importer need to be familiar with?

Transport mode	Document
Sea freight	Bill of lading (B/L)
Air freight	Air waybill (AWB)
Road	International road consignment note (CMR)
Rail	International rail consignment note (CIM)
Multi-modal	Multi-modal transport document (MTD)
	Forwarders negotiable B/L for multi-modal transport (FIATA FBL)
	Combined transport bill of lading (CTBL).

If you are using the services of a freight forwarder or equivalent agent, with the exception of the B/L and the AWB, you will not necessarily come into contact with the above documents.

Insurance

It is important for you to appreciate the need to ensure that your goods are fully insured for the full risk to which they are exposed, and for every leg of the transit to the final destination. Adequate insurance is vital to protect your consignments simply because for the greater part of any international movement, goods are beyond the effective control of both the exporter and importer, and in the hands of third parties.

It is recommended that wherever possible you should buy on terms which permit you to be responsible for insurance arrangements - e.g. FOB. The reason being that you are the best judge of what constitutes adequate cover for your purposes and, should you need to make a claim, it is much easier to do so in the UK, in English, than to attempt to do so abroad in a foreign language and business culture. In addition, despite its recent problems, the Lloyd's insurance market is still the best in the world for underwriting risk and has the keenest rates.

Cargo insurance services are often among the value-added services offered by international transport agents; however, depending on the value of business conducted, you might be wise to take out your own policy for your particular business needs, by contacting appropriate cargo insurance brokers. For further information on insurances contact the Chartered Insurance Institute on Tel: 0171 606 3835 Fax: 0171 726 0131; Association of British Insurers on Tel: 0171 600 3333 Fax: 0171 696 8996; Institute of Insurance Brokers on Tel: 01933 410003 Fax: 01933 410020.

What are the main considerations when buying insurance cover?

* What should the insured value be? The CIF value of the goods plus 10 per cent is a good rule of thumb
* The premium payable
* The risks to be covered
* The terms of purchase
* Transit time and the mode of transport
* Quality of packaging
* The degree of handling - e.g. is transshipment involved?
* Type of product
* Is it a full-load shipment or groupage?

Import Finance and Making Payment

Main types of import finance

* Bank overdraft
* Bank loan
* Credit

Buyer credit - finance provided direct to you by a bank or other financial institution in the supplier's country

Supplier/export credit - finance provided by a bank, export credit agency or other financial institution to the supplier in the country of export, which allows the supplier to extend credit terms to you

Acceptance credit - credit extended to you by UK banks secured on an acceptance term bill of exchange drawn up by you, which the bank discounts in the money market to a discount house.

The main methods of payment

Listed in order of the level of confidence existing between importer and supplier, starting with the most confident:

* Payment in advance
* 'Open account', payment on receipt of invoice: 30, 60, 90, 180 days from date of invoice

- Foreign currency accounts, held by you in the country of export
- Bills of exchange (at sight = on demand, or term = at an agreed future date) allow the supplier to retain control of the goods until you have agreed to make payment. An alternative to using a bill of exchange is the promissory note which differs from a bill of exchange in that it is written by you to the supplier, rather than being drawn by the supplier on you
- Documentary collection ensures the secure delivery of documents from a supplier to you whilst allowing the supplier to retain control of the goods until payment has been agreed. It is usually combined with a bill of exchange, thereby permitting the supplier to extend a term of credit to you. When used in conjunction with a sight bill, you obtain your documents on payment. Alternatively if a term bill is used, you can obtain your documents on 'acceptance' of the bill
- Documentary letter of credit - an undertaking by an issuing bank on your behalf to the supplier through an advising or confirming bank in the supplier's country, to the effect that the issuing bank will pay the supplier for the goods, provided the supplier complies precisely with all the conditions of the credit.

It is important that you obtain a copy of the 'Uniform Customs and Practice for Documentary Credits' aka UCP 500. It is available from the ICC on Tel: 0171 823 2811 Fax: 0171 235 5447 and also from some of the main high street clearing banks.

The main methods of remittance

- Electronic transfer (standard and urgent)
- International money order
- Bank draft by airmail or courier
- Importer's cheque

The main considerations when deciding upon methods of payment and remittance are speed, security and cost. In addition you should ensure that the method of payment agreed takes account of how the goods are moved - e.g. documents necessary for UK customs formalities must travel faster than your goods!

Ways of covering the currency risk

- Pay in sterling (if agreeable to your supplier)
- Currency borrowing
- Currency accounts (in UK or in country of export)
- Currency deposits
- Forward exchange contracts
- Currency options

You are strongly advised to seek detailed guidance on all aspects of financing your intended imports from your banker. It should also be noted that all the main UK clearing banks make available very good literature covering all the above matters, free of charge.

Goods arrival, customs clearance and final delivery

Assuming that you have decided to use an international transport agent - e.g. freight forwarder - you will receive notification of the expected time of arrival of your consignments, whereupon you should prepare clear instructions for your agent on how you would like your goods to be cleared and how final delivery to either you or your customers is to be arranged.

It should be noted that as from January 1, 1993, the beginning of the EC 'Single Market', there are no import clearance formalities in place for goods imported into the UK originating in or already in 'free circulation' in the European Community.

For the purposes of customs clearance, your instructions to your agent should include the following information, as applicable.

- Your import reference
- B/L or AWB no
- Customs classification code
- Classification BTI
- Packing list
- Duty/VAT payment arrangements

- Voyage/flight/trailer reference
- Consignment details
- Import licence - No/ details
- Commercial invoice - No/ details
- Customs procedure code
- Documents to be provided by agent

The documents normally required to effect customs clearance:

- Customs entry C88 SAD (normally completed by your agent)
- Commercial invoice (original)
- Packing list
- Import licence (if applicable)
- Certificate of origin (if applicable)
- Community transit document (if applicable)
- Valuation statement, C105 or C109
- Evidence of freight charges paid (e.g. copy B/L or AWB)
- Copy of insurance certificate
- Other certification, as applicable - e.g. certificates of health, compliance, end-use, analysis etc

Once your agent has lodged the customs entry with Customs and Excise you will be notified of an amount certain to be paid in respect of duty and/or VAT as applicable, which can be paid by your agent on your behalf, or directly by yourself.

When clearance has been successfully effected and all relevant charges have been paid, your agent will be given an 'out of charge note' - C130 - which means your goods have been released from customs control and that they can be collected for onward final delivery, as per your instructions.

The most common form of customs entry is 'entry into free circulation', but importers should be aware that there are a number of other customs options tailored to meet a variety of business needs. The most common alternatives are IPR, OPR, free-zones, customs or excise warehousing and other regimes.

Although there are no customs formalities for goods originating or already in free circulation in the EC, importers trading with EC countries should be aware of the requirement to provide the EC with certain statistical information on its trading activities, via periodic reporting to Customs and Excise, known as 'Intrastats'.

For further advice and assistance on all aspects of customs matters contact your local Customs and Excise Advice Centre, consult the UK Customs Tariff (usually available for reference at such advice centres) and/or request copies of the many H.M. Customs and Excise notices, which are listed in the 'Tariff' and are usually available free of charge from local H.M. Customs and Excise Advice Centres.

This chapter is a summary of the main points and considerations that a prospective importer needs to be aware of. You should realise that whole books have been written on every aspect of importing highlighted above and that this guide should be used as a signpost or a tool for further research on your part.

When considering an importing business venture for the first time, it is important for you to balance the possible benefits of importing against the possible problems.

There is no doubt that importing products can confer a considerable commercial advantage on a business over its competitors, depending on the market. By sourcing abroad, importers can usually benefit from some, all or any combination of the following: lower costs of production leading to a cheaper product; improved quality; wider choice; greater flexibility of specification and supply; and the possibility of discovering and bringing to market a unique or innovative product, as yet unavailable in the UK.

On the downside those new to importing have a steep learning curve to climb before being able to import successfully. As well as the benefits, importing brings with it significant commercial risks and burdens not usually encountered in the domestic market. These risks stem from the difficulties of buying in overseas markets where you are dealing with documents, procedures, regulations, jurisdictions and companies that you are unfamiliar with. Some of the specific risks include: not getting what you ordered; disruption of supply sources due to country, product or supplier specific problems; changes in EC customs duty levels; loss, damage or delay of goods in transit; buying in foreign currencies; and incomplete, improper or inaccurate documentation.

However do not be put off by the downside. If you are willing to put in the hard work and thoroughly research your import venture, it is perfectly possible to develop a successful importing business from scratch.

Christopher E Starns, Director General, The British Importers Association

If price is your only advantage and the main reason for importing, then the extra margin will have to be a good one. Price is the easiest element of marketing strategy to copy and affords the least advantage and for the shortest period. When Tim Waterstone founded his business he did not seek to compete with W H Smith's on price. He saw their weak point as having the wrong opening hours. Smith's were shut in the evenings when working people are free to 'browse', an essential prerequisite to book buying. Smith's limited merchandising and the lack of knowledgeable staff were also key weaknesses.

Using these advantages, in the ten years from 1982 Waterstone built a multi-million pound business and sold it to Smith's, his former employer. His success would not have been so assured if his strategy had been based on price. A big established business will always be able to stand price competition for longer than a new small one.

In my experience . . .

For a new business struggling to get known in the market place, finding the right method of advertising is vital. Free local newspapers can provide a good way of targeting prospective customers in your area, but it is important to monitor how successful your advert has been, and the easiest way is to incorporate a money off voucher. That way you know exactly how many extra customers have visited you as a result of seeing the newspaper advertisement, rather than thinking you know how many!

You should also be aware that within hours of the paper with your advert in hitting the doormat, you will start receiving calls from the advertising sales personnel of other local newspapers encouraging you to run an advert with them too. As it is much easier to be persuaded to run an advert than it is to find the cash to pay for it a week later, make sure you have decided beforehand whether you want to run more adverts, and if so, what your budget is.

One final tip, do haggle on the price. If the paper knows you are interested in buying space, but you wait for them to come back to you a day or two before they go to print, you'll find that, because they want to fill the gap up, the price for the same space may have reduced by as much as a half.

Andrew Walsham, AB's CDs

Selling Abroad

Most small firms in the UK, and elsewhere for that matter, start up and either fail, as about half do, or grow for a few years and then stall, as most of the rest do. The relatively small number of small firms that achieve fast and continuous growth in both sales and profits have one defining feature in common: they export. According to a Cranfield study in 1997, three-quarters of the fastest growing small firms, that is those whose sales and profits have grown by more than 25 per cent in each of the last three years, sell into overseas markets. The most successful of those sell more than a quarter of their output overseas.

In my experience . . .

Some practical tips on how to keep ahead in international trading:

- Be positive and sometimes aggressive with your bank
- Always cover your backside so you are not exposed to currency fluctuations - leave the gambling to the City boys
- Forward Exchange Contracts and Letters of Credit are not difficult - be thorough and organised
- Always know your financial position as soon after the month end as possible
- Litigation is a business tool but it is costly in management time and resources as well as pound notes for the legal fees
- Know your business and the potential market
- Learn from your bad decisions

Mike Seeley, Hugh Jennings Ltd

EXPORTING YOUR PRODUCTS

Whoever said 'exporting is fun' had obviously never actually done any. There are many words that might describe export but 'fun' would not be the most obvious one. 'Frustrating' would be in there somewhere, as would 'complicated', 'confusing', 'unpredictable' even 'infuriating'. But talk to experienced exporters and you will also hear words like 'absorbing', 'fascinating', 'exciting', and most importantly, 'rewarding'. The fact is that exporting, or international trade as it is more currently called, provides an incredible tapestry of experience which balances the good with the bad.

The problem is that many companies entering into international trade are not properly prepared and will only ever experience the bad side. If we are to get to the rewarding parts, both in a personal as well as a commercial sense, then we have to accept that there is an enormous range of pitfalls for the unwary and our job is to prepare ourselves and our companies so that we enter overseas markets in full knowledge of what to expect - and ready to handle it.

We first of all have to accept that overseas markets will inevitably be different from our home market, and it is not just that they speak a foreign language. Good research can reveal a myriad political, legal, economic, technological, social and cultural differences. These have to be considered when we are deciding what we are going to sell and how we will sell it. Then, when we are successful in getting the orders, we are faced with the complex issues of getting the goods there and, most importantly, getting paid.

What sort of questions would an exporter have to answer before entering an overseas market?

- Which markets offer me the greatest potential at the minimum risk?
- What modifications will be needed to make my product saleable there?
- What price is the buyer prepared to pay and on what basis, (ex-works or delivered)?
- Do I need an agent or a distributor and if so, how do I find one?
- How do I promote my products effectively?
- What methods of shipment will be appropriate and how much will they cost?
- Are there any customs barriers that I need to consider?
- How do I cover the risks of theft and damage to my goods in transit?
- How do I make sure that I get my money?

The answers are not always so obvious and will be different from one market to another. However, good research and the use of the many sources of information and advice available both in the UK and overseas might mean that you are not the exporter who lost money because :

- Their bone china dinner services specially designed for the Italians were useless because they lacked a pickle bowl
- The brand name of their product was actually an extremely rude word in the buyer's language
- The Libyan flags in the left paws of the toy teddy-bears were seen as an insult to the flag and were destroyed. (In most Muslim countries the left hand is for toilet purposes only!)
- The sole distributor they appointed was actually contracted to sell a direct competitor's products - which they did with great success
- The 'before and after' photographs which had worked so well for the sale of depilatory creams in English-speaking countries did not work so well when translated into Arabic, which reads from right to left. They forgot to reverse the pictures !

And how about the loss of £155,000 worth of goods because a comma instead of a full stop on an invoice presented against a letter of credit meant the bank rejected the documents. The buyer, quite legitimately, refused to pay and, because the exporter did nothing, the original buyer picked them up at the auction in the port of destination some 10 weeks later at a tenth of the original price.

Exporting offers huge rewards to both the people and the companies involved but the 'amateur abroad' will not survive in this dangerous but fascinating jungle.

Jim Sherlock, The Institute of Export

SELLING ABROAD

SOME PROS AND CONS

Companies begin exporting for a variety of reasons, but the majority of experienced exporters took a conscious decision to start exporting. These companies now take a strategic approach to overseas selling and are widely regarded as being successful exporters.

Whatever triggers off a company's desire to export, consideration must be given at the earliest stage to the potential advantages and disadvantages associated with exporting. If a company carefully plans its move into exporting the rewards can be substantial.

Advantages of Exporting

- Spread risk to counter any UK downturn
- Increase production and reduce unit costs
- Command higher prices and increase profits
- Sell existing products which have reached their full potential in the UK
- In some markets receive better payments
- Expose business to world class standards and competition

Disadvantages of Exporting

- Can take considerable time to get established
- Initial set-up costs can be high
- Any weakness in the business will be exposed and could be exploited
- Can expose businesses to additional risks - i.e., currency fluctuations, payment delays in some markets
- Personal contact with overseas customers and representatives can be difficult and costly
- Appointment of the wrong overseas representative can be costly, damaging and waste valuable time

In view of the above, businesses must seek impartial expert advice at the earliest opportunity, certainly well in advance of starting to export. This is available through the export development counsellor at your local Business Link, who can advise on the full range of support available.

The cost of exporting

In the early stages of researching export potential, businesses cannot afford to gamble on what may be a speculative venture. It is often the Managing Director or owner-manager of a business whose time is used in the planning and development stage. This can be expensive for the business in view of other demands.

Some additional costs to exporting:

* Market research
* Specialist training
* Adaptation of literature and packaging
* Translation of literature and packaging
* Cost of market visits
* Adaptation of product
* Special packaging
* Freight and insurance

Initial costs can be reduced by using a number of methods at the start:

* Choose starter markets close to home
* Select English speaking markets
* Use DTI subsidised market research, trade missions, overseas exhibitions and trade fairs
* Some Business Links may have additional subsidised services
* Try to obtain proforma payment for initial orders
* Use overseas representatives for translations, but make sure you have them checked in the UK
* Use the export development counsellor in Business Link for advice

Over half of exporting businesses have had some sort of failed attempt at exporting but most felt this was due to internal weaknesses, usually not dedicating sufficient time and resources to the project. That is why experienced proactive exporters employ professional staff to manage their exports.

There is no absolute guarantee of success in exporting but the risks and costs can be minimised through careful research and planning.

Remember, it is not sufficient just to mark up your UK prices, by adding on the extra costs for exporting. You should aim to recover your direct costs and make a sufficient margin.

It makes sense to use a local representative in overseas markets as your business's 'eyes and ears'. Valuable feedback can be gained on local selling conditions, pricing and marketing your product or service.

It is imperative that you select the right representative. This should not be done through chance meeting or by sticking an 'Agents Wanted' notice on your overseas exhibition stand.

Overseas representatives can be found and selected through the DTI's Overseas Trade Service, available through Business Links. It is vital to give as much detail as possible about your business and its product or services and what you hope to achieve in the market. Selection can be made from a shortlist of potential candidates who should answer specific questions designed to match your aspirations. They should provide at least the following:

- Registered details of the business
- Any other companies represented or other partnerships
- Financial and personal references
- Existing customers, leads and contacts
- Language and technical skills
- Premises and facilities available
- Staff available
- Exactly what responsibilities the representative will take on

Final selection can be made by visiting the shortlisted representatives, when valuable information can also be gathered about the market. An agreement must be drawn up between the UK exporter and the overseas representative which will include both parties' rights and responsibilities. This must be checked by both parties' legal representatives.

Whether you choose to appoint your local representative as an agent or a distributor depends on a number of factors including market selected, type of product and the distribution methods common in your market. There are advantages and disadvantages in both.

Distributor

- Limited control - largely independent
- Should be allowed to determine prices and terms
- Takes full responsibility for sale of all goods purchased
- You despatch product to one destination only
- Responsible for the financial risk - only one credit risk to UK exporter
- Normally no compensation on termination of agreement

Agent

- Works on the instructions of the UK exporter
- Prices and terms usually fixed by UK exporter
- UK exporter responsible for any unsold goods
- UK exporter responsible for credit risk with all customers in market
- In the EU, compensation usually payable to agent on termination of agreement.

The main point to remember is that any arrangement with an overseas representative must be a partnership, with both parties trusting and supporting each other. This should ensure that both businesses benefit from the growth in sales and profits in the overseas market.

Eric Brown, Business Link, Hereford and Worcester

UNDERSTANDING A FOREIGN MARKET

No two markets are the same and market research, analysis of information gathered and planning are the keys to success in exporting.

Market research begins at home and information on selected starter markets can be obtained from a number of sources available through Business Link.

- Export Development Counsellors
- Online databases and directories
- Export Market Information Centre in London
- DTI's overseas trade services
- DTI's country helpdesks
- DTI's export promoters
- Meetings with commercial staff from the UK's overseas posts

The export development counsellor in your Business Link can help you to choose the most appropriate starter markets which will be decided by your company's resources, skills and products or services. Further initial information can be obtained through visiting the Export Market Information Centre in London. This is the largest library of information on overseas markets in the UK and free to personal callers.

Alternatively, information can be researched for you by one of the EMIC's experienced researchers for a reasonable cost which can be discounted if the service is accessed through Business Links. You can gain basic information about the size of the market for your product, details of companies selling and buying similar products, general economic conditions, terms of payment, cultural differences and methods of doing business. This information can be used to select one or two starter target markets where more detailed research can be commissioned through the Business Link and this will determine the strategy for market entry.

It is well worth making a visit to your chosen markets to gain further valuable local insight into how your product is sold by competitors, packaging, prices, and cultural differences and methods of doing business. Visits can coincide with trade fairs or exhibitions being held for your sector where valuable initial contacts can be made. Alternatively, you could consider one of the DTI's Supported Trade Missions. During your visit you may be able to establish details of the best local distributors or agents from existing importers of products in your sector.

The key to success is to know your markets, and understand your customers' needs. Recognise the differences that exist in selling overseas and adapt your approach accordingly.

Getting Paid

This is one of the most critical areas in export. Research done at the earliest stage can prevent problems later. The main points to bear in mind are:

 Assess the country risk first - both the political and the exchange control element and the likely payment delays.

 Obtain credit information well in advance in order to assess the commercial risk, set the terms and the credit limit.

 Use independent business reports, together with information from the overseas representatives and the customer.

 Make the credit terms an integral part of the negotiations. It is often at this stage that the scene is set for success in collecting money on time.

Payment in advance

This is normally used for smaller value transactions where the importer requires goods promptly, is domiciled in a high risk territory, or is not considered credit-worthy. Payment must be received before the goods are dispatched.

Open account

This method of payment is widely used in the UK market and involves the exporter granting credit against agreed terms - e.g. 30 days from date of invoice.

Documentary bills for collection

These are normally used in medium risk countries, where more security is required with a buyer. Obtaining payment involves documents being sent through your own bank to the customer's bank. The advantages for the exporter are that it is reasonably inexpensive, control of documentation and in some cases goods, is retained and the banks will assist in collecting funds.

Letters of credit

A letter of credit is a written guarantee of payment given by a bank to the exporter in exchange for documents that must comply exactly with the requirements of the letter of credit.

This is a complex method of payment and exporters who are either unfamiliar with letters of credit, or who regularly have problems, must seek further advice from their Business Link or bank.

Obtaining payment

Companies that take a systematic approach to chasing payments are less likely to have to resort to taking legal action to recover money. Often the main reasons for delay can be due to the exporter rather than a difficult customer. The main points to bear in mind are:

- Ensure that all your documentation is accurate and reaches the customer or bank in time
- Survey your own documentation on a regular basis to eliminate any reasons or excuses for late payment
- Ensure that customers' queries and complaints are followed up and that credits are issued promptly
- Make your payment terms clear and unambiguous on open account invoices and display your full bank details prominently
- Contact for payment of larger amounts or invoices on extended credit terms must be proactive - encourage friendly but persistent chasing of accounts using the telephone to remind the customer a week or so before payment is due
- Chase payment of smaller amounts by fax - you can often use a standard fax format and simply fill in the details applicable to those accounts
- Vary your chasing with customers who pay late and become accustomed to your approach
- Ask for sterling cheques to be payable in the UK. Sterling cheques payable abroad have to be collected from the issuing bank which takes several weeks. In addition, the collection charges are expensive and for the beneficiary's account.

The objective should be to maximise profitable sales commensurate with the shortest possible credit period and the minimum bad debt. This is particularly important in export markets where the delays can be longer and the risks can be greater.

EXHIBITING OVERSEAS

Taking space at an overseas trade fair or exhibition can be an extremely cost-effective way of exploring a new market, introducing new products to existing markets or simply maintaining your profile amongst existing and potential customers.

The choice of trade shows throughout the world is staggering and it can often be difficult to decide whether an event is going to be useful for you. If possible a preliminary visit to a trade show purely as a visitor will help you make up your mind before you decide to exhibit the following year. You should review the published list of events that receive DTI support and this may help narrow the choice.

Each event that receives financial support from the DTI will have an organising body within the UK handling the arrangements. So as well as benefiting from significant savings in stand space costs and a contribution towards travel costs for events outside Europe, participating companies will also have a UK point of contact for queries on the event. In addition assistance is given in organising your participation and promoting your presence.

If you do decide to take space at an exhibition, good preparation is vital. Make sure your stand conveys the correct image for your company.

Organisers can provide guidance in maximising your participation in your chosen event. In general terms the following must be observed:

- Ensure that staff manning the stand are properly trained
- Pre-arrange visitors rather than relying on passing trade
- Consider the language skills and translated literature needed
- Prepare comprehensive enquiry forms
- Ensure speedy follow up to enquiries

In summary, with the right preparations and follow up, overseas fairs and exhibitions can be a valuable source of new contacts and business.

Eric Brown, Business Link, Hereford and Worcester

Selling Abroad - A Legal Overview

If you intend to sell overseas you will usually need a local representative who knows and understands your target market. This will usually be either an agent or a distributor depending on the nature of your product.

An agent is a direct representative of your company either making contracts in your name or referring orders to you. The agent is paid a commission for each order obtained. An agent is best suited to low-volume, high-value sales, particularly bespoke projects, goods with after-sales support, long term or repeat sale contracts and other sales where you need to retain familiarity with the end customer, and where you wish to retain price control.

Distributors are widely used by exporters of consumer goods. A distributor buys goods from you and resells them himself within defined territorial limits. The distributor's profit arises between his purchase and resale price. In contrast to an agency, the contract with the end customer is made by the distributor. Your involvement ends with the sale to the distributor and that is your sole credit risk in the territory.

Whatever type of representative, have a written contract taking account of relevant national and supra-national law. Within the EU, agents have substantial statutory rights not available to distributors and you must therefore clearly distinguish between them or your agent's rights may surprise and appal you! Terms restricting competition within the EU will require specialist legal advice. Other parts of the world are subject to their own import and currency export controls and licensing requirements on which legal advice will be needed.

The contract must set out sales targets (linked to termination provisions where these are not met), your agreement on whether either party should be prevented from dealing with others in the territory, the scope of an agent's authority and the precise terms of commission/price discounts available to the representative to ensure that your sales are made on terms which are both commercially advantageous to you and provide the right incentive to the representative.

Manage overseas distributors' debts as you would UK debtors and ensure that the contract is clear on your payment terms. Consider appropriate credit limits within the value of any documentary credit but remember that getting a payment up front is not impracticable and should be considered.

Take advantage of the DTI overseas trade services, either directly or via your local Chamber of Commerce.

David Cranfield and Marcus Reynolds, Shoosmiths

The Logistics of Overseas Trade

FREIGHT FORWARDING: A BUSINESS PARTNERSHIP

Getting your goods to and from overseas markets can be a daunting prospect for the those with no experience, but there is help at hand. Probably the most effective partner for those whose businesses involve importing or exporting is the freight forwarder - the organiser of the international transport market whose services can include:

* Advice and consultancy
* Documentation
* Pricing of services
* Arranging any method of transportation
* Customs documentation and presentation
* Packing and warehousing
* Transit insurance

There are probably over two thousand companies operating as freight forwarders in the UK. They vary considerably in size and in the diversity of their services. For example, the British International Freight Association (BIFA) has in excess of 1200 members accounting for over 85 per cent of all business handled by freight forwarders in the UK.

Basically, there are three different types of company:

Local companies These are small single office firms which tend to deal with clients in their immediate local area or operate at a sea or airport concentrating on particular types of traffic.

National companies Many forwarders have offices in the major ports and airports throughout the country as well as in the largest industrial towns. They may also have warehousing or handling depots from which they operate their own services, as well as agents or correspondents overseas in the markets with which they trade.

International companies The truly international company will have its own offices overseas and offer a wide range of worldwide services.

There are no hard and fast rules about the way a particular company is organised and there will be considerable overlap between the types. Neither should size be considered as a criterion for measuring the standard of service. The industry is made up of many specialist operators and those interested in using a freight forwarder or working in the forwarding profession will find that there is an enormous range of firms to choose from.

It is vital at an early stage of your planning to form a partnership with a freight forwarder to provide advice and information, and it is recommended that you choose one who is a member of the British International Freight Association (BIFA).

It is also essential to agree on the terms under which you will contract with your customer. International trading terms are those which specify the responsibilities of the buyer and the seller. Obtain a copy of the Incoterms 2000, about to be published, which sets out a step by step process to determine the respective obligations. This can be purchased from the International Chamber of Commerce and others.

It may seem rather obvious but getting paid by the customer and making a profit on the deal is essential in any transaction. This becomes more complicated when trading with companies in other countries where different cultures and ways of doing things can confuse the uninitiated. Banks are a very good source of information on this, and advice can also be sought from the freight forwarder.

Another obvious, but often poorly managed function, is the transfer of information. An international sale or purchase can involve communications with many different people. Always give instructions in writing. Always obtain quotations in writing for services to be provided. Never rely solely on the telephone or verbal instructions. More problems are encountered by failing to follow these simple disciplines than any others.

Goods in transit are exposed to risk and you cannot assume that loss or damage to goods in transit will automatically be covered by your subcontracted carrier. Always insure goods if the transport element is your responsibility.

Before you import goods understand that in most cases you will have to pay VAT and import duty upon arrival in the UK. Your freight forwarder can organise this for you but it is vital to know what these costs are because they will have to be added to the price for delivery. Some goods are subject to import licence, others are covered by import quotas - a set annual quantity which is allowed to be imported at a preferential rate of duty. When the quota runs out there may be a substantial increase in the duty rate. You will have no control over this so you may need to take a sudden cost increase into consideration.

The subject of importing and exporting is a vast one and there are many other sources of information available. The final section 'Useful Addresses' lists some of these.

Although there are pitfalls and mistakes can be costly, importing and exporting can be enjoyable and profitable provided that the necessary groundwork is done in advance.

Colin Beaumont, British International Freight Association

THE EURO HAS ARRIVED - AND SMALLER BUSINESSES MUST BE EURO AWARE

Is the single currency an issue for smaller businesses?

Absolutely. Now that the single currency is a reality every business needs to access and monitor its impact. For many this will mean the installation of accounting systems that can cope with the Euro currency. Much has been written about the impact of the single currency in large multi-national companies but there has been little discussion concerning small and medium sized enterprises. For these companies the issue is, if anything, more pressing than for larger organisations which have the expertise and resources available to cope.

What stage are we at with the single currency?

For businesses in Ireland and other member countries the position regarding the single currency is clear. Organisations have until 2002 to convert their accounting functions to the Euro. Unfortunately, for businesses in the UK the single currency is at present characterised by political uncertainty and a lack of precise detail. As a leading member of the IT community, Sage will be working with accounting and government organisations to clarify the position when the political decision is made.

So why must SMEs be ready?

Sage is working to raise awareness of the issue for the UK's smaller businesses, because whatever the outcome of the single currency in the UK, the widespread adoption throughout the rest of Europe of the Euro will have significant implications for the accounting software at the heart of all SMEs.

Sage will guide its customers through the process of adapting to the Euro when the time comes. In the meantime, we are helping our customers to prepare by providing relevant information as and when it becomes available.

Why does the Euro affect SMEs?

Small and medium sized businesses play an important role in the UK's trade with Europe. A recent Sage survey of 1371 SMEs in the UK and Ireland found that 56 per cent had overseas customers. SMEs quite rightly see the single currency as a positive thing. One of the major benefits will be that, once the Euro is introduced, there will be many more people using the Euro than are presently using any other single currency. This will enable companies to extend their trade into Europe much more easily.

I don't have any European customers - so will I be affected?

Yes. The single currency is an important issue for the UK's SMEs regardless of their size, business specialism or whether they trade in Europe - from the self-employed builder through to the £500,000 European exporter. For instance, SMEs that trade with UK subsidiaries of parent companies based in countries where the Euro has already been introduced will find that they have to submit invoices in the Euro currency.

What can SMEs do to be ready?

It is absolutely crucial that these companies look to partner a software supplier that can help to prepare their accounting system for every eventuality - and support it as financial developments occur.

How can Sage help me?

The bottom line for SMEs is that, although the future of the single currency in the UK is as yet undecided, the Euro is here and it will have a big impact throughout Europe. Whatever the nature of your business, it is important that you are aware of the issues that affect you.

Sage, the UK's market-leading PC accountancy software company, is committed to helping its customers with the single currency issue and to providing products that meet their needs. For example, Sage has co-sponsored a briefing document and seminar series, staged by BASDA, the Business and Accounting Software Developers Association. These activities will ensure that Sage customers always have the most up-to-date information on the progress of the single currency in Europe.

Paul Stobart, Business Development Director, Sage Group PLC

Where you sell overseas will be governed by opportunity and demand. But the markets that small firms have had the greatest success in penetrating are, in order:

> Germany
> France
> USA
> Netherlands
> Belgium/Luxembourg
> Italy

Naturally, much will depend on your product, your expertise and your planning. Export can be dramatically rewarding and provided the home fires are kept burning and the markets carefully watched abroad then your business should prosper further.

The Geese that Lay Golden Eggs

Most business people agree that probably one of the best ways of growing a business is through referred clients. No money wasted on advertising that may or may not work and no time spent trying to convince strangers to do business with you. Referred leads are almost ready sold, because trust and confidence already exists, to some degree, through the introducer.

One of the most effective ways to get leads is to focus on those people who pass you referrals already and to encourage them to do it more often. How are you doing in the area of rewarding your introducers for referring you in the first place?

Most business people provide a referral reward or even an introduction fee to people helping them to obtain a lead that ends with a sale. Additionally some make it a standard practice to refer the source to their own potential clients when the opportunity arises. Some people have different rewards for different types of leads. It's one thing to mention your name - another to urge the prospect to contact you.

Probably the most common, and usually the biggest mistake business people make in this area is rewarding contacts only for leads that result in business. Just think, if the prospect does not avail him or herself of your services, that doesn't mean that the introducer didn't do the job! You might feel that 'the lead was poor quality'. That might be true. In any event, you need to reward the behaviour of your introducers, so that in the future that person, when in a similar situation, again thinks of you instead of someone else.

A colleague of mine sends a bottle of bubbly for every referral received. I send a variety of things - motivational books, posters etc. It might be a theatre or cinema ticket or just a thank you note - a gift voucher or more substantial gift, depending on the type of business and the potential lifetime value of the sale.

Just a few pounds. The value? Enormous. You will be delighted with the ongoing benefits you get from giving those little gifts when you begin to invest in your business through referrals, and follow up not only on leads but also your referral sources. For every lead you receive, give something back.

Take care of the golden geese that lay the golden eggs

Tony Walker Senior Partener - Walker Longfood & Co

Managing Change

Chapter Ten

The first task of a leader of a small business is to define the company's mission. In a world where product life cycles are shrinking, new technologies have an ever shorter shelf life and customers demand ever-higher levels of both quality and service, entrepreneurial leadership means inspiring change.

Whilst managers may accept the status quo, leaders must always challenge it. In adapting the business to an increasingly volatile and competitive environment, the boss must become the change master in the firm.

But recognising the need for change falls a long way short of being able to implement it successfully. Few people like change and even fewer can adapt to new circumstances quickly and without missing a heartbeat.

By definition, a business seeking fast growth must be able to manage a rapid rate of change. Entrepreneurs must see change as the norm and not as a temporary and unexpected disruption, which will 'go away' when things improve.

Managing Difficult Times

All economies are cyclical. That is they move between periods of growth, stagnation, decline and back to growth again. As well as this cyclical pattern other forces are at work. There is, or certainly has been for several hundred years, a general upward trend in economic well-being. So each new high point on the cycle ends up a little higher than the last. Within each year most businesses experience seasonal pressures that create temporary ups and downs.

Within all this turbulence a business - especially a small one - can expect to be tossed around a fair bit.

STAYING AFLOAT - AVOIDING A CASH CRISIS

There is no escaping the fact that running a business is hard work. Along with the freedom to determine your own destiny and reap the rewards comes the burden of responsibility - you make your own success, or suffer your own distress!

To state the obvious, succeeding in business is much more difficult than failing. Very many small businesses do not make it past the first few years. But if you are determined to succeed by overcoming whatever problems arise, you stand a good chance of success. With the right preparation, advice, planning - and a little luck - there is no reason for pessimism.

That said, a prudent and cautious attitude is probably the ideal accompaniment to entrepreneurial zeal. Being aware of what could happen, and planning accordingly, is not just good business practice - if things do get difficult it could make the difference between survival and failure.

A survey carried out by the Society of Practitioners of Insolvency showed that inadequate management - including over-optimism, imprudent accounting, and a lack of management information - was the main cause of nearly one in four company failures over a twelve month period. What can you do to avoid such a disastrous end?

There is no single perfect way to manage a business - there are countless decisions to be made in every situation, making each business unique. The basic rules for reducing the risk of your business collapsing, however, can probably be summed up by the following: know your company's exact financial position, and take advice as soon as problems appear - that is before they become insoluble.

A lack of accurate financial information can ruin the most sound business. Suddenly finding yourself without cash will be a serious problem no matter how many orders are coming in, or customers are filing through the door. At the simplest level this means that you should know who owes you what, how much you owe, to whom, and when, and have a good idea of any significant costs that are likely to arise in the future.

Secondly, are your margins sufficient to allow the business to meet its overheads? Even high sales at inadequate margins will gradually lead to a cash shortage. If you do not keep proper management accounts, you may not find out until it is too late.

A further effect of a lack of information is that it can mask more serious problems in the performance of a business. Costs may be too high, or sales simply insufficient. Once acknowledged these issues can be addressed, but ignorance will only compound the problem.

Many of the factors that can bring about insolvency can be identified at a relatively early stage, if you know what to look for. These are some of the symptoms to be aware of:

 Diminished cash balances - either the business is over-reaching itself or the volume of sales is insufficient

 Poor collection of debtor's book. Many directors are unwilling or unable to collect their debts. Invoices due are not the same as cash in the bank

 Lines of credit - have you delayed payment to suppliers, and now find that everything that can be postponed has been postponed?

 Are you behind in payments to the Inland Revenue or Customs and Excise? - If you are, seek advice soon as these are not usually patient creditors, and they have the power to seize your equipment

Do you prepare annual forecasts? - If you don't you can have only the vaguest notion of where your business is going. Even annual forecasts are no use if you don't plot actual progress against them

 Poor cost control. How sure are you that you are getting the best deals? When did you last check?

 How often do you receive final demands or writs from suppliers?

How many of your suppliers are longstanding? Or are you forced to keep finding new suppliers?

This is not an exhaustive list of danger signs, of course - but while they would not necessarily spell the end of your business, they should not be ignored. The best course of action is always get advice, either from your own advisers or from a licensed insolvency practitioner, sooner rather than later.

Many business people are reluctant to take professional advice unless there is either a statutory need for it, or a crisis that needs emergency action. The perceived high cost of getting help is believed to be the most common reason for this reluctance.

Professionals frequently urge businesses to take advice as soon as a problem arises. Of course, the advisers want to sell their services as much as anyone else, but it really is true that early advice can make all the difference. This adage is especially true when insolvency is a possibility. Early action can at least lead to a more constructive outcome, and very often prevents potentially critical situations - when liquidation may well result.

The consequences of allowing a problem to worsen before getting help cannot be overstated. If it means saving your business and livelihood, taking action is surely better than taking the risk.

Simon Freakley, Society of Practitioners in Insolvency

LEGAL MATTERS TO CONSIDER WHEN THE PRESSURE IS ON THE BUSINESS

When robbing Peter to pay Paul, the last thought crossing any businessman's mind is whether it is a crime or merely something that may have to be paid for later.

The main legal problems arise where the business is a limited company or a partnership. Sole traders just go bankrupt. The reason is that directors or partners are likely to have assets, such as houses and cars, or racehorses and aeroplanes, which are not otherwise available to meet the claims of a business' creditors.

Any legal problems for a sole trader are more likely to be criminal, as most assets will be included in a bankruptcy, which may include pensions payable on retirement many years later.

When suppliers start issuing court proceedings or refusing to supply, or the bank bounces cheques, a business should prepare up-to-date financial information and take appropriate professional advice. It is no good asking a friend at the golf club, who has been made bankrupt. If he could help, he would not have had the same problem.

Since 1986, a director can be made personally liable for all or some of the debts of a company. This can also apply where the old business is closed and a new one started up with the same name. The basis for this is that there comes a point where no director could avoid knowing that a company will go into liquidation sooner or later. At this time, the directors have to put the interests of the creditors first, not the shareholders or themselves.

In addition, directors must avoid showing a preference among creditors by paying one at the expense of others. For example, if the bank overdraft is secured against personal guarantees and the directors, faced with liquidation, decide to pay off the overdraft, the bank can be ordered to refund the payment since this constitutes a preference. The guarantees will then be claimed against. In a liquidation, creditors share equally after secured claims and preferential creditors (such as VAT, PAYE and employees) have been met.

Any disposals of a business's assets for less than full value can also be attacked. When the writing is on the wall, don't sell any of the assets to a friend or relative for £1 without obtaining a proper valuation. As no two valuations ever seem to agree, it can be expensive to defend such claims, even if ultimately successful.

It is possible to obtain protection from the claims of creditors, no matter what form a business takes. A Voluntary Arrangement is available to allow your company to survive temporary difficulties, for example caused by the insolvency of a major customer. If necessary, if three-quarters of all the creditors by value agree, less than full payment can be required.

The best way to avoid the risk of future claims is to obtain and heed professional advice. Many businesses have been saved by Insolvency Practitioners, where they are consulted early enough. It is no use waiting until a bankruptcy or winding-up petition is served. It may be too late by then.

Neil Bradshaw, Partner, Business Support & Insolvency, Shoosmiths

In the life-cycle of a business, most will go through an initial phase of growth while they effectively exploit the opportunities in their market. As the market matures and awareness grows, so new entrants come into the market. This process continues until high returns are no longer to be had. The market is over-saturated and only the fittest survive - those who see the need to change soonest, and respond to it.

The Four M's

Governments, investors and national lottery enthusiasts all know the difficulties of picking winners. Picking losers is no easier but there are some indicators that are familiar to business rescue and insolvency practitioners. Although not infallible these at least suggest that caution or further enquiry might be warranted. These warning signs can be categorised as the four M's - Management, Markets, Mistakes and Money.

Management

Autocrats or dictators This all-powerful type operates alone. He may reinforce his isolation by ensuring that he is also chairman of the company. He surrounds himself with yes-men and in a smaller business he will probably be the major shareholder so there is no sanction to temper excess.

Unbalanced teams Typically dangerous combinations might be two marketing people who support each other's over-optimism or two engineers, each with brilliant ideas but lacking marketing or organisational skills. Any combination that does not include financial skills is likely to be weak.

Succession unplanned Common in family businesses where control is handed down from father to son without any thought as to whether son is competent or even interested. Autocrats also fail to give sufficient responsibility to successors to enable them to learn and to take up the reins effectively.

High staff turnover (Or rats and sinking ships) People may doubt the quality of the management and usually the best people are the first to walk. This weakens the skill base and demotivates those who remain. This type of turnover at board level is particularly worrying.

Long stayers Excessively long-service staff can also be a problem. The company becomes set in its ways and misses new ideas. Resistance to change will also be higher in such an organisation.

Poor industrial relations A disaffected workforce can undermine plans simply by not caring about what they are doing. Management takes decisions without necessary information from the coalface and may even be unaware of the problems.

Inability to change If management responds quickly to change the business has a chance. If they don't, the rot takes hold. Management stops listening to advisers, the marketplace, their employees or their colleagues. Weak managers go into a form of denial, burying their heads in the sand. They become nostalgic about the good old days and continue to fight the last war instead of preparing for the next. The corporate motto echoes Mr Micawber's dictum 'something will turn up'. It usually does - in the form of a receiver!

Markets and products

Cyclical markets Just as boom-and-bust cycles put businesses under pressure, so do cyclical markets - commodities for example.

Reliance on single customer/supplier The risk is significantly increased. The business is not only exposed to failure of the third party but also to economic blackmail or the risk of simple changes in policy.

Marginal operators Some businesses offer additional production capacity at a high price in times of high demand or take surplus output at a low price in times of low demand. In the short term they may get premium prices but when the temporary over-or under-capacity in the industry ceases, they have no business at all.

Poor market research Strategic planning is out of step with the realities of the market, inhibiting the business's ability to respond. Being out of touch with customers can mean lost turnover.

Poor marketing thrust Either the level of marketing is insufficient for the product or there is inadequate finance to sustain marketing. Failure is common where a small company tries to enter a market dominated by large players.

Product quality If the competition does it better, failure is inevitable in an open market. Some businesses, especially in less developed economies, can overcome this with state subsidies and trade barriers, but this is not sustainable in an increasingly global marketplace.

Failure to develop new products A high risk activity for both new and established businesses, but development is essential as product life cycles shorten. Failure is common in companies which have one good idea, never to be repeated.

Mistakes

Over-trading A company can run out of money as a result of growing too fast or run out of management capacity to control its levels of activities.

High organic growth rates Studies of major business failures in 1989 and 1990 showed that high sustained growth rates pointed to a substantially increased risk of failure. Of 45 companies surveyed, the average annual compound growth in turnover was more than 50 per cent over a four year period. By contrast, the average growth in companies which survived was just 6 per cent.

Acquisitions These are sometimes unhappy affairs. Sometimes so unhappy that the acquisition brings down the acquirer. A classic example was Atlantic Computers which brought down British and Commonwealth. A bad acquisition is a form of fast suicide.

The big project Diverts funds and management concentration with disastrous consequences. The safety test to apply is to estimate whether the business could survive the complete failure of the project. John Harvey-Jones said he would never 'bet the company'.

Money

Planning and forecasting Over-optimism is a recurring feature of business failures. Review business plans for realism, accuracy and above all sensitivity - how serious are the consequences if a key assumption is wrong by 5 per cent or 10 per cent?

Inadequate or absent management accounts If management accounts are absent or poorly presented, either the management feel they have something to hide (possibly even from themselves) or they are not using the information effectively.

Availability of long term finance Does the business have access to sufficient long term finance? Can it generate sufficient cash to repay commitments which are due in the short term?

High gearing This may indicate an underlying problem of an inappropriate capital structure. High gearing is easy to achieve, but results in a relatively fixed overhead (i.e. interest) making the company more vulnerable to market changes.

Relationship with providers of finance This is particularly important for secured lenders. Banks like customers who instigate meetings with lenders, whose requests are supported by sound business plans, who provide pertinent management information and whose overdrafts swing with seasonal cycles and do not become 'hard core'. They worry about the business where lenders and investors are suddenly getting no information or even misinformation.

Excessive boardroom pay Not Greenbury and all that. Sometimes desperate men do desperate things and, faced with inevitable failure, directors may just go for broke, taking what they can while the going is (relatively) good.

It may be hard to establish whether or not all these warning signs apply - it will depend on the nature of relationship you have with your business partner. But you should never be afraid to ask questions. Do they want to do business with you or not? If nothing else, evasive answers to open, reasonable questions give cause for concern. Spend time with your business partner - ideally on their premises rather than in a restaurant. How does the company compare with those of its competitors you know? Are the people happy and motivated? Is the plant well maintained and of good quality? Is the stock well presented? Does the company have the look and feel of a business that knows where it is going and why?

Finally, what if it is clear that your customer's or supplier's business (or dare we say even your own) fails enough of these tests to raise serious concern about its future? Effective change may well require the introduction of a third party. The best entrepreneur may never have acquired the skills needed to carry out an effective business rescue. Yet people who would not dream of buying a house without the help of a solicitor so often assume that they automatically have these skills.

Avoid some of the rather seedy, unqualified, ambulance chasers and asset strippers who will gather like vultures. There are some good company doctors. Seek professional help from an organisation which has a good track record and the credibility necessary to get key lenders and investors to buy in to any recovery plan.

Despite the fact that many of these warning lights are already flashing when we are instructed, our business recovery and insolvency practice keeps 70 per cent of these businesses out of formal insolvency proceedings. Receiverships and liquidations are a failure for everybody and we would rather avoid them.

Steve Hill, Partner Business Recovery and Insolvency, Coopers & Lybrand

PRECAUTIONARY MEASURES

Nobody plans to fail - they simply fail to plan. Plans should include the possibility that the business is unlikely to last for ever. It may be a cliché, but the objective is to exit at the top of the market - when the most value can be realised for all stakeholders, including the owners of the business. This could be achieved by selling the business, for example to someone who is prepared to pay a premium because he considers it will complement his existing business, or by way of a solvent (members' voluntary) liquidation. The assets are then sold off and, after paying all debts, the surplus is distributed to shareholders.

It is not uncommon for businesses to have liabilities in excess of assets. Although not necessarily a fatal problem, this is an indicator that the business may need expert help. Once shareholder value is negative, and unless it can be restored, the directors are personally at risk if the position continues to deteriorate. These risks include the possibility of being sued for wrongful trading, to make good the additional losses to creditors, or being disqualified as a director. Additionally, the directors must recognise that they are, at this stage, risking creditors' money rather than shareholders' funds, and without specialist help they could inadvertently take steps that favour some creditors at the expense of others. This too, should liquidation ensue, can result in legal action against directors.

Directors need to understand that whilst they may well understand their company's product, and may well have experience of managing growth, managing (or reversing) decline requires specialist skills. Many entrepreneurs assume, often wrongly, that they have such skills - even if they would not dream of, say, buying a house without the assistance of a solicitor. Many insolvencies can be avoided if the right expertise is brought to bear at the right time. Corporate rescue skills are learned over many years - nobody is born with them. The issue is not only about understanding what is best for the business, important though that may be. It is also essential to understand the attitudes, expectations and interests of other key players such as bankers, tax authorities, trade creditors and investors. There are unwritten rules of the game that need to be recognised.

A common response to an emerging problem is to seek further bank facilities. The bank in turn may, prior to considering such a request, seek an independent business review, carried out by an accountant well versed in business recovery and insolvency. This request may often come not from the company's normal relationship manager, but from a senior banker to whom the request has been referred in accordance with the bank's usual procedures. Directors often, wrongly, see this as a precursor to an almost inevitable receivership or liquidation. In fact the overwhelming majority of such appointments do not result in a recommendation for insolvency. Banks would generally rather retain their customers.

In an attempt to shed more light on a process which is often misunderstood, and is sometimes regarded as confrontational, the major UK banks have subscribed to a statement of principles called "Banks and Business - Working Together", with effect from I July 1997. This document, available from banks, is an excellent guide to what the bank is entitled to expect of its customer, and vice versa, when storm clouds are looming. Too many receiverships ensue simply because the customer refuses to cooperate in the process. This is the ultimate self-defeating strategy - a form of corporate suicide - especially if the business has a good story to tell, but simply refuses to tell it. When the process works well, it is because all parties are committed to repairing any breakdown in the banker/customer relationship that may have occurred.

- First option is always to exit while shareholder value can be maximised
- When shareholder equity is negative, directors are personally at risk, and owe a duty of care to creditors - not shareholders

- Corporate recovery is not for beginners - seek expert help sooner rather than later
- If the bank seeks to introduce expert help, make sure you understand the bank's expectations as well as your own, and cooperate in making the process work for both sides

Avoiding the drop

During the 1990s, the term 'rescue culture' has entered the English language. What does this really mean?

Long before the 1990s, many businesses were rescued informally. This continues to be the case. Informed creditors, as long as they do not feel that they are being strung along, recognise that they have a far better chance of recovering their money from a trading entity than they do from a liquidator. Normally the process requires the intervention of a third party such as a company doctor or an insolvency practitioner, to act as honest broker between the company and its creditors. Thousands of UK businesses - including some very well known names - have been through such a process in recent years.

The wholesale reforms to UK insolvency law in 1986 also included some important innovations, not least a recognition that even a business which was insolvent - i.e., unable to pay its debts when due - was not necessarily a terminal case, fit only for liquidation. Accordingly, statutory rescue procedures, notably voluntary arrangements (for companies, individuals and partnerships) and administrations (for companies and partnerships) were created.

These procedures are complex, and must by law be supervised by a licensed insolvency practitioner. That does not mean they are insolvency procedures in the classic sense (a receivership by any other name). Used properly, they enable a business to be restructured, and to buy time to come to terms with creditors. The quid pro quo, reasonably enough, is that the creditors have to vote in favour of the proposals being put to them.

Whilst all insolvency practitioners are licensed, regulated professionals, it is true to say that some are better than others. Sadly, voluntary arrangements or administration proposals are sometimes unrealistic or unworkable. Some creditors, disappointed too often by unfulfilled promises of 'jam tomorrow', have formed fairly cynical opinions of these procedures. This does not mean that they cannot work. The important point, for the directors, is to ensure that they instruct a practitioner who enjoys the confidence of creditors and has a good track record. Ask probing questions and (it is probably unnecessary to state) do not assume that the cheapest job will be the best job. When survival is at issue, do you really want to go with the lowest quote?

Beware of unlicensed, unregulated people who - especially once the company's problems are a matter of public record (e.g. because a creditor is suing for his money) - will often make unsolicited approaches. They may describe themselves as "insolvency consultants" or "rescue consultants", or some such phrase. Some of them may provide sound advice and a valuable service. Others just want a substantial cheque in advance for a 'service' of dubious value, and a small but significant minority are crooks looking to gain control of the business to sell off the assets and pocket the proceeds regardless of creditors' interests.

Do not instruct anybody in whom you have less than complete confidence, and if in doubt ask your lawyer, bank or auditor to recommend somebody who has a good reputation and is a member of a regulated profession. Professionals have licences to lose if they act improperly, and they have negligence insurance to cover against the consequences of poor advice. If you are seriously ill, whose advice do you want - that of a qualified doctor, or a snake-oil salesman?

- Informal rescues, workouts or turnarounds (these terms are more or less interchangeable) are widely used and can work well - this is always the first option
- Failing that, voluntary arrangements or administration can be used to rescue a business - these are not simply insolvency procedures
- Make sure you choose someone who has a good reputation and track record. Is this a person my creditors are likely to know and trust?
- When survival is at issue, price is only one factor to consider
- Beware purveyors of snake oil!

In my experience . . .

Several years after starting our company, and after a lot of late nights and a lot of hard work, we were just starting to show a profit. We had also established a supplier relationship with a much larger international company that did not have an office in our city. It turned out they wanted to set up their own operation and asked us if we would merge with them. The deal offered some benefits of expansion and security but I didn't think it rewarded the past effort. Also the deal was to their advantage as they would eliminate a possible competitor by taking us over.

I declined the deal but a further meeting was arranged and the chairman and senior executives flew in for a meeting. I was outnumbered six to one, but just kept saying No. Finally, as much to get out of the situation as anything, I stole a line from the movie The Godfather and said, "Make me an offer I can't refuse". The chairman's honour was now at stake and he put forward a deal that was the business equivalent of winning the lottery.

- Never be afraid to say No
- Always deal with the top man

Barry Roxburgh, Public Relations Consultant

Not every business is rescuable. Some reach the end of their natural life and, if they are insolvent, all that remains is to give them a 'decent burial', distributing their 'estate' to creditors in due order of priority.

There is less stigma attached to business failure than was once the case. Indeed, the whole raison d'être of limited liability companies is to stimulate enterprise by enabling the directors and shareholders to walk away from a liquidation (in the absence of any misconduct by themselves) free to try again another day. Encouraging an enterprise society means recognising, and perhaps even encouraging to some extent, a percentage of failures. A risk-free business environment would be stagnant and somewhat uninteresting for the participants. Frank Borman, CEO of Eastern Airlines, a large American insolvency, said "Capitalism without bankruptcy is like Christianity without hell".

Recognising that a business is irretrievably insolvent and letting go may be the greatest challenge an entrepreneur is ever asked to face. As well as a personal sense of bereavement, he may feel that he has let down customers, creditors, fellow-directors and shareholders, and employees. Understandably, some people are reluctant, or simply unable, to accept that burden, and go into a form of denial. A common metaphor in insolvency work is the ostrich with his head in the sand. Unfortunately, the longer the period of denial lasts, the worse things become, and the lower the funds ultimately available to help repay creditors.

If the company is simply unable to accept its fate, ultimately a creditor will force the issue by imposing insolvency against the will of the company. Any creditor owed more than £750 can serve a statutory demand requiring payment within 21 days. In the absence of payment he can petition the court for the company to be compulsorily wound up. In that case the Official Receiver (a government official) will simply close down the business, except in the most exceptional circumstances. Court and other statutory costs, together with the reduced opportunity to maximise asset values once trading has ceased, mean that compulsory liquidation rarely provides a worthwhile outcome for anybody.

Preferable by far is creditors' voluntary liquidation. In this case, the directors approach an insolvency practitioner directly and resolve to wind up the company. Meetings of shareholders and creditors are convened, and the Insolvency Practitioner will generally take appropriate steps to ensure that asset values are maximised. Creditors are likely to hold the directors in higher esteem for having taken steps to bring the business to an orderly end, without creditors having had to spend significant sums in legal fees.

The remaining option is administrative receivership, which may often be the best option by far. An administrative receiver can only be appointed by a secured creditor holding a debenture over all of the company's assets. The process can be used to good effect to rescue a business (although not the company itself). Assuming a willing purchaser can be found, the assets are sold as a complete package, indeed as a going concern business, with the purchaser taking over the workforce and possibly also the management. The company's debts are left behind, and the proceeds of the sale of the business are then distributed amongst the creditors according to their rights and priorities. Receivership is thus an effective way to bring into the business additional resources - financial or managerial - and give it a new lease of life. A business sold as a going concern will normally realise significantly more than the sum of its parts.

There is no reason why the existing management cannot buy the business from a receiver. What is often disparagingly referred to as 'phoenixism' can in fact be done perfectly legally and properly. The main requirement is simply that the management should pay an open market price for the assets they are acquiring, and that there is the maximum degree of openness with creditors as to what has been done, and why. It has even been known for the bank that appointed the receiver to fund the management buy-out, because the bank recognises that the restructuring that has taken place during, or as a result of, the receivership process is sufficient to put the business back on a sound footing.

Where there is no debenture holder able to appoint a receiver, the administration procedure can be suitably adapted to provide the same result. This does not mean that, as noted earlier, administration is not a pure rescue procedure, although it must be acknowledged that the fact that it can be used in both of these ways is sometimes a source of misunderstanding.

In summary, even if rescue is impossible, it is still possible to get a better outcome for all stakeholders if the right steps are taken at the right time.

 Seek expert advice from an insolvency practitioner. Nobody else is legally allowed to deal with an insolvency.

 Do not leave it too late - most of the better options tend to have sell-by dates!

 Consider administrative receivership or administration if there is a chance that somebody might want to buy the business.

If the business has no future, accept that liquidation is inevitable - do not put it off, making matters worse.

 Voluntary liquidation is preferable to compulsory liquidation, and will earn more respect from creditors.

 Directors who act properly will not be penalised, and will live to fight another day.

Steve Hill, Partner Business Recovery Services, PricewaterhouseCoopers

Managing in difficult times means having robust strategies. In the UK context that means having the cash to survive a twenty per cent drop in sales, and having the resources to exploit a similar and equally sudden increase in demand. That is a tall order and it has to be said that most small firms would have difficulty meeting that standard. But the most successful entrepreneurs are not gamblers. They take calculated risks and keep a very careful eye on the economy. The late Sir James Goldsmith is credited with being amongst the very few entrepreneurs to spot the 1987 stock market crash and liquidate his holdings. But others took less drastic action and survived, whilst many hundreds of thousands of less prudent enterprises went to the wall.

Managing Growth

Growth can be even more of a challenge than getting the business started in the first place. After all, when you start out you usually have only yourself to convince. Once you are under way there are employees, shareholders, bankers, customers and suppliers - to name but a few - who all have a part to play in helping you to grow successfully and so have to be 'sold' on your new strategies.

If you want to create a valuable business - one that is worth something to others rather than just one that creates a good income for you and perhaps your family - then you will have to go for growth.

You will need to build up a business that has a management team running it and does not need you for day-to-day decisions. Whilst not being needed may bruise your ego, it should do wonders for your bank balance when you sell up.

PLANS ALWAYS CHANGE

So you've won that big order - but you can only make 7000 Spice Girls dolls a month. Why are they suddenly so popular in Brazil?

Suddenly the success of your business has rendered your business plan redundant. You now need to add an extra productionline to meet demand, but there is not enough space in the factory. You need a larger stock of raw materials but don't have the cash to pay for them. You need more staff. You need to understand how to manage foreign exchange cash management. In short, you need a new business plan.

Change comes in many guises. It may be immediate like the scenario above or it may happen slowly over time. It may change your business beyond all recognition. Change can be internal - such as the loss of key staff - or external - such as markets contracting or new technology. Your original business plan with its three year projections may no longer be viable but this doesn't mean that you no longer need a plan.

It is crucial to review the basic assumptions underpinning your business and to assess the impact of changes on all fronts - management, staffing, capital expenditure, cash requirements, profitability and even equity and ownership.

Don't be afraid to alter your basic strategy. For example, organic growth may be the original and successful strategy to achieve a strong market position. Continuing to invest in production may be inappropriate as the added value is now in the strong brand name, and production can be subcontracted more cheaply. Thus the business could divest itself of manufacturing and could concentrate on developing new markets for complementary brands. Proceeds from the sale of the manufacturing business could be used to acquire or develop new brands.

You need to stand back regularly and take a critical look at your business. Go back to basics and if necessary challenge vested interests and ideas. Don't get struck in a rut and do something simply because 'it has always been done that way'. Think laterally.

It may be necessary to 'hire and fire' the management team to achieve the correct mix of skills - although it is often better to look at training and redefining an individual's role if they have valuable experience, expertise and knowledge. Consideration should be given to how the business is financed so that it is appropriate for your new needs. You may have found relying on an overdraft to be adequate for a number of years, but a growing business can be constrained by the local bank manager. Cash may be more important than profit and you need to be sure that you will have cash available - for example for necessary capital expenditure. It is useful to maintain a forecasting model of your cash flow on a spreadsheet - which should be integrated with a budget profit and loss and a budget balance sheet.

The most important thing to remember is that your business plan is not set in stone. It is more like a living tree which grows and adapts to its changing environment.

Andrew Godfrey, Head of Growth and Development Services, Grant Thornton

GROWING BUSINESSES

Many businessmen and women immediately answer the question "Why are you in business?" with the stock response of "To make lots of money!" accompanied by a pitying look that conveys what a moron you are for having asked the question in the first place. If you follow up with "And how are you going to make lots of money?" the response is often "By growing the business to make big profits!" or "By growing the business to sell it!"

Growth often seems to be a lodestone to small and medium sized businesses; seen as a panacea for all the problems from low levels of profitability, through poor purchasing power, to a lack of human resource and finances to seize commercial opportunities, with a host of other difficulties faced by small enterprises thrown in along the way.

But is growth universally good for business? No, is the answer. Growth is unlikely to rectify the problems of a basically unprofitable business. Cash shortage and a propensity to over-trade are also endemic amongst small growth-aspirant companies - often terminally so. Companies that have not looked ahead and anticipated the problems of growth and understood how they will address them can find the experience uncomfortable, expensive and in the worst case fatal.

On the positive side the creation of a larger business and the accompanying achievement, profits, opportunities and kudos cannot be overlooked. The message must be that growth is best achieved as a planned and controlled strategy rather than as a piecemeal and chaotic reaction to market demand.

Key business issues in a growth situation

Cash is almost invariably an issue. Rapid growth tends to exhaust credit with suppliers, and increasing activity levels can detract focus from debt collection. Factoring might provide a short to medium term solution and an empathy between the bank and the business also won't go amiss. However, what is really needed is an understanding of what the financial requirements of growth will be and a plan to provide for these.

Nearly all other business disciplines follow a similar logic. There is a limit to the amount of work that existing staff can undertake even if it's in an atmosphere of exciting growth challenge. But short term remedies such as temporary employment can prove costly both in absolute terms of wage bill but also in the areas of the opportunity cost of training or disruption to services. Human resource planning, addressing the issues before they occur, will mitigate the worst effects at the least cost.

Production capacity may become fully utilised. It is easier to deal with this if, in advance of the growth, alternative methods of production - subcontracted production or capital purchase of new plant - have been properly evaluated and the appropriate option provided for.

The list goes on but the message is clear. If you have planned to grow and examined the various ways in which it will impact on the business then it is easier to control and accommodate. Straightforward application of this sound management practice is more than half the battle. Knowing when you are reaching the limit of your experience or abilities and where to go to get help and support is the other part of the equation.

What should you consider before deciding whether to grow? First and foremost you should decide why you are in business and what you are ultimately trying to get out of it. A 'life-style' or 'hobby' business might lose all its appeal and the very reason for establishing it if it is grown into a large corporate entity. Equally the character of the individual who owns or runs the business should be taken into account - many entrepreneurial businessmen and women become uncomfortable with the administrative and management disciplines concomitant with a larger corporate organisation.

Once you have established why you want to grow and have a clear idea of how this is going to be achieved, it is important to understand your own position (taking realistic stock of your strengths and weaknesses) and the part you are going to play in the growth. Do you want to be the head of a complex business running it through delegation, or do you relish rolling your sleeves up and getting stuck in. Either is a completely valid option but it is important to recognise it in advance and ensure that the growing business can accommodate what you want.

 Establish why you want to grow and be clear that this is the correct option

 Decide how you're going to grow and plan to accommodate all the business disciplines in this growth

 Ensure you communicate this plan to not only your own employees but also your professional support, at the very least your banker and your accountant

 Control your own growth, keep an eagle eye on both gross and net profitability and do not fall into the common trap of becoming a busy fool

 Do not allow yourself to lose control of your working capital - it is easy to do and hard to rectify in a growing company

Financial Project Manager, Business Link, Hereford and Worcester

Managing Growth from Private to Public Company

Private companies generally meet their funding requirements from a restricted number of sources such as private investors (often managers and employees of the business) banks and venture capitalists.

A private company (except a private company limited by guarantee) may not offer its shares to the public. Thus if a private company wishes to expand rapidly it may have to raise finance by 'going public'. This does not mean being listed on the London Stock Exchange. A relatively small number of public companies are quoted companies - i.e. listed on the Stock Exchange.

But before the decision is made to become a public company a number of matters need to be thought through.

Public companies are subjected to far tighter restrictions than private companies, including amongst other things:

- At least two directors must be appointed
- A minimum issued share capital of £50,000 must be allotted
- They are not permitted to file abbreviated accounts
- They are not permitted to purchase their own shares from capital
- Financial assistance cannot be given by the company for the acquisition of its shares
- They are not permitted to use written resolutions
- Public companies are subject to the more stringent provisions of both the Companies Act 1985 and the City Code on Takeovers and Mergers

Certainly a company wishing to 'go public' should weigh up the pros and cons very carefully.

If the directors and shareholders then still wish to re-register as a public company, the conversion is governed by Sections 43–47 of the Companies Act 1985, which require that the following be filed at Companies House:

A special resolution that the company be re-registered as a public company and that the memorandum and articles of association be amended, and

An application to re-register, signed by a director or secretary, and enclosing:

- The memorandum or articles of association as altered pursuant to the special resolution made to convert the limited company to a public limited company
- A written statement from the auditors that the company's net assets are not less than the aggregate of its called up share capital and its undistributable reserves
- A copy of the latest balance sheet
- An unqualified auditors report
- A statutory declaration made by a director or the secretary that the special resolution to convert to a public company has been passed; the requirements of the Companies Act have been complied with; the minimum share capital requirements (£50,000) have been satisfied;

the company's net asset position, as reflected in the report of the auditors, has been maintained

- The relevant fee

If the Registrar of Companies is satisfied that all requirements have been met, a certificate of re-registration as a public company is issued.

C M St J O'Grady and Helen Engelhart, Shoosmiths

In my experience . . .

My husband left a national company to set up his own commercial refrigeration business. One of his great strengths had been his ability to communicate and empathise with the engineers - because he had started as an engineer himself. This worked splendidly and the business grew so rapidly that the original working team was split into three, each with its own supervisor and a Service and Maintenance Manager to pull the whole thing together.

This is where the problems started. The men continued to maintain their direct links with my husband, which he enjoyed because it kept him in touch with what was going on. However, the middle managers were aware that they were being bypassed and felt undermined. Eventually there was a mutiny when one of the middle managers sacked an engineer. He came to my husband who reinstated him without reference to the middle manager. The manager resigned in protest and the bad blood that was caused soured a once-happy company, with everyone in either one camp or another.

- Keep updating your skills - behaviour that is useful at one stage may not be appropriate when circumstances change
- Give your managers the power to do the job you hired them for - and trust them to do it
- Recognise that, as the business grows, you will not be able to know everything in fine detail - use performance targets and budgets to monitor the important aspects

Karen Ryan, Ryan Refrigeration Ltd

Managing Growth - What to Watch for When Expanding

Expanding the Range of Products or Services/Selling More

The growth of the business will depend on obtaining additional customers, increasing the transaction frequency with each customer and increasing the average sales value of each transaction. The effectiveness of the processes in place to achieve these objectives should be regularly reviewed and improved.

Although obtaining new customers is essential to the growth of a business, care should be taken to review the financial position of those customers before any trading on credit terms commences. There are agencies that will investigate companies' credit-worthiness and in certain industries it is possible to take out insurance cover on outstanding monies in order to minimise the impact of any bad debts.

An increase in transaction frequency and average sales value can be achieved by expanding the range of products or services available to customers. However, care should be taken to include in the business plan the costs of development and marketing of the new products/services to ensure that they are cost-effective. Also, it is necessary to assess the financial security of any key suppliers whose business failure could affect the continuance of the supply to the customer base. Although most businesses have a number of main customers, it is vital to ensure that the business does not become reliant on a particular customer or group of customers for its continued survival. An increase in the level of business with an existing customer may not be as advantageous to the future of the business as additional business obtained from new customers.

Change in premises

Any change in business premises needs to be considered closely in the context of the overall business plan. The level of the expected growth of the business may determine whether it is advisable for new premises to be rented or bought outright. Purchase of premises can be tax efficient and has the advantage of providing an asset for the future benefit of the owners. However, renting can be more flexible in that the length of a lease can be determined by reference to the period for which it is anticipated that the premises will meet the changing needs of the business. The availability of additional space to allow for expansion in the future would be a prime consideration in selecting premises. In some businesses location of the premises can be important to the customer base.

Change in personnel

The average business loses 50 per cent of its employees every four years. When management time, recruitment fees and learning curves are taken into account it is clearly in the interests of the business to keep its existing employees satisfied in terms of their working conditions and remuneration packages. Creation of loyalty within the existing workforce has great value to the business. When it becomes necessary to recruit additional or replacement employees it is essential that the recruitment procedures maximise the chances of finding the appropriate applicant. Where significant recruitment takes place it is advisable to obtain professional assistance with the recruitment process, recognising that the key to any business, particularly an expanding business, is the quality of its personnel.

How to cut costs

As a business grows, it is important that the management information systems used to monitor the business keep pace. The old adage "What you can measure you can manage" certainly applies to an expanding business. Management information systems should be sufficient to ensure that the profitability of different products and the effectiveness of marketing methods are monitored. It is important not only to measure the results achieved by the business but also the activities that produce those results.

Each business process needs to be examined regularly to ensure that it is still effective. Rather than making small changes to an existing system it may be more effective to abandon it and devise an entirely new operating system. Systems will need to become more sophisticated over time and it is essential to overcome any resistance to change.

The managers of the growing business need to spend time working on the business rather than in the business. A danger is that management personnel will spend time assisting in production areas rather than in the key area of management. Businesses should not be afraid of paying for outside professional advice in circumstances where this is cost-effective and adds value to the business. The key to cutting costs is control - and this is brought about by adequate operating and management information systems.

What to be careful of when expanding

During a period of growth it is essential to maintain the quality of the products/services supplied by the business. Care should be taken not to ignore the existing customer base by directing efforts towards attracting new customers. Any marketing processes should be aimed at the existing customer base as well as new customers. The average business loses 50 per cent of its customer base in a period of five years which illustrates how important it can be to encourage the loyalty of existing customers. As with employees, loyalty creates value.

Overall

To achieve successful growth a business requires adequate management information and operating systems and must be flexible and adaptable to the changing needs of its customer base.

Michael Wasinski, Hacker Young

RENEWING YOUR BRAND

Successful brand management can be a life's work. Creating a distinctive brand for a new business is just the first stage of a long process. Over time, as a business grows and develops, the brand (or brands) should be monitored carefully on a regular basis. The legal foundation of the brand (its trademarks), the brand strategy and personality and the brand identity should be reviewed and, where necessary, refreshed to keep them relevant and appealing.

Of course, the heart of the brand - its purpose and core brand values - should remain constant wherever possible. Nothing is more damaging for a brand than constant changes in direction. That approach can result in a brand that is as superficial and unappealing as a friend or colleague who transforms, chameleon-like, as his or her environment or circumstances change.

Brands must have integrity and depth, but aspects of their visual presentation and communication must be flexible enough to adapt to significant changes in the scale and character of the business that they represent. As a person, I have my own style when it comes to clothes but I might choose to wear a suit to work and jeans to a football match.

The prospect of entering a new geographic market or product category, an acquisition or merger, a step change in the size of the business or a dramatic change in the competitive environment are all examples of corporate developments which might prompt a refocusing and renewal of brand strategy and identity.

Brand names

It is generally accepted that the brand name is the one feature of a brand that should never change. Perceptions of a brand that accumulate over time attach to and are bound up in the brand name. In those exceptional circumstances when the brand name does need to be reappraised, the business owner should devote time and attention to ensure that brand identity is transferred to the new brand name and not lost, at a cost to the business.

Developing new brand names is a difficult task in itself and should not be undertaken lightly. Trademark classes are increasingly crowded with competing marks and finding a brand name that is appropriate, legally available, linguistically acceptable and distinctive can be a complex and costly job.

Trademarks

The trademark registrations that underpin the brand must be kept up-to-date through constant vigilance. Keeping a brand protectable depends to a large extent on evidence that the trademark rights are actually being exerted when an infringement occurs. So, if a competitor or new brand is suspected of 'passing-off' and infringing a brand name or identity, a professional trademark attorney should be consulted as soon as possible.

Brand identity

Like a brand name, a visual identity (logo, colour scheme and typeface, retail environment or corporate 'look') should always be designed for the long term. Awareness and identity can be built up over time through having a unique visual style that reinforces the brand's heritage and personality.

But identity management is about much more than the consistent application of a logo to letterheads and signs. The presentation of the brand to different audiences in each 'brand experience' must be carefully managed so that the brand's personality comes across powerfully and consistently. Wherever necessary, the brand identity should be assessed and carefully updated. Everything, from the tone of voice of a receptionist and the design of a web site, to a showroom or trade stand, should be infused with the brand's personality to build a distinctive and memorable brand style.

Brand architecture

As a business grows and develops it is likely that its product range will expand, its offices and facilities will multiply and it will face a number of different competitors in different segments. In these circumstances a single brand image may need to be developed into a broader brand structure or 'brand architecture'. Finding the right brand architecture for the business is vitally important. Is a single, 'monolithic' brand (in the BMW mould) best, or should different brands or 'sub-brands' be developed that are more focused and suited to specific products or markets (as practised by Vauxhall, for example)? For the small business, a monolithic approach may well be best as it is cost-effective and allows maximum focus.

Branding works best when brand management can be conducted within a clear framework, with new products or services slotting easily into an architecture that has been set up with the long term development of the business in mind. For a new business, getting noticed is the hardest challenge. Developing a distinctive brand can be the best way to stand out from the crowd.

Interbrand Newell & Sorrell

THE ALTERNATIVE INVESTMENT MARKET

The Alternative Investment Market (AIM) started in June 1995 as the successor to the Unlisted Securities Market. The purpose of AIM is to provide smaller companies with the opportunity to raise capital and have their shares quoted so that buyers and sellers are able to trade the shares on a ready market.

Companies often seek a quotation on AIM as it is considered less costly and with fewer requirements than a full listing on the London Stock Exchange. In many cases, joining AIM is the stepping stone for a full listing on the London Stock Exchange.

Companies wishing to join AIM have to fulfil certain requirements and it is only possible to give an outline of the some of the requirements here. Prior to admission to AIM, companies should:

- Publish a prospectus and deposit it with the London Stock Exchange
- Appoint a nominated adviser
- Have published accounts conforming to the statutory requirements. It is very unusual for a company to join AIM before it has traded for at least two years but, theoretically, it is possible. In this case, all directors and employees must agree not to sell any interests they have in the company's shares for at least one year from the time the company has joined AIM
- State that the company has sufficient working capital for present requirements

Companies trading on the AIM for at least two years may, on application, be admitted to the Official List without having to supply full listing particulars.

C M St J O'Grady, Shoosmiths

AIM IN THE RIGHT DIRECTION

Gaining access to capital can often prove the biggest growing pain for businesses. Many traditionally look to banks and venture capitalists but there are other routes to consider.

Launched in June 1995, the Alternative Investment Market (AIM) replaced the Unlisted Securities Market (USM) as the junior market of the London Stock Exchange (LSE). From its inception AIM has attracted smaller, young and fast growing companies who have raised approximately £1.42 billion. The market includes some 299 companies whose combined worth is now nearly £5.5 billion.

AIM offers small to medium sized businesses an effective way to appeal to a wider spectrum of businesses, including start-ups, management buy-outs and buy-ins and family owned businesses.

Unlike a full listing where at least 25 per cent of the shares must be available to the public, no minimum number of shares has to be sold on admission to AIM. This is one of the benefits of AIM and differentiates it from the main list. However, commercial reality means that a sufficient number of shares must be issued in order to create a market in them. This makes it suitable for smaller companies in the second stage of growth and those where control is important, perhaps family owned businesses that want to float without allowing such a substantial proportion of the shares into the public's hands.

The majority of AIM companies are capitalised in a range between £3 million and £30 million and feature a wide range of business types. Another misconception is that AIM is only for high-tech or blue-sky companies. While it does attract and support such businesses the market's focus is moving towards more straightforward businesses such as manufacturing, mining, retailing and nursing homes. It is also not necessary to have a trading record, but there must be a published prospectus that complies with the LSE's rules and the nominated adviser must be satisfied with the management and financial controls.

Determining whether or not your business should go public is probably one of the most significant business decisions you and your fellow directors will have to make. It is a major landmark in a company's development. But it can bring challenges for the business and demands on its owners and directors which must also be considered very carefully.

No two businesses are alike and for every company contemplating going public the considerations are very different. Companies decide to float for a number of reasons - a means of raising capital for expansion, restructuring existing debt or as a way of providing shareholders with a dealing facility. Going public provides one way of achieving these goals and one that has enabled many companies to progress to the next stage of their development.

Not only can floating on AIM raise funds to pay off loans or expand the business by creating a market for shares in a company, it can also provide a way forward for mergers and acquisitions. It increases credibility with lenders, customers and suppliers - and in certain markets can confer significant tax breaks, including capital gains and inheritance tax.

Nominated advisers can help businesses to think through whether going public is the right option for the business. After considering all the issues owners may decide that flotation is not the right step. If, however, they decide to go the AIM route then the nominated adviser is not only required by AIM rules but can also prove a useful asset in helping to steer the business through the flotation process, or even help to start the planning process and getting the business into shape for flotation.

The interest for AIM has come from entrepreneurial business all over the UK and increasingly from overseas companies as well. Should you explore the possibilities?

Ian Smart, Corporate Finance and Investigations Partner, Grant Thornton

Exit Stage Right

Sooner or later, the issue of exit arises for virtually every business. Why? Because at some point some or all of the shareholders will wish to realise their investment. This does not apply solely to smaller and medium sized businesses. We have seen during the 1980s and the 1990s that even the major multinationals can be subject to billion dollar and billion pound takeover bids and that they too have to consider the wishes of their shareholders.

Exit considerations

What are the key factors that can occur, sometimes unexpectedly, that can force the issue of exit on the shareholders' agenda?

Privately owned businesses

The business may be a small family-owned, privately-run operation that has been in existence for generations. However any of the following could occur to upset the status quo:

- Death/retirement of the founder/major shareholder
- No management succession
- Major shareholder(s)' need to realise funds
- Family/shareholder dispute
- Unsolicited approach from a third party interested in acquiring the business

The presence of institutional shareholders

The business may have been established and financed by debt and/or equity provided by banks and/or private equity investors (institutions such as the well known insurance companies or pension funds providing venture and development capital). Such institutions as shareholders will have no day-to-day involvement in the running of the business but are likely to have a significant stake in the business and will usually have a seat on the board. Moreover they will be a significant influence as far as exit is concerned and this can be a cause of disagreement.

Whilst institutional investors and the management team will be united in wishing to maximise the value of their investment they may disagree as to timing. Their interests will inevitably diverge because:

- Management may have further aspirations about the growth and direction of the business
- Institutional investors are investing other people's money and are driven by the need to maximise and maintain the returns achieved from their funds

Putting it more simply an institution will typically invest on the basis of a five year time horizon and will often structure the initial investment in such a way that a form of exit has to be achieved within this time scale.

The exit route - pros and cons

Whilst there are a variety of elaborate and sometimes complex routes available for unlocking some or all of a company's capital structure, the most common exit routes are flotation and trade sale.

Flotation

In the United Kingdom the main stock market (the Official List) is a long established and well developed market which for centuries has provided a mechanism for companies to raise capital, either to realise investments or to finance growth or both. More recently it has been recognised that a junior market should be available to cater for smaller developing businesses and for investors specifically interested in investing in those businesses. Currently the junior market is the Alternative Investment Market (AIM) which was launched in June 1995 and which provides a lower cost, less regulated platform for smaller businesses to access capital for exit or expansion. Since it was established, almost 300 companies have joined AIM, the market's total capitalisation was £5.5 billion as at September 1997 and over £1.4 billion of fresh capital has been raised from investors.

Flotation may be an attractive exit route for a number of reasons:

- It may achieve a higher value for the business
- Some shareholders can realise their investment while the company's independence is maintained
- The market is available for ongoing access to capital for future sales by shareholders or to finance expansion

Flotation does bring with it a number of regulatory obligations and increased public scrutiny which can deter some businesses. In addition flotation is not an option if all shareholders wish to sell.

Trade sale

Outright sale of the business is an obvious exit route. If properly handled it can be a simpler and less expensive process than a flotation. It has a number of other advantages:

- A successful auction process could secure a premium price
- A full exit for all shareholders
- Possibility of new commercial opportunities through tying up with a larger group

The sale process, however, is not without its drawbacks. The process can be lengthy and contract discussions over key issues such as warranties and indemnities sought from the seller can be major stumbling blocks. Once sold, of course, there is no opportunity to participate in the future success of the business and, for management staying with the business, independence has been lost.

The way forward

Any company thinking about exit and wondering which route to take will certainly need to take advice. There is a huge industry of financial advisers including merchant banks, stockbrokers, specialist advisory firms, accountants and lawyers, all of whom will have experience and expertise of flotations, trade sales and other routes. Knowing where to start will be daunting and confusing for the uninitiated seeking help and perhaps the following suggestions will help:

 Personal contacts and introductions are often the most useful way forward - shareholders should tap the knowledge of their company's auditors and solicitors and speak to other companies, either in their geographic area or in the same business, who have recently sold or floated

 Aim to set up a 'beauty parade' of three or four potential advisers and seek a full presentation of their credentials

 Do not be seduced by extravagant claims as to what price can be achieved. Be wary of advisers who may be pitching high to secure the business but then cannot deliver

 Select advisers on a 'horses for courses' basis. Certain firms specialise in advising smaller and medium sized businesses and others specialise in specific sectors - these advisers are more likely to provide a higher degree of attention and a better level of service

Finally, and perhaps most important, it is essential that client and adviser will get on. Some transactions can take months to complete and may include long days and nights of meetings. Companies (and, for that matter, advisers) should make sure they will be able to put up with each other!

Botts & Company Limited

Most small firms see entering new markets and launching new products as the way to grow. Whilst it is true that entering new markets (particularly overseas) and launching new and innovative products and services are hallmarks of fast-growing firms, these are not the only strategies that will achieve that result.

Many of the fastest growing and most profitable small firms achieved those results by sticking to their core products and markets. In other words selling more of their existing products and services to more people like the customers they have now. They concentrate on keeping customers rather than just finding ever more people they know less and less about, to sell to.

The most successful enterprises have a superior product or service, a superior reputation and a better understanding of customer needs. All these factors are achieved by concentration and focus, rather than diffusion of effort.

Remember it's the bottom line and not the top one that matters most.

Conclusion

Those of you who have taken the trouble to read this far will in all probability already have been amply rewarded. Without the benefit of outside advice, too many ventures can set off in the wrong direction and flounder. Sophie Mirman, the Sock Shop founder, described her own business failure in just those terms. Her expansion into America was a disaster that killed off a promising business. In her words, when she hit New York she turned left instead of right.

Knowledge is the key, but too many would-be entrepreneurs prefer rumours. Gaining information on markets and competitors to keep your offering superior can take time and resources. But to borrow the words of a former Harvard Business School Dean, when faced with a student who was dismayed at the cost of a course there, "If you think knowledge is expensive you should try ignorance".

In my experience . . .

In this revolutionary internet age and in the early dawn of the millennium some of you may think my advice somewhat outdated. Always confirm agreements in writing. If you are worried about pushing your client to confirm a deal it is just as easy for you to follow up in writing with all the arrangements as you understand them. For suppliers big and small and customers of all types always confirm in writing - fax, email, whatever, but don't forget!

A Turner, Hope Cove Developments

3i plc
91 Waterloo Road
London SE1 8XP
Tel: 020 7928 3131
Fax: 020 7928 0058
www.3i.com
*Offers venture capital and assistance
to businesses*

Abacus Research*
Eden House
River Way
Uckfield
Sussex TN22 1SL
Tel: 01825 761788
Fax: 01825 765755
✉ enquiries@abacus.uk.com
www.abacus.uk.com

The Advertising Association*
Abford House
15 Wilton Road
London SW1V 1NJ
Tel: 020 7828 2771
Fax: 020 7931 0376
✉ aa@adassoc.org.uk
www.adassoc.org.uk

**Advertising Standards
Authority**
2 Torrington Place
London WC1E 7HW
Tel: 020 7580 5555
Fax: 020 7631 3051
www.asa.org.uk

**Advisory, Conciliation and
Arbitration Service (ACAS)**
Head Office
Brandon House
180 Borough High Street
London SE1 1LW
Tel: 020 7210 3613
(main switchboard)
www.acas.org.uk

**Alliance of Independent
Retailers & Businesses**
Alliance House
14 Pierpoint Street
Worcester WR1 1UW
Tel: 01905 612733
Fax: 01905 21501
✉ alliance@indretailer.co.uk
www.indretailer.co.uk

**Association for Management
Education & Training in
Scotland**
Cotterell Building
University of Stirling
Stirling FK9 4LA
Tel: 01786 450906
Fax: 01786 465070
✉ amets@stir.ac.uk

**Association of British
Chambers of Commerce**
Export Marketing Research Scheme
4 Westwood House
Westwood Business Park
Coventry CV4 8HS
Tel: 02476 694484
Fax: 02476 695844
✉ enquiry@britishchambers.org.uk
www.britishchambers.org.uk

Association of British Insurers*
51 Gresham Street
London EC2V 7HQ
Tel: 020 7600 3333
Fax: 020 7696 8996
www.abi.org.uk

**British Market Research
Association**
16 Creighton Avenue
London N10 1NU
Tel: 020 8444 3692
Fax: 020 8883 9953
✉ admin@bmra.org.uk

**Association of Business
Executives**
William House
14 Worple Road
London SW19 4DD
Tel: 020 8879 1973
Fax: 020 8946 7153
www.abeuk.com

**Association of Chartered
Certified Accountants***
29 Lincoln's Inn Fields
London WC2A 3EE
Tel: 020 7242 6855
Fax: 020 7831 8054
www.acca.org.uk

Association of MBAs
15 Duncan Terrace
London N1 8BZ
Tel: 020 7837 3375
Fax: 020 7278 3634
www.mba.org.uk

Baker Tilley*
2 Bloomsbury Street
London WC1B 3ST
Tel: 020 7413 5100
Fax: 020 7413 5101
www.bakertilley.co.uk
Chartered Accountants

**Bankruptcy Association of
Great Britain & Ireland**
4 Johnson Close
Abraham Heights
Lancaster LA1 5EU
Tel: 01524 64305
Fax: 01524 389717
www.theba.org.uk

BDO Stoy Hayward*
8 Baker Street
London W1M 1DA
Tel: 020 7486 5888
Fax: 020 7487 3686
✉ tony.perkins@bdo.co.uk
www.bdo.co.uk

Botts & Co*
Lintas House
15-19 New Fetter Lane
London EC4A 1BA
Tel: 020 7427 6300
Fax: 010 7427 6301
www.bottscompany.com

**British Association of
Communicators in Business**
42 Borough High Street
London SE1 1XW
Tel: 020 7378 7139
Fax: 020 7378 7140
www.bacb.org

British Bankers' Association*
Pinners Hall
105 - 108 Old Broad Street
London EC2N 1EX
Tel: 020 7216 8800
Fax: 020 7216 8811
www.bva.org.uk

British Exporters Association
Broadway House
London SW1H 9NQ
Tel: 020 7222 5419
Fax: 020 7799 2468
www.bexa.co.uk

British Franchise Association*
Thames View
Newtown Road
Henley on Thames
Oxfordshire RG9 1HG
Tel: 01491 578050
Fax: 01491 573517
✉ mailroom@british-franchise.org.uk
www.british-franchise.org.uk

British Importers Association*
Suite 8 Castle House
25 Castlereagh Street
London W1H 5YR
Tel: 020 7258 3999
Fax: 020 7724 5055

**British Insurance Brokers
Association**
Biba House
14 Bevis Marks
London EC3A 7NT
Tel: 020 7623 9043
Fax: 020 7626 9676
✉ enquiries@biba.org.uk
www.biba.org.uk

British International Freight Association*
Redfern House
Browells Lane
Feltham
Middlesex TW13 7EP
Tel: 020 8844 2266
Fax: 020 8890 5546
✉ bifa@btconnect.com
www.bifa.org

British Library - Lloyds TSB Business Line
96 Euston Road
London NW1 2DB
Tel: 020 7412 7454
Fax: 020 7412 7453
Call or fax to arrange a readers pass for addmission to the reading room

British Quality Foundation*
32-34 Great Peter Street
London SW1P 2QX
Tel: 020 7654 5000
Fax: 020 7654 5001
www.quality-foundation.co.uk

British Retail Consortium
5 Grafton Street Mayfair
London W1X 3LB
Tel: 020 7647 1500
Fax: 020 7647 1599

British Safety Council
70 Chancellor's Road
London W6 9RS
Tel: 020 8741 1231
Fax: 020 8741 4555
www.britishsafetycouncil.co.uk

British Shops & Stores Association
Middleton House
Main Road Middleton Cheney
Banbury OX17 2TN
Tel: 01295 712277
Fax: 01295 711665
www.training.british-shop.co.uk

British Standards Institute
389 Chiswick High Road
London W4 4AL
Tel: 020 8996 9000
Fax: 020 8996 7400
www.bsi.org.uk

British Technology Group
10 Fleet Place
Lyme Burner Lane
London EC4M 7SB
Tel: 020 7575 0000
Fax: 020 7575 0010
www.btgplc.com

British Venture Capital Association*
Essex House
12-13 Essex Street
London WC2R 3AA
Tel: 020 7240 3846
Fax: 020 7240 3849
✉ bvca@bvca.co.uk
www.bvca.co.uk

Business Connect - Wales
Tel: 0345 969798
The Business Connect Line will direct you to your nearest Business Connect office in Wales

Business in the Community
44 Baker Street
London W1M 1DH
Tel: 020 7224 1600
Fax: 020 7486 1700
www.bitc.org.uk

Business Link
Tel: 0345 567765
www.businesslink.co.uk
The Business Link Signpost line will direct you to your nearest Business Link in England

Business Link, Coventry & Warwickshire*
Enterprise House
Courtaulds Way
Foleshill
Coventry CV6 5NX
Tel: 0345 124692
Fax: 024 7666 1453

Business Link, Gloucester*
Chargrove House
Main Road
Shurdington
Cheltenham GL51 5GA
Tel: 01452 509509
Fax: 01452 509500
✉ enqbl@glos.businesslink.co.uk
www.glos.businesslink.co.uk

Business Link, Hereford*
Crossway House Holmer Road
Hereford HR4 9SS
Tel: 01432 356699
Fax: 01432 274499

Business Link, Leicestershire*
10 York Road
Leicester LE1 5TS
Tel: 0116 255 9944
Fax: 0116 255 3470

Business Link, Leominster*
Corn Square
Leominster
Herefordshire HR6 8LR
Tel: 01568 616344
Fax: 01568 616355

Business Link, Wolverhampton*
Technology Centre
Wolverhampton Science Park
Glaisher Drive
Wolverhampton WV10 9RU
Tel: 01902 824200
Fax: 01902 824201

Business Link, Worcester*
St Swithins House
Trinity Street
Worcester WR1 2PW
Tel: 0800 104010
Fax: 01905 611611

Business & Technology Education Council
Steart House
32 Russell Square
London WC1B 5DN
Tel: 020 7413 8400
Fax: 020 7393 4445
www.decksale.org.uk

Cable & Wireless Communications*
26 Red Lion Square
London WC1R 4HQ
Tel: 0500 100 001
www.cwcom.co.uk

Chamber of Commerce - Hereford & Worcester*
Chamber Court
Castle Street
Worcester WR1 3AD
Tel: 01905 723200
Fax: 01905 613338
✉ enquiries@hwccte.co.uk
www.hwccte.co.uk

Chantrey Vellacott*
Prospect House
58 Queens Road
Reading RG1 4RP
Tel: 0118 959 5432
Fax: 0118 959 8532
www.cvdfk.com

* Contributors
✉ e-mail address

Charity Commission Registration Division
St Albans House
57-60 Haymarket
London SW1Y 4QX
Tel: 020 7210 4477
Fax: 020 7210 4545
www.charity-commission.gov.uk
For companies intending to register as a charity

Chartered Institute of Management Accountants*
63 Portland Place
London W1N 4AB
Tel: 020 7917 9254
Fax: 020 7580 2493
✉ pstandards @cima.org.uk
www.cima.org.uk

Chartered Institute of Patent Agents
Staple Inn Buildings
High Holborn
London WC1V 7PZ
Tel: 020 7405 9450
Fax: 020 7430 0471
www.cipa.org.uk

Chartered Insurers Institute
20 Aldermanbury
London EC2V 7HY
Tel: 020 7606 3835
Fax: 020 7726 0131
www.cii.co.uk

City Business Library
1 Brewers Hall Gardens
London EC2V 5BX
Tel: 020 7332 1812
Fax: 020 7600 1185
For people who live and work in the city of London. The library has a fee-based service called Business Information Focus call
Tel: 020 7600 1461

Commission for Racial Equality
Elliot House
10-12 Allington Street
London SWIE 5EH
Tel: 020 7828 7022
Fax: 020 7630 7605
www.cre.gov.uk

Commission of the European Communities
Jean Monet House
8 Storey's Gate
London SW1P 3AT
Tel: 020 7973 1992
Fax: 020 7973 1900
www.europa.eu.int

Companies House
Crown Way
Maindy
Cardiff CF4 3UZ
Tel: 029 2038 0801
Fax: 029 2038 0517
Guidance on forming a limited company

Computer Services Association
20 Red Lion Street
London WC1R 4QN
Tel: 020 7395 6700
Fax: 020 7404 4119
www.cssa.co.uk

Confederation of British Industry
Centre Point
103 New Oxford Street
London WCIA IDU
Tel: 020 7379 7400
Fax: 020 7240 1578
www.cbi.org.uk

Consultative Council of Professional Management Organisations
c/o Institute of Chartered Secretaries
16 Park Crescent
London W1M 4HA
Tel: 020 7580 4741
Fax: 020 7323 1132
www.icsa.org.uk/icsa/

Crafts Council
44a Pentonville Road
London Nl 9BY
Tel: 020 7278 7700
Fax: 020 7837 6891
www.craftcouncil.org.uk
Offers a range of schemes for artists and craftsmen, including training, grants, loans and bursaries

Cranfield School of Management*
Cranfield
Bedford MK43 0AL
Tel: 01234 751122
Fax: 01234 751806
www.cranfield.ac.uk/som

Deloitte & Touche*
Hill House
1 Little New Street
London EC4A 3TR
Tel: 020 7936 3000
Fax: 020 7583 8517
www.deloitte-touche.co.uk

Department for Education and Employment
Moorfoot
Sheffield S1 4PQ
Tel: 0114 275 3275
General enquiries: 0870 0012345
www.dfee.gov.uk

Department of Social Security (DSS)
Richmond House
79 Whitehall
London SW1A 2NS
Tel: 020 7210 5983
www.dss.gov.uk

Department of Trade and Industry (DTI)
Loan Guarantee Section
Level Two
St Mary's House
Moorfoot
Sheffield S1 4PQ
Tel: 0114 259 7308
Fax: 0114 259 7316
www.dti.gov.uk

Department of Trade and Industry (DTI)
Import Licensing Branch (ILB)
Queensway House
West Precinct
Billingham TS23 2NF
Tel: 01642 364333/4
Fax: 01642 533557
www.dti.gov.uk

Department of Trade and Industry (DTI)
Business in Europe Branch
Kingsgate House
66-74 Victoria Street
London SW1E 6SW
www.dti.gov.uk
Separate telephone numbers for enquiries for different countries can be obtained from the DTI Enquiry Unit
Tel: 020 7215 5000

Department of Trade and Industry (DTI)
Overseas Promotion Service
Bridge Place
88-89 Eccleston Square
London SW1V 1PT
Tel: 020 7215 0572
www.dti.gov.uk

Department of Trade and Industry (DTI)
Small Firms Business Support
Ashdown House
1 Victoria Street
London SW1H OET
Tel: 020 7215 5000
www.dti.gov.uk
Provides advice, support and information. Business Link helps small firms identify business problems, produce action plans and access a wide range of business support services, including finance, management best practice, exporting and overseas trade.There is also grant support for innovation and research, and extra help for firms in Assisted Areas

Design Council*
34 Bow Street
London WC2E 7DL
Tel: 020 7420 5200
Fax: 020 7420 5300
www.design-council.org.uk

Welsh Development Agency - Mid Division
Ladywell House
Newtown
Mid-Wales SY16 IJB
Tel: 0345 775577
Fax: 01686 627889
✉ inquiries@ddrw.org
www.wda.co.uk
Help for small businesses in mid-Wales (advice, factories and workshops, loans)

Direct Marketing Association
Haymarket House
1 Oxendon Street
London SW1Y 4EE
Tel: 020 7321 2525
Fax: 020 7321 0191
✉ dma@easynet.co.uk
www.dma.org.uk

Direct Selling Association*
29 Floral Street
London WC2E 9DP
Tel: 020 7497 1234
Fax: 020 7497 3144
✉ ukdsa@globalnet.co.uk
www.dsa.org.uk

Dun & Bradstreet*
Holmers Farm Way
High Wycombe
Bucks HP12 4UL
Tel: 01494 422000
Fax: 01494 422260
www.dunandbrad.co.uk

University of Durham Business School*
Mill Hill Lane
Durham
DH1 3LB
Tel: 0191 374 2211
Fax: 0191 374 3748
www.dur.ac.uk/dubs

Engineering Employers Federation
Broadway House
Tothill Street
London SW1H 9NQ
Tel: 020 7222 7777
Fax: 020 7222 2782
www.eef.org.uk

English Partnership (EP)
St George's House
Kingsway
Team Valley
Gateshead NE11 ONA
Tel: 0191 487 8941
Fax: 0191 487 5690
www.englishpartnership.co.uk
Builds small workshop premises in areas of high unemployment

English Tourist Board
Development Advisory Services Unit
Thames Tower
Blacks Road Hammersmith
London W6 9EL
Tel: 020 8846 9000
Fax: 020 8563 0302
www.visitbritain.com
Grants and advice for tourism-related businesses

Equal Opportunities Commission
Overseas House
Quay Street
Manchester M3 3HN
Tel: 0161 833 9244
Fax: 0161 835 1657
www.eoc.org.uk

Ethical Consultancy Services Ltd*
Burlington Buildings
11 Orford Place
Norwich NR1 3RU
Tel: 01603 615200
Fax: 01603 613500
✉ ethicalco@aol.com

Export Credits Guarantee Department (ECGD)
2 Exchange Tower
PO Box 2200
Harbour Exchange Square
London E14 9GS
Tel: 020 7512 7000
Fax: 020 7512 7649
www.ecg.gov.uk

Export Marketing Research Scheme
British Chambers of Commerce
4 Westwood House
Westwood Business Park
Coventry CV4 8HS
Tel: 02476 694484
Fax: 02476 695844
www.britishchambers.org.uk

Federation of Crafts and Commerce
Federation House
4 The Briars
Waterberry Drive
Waterlooville PO7 7YH
Tel: 023 9223 2099
Fax: 023 9223 2120
www.fcc.org.uk

Recruitment & Employment Confederation
36-38 Mortimer Street
London W1N 7RB
Tel: 020 7323 4300
Fax: 020 7255 2878
www.rec.uk.com

Federation of Small Businesses*
Press & Parliamentary Office
2 Catherine Place
Westminster
London SW1E 6HF
Tel: 020 7592 8100
Fax: 020 7233 7899
www.fsb.org.uk

Federation of Small Businesses - Head Office
Whittle Way
Blackpool Business Park Blackpool
Lancashire FY4 2FE
Tel: 01253 336000
Fax: 01253 348046
✉ ho@fsb.org.uk
www.fsb.org.uk

Federation of Small Businesses
- Scotland
74 Berkeley Street
Glasgow G3 7DS
Tel: 0141 221 0775
Fax: 0141 221 5954
www.fsb.org.uk

Federation of Small Businesses
- Inverness
22 Market Brae
Inverness IV2 3AB
Tel: 01463 237772
Fax: 01463 711299
www.fsb.org.uk

Federation of Small Businesses
- Wales
6 Heathwood Road
Birchgrove
Cardiff CF4 4JP
Tel: 029 2052 1230
Fax: 029 2052 1231
www.fsb.org.uk

Federation of Small Businesses
- Northern Ireland
3 Farrier Court
Glengormley
Newtownabbey
Co Antrim BT36 7XB
Tel: 028 9084 4079
Fax: 028 9034 2441
www.fsb.org.uk

Federation of Small Businesses
- Birmingham/West Midlands
113 Vibart Road
Yardley
Birmingham B26 2AB
Tel: 0121 784 8268
Fax: 0121 783 7798
www.fsb.org.uk

Federation of Small Businesses
- Lancs & Cumbria
347A Garstang Road
Fulwood
Preston PR2 4UP
Tel: 01772 712033
Fax: 01772 788033
www.fsb.org.uk

Federation of Small Businesses
- Lincoln
8/10 Guildhall Street
Lincoln LN1 1TT
Tel: 01522 523380
Fax: 01522 514458
www.fsb.org.uk

Federation of Small Businesses
- North Yorkshire
Tower House
Fishergate
York
North Yorkshire YO10 4UA
Tel: 0I904 629777
Fax: 01904 629666
www.fsb.org.uk

Federation of Small Businesses
- Staffordshire & West
Midlands
12 Pinetree Drive
Sutton Coldfield
West Midlands B74 3SE
Tel: 01922 744044
Fax 01922 744044
www.fsb.org.uk

Federation of Small Businesses
- North East
Quayside Business Centre
Ouseburn Building
Albion Row
East Quayside
Newcastle Upon Tyne NE6 1LL
Tel: 0191 276 6770
Fax: 0191 276 6770
www.fsb.org.uk

Finance & Leasing
Association*
Imperial House
15-19 Kingsway
London WC2B 6UN
Tel: 020 7836 6511
Fax: 020 7420 9600
www.fla.org.uk

Forum of Private Business*
Ruskin Chambers
Drury Lane
Knutsford WA16 6HA
Tel: 01565 634467/8/9
Fax: 01565 650059
[email] fpbltd@aol.com
www.fpb.co.uk

Freight Transport Association
Hermes House
St John's Road
Tunbridge Wells TN4 9UZ
Tel: 01892 526171
Fax: 01892 534989
www.fta.co.uk

Grant Thornton*
Grant Thornton House
Melton Street
Euston Square
London NW1 2EP
Tel: 020 7383 5100
Fax: 020 7383 4715
www.gti.org

The Guild*
Burlington Buildings
11 Orford Place
Norwich NR1 3RU
Tel: 01603 615200
Fax: 01603 613500
[email] services@the-guild.co.uk
www.the-guild.co.uk

Hacker Young*
St James Building
79 Oxford Street
Manchester M1 6HT
Tel: 0161 236 6936
Fax: 0161 228 0117
[email] hymail@hymcr.u-net.com
www.hackeryoung.co.uk

Hays Information Managment*
Quadrant House
15 - 1tockwell Green
London SW9 9JJ
Tel: 0800 019 0919
Fax: 020 7526 3140
[email] info@stk.hays-hjim.co.uk
www.hays-him.co.uk

Health & Safety Infoline
HSE Information Centre
Broad Lane
Sheffield S3 7HQ
Tel: 0114 289 2333 or
Tel: 0541 545500
www.open.gov.uk/hse/hsehome.htm

Her Majesty's Stationery
Office (HMSO)
51 Nine Elms Lane
London SW8 5DR
Tel: 020 7873 0011
Fax: 020 7873 8347

HM Customs & Excise Head
Office
22 Upper Ground
London SE1 9PJ
Tel: 020 7620 1313
*Advises all businesses on import and
export requirements*

IBM United Kingdom Ltd*
Customer Response Centre
PO Box 41 North Harbour
Portsmouth PO6 3AU
Tel: 0990 426426
www.ibm.com

* *Contributors*
[email] e-mail address

Incorporated Society of British Advertisers
44 Hertford Street
London W1Y 8AE
Tel: 020 7499 7502
Fax: 020 7629 5355
✉ info@isba.org.uk
www.isba.org.uk

Independent Banking Advisory Service
Suite A North View
North Fen Somersham
Huntingdon PE17 3HW
Tel: 01487 843444
Fax: 01487 740607
✉ help@ibas.co.uk
www.ibas.co.uk

Industrial Common Ownership Movement (ICOM)
74 Kirkgate
Leeds LS2 7DJ
Tel: 0113 246 1737
Fax: 0113 244 0002
✉ icom@icom.org.uk
Advice and assistance with setting up worker co-operatives

Industrial Society*
Robert Hyde House
48 Bryanston Square
London W1H 7LN
Tel: 020 7479 2000
Fax: 020 7479 2222
www.indsoc.co.uk

Inland Revenue
Somerset House
The Strand
London WC2R 1LB
Tel: 020 7438 6622
www.inlandrevenue.gov.uk
This central telephone number will give you the number of your local Inland Revenue office

Institute for Independent Business
33 Brydale Path
Claringdon House
Watford
Herts WD2 4AA
Tel: 01923 239543
Fax: 01923 239643
✉ postmaster@iib.org.uk
www.iib.org.uk

Institute of Administrative Managers
40 Chatsworth Parade
Petts Wood
Orpington BR5 1RW
Tel: 01689 875 555
Fax: 01689 870 891
✉ iadmin@cix.compulink.co.uk

Institute of British Administrators
16 Park Crescent
London W1N 4AH
Tel: 020 7580 4741
Fax: 020 7323 1132
✉ icsa@dial.pipex.com
www.icsa.org.uk

Institute of Business Advisers*
PO Box 8
Harrogate
North Yorks HG2 8XB
Tel: 01423 879208
Fax: 01423 870025
✉ enquiries@iba.org.uk
www.iba.org.uk

Institute of Chartered Accountants in England and Wales
Chartered Accountants Hall
PO Box 433
Moorgate Place
London EC2P 2BJ
Tel: 020 7920 8100
Fax: 020 7920 0547
www.icaew.co.uk

Institute of Chartered Accountants in Ireland
Chartered Accountants House
87-89 Pembroke Road
Dublin 4
Tel: 00 353 1 668 0400
Fax: 00 353 1 668 0842
✉ ca@icai.ie
www.icai.ie

Institute of Chartered Accountants of Scotland
27 Queen Street
Edinburgh EH2 1LA
Tel: 0131 225 5673
Fax: 0131 225 3813
✉ icas@icas.org.uk
www.ocas.org.uk

Institute of Chartered Secretaries and Administrators
6 Park Crescent
London WIN 4AH
Tel: 020 7580 4741
Fax: 020 7323 1132
✉ icas@dial.pipex.com
www.icas.org.uk/icas

Institute of Commerce
William House
14 Worple Road
Wimbledon
London SW19 4DD
Tel: 020 8879 1973
Fax: 020 8946 7153
✉ info@abeuk.com
www.abeuk.com

Institute of Company Accountants
40 Tyndales
Park Road
Clifton
Bristol BS8 1PL
Tel: 0117 973 8261
Fax: 0117 923 8292

Institute of Direct Marketing
1 Park Road
Teddington
Middlesex TW11 0AR
Tel: 020 8977 5705
Fax: 020 8943 2535
✉ name@theidm.co.uk
www.theidm.com

Institute of Directors
116 Pall Mall
London SW1Y 5ED
Tel: 020 7839 1233
Fax: 020 7930 1949
www.iod.co.uk

Institute of European Trade & Technology
29 Throgmorton Street
London EC2N 2A T
Tel: 020 7628 3723
Fax: 020 7628 7692
✉ iett@dial.pipex.com
www.iett.co.uk

Institute of Export*
Export House
64 Clifton Street
London EC2A 4HB
Tel: 020 7247 9812
Fax: 020 7377 5343
✉ institute@export.org.uk
www.export.org.uk

Institute of Financial Planning*
Whitefriars
Lewins Mead
Bristol BS1 2NT
Tel: 0117 930 4434
Fax: 0117 929 2214
✉ enquiries@institutefinplan. demon.co.uk
www.financialplanning.org.uk

Institute of Insurance Brokers
Higham Business Centre
Higham Ferrers
NN10 8DW
Tel: 01933 410003
Fax: 01933 410020
✉ inst.ins.brokers@iib/uk.com

Institute of Management
3rd Floor 2 Savoy Court
Strand
London WC2R 0EZ
Tel: 020 7497 0580
Fax: 020 7497 0463
✉ mic.enquiries@imgt.org.uk
www.inst-mgt.org.uk

**Institute of Management,
Small Firms Information
Service***
Management House
Cottingham Road Corby
Northants NN17 1TT
Tel: 01536 204222
Fax: 01536 400388
✉ mandev@inst-mgt.org.uk
www.inst-mgt.org.uk

**Institute of Management
Consultants**
32-33 Hatton Garden
London EC1N 8DL
Tel: 020 7242 2140
Fax: 020 7831 4597
✉ consult@imc.co.uk
www.imc.co.uk

**Institute of Management
Specialists**
Head Office
Warwick Corner
42 Warwick Road
Kenilworth
Warwickshire CV8 1HE
Tel: 01926 855498
Fax: 01926 851310

**Institute of Personnel
Development**
35 Camp Road
Wimbledon SW19 4UX
Tel: 020 8971 9000
Fax: 020 8263 3333
✉ ipd@ipd.co.uk
www.ipd.co.uk

Institute of Public Relations*
The Old Trading House
15 Northburgh Street
London EC1V 0PR
Tel: 020 7253 5151
Fax: 020 7250 3556
www.ipr.org.uk

Institute of Quality Assurance
12 Grosvenor Crescent
London SW1X 7EE
Tel: 020 7245 6722
Fax: 020 7245 6788
✉ reception@iqa.org
www.iqa.org

**Institute of Sales & Marketing
Management**
Romeland House
Romeland Hill
St Albans
Herts AL3 4ET
Tel: 01727 812500
Fax: 01727 812525
✉ sales@ismm.co.uk

Institute of Sales Promotion
Arena House
66-68 Pentonville Road
Islington
London N1 9HS
Tel: 020 7837 5340
Fax: 020 7837 5326
www.isp.org.uk

**Insurance Brokers
Registration Council**
Higham Business Centre
Midland Road
Higham Ferrer
Northants NN10 8DW
Tel: 01933 359083
Fax: 01933 359077

Interbrand Ltd*
40 Long Acre
Covent Garden
London WC2E 9JT
Tel: 020 7240 4040
Fax: 020 7836 0516
✉ info@interbrand.co.uk
www.interbrand.com

**International Chamber of
Commerce**
14-15 Belgrave Square
London SW1X 8PS
Tel: 020 7823 2811
Fax: 020 7235 5447
www.iccwbo.org

Knight Frank*
20 Hanover Square
London W1R 0AH
Tel: 020 7629 8171
Fax: 020 7493 4114
✉ kf@knightfrank.com
www.knightfrank.com

**Language Excellence Centres
(ALEC)**
Secretary to the Association
London
Tel: 020 7224 0172
*The telephone number above will give
you the number of the language centre
nearest to you*

The Law Society
113 Chancery Lane
London WC2A 1PL
Tel: 020 7242 1222
Fax: 020 7831 0344
www.lawsociety.org.uk

Lawyers For Your Business*
Helpline - Tel: 020 7405 9075

**(LEDU) Local Enterprise
Development Unit**
LEDU House
Upper Galwally
Belfast BT8 6TB
Tel: 028 9049 1031
Fax: 028 9055 9217
✉ ledu@ledu-ni.gov.uk
www.ledu-ni.gov.uk
*The helpline will connect you with
your nearest LEDU office in Northern
Ireland*

Lexicon Public Relations Ltd*
Nidd Bank House
Station Road Darley
Harrogate HG3 2PW
Tel: 01423 781515
Fax: 01423 780881
✉ lexiconelt@aol.com
www.lexiconpr.co.uk

Life Insurance Association (LIA)
Lia House
Station Approach Chorleywood
Rickmansworth WD3 5PF
Tel: 01923 285333
Fax: 01923 285395
www.lia.co.uk

Livewire - England
Hawthorn House
Forth Banks
Newcastle upon Tyne NE1 3SG
Tel: 0191 261 5584
or 0345 573252
Fax: 0191 261 1910
✉ livewire@projectne.co.uk
www.shell-livewire.org

Livewire - Northern Ireland
5 Airport Road
Belfast BT3 9EU
Tel: 028 9055 3800
Fax: 028 9055 3822
✉ enterprise@livewire.nireland.com
www.shell-livewire.org

* Contributors
✉ *e-mail address*

Livewire - Scotland
PO Box 2 Penicuik
Midlothian EH26 0NR
Tel/Fax: 01968 679915
www.shell-livewire.org

Livewire - Wales
Greenfield Business Centre
Greenfield Holywell
Clwyd CH8 7QP
Tel: 01352 710199
Fax: 01352 715210
www.shell-livewire.org
Livewire is an enterprise agency specifically aimed at the 16 to 30 age group

Local Enterprise Agencies (LEAS)
Business in the Community
44 Baker Street
London W1M 1DH
Tel: 020 7224 1600
Fax: 020 7486 1700
✉ information.@bitc.org.uk
www.bitc.org.uk
There are over 400 Local Enterprise Agencies throughout the UK, offering business advice and counselling to new and expanding businesses - addresses can be obtained from local TECs, LECs and Jobcentres

Paulette Lockington*
Development and Training Consultant
39 Melrose Place
Watford WD1 3LU
Tel: 01923 210632
Fax: 01923 210632

London Business School
Sussex Place
Regents Park
London NW1 4SA
Tel: 020 7262 5050
Fax: 020 7724 7875

London Chamber of Commerce and Industry
33 Queen Street
London EC4R 1AP
Tel: 020 7248 4444
Fax: 020 7489 0391
www.londonchamber.co.uk

London Enterprise Agency
4 Snow Hill
London EC1A 2BS
Tel: 020 7236 3000
Fax: 020 7329 0226
www.lenta.co.uk

Mailing Preference Services
5 Reef House
Plantation Wharf
London SW11 3UF
Tel: 020 7766 4410
Fax: 020 7978 4918
Regulatory body of the direct mail industry

Market Research Society
15 Northburgh Street
London EC1V 0JR
Tel: 020 7490 4911
Fax: 020 7490 0608
✉ info@marketresearch.org.uk
www.marketresearch.org.uk

Michael Page International*
Savannah House
11-12 Charles II Street
London SW1Y 4QZ
Tel: 020 7269 2532
Fax: 020 7930 9734
www.michaelpage.net

Microsoft Ltd
Microsoft Campus
Thames Valley Park
Reading RG6 1WG
Tel: 0870 601 0100
Fax: 0870 602 0100
www.microsoft.com/uk

Miller Freeman UK
630 Chiswick High Road
London W4 5BG
Tel: 020 8742 2828
Fax: 020 8747 3856
www.unmf.com
Franchise exhibition organisers

Moore Stephens*
St Paul's House
Warwick Lane
London EC4P 4BN
Tel: 020 7334 9191
Fax: 020 7248 3408
✉ nick.hilton@moorestephens.com
www.moorestephens.com

MOPS Scheme
16 Tooks Court
London EC4A 1LB
Tel: 020 7269 0520
Ensure that mail order advertisers are solvent and on the level

National Approval Council for Security Systems
Queensgate House
14 Cookham Road
Maidenhead SL6 8AJ
Tel: 01628 637512
Fax: 01628 773367
✉ macos@macos.org
www.macos.org

National Association of Self-Employed
Lynch House
91 Mansfield Road
Nottingham NG1 3FN
Tel: 0115 947 5046
Fax: 0115 950 9139
✉ nasgbni@btclick.com

National Computing Centre
Oxford House
Oxford Road
Manchester M1 7ED
Tel: 0161 242 2200
Fax: 0161 242 2400
eee.nccglobal.com
The AA for computer users - provides a range of products and services to members but also a free public website

National Federation of Enterprise Agencies
Trinity Gardens
9 - 11 Bromham Road
Bedford MK40 2UG
Tel: 01234 354055
Fax: 01234 354055
www.nfea.com
Speaks nationally on behalf of Enterprise Agencies

Nomadic Display*
71 St johns Road
Isleworth
Middlesex TW7 6QX
Tel: 020 8326 5555
Fax: 020 8326 5566
✉ adavis.nduk@btinternet.com
www.nomadicdisplay.com
Supplier of portable and modular exhibition and display equipment

Northern Ireland Department of Economic Development
64 Chichester Street
Belfast BT1 4JX
Tel: 028 9023 4488
Fax: 028 9054 5000
www.idbni.co.uk
For registration of Northern Ireland partnerships. Can assist with start-up capital and expansion for new manufacturing enterprises

Northern Ireland Tourist Board
St Anne's Court
59 North Street
Belfast BT1 1NB
Tel: 028 9024 6609
Grants and advice for tourism-related businesses

Office of Fair Trading - (Head Office)
Field House
15-25 Breams Buildings
London EC4A 1PR
Tel: 020 7211 8000
✉ enquiries@oft.gov.uk
www.oft.gov.uk

Office of the Banking Ombudsman
7 Graze's Road
London WC1X 8NB
Tel: 020 7404 9944
Fax: 020 7405 5052
✉ banking.ombudsman@obo.org.uk
www.obo.org.uk

Office of the Data Protection Register
Wycliffe House
Water Lane
Wilmslow SK9 5AX
Tel: 01625 545 745
Fax: 01625 524 510

Office of National Statistics
Government Buildings
Cardiff Road
Newport NP10 8XG
Tel: 01633 815696
Fax: 01633 812863
www.ons.gov.uk

Pannell Kerr Forster*
New Garden House
78 Hatton Garden
London EC1N 8JA
Tel: 020 7831 7393
Fax: 020 7405 6736
✉ rhodri.whitlock@uk.pkf.com
www.pkf.co.uk

Patent Office, Design Registry & Trademarks Registry
Cardiff Road
Newport
S Wales NP10 8QQ
Tel: 0645 500 505
Fax: 01633 814 444
✉ enquiries@patent.gov.uk
www.patent.gov.uk

PCMC Marketing Services*
Opus House
Basingstoke Road
Riseley
Berks RG7 1QQ
Tel: 0118 988 0410
Fax: 0118 988 0401
✉ mail@pcmc.co.uk
www.ohi.co.uk

Personal Investment Authority
25 The North Colonade
Canary Wharf
London E14 5HS
Tel: 020 7676 1000
Fax: 020 7676 1099

PICKUP Europe Unit
The PICKUP European Briefing Unit
University of Bradford
Bradford BD7 1DP
Tel: 01274 235 821
Fax: 01274 235820
✉ ebu@bradford.ac.uk

PriceWaterhouseCoopers*
Plumtree Court
London EC4A 4HT
Tel: 020 7583 5000
Fax: 020 7822 4652
www.pwcglobal.com

Prince's Trust
18 Park Square East
London NW1 4LH
Tel: 020 7543 1234
Fax: 020 7543 1200
www.princes-trust.org.uk
Grants and loans to the under 30s

Project North East*
Hawthorn House
Forth Banks
Newcastle upon Tyne NE1 3SG
Tel: 0191 261 7856
Fax: 0191 261 1910
✉ staff@projectne.co.uk
www.pne.org

Public Relations Consultancy Association
Willow House
Willow Place
London SW1P 1JH
Tel: 020 7233 6026
Fax: 020 7828 4797
www.prca.org.uk

Race Relations Employment Advisory Service (RREAS)
Head Office
14th Floor Cumberland House
200 Broad Street
Birmingham B15 1TA
Tel: 0121 244 8141
✉ hq.rreas@dfee/gov.uk

Recruitment & Employment Confederation*
3rd Floor Steward House
16a Commercial Way
Woking GU21 1ET
Tel: 01483 766442
Fax: 01483 714979
✉ info@rec.uk.com
www.rec.uk.com

Regional Supply Network Office - Devon/Cornwall
Tel: 01752 772 122
Fax: 01752 788 660
www.rso.co.uk

Regional Supply Network Office - East
Tel: 01727 813 704
Fax: 01727 813 463
www.rsneast.co.uk
www.rso.co.uk

Regional Supply Network Office - East Midlands
Tel: 0115 988 8300
Fax: 0115 853 3666
www.enda.org.uk

Regional Supply Network Office - London
Tel: 020 7203 1953
Fax: 020 7203 1954

Regional Supply Network Office - North East
Tel: 01642 330 100
Fax: 01642 330 101
www.onenortheast.co.uk

Regional Supply Network Office - South East
Tel: 01732 873 939
Fax: 01732 874 821

Regional Supply Network Office - West Midlands
Tel: 0121 770 2700
Fax: 0121 770 2727
www.wmda.co.uk

Regional Supply Network Office - Yorkshire & Humberside
Tel: 0113 243 9260
Fax: 0113 246 8443

Regus*
300 Hillswood Drive
Chertsey
Surrey KT16 0RS
Tel: 01784 898073/895005
Fax: 01784 898502
www.regus.com

The world's largest operator of fully serviced business centres with more than 250 locations in 45 countries

Royal Institute of Chartered Surveyors
12 Great George Street
Parliament Square
London SW1P 3AD
Tel: 020 7222 7000
Fax: 020 7222 9430
www.rics.org

Royal Mail
148 Old Street
London EC1V 9HQ
Tel: 0345 950950
www.royalmail.co.uk

Royal Society for the Prevention of Accidents*
Edgbaston Park
353 Bristol Road
Birmingham B5 7ST
Tel: 0121 248 2000
Fax: 0121 248 2001
www.rospa.com

Rural Development Commission
141 Castle Street
Salisbury SP1 3TP
Tel: 01722 336 255
Fax: 01722 332 769
www.countryside.gov.uk

Sage Group PLC*
Sage House
Benton Park Road
Newcastle upon Tyne NE7 7LZ
Tel: 0191 255 3000
Fax: 0191 255 0308
✉ name of person@sage.com
www.sage.com

Scottish Business Shops
Tel: 0141 248 6014
(0800 787878 within Scotland)
This helpline will connect you with your nearest Business Shop in Scotland

Scottish Enterprise Agency
120 Bothwell Street
Glasgow G2 7JP
Tel: 0141 248 2700
Fax: 0141 221 3217
www.scotent.co.uk

Scottish Executive
Meridian Court
5 Cadogan Street
Glasgow G2 6AT
Tel: 0141 242 5500
Fax: 0141 242 5589

Scottish Tourist Board
23 Ravelston Terrace
Edinburgh EH4 3TP
Tel: 0131 332 2433
Fax: 0131 343 1513
www.holiday.scotland.net
Grants and advice for tourism-related businesses

Shoosmiths Solicitors*
52-54 The Green
Banbury OX16 9AB
Tel: 01295 267971
Fax: 01295 265620
✉ Firstname.Lastname
@shoosmiths.co.uk
www.shoosmiths.co.uk
Partner Contact: John Spratt

Shoosmiths Solicitors*
The Lakes
Northampton NN4 7SH
Tel: 01604 543000
Fax: 01604 543543
✉ Firstname.Lastname@
shoosmiths.co.uk
www.shoosmiths.co.uk
Partner Contact: Kit O'Grady

Shoosmiths Solicitors*
Lock House
Castle Meadow Road
Nottingham NG2 1AG
Tel: 0115 906 5000
Fax: 0115 906 5001
✉ Firstname.Lastname@
shoosmiths.co.uk
www.shoosmiths.co.uk
Partner Contact: Oliver Brookshaw

Shoosmiths Solicitors*
Regents Gate
Crown Street
Reading RG1 2PQ
Tel: 0118 949 8765
Fax: 0118 965 8700
✉ Firstname.Lastname@
shoosmiths.co.uk
www.shoosmiths.co.uk
Partner Contact: Marshall Leopald

Shoosmiths Solicitors**
Bloxam Court
Corporation Street
Rugby CV21 2DU
Tel: 01788 573111
Fax: 01788 536651
✉ Firstname.Lastname@
shoosmiths.co.uk
www.shoosmiths.co.uk
Partner Contact: Chris Hill

Shoosmiths Solicitors*
Russell House
1550 Parkway
Solent Business Park
Whiteley
Fareham
Hants PO15 7AG
Tel: 01489 881010
Fax: 01489 881000
✉ Firstname.Lastname@
shoosmiths.co.uk
www.shoosmiths.co.uk
Partner Contact: Sally Norcross-Webb

Simpler Trade Procedures Board (SITPRO)
151 Buckingham Palace Road
London SW1W 9SS
Tel: 020 7215 0825
Fax: 020 7215 0824
www.sitpro.org.uk

Small Business Bureau*
Curzon House
Church Road
Windlesham
Surrey GU20 6BH
Tel: 01276 452010
Fax: 01276 451602
www.smallbusinessbureau.org.uk

Small Firms Enterprise Development Initiative (SFEDI Ltd)
7 Britten's Court
Clifton Reynes
Olney
Buckinghamshire MK46 5LG
Tel: 01234 241255
Fax: 01234 241593
✉ bab_ltd@compuserve.com
www.sfedi.org.uk
"sharing successful business practice"
by rasing the standards of business advice, information, training and development programmes available to owner managers

Society of Pensions Consultants
St Bartholomew House
92 Fleet Street
London EC4Y 1DG
Tel: 020 7353 1688
Fax: 020 7353 9296
✉ john.mortimer@spc.uk.com
www.spc.uk.com

Society of Practitioners of Insolvency*
4th Floor Halton House
20 - 23 Holborn
London EC1N 2JD
Tel: 020 7831 6563
Fax: 020 7405 7047
✉ gensec@spi.org.uk
www.spi.org.uk

Speechly Bircham*
6 St Andrew Street
London EC4A 3LX
Tel: 020 7427 6400
Fax: 020 7427 6600
✉ speechly@speechlys.co.uk
www.speechlybircham.co.uk
Solicitors

Stationers Hall
Ave Maria Lane
Ludgate Hill
London EC4M 7DD
Tel: 020 7248 2934
Fax: 020 7489 1975
✉ admin@stationers.org
Registration of copyright

TEC National Council*
Westminster Tower
3 Albert Embankment
London SE1 7SX
Tel: 020 7735 0010
Fax: 020 7735 0090
✉ info@tec.co.uk
www.tec.co.uk

THE (Technical Help for Exporters)
British Standards Institution
389 Chiswick High Road
London W4 4AL
Tel: 020 8996 9000
Fax: 020 8996 7400
✉ info@bsi.org.uk
www.bsi.org.uk

TNL*
Mallan House
Bridge End Industrial Estate
Hexham
Northumberland NE46 4DQ
Tel: 01434 600555
Fax: 01434 600590
✉ tnl@tnl.co.uk
www.tnl.co.uk

The UK 200 Group*
2nd Floor Stafford House
33 - 39 Station Road
Aldershot
Hants GU11 1BA
Tel: 01252 327666
Fax: 01252 310890
✉ info@turnbulls.co.uk

Venture Capital Report Ltd
166 Foxglove House
Piccadilly
London W1V 9DE
Tel: 020 7907 2900
Fax: 020 7907 2930
✉ vcr@vcr1978.com
www.vcr1978.com

Welsh Development Agency
Principality House
The Friary
Cardiff CF10 3FE
Tel: 0345 775577
Fax: 01443 845589
✉ enquiries@wda.co.uk
www.wda.co.uk

Welsh Office
Industry Department
Crown Building
Cathays Park
Cardiff CF10 3NQ
Tel: 029 2082 5111
Fax: 029 2082 5214
www.wales.gov.uk

Welsh Tourist Board
Brunel House
2 Fitzalan Road
Cardiff CF2 1UY
Tel: 029 2049 9909
Fax: 029 2048 5031
www.visitwales.com
Grants and advice for tourism-related businesses

WWAV Rapp Collins*
1 Riverside
Mambe Road
London W6 9WA
Tel: 020 7727 3481
Fax: 020 7221 0520

Index

S

Sage Group plc - 96, 165, 229, 345
sales day book - 172-173
sales forecasts - 85
sales invoices - 102, 169
sanctions - 228, 231, 265
search engines - 203, 249-251, 262, 276
searching trademark register - 109
seasonal patterns - 185-186
secure server - 271, 275
self - employed - 34
selling - 77, 88, 172-173,205, 235, 241, 267-268, 300-302, 312-313, 320, 332, 334, 336-338, 341, 366, 376
Sex Discrimination Act - 122, 135-136
shareholders - 38-39, 41-43, 51, 61, 78, 93-96, 103-104, 292, 351, 355-356, 359, 361, 365, 372-375
shares - 32, 38, 42, 50, 93-95, 101-103, 365, 370-372
shopping cart - 271
sick pay - 123, 182
single market (EU) - 329
Small Firms Loan Guarantee Scheme - 97
SMART Scheme - 100
social businesses - 60-63
social contract (EU) - 124
software, accountancy - 345
sole traders - 36-37, 43, 54, 149-150, 350
solicitors - 21, 37, 39, 49, 53, 56, 58, 71-75, 157, 375
specialist lending schemes - 99
staff and employees - 27, 31, 128, 219-221, 309
starting up - 26, 95, 101, 165, 216
statutory obligations - 146-147
statutory protection - 108, 128
stock control - 70, 179, 184, 244, 272
Stock Exchange - 38, 365, 371
stock markets - 100
structure business - 24
suppliers - 22, 36-37, 39, 43, 45, 85-87, 101, 117, 171-172, 180, 187-190, 244, 265, 272, 323
stakeholder pensions - 152-154

T

takeovers - 365
tax - 29-32, 36, 42-46, 50-51, 62, 69, 82, 84, 95, 98, 104, 122, 129, 145, 147-153, 158, 179, 181-182, 197, 265, 356, 367, 372
TECs (training and enterprise councils) - 27, 66, 139, 322
telephone techniques - 205
temporary staff - 126
termination of employment - 123, 134, 219

term loan - 92
terms of employment - 124
theft insurance - 156-157
third party motor insurance - 155
Town & Country Planning Acts - 114
trade credit - 223-224
trade finance - 98
trademarks - 108-110, 297-298, 369
trade sale - 374
Trade Union & Labour Relations Act - 122
Trading Schemes Regulations - 313
training - 27, 40, 59, 63, 67, 70, 123, 128-129, 133, 136-140, 143, 145, 161-162, 186-187, 215, 221, 301, 319, 335, 362-363
transit insurance - 157, 342
transport documents - 326
TV advertising 284, 286-287

U

unfair dismissal - 128, 157, 221
Unlisted Securities Market - 370-371
US Patent Office - 108
USP (unique selling point) - 299

V

variances - 85, 87
VAT (value added tax) - 24-25, 36, 42, 48, 69, 82-83, 144-145, 147-148, 150-151, 158, 171-173, 177-178, 189, 223, 226, 265-266, 272-273, 313, 322, 329, 343, 351
venture capital - 95-97, 99, 104
video conferencing - 209

W

wages - 42, 70, 81, 84, 123, 128-134, 145, 169, 171, 175, 182
warranties - 189-190, 375
web site competitions - 260
web site design - 253-258
web site, establishing - 242-252
winding - up petition - 229
Windows PC - 235
Woolf reforms - 230-231
working capital management - 86
world wide web - 197, 202, 276

Y

Yellow Pages - 54, 104, 291

Setting Up and Managing
Your Own Business

In my experience . . .

Name:

Company:

Tel: Fax:

Setting Up and Managing Your Own Business

In my experience . . .

Name:

Company:

Tel: Fax:

Setting Up and Managing
Your Own Business

In my experience . . .

Name:

Company:

Tel: Fax:

Notes

Notes

Notes